Praise for En

"A field guide to reactionary a
Enemy Feminisms surfaces a hid
A welcome alternative to political instory as an accumulation of social media screenshots." —Malcolm Harris, author of *What's Left: Three Paths Through the Planetary Crisis*

"Sophie Lewis's book is honest, brutal, historically comprehensive, and brilliant. She relays the sorry news that 'women are horrible, quite often' and that the history of Anglophone feminism includes many who cling to patriarchy, follow fascism, support racism and lynching, and engaged in forms of 'Enlightenment fundamentalism' that are enthusiastically Islamophobic.

One could hang one's head in shame or disavow the term. At the same time, however, Lewis insists in theoretical and historical terms the way that feminism is committed to 'building an abundant and livable world,' the abolition of all 'organized scarcities,' the destruction of markets, interspecies obligations, the communization of shared public goods. After a seething and convincing critique of feminism as whiteness, she calls for an understanding of abolition as 'a rebirthing of the world such that the humanism embodied in the slave economy is at once turned inside out, destroyed, transformed, and realized for the first time.' After exposing the fascist alliances within feminism, she counters with a searing vision of renewed Marxist feminism and transnational alliance: 'an extraordinary coalition is denaturalizing capitalist gender, building monstrous affinities, and seeking ways to communize care.' Where would we be without Sophie Lewis? In a more impoverished political world. This book is mandatory reading for anyone interested in a rough and compelling vision of the feminist past, present, and future." —Judith Butler, author of *Who's Afraid of Gender?*

"*Enemy Feminisms* is a compelling, provocative, ferocious book that shreds one received wisdom after another in a poised balance of incisive argument and elegant writing. Sophie Lewis has become an indispensable thinker for our era." —Torrey Peters, author of *Detransition Baby*

"Lewis's *Enemy Feminisms* evidences the need for animosity between feminists and the histories of violence through which fascistic and reactionary accounts of feminism emerge. They warn us against the falsity of sisterhood, examining how and why we must be prepared to break with this myth in order to assert what feminism can and should do. With daring and inventive prose, they remind us that if ours is a liberatory vision, we must be able to identify our enemies." —Lola Olufemi, author of *Feminism Interrupted*

"Lewis treats feminism not as an inherent moral good, but as a thick tangle of partial, contradictory practices that must be judged on their material effects—and shows us how we might cut our way through. Fearsome and deeply needed." —Andrea Long Chu, Pulitzer Prize–winning critic at *New York* magazine

"Sophie Lewis is sharp, bold, compassionate, and fearless." —Amia Srinivasan, author of *The Right to Sex*

"Everything about the necessity of Sophie Lewis to contemporary discourse on the left has been said, and rightly so! Her work and voice are crucial, learned, and stylistically a joy to read. But what needs to be said, more than this, is that Sophie Lewis is absolutely clear on the urgent material stakes of her writing. *Enemy Feminisms* expertly and painstakingly parses the historical and contemporary landscapes of reactionary fascist feminisms for our sake, and for the sake of a struggle we simply need to win." —Jordy Rosenberg, author of *Confessions of the Fox*

Enemy Feminisms

TERFs, Policewomen, and Girlbosses against Liberation

Sophie Lewis

Haymarket Books
Chicago, IL

Published in 2025 by
Haymarket Books
P.O. Box 180165
Chicago, IL 60618
773-583-7884
www.haymarketbooks.org
info@haymarketbooks.org

ISBN: 979-8-88890-249-3

Distributed to the trade in the US through Consortium Book Sales and
Distribution (www.cbsd.com) and internationally through Ingram Publisher Services International (www.ingramcontent.com).

This book was published with the generous support of Lannan Foundation, Wallace Action Fund, and the Marguerite Casey Foundation.

Special discounts are available for bulk purchases by organizations and
institutions. Please email info@haymarketbooks.org for more information.

Cover design by Rachel Cohen.

Library of Congress Cataloging-in-Publication data is available.

10 9 8 7 6 5 4 3 2

Contents

Women Are Not Horrible

*Newsflash: women weren't really involved
in that whole Empire thing.*

—Twitter[1]

"Women are not horrible," said the artist Jenny Holzer in an interview in 2023, in answer to a question about "the future of the feminist movement."[2] If Holzer could speak to her former self, she went on, she'd advise the young Jenny not to feel "guilty" for making feminism a "constant, out-loud" focus. Implicit in Holzer's statement is the idea that if women *were* horrible, it would make sense to be apologetic about being a feminist. In a way, it's lucky that women *aren't* horrible, because our non-horribleness is part of what legitimizes a full-throated feminist position. "We're largely not the problem," Holzer repeats.

I think I know why feminists say this, and why we believe it, not least because I've spent twenty years doing so myself. But "women are horrible" and "women are not horrible" are really two sides of the same coin, and both are bad reasons to do feminism. The one claim merely reverses the other, leaving intact the premise that gendered oppression is some kind of public relations matter—a question of people misjudging the group's inherent value. Pedestals and pillories and exculpatory and incriminating gestures have all been part of the construction of womanhood for a long time, and touting women's innocence or niceness relative to men doesn't get us out of that circuit. It's not liberatory—it's as dehumanizing as saying "women suck." Why would women not be horrible; aren't they part of history?

At the risk of sounding dramatic, I've been able to sniff out antifeminism like a bloodhound ever since I was able to form complex sentences. I can easily catch the scent of gynophobia, but I also detect hatred of *feminists*, specifically. Both can emanate from women—even from feminists. After all, why wouldn't this be the case? I have noticed glimpses of sexist, misogynist formations in myself, too.

I reckon I have harbored feminist emotions ever since I was five years old, parked in front of a TV watching a VHS cassette of Ingmar Bergman's adaptation of Mozart's opera *The Magic Flute* (1975), only to be chastised for identifying with the Queen of the Night (*die Königin der Nacht*). In case you don't know, the Queen of the Night is an emotionally wounded lady who hangs out in exile with a bunch of other witchy women. She is enraged, bereft of her daughter Pamina (who's been abducted by Pamina's dad), and she sings some of the hardest arias ever.

It has to be said that my little brother and I would watch anything. But options were limited on the shelves of our dusty home video-cassette collection circa 1993, so, usually, it was *The Magic Flute—Die Zauberflöte*, as it is known in German—or Disney's *Bambi* (1942), in which the mom, terrifyingly, gets shot dead. We were part-time latchkey kids in a mixed-nationality (German/English), white, expatriate household in France that was, as you can probably guess, middle class. He and I liked to wear long veils made of old sheets, "fancy" dresses, and plastic tiaras, tearing around outdoors and indoors, yodeling our best approximations of the famous coloratura soprano. We were utterly uninterested in the end of the opera movie, when the queen gets unmasked as evil, and the king she's trying to murder, Sarastro, turns out to be an enlightened sun god—the lord of the Masonic temple everyone joins in the happy ending.

You'd have thought that when our dad stopped us one evening, it would have been because our operatics were untuneful. But, as it turned out, Dad was irritated about something else. He said we were wrong to side with Princess Pamina's wicked mother. Instead, we ought to sympathize with her wrongfully maligned father. Did we not think Sarastro likely had good reason to banish his wife? Had we stopped watching before the part when he's revealed to be good? (We had.) Why did we like the queen so much?!

We both burst into hysterical tears. *Banished*? Can moms be banished? We screamed in terror. I beat my fists against a wall. "No," I shrieked, in loyalty to *die Königin der Nacht*, "no, no, no." But Dad, according to the story, stood firm and bawled right back at me: "The Queen of the Night is not the goodie!" Even to this day, I feel the itch in my fingertips to type "yes she is, yes she *is*." But for the record, Dad was right, and I was wrong. The Queen of the Night *is* the baddie. And even so, to this day, a vein in my body jerks to life, ready to fight, whenever a weird woman is villainized or a matriarch taken down a peg. "Women are not horrible!" I want to yell. "We are largely not the problem!"

When I was thirty-one, a lot of women yelled the same thing at me. A newspaper editor had asked me to write an op-ed that would introduce American readers to "trans-exclusionary radical feminism" (TERFism), a deeply un-radical "sex-based rights" phenomenon that had dominated mainstream discussions of gender justice in the UK for years.[3] The "hook" was a 2019 trip to Washington, DC, funded by the right-wing Heritage Foundation, by a small group of feminists from Britain, who protested "transgender ideology" by ambushing the trans national press secretary of the Human Rights Campaign, Sarah McBride.[4] "Stop the erasure of the female!" the uninvited "female rights activists" had shouted while filming McBride's dismay on their cell phones. This species of anti-trans hostility was, to many Americans, something new in 2019. Why was feminism in Britain *this* paranoid about a supposed existential threat that trans women pose to cis women, when no comparably resourced anti-transfeminism even existed in the US? I tried my best to answer. I explained that a national culture of "no-nonsense" anti-utopianism prevails on TERF Island. The "commitment to misery, to being a "bloody difficult woman,'"[5] as writer Asa Seresin puts it, notably by mocking and blocking others' attempts at self-actualization, is one of the main things driving the stubborn insistence on anti-trans prejudice there. That's the context in which UK feminists routinely frame "gender" as somehow self-indulgent and frivolous. To have or mention (let alone reinvent) a gender identity is for TERFs a form of individualism that holds "ordinary" women in contempt.

This posture allows them to tell themselves that their opposition to National Health Service (NHS) provisions for trans people constitutes punching up, instead of down. It's a narrative of righteous self-defense against rapacious neoliberal invasion, but in its panic-mongering about genderfluid foreignness, it fuses seamlessly with a much older British feminism of fear. The construct of the trans woman freighted with sexual menace is, after all, one that imagines her not only as an un-woman, but as fundamentally *un-British* too (European xenophobia has frequently used anti-"American"-ism as the more acceptable cover for feelings about aliens more generally). I hence hear strong echoes, in TERFism, of two centuries' worth of "proudly Anglo-Saxon" feminist participation in eugenicist colonial efforts to clean up messy gender (and prostitution) in colonies like British India, where there were substantial populations of non-cisgender indigenes.[6] Bottom line, the biggest reason for British feminism's transphobia is empire. I knew in advance that ridiculing antiracism—or at least, imagining it as necessary *for Americans only*—is the official sport of Britain's intellectual establishment. If you're English or, like me, half-English, it's likely you were reared at least a bit on Middle England's idea of its own national character as skeptical, fair, rational, ascetic, devoted to debunking, and above all, responsible for the abolition of slave trading. I naturally anticipated the possibility of indignation on the part of people I had written about. Still, it was a shock when furious TERFs told me that "women weren't really involved in that whole empire thing."[7]

Sarah Ditum, a *Sunday Times* columnist, ridiculed my idea that British women might learn something from indigenous feminists.[8] "Who the fuck is she talking about?" she tweeted, pretending to have no idea what indigeneity means in relation to empire. "The Celts? Anglo-Saxons?" Likewise, Kathleen Stock OBE, the "gender critical" academic, hadn't heard of native feminism in a UK context. Stock speculated that, by *indigenous*, I perhaps meant autochthonous Germanics like the twelfth-century mystic Hildegard von Bingen.[9] (In fact, I meant Kenyan, Indian, or Sri Lankan feminists, for example.[10]) Even I felt startled by the parochialism and xenophobia of my reception by those I had written about. For the TERFs dogpiling on my op-ed, not only does trans activism undermine feminism (writ large), but feminist criticism from the left *of* feminism is antifeminism. It *silences women*, or so the silenced women in question tell the world every other day on talk shows—or in the pages of the *Guardian* and (since circa 2021) the *New York Times*.[11]

The cry of censorship distracts from what is, in reality, simply a refusal to engage with unwelcome lessons. Of course it's not necessarily "anti-woman" to explore how European feminists were active in colonial governance—for instance, in the policing of gender via eugenic education, or in sexual hygiene policy and missionary work. It is a vital feminist process. But in the face of the West's cultural allergy to this kind of self-knowledge, regarding women's involvement in empire, scores of historians have had to create an entire academic field. Scholars such as Anne McClintock, Saba Mahmood, Chandra Mohanty, Antoinette Burton, and Vron Ware have painstakingly researched, stated, and restated the apparently indigestible facts.[12] The jury really is in. Middle- and upper-class ladies (especially) participated *feministly* in racial domination on a planetary scale. Only by facing these truths can feminism become accountable to itself, mutate and split accordingly, and thrive. Yet in the stubbornly defensive minds of the West's decorated public intellectuals, national treasures, talking heads, and curriculum writers, to bring this stuff up is to display craven ingratitude, rank hypocrisy, bad taste, and a dishonorable capitulation to today's woke-decolonial youth tyranny.

I count myself among the card-carrying allies of those phantasmatic upstarts, the young people fighting for their bodily autonomy, the ones TERFs call "blue-haired bullies," as though they have the power to oppress their educators. That said, not long ago, I might have reacted violently, too, if I thought someone was calling feminism itself bad or counterrevolutionary. A leftist said to me in an elevator in 2012 that feminism was a bourgeois enterprise—I almost shoved him. I understand, profoundly, the impulse to attack critiques of feminism. I know it can be upsetting to learn that feminisms have been eugenic, colonial, deadly to indigenous lifeways, explicitly antiblack, knowingly dangerous to sex workers, violent to queer and feminine people, and even, weird as it may sound, misogynistic and patriarchal. It can be tough to get one's head around Western feminism's role in the counterrevolutionary logic of cisness, a modern notion which has harmed all women by bifurcating and hierarchizing us in relation to maternal potential, very narrowly defined. The temptation is strong to immediately say, at least, "OK, but feminists clearly aren't the *main* culprits here. What about *antifeminists'* much, much bigger role?" Yet the valid concerns embedded in these objections still do not justify institutionalized avoidance of the topic. If these oppressors are such a minor thread in human history, what's wrong with getting to the bottom of their oppressing?

Women *are* horrible, quite often. Feminists, even, are part of the problem. That's what this book is about, because I think we have no choice but to name enemy feminisms, if we are to build an abundant and livable world while calling that project feminism. We have to let go of the comforts of both self-castigation and defensiveness.

Speaking of which: I'm aware that when I told you the story of my passionate defense of the Queen of the Night just now, I let myself imply that I'm the writer I am today because I never backed down. That story would go something like this: unlike Mozart's Prince Tamino and Princess Pamina, I never transferred my allegiance away from the "irrational," dark, unruly circle of women, never submitted to the patriarchal temple of reason. This gives me the pleasure of casting my biography as one long man-disdaining rebellion, an uninterrupted hangout with the crone sisterhood on the heath. I'd love to tell myself this story. I imagine it's the kind of story Kathleen Stock tells herself. But in truth, my dad's campaign against the night queen worked.

In our middle-class nuclear household, the father scapegoated the mother, and we all ganged up on her: a somewhat rational strategy since, as anti-psychiatry activist and radical feminist Bonnie Burstow writes, "identification with mother means drudgery and powerlessness."

> Often, father and daughter look down on mother (woman) together. They exchange meaningful glances when she misses a point. They agree that she is not bright as they are, cannot reason as they do. This collusion does not save the daughter from the mother's fate.[13]

All the way into my early twenties, I stepped in and out of the role of the daddy's girl, now belligerent and fugitive, now bought off and treacherously fluent in sexist chauvinism. Femmephobia—the denigration of artful or self-conscious femininity—was a strategy I sometimes used to please my favored parent (actually, my mother modeled it for me). And if I then felt dirty or dissociated, I changed tack abruptly, "owning" my assigned gender, and fighting tooth and nail, on behalf of Woman generally and women everywhere. Dad did not encourage sympathy for Mum's depression. Reader, my collusion with him did not save me from her fate. The way I *do* escape her fate nowadays has to do with the collective arts of a non-dyadic queer household and a local web of care.

Announcing oneself to be *not like the other girls* expresses a hope and even a malformed desire for freedom. By joining in the belittlement of one's group, one gambles on the chance of being marked as an exception, and thus getting to be part of mankind. Mary Wollstonecraft tried it, and so did the ex-suffragettes who invented women's policing, and so did the anti-pornography radical Robin Morgan. As we'll see, it doesn't work very reliably, and often, women even *know* it won't. But then again, neither does the opposite move. Yes—heroization is a trap too. My mom will not get justice via being idealized and turned into the goodie, any more than the Queen of the Night would. (Let's face it, how good is any royal likely to be anyway?) It is possible not to idealize an abused wife even while imagining solidarity with her. Solidarity, actually, requires us not to idealize. Think of the daughter at the heart of the *Magic Flute* custody battle—she is never consulted on her views, nor would we need her innocence in order to support her. Feminists, perhaps, should try to avoid heroes. *No girlbosses, no heroines, no masters.*

It's so natural feeling, though, to be on the defensive. Hey, the Queen of the Night sings the hardest aria. She is, we want to say, a total queen. I wasn't even old enough to attend school when I learned this script. And while my inauguration was a preschool run-in with a literally patriarchal outburst against a "feminist" figure from a German VHS tape—an unusually stark case—I wonder how many other feminists were born more or less the same way. How many of us have had our liberal feminism sparked, early in life, by a collision with a matrophobic (anti-mother) or femmephobic narrative that unintentionally misfired, eliciting the "wrong" affinities, loyalties for which we were inexpertly, counterproductively, punished?

I wonder above all whether the attendant habit of thought—of stubbornly making goodies out of baddies—serves us well. Think of the sheer volume of diary entries, blog posts, and undergrad or high school essays in the West (perhaps you wrote some of them? I did) that have been dedicated to redeeming and then hyping the reputations of jezebels, madwomen, wicked stepmothers, evil nurses, murderesses, and sadistic crones—figures like Pandora, Medusa, Medea, Baba Yaga, Lilith, Lady Macbeth, Bertha Mason, Miss Havisham, Annie Wilkes, Cruella de Vil, or indeed Eve. You name it: from Ursula the sea witch did nothing wrong, to Aileen Wuornos for president, I've likely tried it out in print or in conversation. But what if the whole logic of redemption is a trap? How far does it take us, and where does it end? There's no shortage of articles contending that Condoleezza Rice, Kamala Harris, or Priti Patel are inspirational overcomers of misogynoir even when they are wielding giant apparatuses of racist state violence.

It took me long enough, but slowly I began to grasp the limits of villainess-redemption feminism. Any ideology premised on women being either "the goodies" or "victims" would, after all, definitionally have nothing to offer my enraged-yet-suicidal mom. In 2016, at US election time, I asked myself why everyone, seemingly, was equating feminism with "loving women." Clearly, "pro-women" sentiments were not correlated with pro-all-women outcomes, since they were present in everything from paeans to racial profiling to advocacy for forced birth (that year, "tradwives" were already gaining momentum). Remember when Ivana Trump said her ex-husband "loves women"—and Ivanka, their daughter, echoed her, saying Donald is a "feminist"? These news stories stuck in my memory because my avowedly left-liberal dad used to strike a similar note every time I accused him of antifeminism. "An antifeminist?!" he'd exclaim. "But I *love* women. Women are so much nicer than men." True enough, but I never thought to ask him what, in that case, was the sex or species of the decidedly non-"nice" person he was married to.

They say that "to understand all is to forgive all." But if this is true, then a commitment to "impurity" in politics (a commitment I think of as key to anti-fascism) must walk hand in hand with the courage to draw lines and fight people if necessary. Even kin. In other words, feminists who, like me, are committed anti-fascists— or anti-fascists who are also feminists, as they must be—need to know the difference between forgiving enemies and giving up the fight against them. This has to be crystal clear. It's a question of learning to more confidently oppose people whom we understand: a cop is still my enemy when she's my neighbor. We can feel compassion for QAnon moms and still liquidate their armory. We can *forgive* a pro-life feminist and still destroy the forced-birth judiciary.

For centuries, "women are not the problem" has been an eminently publishable take, from feminists and antifeminists alike. Contrariwise, many of us on the radical left are glad that so many of us *are* a problem for the survival of the present state of things. We dream, in fact, of being bigger—much, much bigger—problems. As we expand our desire for revolution, I hope we can start to reject pantheons and, instead, practice remembering and admiring flawed comrades whom we care for, in part, *by* criticizing them. My teachers include Pat Parker, Shulamith Firestone, Mario Mieli, Donna Haraway, and Emma Goldman, all of whom I defend vehemently even as I disagree with them on many things. Heroization is a dangerous game, even a regressive one. But it's so pleasurable! It's hard to go without it.

For now, what I know is that if I could go back, like Jenny Holzer, and speak to the pint-sized version of myself beating her fists against that wall, I would want to say:

> Hey, little Saffoo. Don't worry about liking the Queen of the Night, the baddie. Don't worry about not liking the sun king. Real talk? The two of them are definitely part of the same monarchy, and she uses her kids like pawns as well. One day, we'll almost certainly need to fight them both, perhaps even getting rid of the difference between mommies and daddies altogether. But taking joy in something doesn't mean we have to make that thing a political principle. In the real world there aren't goodies and baddies. It's more like: comrades and enemies. You are currently on enemy ground! The nuclear family is an injustice machine. So, sing on. And then, get out, and find your comrades.

All of us deserve the freedom and safety to be foolish. I am fond of the 1909 illustration of the "zero" card in tarot—the "Fool" card that comes before all other cards—for this reason, with its lackadaisical and unsuspecting wanderer gaily gathering flowers with her little dog on a cliff edge. It's a card that speaks to me of the nonuniversal design of childhood: the fact that our society tries to shield only some, not all, harmless babes from having to grow up via trauma and injury: "the hard way." Every child deserves access to what is currently white upper-class childhood. That is, the right not to pay for ignorance with their life, and space to safely fall off cliffs.

However, there is another, very different sense of the word "fool." It's one I almost used in the title of this book, which at one point was going to be *The Feminism of Fools*. This other usage, though, is infinitely heavier, albeit it sounds to the uninitiated as though it's *only* about ignorance. (That's why I ended up invoking "enemies" instead.) The foolishness in the "of fools" formulation is an enemy foolishness: there's no aimless, head-in-the-sky, radical openness here at all. Rather, there is comfortable, calcified, willful certainty with regard to what's what, a disavowed incuriosity vis-à-vis the impossible. Can one type of fool become the other? Sure—in an anti-child society intent on turning unproductive youth into productive adults as fast as possible, it happens all the time. I've seen fools of the utopian type suddenly seek to "get real" and "grow up" by rapidly embracing the pseudo-realism of the latter type. This is what happens, for example, when you decide, as a baby feminist, that *all Night-Queen ends justify the means.*

A century and a half ago, in German-speaking leftist circles, a popular apothegm emerged, typically attributed to August Bebel, world-famous author of *Woman and Socialism*.[14] The line was: "Der Antisemitismus ist der Sozialismus der dummen Kerle"—in other words, *antisemitism is the socialism of fools.* The phrase swiftly went viral, since it so helpfully put a name to a pernicious form of xenophobic anti-banker populism that makes hay out of the phobic association between the figure of "the Jew" and finance capital, on the one hand, and communism, on the other. In the socialism of fools, capitalism *is* finance *is* the Jews—but Jews are somehow also trying to undermine nationhood, overthrow class society, and usher in a Marxist world order. The soi-disant "socialists" in question said they *loved* the working class, but what they loved was actually an idea of artisanal purity and clean-living very different from the slum dwellers, garment factory laborers, and sweatshop rabble of the actual (also substantially Yiddish-speaking) proletariat.

Still, as writer Naomi Klein discusses in her study of conspiracism, *Doppelganger: A Trip into the Mirror World*, these self-contradicting stories are easy to fall into, even for nominally well-intentioned people, under present conditions of rampant dispossession and alienation. Which is not to say that they are only a little bit off. No: the socialism of fools is the royal road to National Socialism—in other words, fascism. What is distinct about the phrase "socialism of fools" is that it highlights a tragedy: the original impulse of someone who ends up in that camp may have at one point been anti-capitalist.

Someone may have looked about and said to herself that something is drastically wrong with market society, something that liberal democracy cannot solve. That much is true. But then, instead of persisting toward an understanding of capital as an impersonal system of social relations (something that certainly can feel vertiginous), she chokes. With the value-form too big and individual bosses and property owners too small, she has nothing of the right size toward which she can direct her rage. She finds the feeling of ambiguity intolerable. So she falls into the still subversive-feeling (but fundamentally consoling) belief that only *some* of capitalism's modern manifestations are what's wrong: speculation, debt, usury, human trafficking, "greed."

Perhaps, she thinks, these evils have a common source in a social parasite preying on what would otherwise be a healthy state of economic nature characterized by honest labor and fair trade. Perhaps, instead of the banal planetary violence that is the relationship of class, the heart of the matter is more spectacular, and easier to visualize: *a race of super powerful yet only indirectly discernible aliens; a craven fifth column walking among us, undermining us, leeching off us, profiteering.* . . . It is sometimes forgotten that fascists understand themselves as an emancipatory anti-elite revolt against politics. Make no mistake: the point here isn't that leftism is somehow closer to fascism than liberalism is, but that a fleeting radical instinct or canny inclination toward systemic analyses can, in some cases, slip, plunge, and turn into an enemy politics.

We can understand various moments in feminist political philosophy over the past two centuries in similar terms. Like the socialism of fools, the feminisms I'm thinking of typically began with a radical impulse. In each case, women said to themselves, *Something is deeply wrong in gendered life, something that humanism as we know it cannot solve.* (True.) Instead of then persisting, though, toward an understanding of gender *itself* as unnatural all the way down— which certainly can feel vertiginous—they cop out. Divisions like "productive-reproductive" and "private-public" feel rather abstract, while individual workplaces (be it the hearth where unwaged care happens, or the waged domestic sphere, or the call center, or the commercial kitchen) feel overly specific. It would be easier to be able to paint a picture of our tormentor! So, maybe we can all agree that some of gender's manifestations are bad: prostitution, femme-ness, transfemininity, contract pregnancy, oriental patriarchy, intimate partner violence, sexed access bars to education, the pay gap, stigma on abortion, or even an imagined lack of stigma on abortion. Any one of these things can surely be attacked, for starters, in the name of a sex-egalitarian world? Easier, anyway, than figuring out what unmaking the mode of production that *underlies* the logic of gender would entail. Easier to visualize the problem as a glass ceiling, a wage differential, an office sex pest, a pimp, a foreign rapist, a male doctor, a husband's drunkenness, "the" penis, or "gender ideology." We can destroy these things—right?—by legislating against outrages to motherhood and girlhood; against porn, the veil, sex work, sexual misconduct, intemperance, workplace discrimination, or trans self-determination.

I wish I'd had a concept like "the feminism of fools" twenty years ago. No one ever explained to me, when I was cutting my teeth as a feminist in my late teens, that certain feminisms actively wreak a great deal of evil. As a result, I spent over a decade equating feminism with "good" politics in a world that reflected anything but. I simply pushed down my unease. Just like all the other feminists around me plumping for this strategy, whenever I encountered reactionaries calling themselves feminist (something that happened disconcertingly often), I'd breezily define them as a non-feminist. *That's not real feminism,* I'd say. *Whatever they may think, these people aren't feminists. In order to count, a feminism has to fill some kind of criteria to do with antiracism and anti-capitalism.* This purgative approach is understandably very popular. As far as I know, pretty much all my friends do it sometimes, and it's easy to understand why.

For one thing, clarifying that "these so-called feminists do not speak for me" is a valuable form of solidarity with the hardest-hit victims of imperial feminism or girlbossery. When we say "that's not feminism," we are letting the harmful pro-woman actors know that they are not our people, while letting their targets know we have their back. For example, civilizing crusaders against the hijab aren't feminists, we affirm, building our barricades around the term. Whorephobic humanitarians aren't feminists. If you're a racist rape prosecutor like New York's head of sex crimes in 1989, Linda Fairstein, you aren't a real feminist![15] If you're a kink shamer, you're not doing feminism! "Pro-life" feminism? No such thing! Or, as some wags have proposed, TERFs aren't even feminists, they're FARTs: Feminism-Appropriating Radical Transphobes. At the time of writing, a web search for the term "real feminism" returns just under one hundred thousand results.[16]

Our uneasiness here is palpable. Do we even know when "real feminism" began? It turns out that the word itself was likely coined a few years after Mary Wollstonecraft's *A Vindication of the Rights of Woman* (1792) was published—a treatise itself preceded by the French revolutionary Olympe de Gouge's *Declaration of the Rights of Woman* (1791). Meanwhile, good anthologies of "feminism" nowadays tend to provincialize the Western canon altogether, beginning anywhere in the last four thousand years, perhaps with undated Cheyenne proverbs or Apache storytelling, or an invocation by the Sumerian priestess Enheduanna, verses by Sappho, selections from the Hebrew Bible, or poems from the *Therigatha* (a collection written by Buddhist nuns).[17] But the original self-styled "feminism," as I love to remind people, was probably the early nineteenth-century family abolitionism of the French utopian socialist and sex liberationist Charles Fourier.[18] While anglophone histories typically start the story with Wollstonecraft's vindication of bourgeois motherhood, we could easily start with Fourier, who vindicated the reverse—namely, abolition of the private nuclear home. How can a single movement's two "parents" want such opposite things? The disunity of Western, colonial feminism's origins is a source of great subliminal anxiety to today's feminists. And no wonder! In the context of new awareness forced on our collective memory by Black Lives Matter, several figures in the authorized woman-suffrage pantheon have come into unflattering focus lately as committed white supremacists.[19]

Traditional accounts about the foremothers of the Western women's movement are stuck in our collective gullet. Many of us learned how those brave bluestockings stepped out from the private sphere and said, "No! we shall NOT be slaves!" even while, ostensibly, supporting other people's struggles to break actual slave chains around their ankles. It's a tale most of us know—that *A Vindication* was bourgeois-revolutionary feminism's opening gambit in English—but it's still worth recalling its core proposition, penned during the Haitian Revolution: that domesticated Western women are in a comparable situation to enslaved Africans laboring in the Caribbean and thus deserving of social emancipation (like them, or possibly even more so). Wollstonecraft's opposition to (real) slavery was sincere, to be sure, if not meaningfully antiracist. Her overarching argument was that one should oppose European gentlewomen's lack of access to education *because* one already opposes the colonial system of slave labor.[20] We have this conceptual strategy to thank for kickstarting the past 233 years of liberal-democratic gender progress.

Organized bourgeois womanhood taking inspiration from anti-colonial struggle and then seeking to take precedence over it persists, as a pattern, to this day. That said, the massive uptick in conversations about white feminism in recent years proves that many feminists in the West *are* chewing on the legacy of the slavery analogy. A massive surge in antiwhite feminist discussions indicates some real willingness on the part of "nice white ladies" to unlearn imperial feminism.[21] Many have sought tools to help them identify the unmarked, baked-in settler chauvinism and antiblackness in their self-empowerment networks. From 2016 on especially, thousands flocked to lectures, teach-ins, and workshops on decolonial feminism by Black feminists like Gail Lewis and Reni Eddo-Lodge in the UK, while in the US, "hood feminism" (Mikki Kendall) and "abolition feminism" (Angela Davis et al.) gain new recruits every day.[22] Naturally, the publishing industry reflected this turn. Several useful books on feminist whiteness appeared in 2021: Kyla Schuller's

The Trouble with White Women, Jessie Daniels's *Nice White La-dies*, Ruby Hamad's *White Tears/Brown Scars*, and Rafia Zakaria's *Against White Feminism*.[23] Even the former editor of *Vogue*—Koa Beck—published a book that year called *White Feminism: From the Suffragettes to Influencers and Who They Leave Behind*.

Actually, "the trouble with white feminist politics is not what it fails to address and whom it leaves out," writes Schuller, in a gen-tle corrective to Beck's frame. "White feminism is an active form of harm, not simply a by-product of self-absorption." Hence, "ex-panding white feminism's tent will not transform the materials of which it is made."[24] (Unsurprisingly, a counterrevolutionary rash of $30,000-an-hour consultants, such as Robin DiAngelo, tried to transform those suddenly self-conscious and guilty *materials* into cash, co-opting the critique of feminist whiteness into a practice of white feminist self-castigation.[25]) Make no mistake: whiteness cannot be disentangled from any of the enemy feminisms I seek to illuminate in the pages that follow: the feminism of anti-Islam, the feminism of bosses, the feminism of forced gestating, the fem-inism of cisness, and more. It gives me hope that so many of us are now coming to grips with the co-imbrication of gender and racialization. My worry, following Schuller, is that it seems easier for the culture to talk about "white feminism" as a simple matter of "things that were done by feminists who are white" than it is to wrestle with the notion of a feminism that has whiteness baked into its very core.

"White feminism" is a valuable concept. In some hands, how-ever, it has an ambiguity to it that capitalism already exploits. Can you lose the whiteness without fatally damaging the feminism? What if (as some people seem to secretly hope) there's no way to stop being white at all? For those who would prefer to meditate on their privileges forever instead of picking a side and committing to "race treachery" (that is, what the abolitionist John Brown called "loyalty to mankind"), too much talk of white feminism can be-come demobilizing and indulgent. At the same time, some man-ifestations of ethnonationalism, pro-whiteness, class domination, and coloniality in feminist form are *not* actually identified as "bad" feminism on the liberal world stage often enough, on account of the ethnic characteristics of their main stakeholders. (Think of Japanese trans-exclusionary feminism, or Hindu femonationalism.) As Gloria Anzaldúa remarked long ago, some whites "possess women-of-color consciousness, just as some women of color bear white consciousness."[26]

Feminists committed racist mistakes, and their feminisms reflected errors of judgment—this much, at last, we've been dragged kicking and screaming to recognize. But the culture still shows reluctance to contemplate the extent of some feminisms' deeper theoretic entwinements with fascism. What we need now is a bestiary of enemy feminisms, to jolt us into understanding that a woman's cry for women's power is sometimes part and parcel of the oppressor's program. Even as we suffer loss in the short term, we can ultimately only gain, as feminists, when we accept that certain beloved old lines and lineages of feminism weren't just incidentally misogynist but substantively so; that their core definitions were bourgeois, irremediably; that their racism was non-excisable. What are our other options? Shall we attempt the bonkers task of "calling in" people with opposite aims to our own—decolonizing what is squarely a form of colonialism? Or shall we break up the house of feminism, that battered and beloved fortress where so many of us have *not* lived well, and dare to name some feminisms *enemies*?

Contra the aggrieved cries from certain quarters that it can only ever be patriarchy that benefits when feminists criticize other feminists, I affirm with Anzaldúa that lines of affinity, not identity, must be drawn. Some feminisms are obstacles to gender freedom, and asking "which side are you on?" is the most elemental level of political physics. "The side of women" doesn't exist. It never existed.

Let's be brave and swallow our bitter medicine. Feminists across the political spectrum have taken pains to define their troops as chaste and untainted by lust (especially interracial lust); not to mention maternal, i.e., pure, straight, removed from the realm of productive work; and "natural," that is, not artificial, not "femme," neither surgically nor chemically enhanced. Black feminisms have a better track record, but of course some Black feminists too have been thoroughly ableist in this way, or whorephobic, or anticommunist. All in all, a great deal of feminisms have imagined their central subject as hardworking, nondisabled, healthful, and prosthesis-free—these being the unspoken complements to a womanhood that is life-giving (or at least pro-family), economically independent (or at least aspiring), nonviolent (or at least law-abiding), and "self-respecting" (not a body modifier or a bottom).

All of this was feminism, not liberatory feminism, but feminism in the sense that it contested a patriarchal constraint placed upon a certain group of women, no matter how few. Victorious aristofeminists proceed to co-engineer and enforce patriarchal or eugenic constraints for others; they even expect generalized feminist support for their accessions. Is this "worse" than a hypothetical gentlemen-only alternative domination? No, but nor is such equal-opportunity inequality, such counterrevolutionary fairness, remotely what my team is fighting for. We need to be discerning about any given feminism precisely because feminism is so capacious that it comprises, within itself, its own mortal enemies. I say this (as a reluctant feminist killjoy) because I *belong* to feminism. It is thanks to *and* despite people like Wollstonecraft—both!—that feminism can be a force of reaction even as it is an insurgent force that materially creates the right to the city, filling the streets with choreographies and chants denouncing cops, courts, dads, bosses, and the state.[27]

Feminism, in its best instances, is a burning prison: an insistence that life can be worth living and that every person's pleasure matters. It is, too, the practices that make life livable, wresting care free from the market;[28] freely distributing bread, roses, and hormones;[29] desegregating the generations;[30] bailing mamas out of detention;[31] disempowering rapists in kin networks, churches, and social centers;[32] and expropriating golf courses in order to open spaces of erotic (not necessarily sexual—but also sexual!) encounter.[33] Feminism sometimes flashes an unlit pathway toward a world without whiteness or colonizers.[34] In these moments, it's an insurrection halting family policing, forced gestating, and every other reproductive injustice.[35]

For many of us, feminism denotes the task of abolishing all organized scarcities, from the private nuclear household to the nation.[36] It's the deprivatization of love, via the insurgency of mothers of every gender against the patriarchal institution of motherhood, the decoupling of survival from the wage, the destruction of markets, the ecological insistence on interspecies responsibility, the decarbonization of every mégapole, and the communization of continent-wide architecture: waterways, seed banks, and libraries.[37] It's a local proletarian strike against work (that always already gendered and stolen substance otherwise called alienated labor) and a planetary revolution in values that prioritizes care over accumulation. It's a perfectly good name, too, for the horizon wherein work's myriad precarious, abject, wageless, mad, incarcerated, and otherwise remaindered victims are avenged. As a revolutionary movement, feminism abolishes gender *qua* differential, while remaking genders *qua* lush, interesting, and pleasurable difference.[38]

Feminism, in other words, carves out space for autonomous formulations of gender pending revolution. Also known to some as the revolt of femmes against cisness,[39] of sex workers against work,[40] feminism is "black quantum womanism";[41] junkie communism;[42] multispecies reparations;[43] a queer glitch[44] in the matrix of the given. Feminism is necessarily central to any meaningful anti-fascism. But this does not mean that it is always anti-fascist or even non-fascist. We can't just bank on that. Rather, our task is to conspire toward a world where women, if that word still exists, will still be horrible and not horrible, but where counterrevolutionary feminism has been stripped of its capacity for violence, and even *our* feminism is, happily, obsolete.

ONE

The "Enslaved" Englishwoman Goes Abroad

*Woman is the N—r of the world! It's
something Yoko said to me in 1968.*

—John Lennon, New York City[1]

It sometimes feels as though Western feminists are produced to lack
self-awareness by design. This blithe mindset represents one of our
many inheritances from that deeply frustrating ur-comrade, Mary
Wollstonecraft—the women's advocate who first said (in a manner
of speaking, foreshadowing Yoko Ono) that "Woman is the N—r
of the world," not meaning it as a compliment. The placard bearing
this motto at the 2011 "Slutwalk" protest in New York was, one
hopes, hastily dashed off.[2] Wollstonecraft's magnum opus, for its
part, was definitely written in a hurry. Its author, like many of history's other most influential philosophers, was a deeply contradictory
person whose Jacobin radicalism and godly reformism, bourgeois
maternalism and free-love anarchism, personal sex libertinism and
anti-sex repressiveness, all ricochet around her second manifesto,
the haloed wellspring of anglophone feminism. Albeit a mess, the
text was a smash hit. *A Vindication of the Rights of Woman* is the
reason why statues in Mary's honor were built in London centuries

later, only to be deemed antifeminist (because pornographic [because nude]) by trans-exclusionary feminists in 2020.[3]

Ironically, a better place for TERFs to look for misogyny would be in the text itself, which claims femmephobically that ladies and "Negroes" both frequently embrace their subjection out of sheer ignorance: a "passive, indolent" tendency betrayed in both cases by a "fondness for dress, for pleasure."[4] Wollstonecraft even admits her alignment with the vicious misogynists of the early eighteenth century (such as Alexander Pope and Jonathan Swift, who routinely excoriated the coquettish "weakness" of most females): "I cannot help agreeing with the severest satirist, considering the sex as the weakest as well as the most oppressed half of the species."[5] We would do well to remember that most of the world's big progressive tracts hadn't just been non-feminist at this time; they'd been strenuously gynophobic. For instance, Jean-Jacques Rousseau's *Émile* (1762)—a touchstone text of the Enlightenment left—warned extensively against women's civil, psychic, and economic independence. Viewing them as naturally cunning and soft, France's proto-socialist *philosophe* felt that women's emancipation would stymy progress, not least because the free exercise of their insatiable sexual appetites would unleash anarchic effeminacy upon society (not the good kind). Mary stood in the midst of all that leftist misogyny.[6] She was writing right up against it, and at the same time she was *of* it.

Wollstonecraft's slave/lady equivalence was meant to be empirically defensible on the basis of a shared infantilization that slaves and ladies both suffer at patriarchy's hands. I suspect she knew infantilization not to be the main form that violence in slavery takes, but she intended the analogy to shock. The anticipated reader she hoped to convince was, after all, likely to believe the proper order of things to be: white women below white men, no doubt, but surely above blacks. As expected, the "hyena in petticoats" (as one of her critics called her) discombobulated her peers with her suggestion that Englishmen *blackened* their mates. Was it possible that the increasingly widely acknowledged un-Christian brutality of the master-slave relation secretly lurked inside every English home?! Others had denounced middle-class female subjugation using the language of chattel slavery abolitionism before 1792. However, *A Vindication* aired, stretched, and exercised the simile. The diagnosis was designed to appeal emotionally to millions of anti-slavery Europeans. In case you're wondering, though: no, she didn't countenance armed insurrection as a remedy for either group's plight.[7]

Wollstonecraft changed the world by insisting that marriage is nothing but a property relation, that women's inferiority is man-made (not given), and that education—a birthright unjustly denied women—is what creates men's superiority. It is unfortunate, though, that she chose to fight Rousseau on his own terms, adopting his paradigm of a hypersensuous and debased femininity as fact. The feminist and the antifeminist ultimately agree on a lot, as literary theorist Cora Kaplan points out: both think "sexuality and pleasure are narcotic inducements to a life of lubricious slavery."[8] Thus *A Vindication* contends that, because girls get initiated so early into the bestial corruptions of sensuality and sentiment, later, as women, they can no more attain the heights of rationality than a tradeable cotton picker might (that is, Mary thinks, not at all). While the condition of slavery, both metaphorical and non-metaphorical, is unjustly imposed from above, it apparently has to be said that victims cultivate their own slavishness when they don't try very hard to better themselves. There's no excuse for other "slaves" to cling to their ignorance, especially given that exceptional cases—like Wollstonecraft herself—exist. She managed to seize rationality for herself by force of will, didn't she?

To reiterate: these derogations of femininity occur within a breakthrough analysis of the social construction of gender. It makes sense to feel guilty, for this reason, when we point out, to quote the feminist critic Susan Gubar, the huge amount of "feminist misogyny" at work here.[9] Yet it's important to say so: Wollstonecraft clearly *hated* British wives' active cultivation of feeling and bodily pleasures. Why weren't they pursuing reason (the one trait befitting the revolutionary character)? Why, oh, why did they accept their lot? For me, it's fair to call *A Vindication* the original claim to being *not like the other girls*. "I have conversed," Mary boasts, "as man with man, with medical men, on anatomical subjects,"[10] and clearly they all agree: women, as the European ruling classes have constructed them, are a problem. Sure, it's largely the fault of men, with their tyranny and unchastity, that this is so. But that's why her text concludes with a plea, not to women to rise up, but to "ye men of understanding": be chaste, and demand more of the mothers of your children![11] As far as I can make out, nowhere does she present herself as a woman speaking to women (in contrast to Olympe de Gouges, who wrote, "Women, wake up!"[12]). Wollstonecraft speaks as a man, *to* men, placing herself among history's few noteworthy females: "Male spirits, confined by mistake in female frames."[13]

"Could the disgust at fallen, fated, or fatal females be self-disgust," Gubar speculates?[14] I certainly find it poignant that *A Vindication* is so harsh with its own author, denying her (by all accounts appetitive, "libertine") sexuality; her (well-documented) experiences of abject, boy-crazy emotion.[15] Mary can't seem to stop pouring contempt on femmes who swoon, cry, flatter, tyrannize, backstab, and betray bigotry while shunning academic study, spoiling pets, reading only for pleasure, and trafficking in "libertine notions of beauty."[16] Jean Grimshaw, a philosopher, once paraphrased Mary's view like this: "Women are enervated, their feelings are false and overstretched, they have factitious and corrupt manners, a romantic and unnatural delicacy of feeling; they are prone to sensuality, sentimentality, artificiality, coquetry, doting self-love, vapid tenderness, and a deluge of false sentiments. They languish like exotics and supinely dream life away."[17] It's true: Wollstonecraft deploys the misogynist orient—a second racialized reference—to clarify how white women debase themselves. "Surely," she exclaims, "these weak beings are only fit for a seraglio!"[18]

When *Rights of Woman* was taught to me as an English literature undergraduate, it was suggested that the rhetorically terrorist tactics of these canonical first words of feminism were necessary if the immortal hyena was to stand a chance of being heard at all. Thus: white wives are caged (confined to the home), systematically stunted (kept illiterate), auctioned (on the marriage market), and bred (via marital rape). Even disregarding the omission of other planks of the actual slavery experience—things like sweated labor, natal alienation, flogging, kinlessness, and the ungendering of black female flesh—it is all, needless to say, a stretch. "I argue from analogy,"[19] Wollstonecraft eventually concedes, granting that middle-class white mothers "indirectly" actually have a lot of "illicit" power ("too much"!).[20] "When I call women slaves, I mean in a political and civil sense."[21] Oh.

The consistent part is that, as with actual slavery, the horizon for ending women's "slavery" in 1792 was not suffrage and citizenship (a bridge too far at that time, even for Mary): it was overwhelmingly about access to reason, learning, and enlightenment. Like a growing majority of her peers, Wollstonecraft felt that the enslaved would remain lost to God if barred access to religious schooling. And, similarly, she said, the metaphorically enslaved illiterates of the respectable household will always be inadequate to the task of Christian motherhood unless they receive rational educations. By 1833, long after her death, the women's movement of abolitionists going door-to-door to canvas housewives, raising funds at anti-slavery bazaars, and lobbying Parliament to sanction slave colonies, was almost two hundred thousand strong. Tragically, these figuratively enslaved activist women didn't emulate or support the vast number of nonfiguratively enslaved women who were struggling to steal themselves away from planters, liberate themselves from legal non-personhood, and escape "social death." Rather, as they leveraged their power over household spending, started civil society initiatives, and went to school, they took inspiration from the would-be free *male* "Negro."

Feminists did succeed in claiming space in public life over the decades that followed. But—like it or not—this success partly flowed from a craven persuasive gambit. Preempting antifeminists' claim that female power would only jeopardize British rule abroad and social order at home, *Rights of Woman* argued, patriotically, that it was actually feminine subjection that was alien to the nature of the British Empire. For the sake of a *better* empire, "we" not only had to free the Negroes, but we had to give ladies rights, Wollstonecraft proclaimed. Male supremacy, thanks to this reframing, could suddenly be held up as anachronistic—pre-British—or implicitly just as primitive as worshipping idols or trading slaves.

Wollstonecraft still did not demand for women the right to hold political office or abjure marriage altogether. Notwithstanding her criticisms of married misery, her own reluctance to marry, and her comparison of husbands to slave owners, she meant only (for now) for women to gain entitlements to the exercise of reason through being good educators of their children by virtue of being, themselves, educated. Feminism, then, but *for* patriarchy. Feminism for unselfish reasons: an army of enlightened mothers as the geopolitical solution to the gender backwardness in which England was mired. What's called for, she suggested to the gentlemen of the world, is a supplement of virtuous, *masculine* maternalism. All will benefit from the "revolution in female manners" on the horizon, because tomorrow's unsentimental womanhood shall purify the nation of the stain of both slaveries.

Mothers in this picture are unwaged, an unmistakable sign that the women who matter aren't working class. Certainly, there were many other types of womanhood in Wollstonecraft's day—for instance, poor, "fallen," laboring, colonized, and/or captive ones— that simply have no place inside her approach to anti-slavery. Still, Wollstonecraft's ideas soon became the dominant incarnation of proto-suffragism, and its offshoots persist even in the twenty-first century. We could call these offshoots feminist imperialism, or imperial feminism.[22] (That's right: abolishing slavery was also a pro-empire position.) Such success was surely not incidental. Why did "feminist philosophy" take off the way it did, in the moment it did? I'd venture an answer: not least because the power of this legendary treatise derived from imperial-feminist misogyny, a patriarchal dual strategy that harnessed both the abolitionist sentiment of the 1790s and the chauvinist stereotypes of effeminate Eastern societies so dear to theorists of civilizational progress in the 1770s. Mary topped the charts partly because she equated women's liberty with ideas about Britain's destiny as a *progressive* imperial power.

We cannot ignore these facts, disillusioning as they are. In the 2010s, as we shall see, German and American feminists seeking to criminalize male Muslims have trotted out very similar claims, this time referencing *their* respective nations' innate gender progressiveness. To give ("our") women more authority, so the Wollstonecraftian line goes, is to restore something organic about the nation's soul. Hence, insofar as the *Rights of Woman* started modern Anglo-feminism, to be a feminist in the West today requires careful consideration of the question, not of whether feminist imperialism *is* feminism, but rather of *whether all feminisms share the same side.* It is one thing to accept our kinship with that high-handed, overblown, curiously macho double comparison of British ladyhood to the "morally corrupt"[23] conditions of non-Western women and enslaved black men. Exploring that inheritance is part of "claiming bad kin."[24] But it is another thing to assume that Wollstonecraftian feminism is a comrade feminism.

Many things were going on at once in this first foray of gender-progressive activism in the West: anti-slavery, macho cool-girl-ism, weaponized ladylike niceness, and pro-market patriotism. Early nineteenth-century European women, urged on by Wollstonecraft's writing, first flexed their ambition to move beyond the sphere of mere influence toward that of power with a consumer boycott: "abstaining" from slave-grown household produce. Quakers in America and Britain had boycotted sugar—because it was slave-grown—already in the 1780s. By the 1800s, though, this ongoing initiative was multidenominational and predominantly led by women. Substantial pressure was put on the slave economy, in the manner of any good BDS (Boycott, Divestment, and Sanctions) campaign. Simultaneously, the sugar boycotts targeted the dynamics of sexed life among the well-to-do Britons by vindicating a strong, informed, and active motherhood in lieu of indolent wifely ignorance—and by raising the question of white women's *political* relationship to the global slave economy in their own right, as sugar consumers.

Feminist abstainers like Mary Birkett, Mary Morris Knowles, Elizabeth Heyrick, Lucy Townsend, and Ann Yearsley linked the barbarous "excesses" of imperial capitalism to male chauvinism, and believed that the key to a calmer, more peaceful and prosperous imperialism lay in women's hands. This new geopolitically oriented feminist notion lent real moral weight to the woman's sphere. It revolutionized traditional domesticity by making it into an explicit resource in the service of the British Empire, even while pretending to seek only minor reform. Doubling down strategically on the conventional idea that (white) women are *women* (meaning: bleeding hearts), feminist sugar abstainers carved out niches in the slavery abolition movement for themselves; then they negotiated and bargained, with their male counterparts from there, for even more power sharing.

Boycotting sugar, according to feminist historian Clare Midgley, transformed British ladies "from self-indulgent weepers over poems on the sufferings of the poor slave into women willing to take action to right wrongs."[25] *A Vindication* had asked rhetorically whether "one half of the human species, like the poor African slaves, [is] to be subjected to prejudices which brutalize them, when principles would be a surer guard, only to sweeten the cup of man."[26] The conceit here was to say that colonizers enslave and debase black people just to extract a granulated tea sweetener; while by the same token, the imposed norm of hyperfemininity is a bad way to extract women's true propriety and motherly productivity at home. (In short: allowing the weaker sex access to reason is a better way to secure our hard work and virtue, just as allowing the darker races access to wages is economically more efficient.) As one might expect, the protest that grew from this opportunistic thought consisted of a lopsided, one-way pseudo-solidarity at best, embodied in the compassionate refusal to buy, drink, or eat sugar made in an evil way.

The way into gender politics, then, was race. It was by doing the humanitarian work of caring for the wretched of the earth overseas that respectable women gained access at home to a position from which feminism could be waged. By refusing to enjoy a commodity of unethical sweetness, and by organizing a mass decades-long "no" to consumer complicity, white pro-abolition ladies began to challenge patriarchy in their lives, beginning with what the communist feminist Angela Davis has called "the insufferable male supremacy within the anti-slavery campaign."[27] They grew less afraid to leave their husbands, fundraised for girls' schools, and formed reading groups. No sooner had Wollstonecraftism asserted itself in these ways, though, that "waves of counterrevolutionary anxiety swept through upper-class homes in England" (to quote historian Barbara Taylor); and amid the backlash that was the Evangelical Revival, gender radicals lost almost all their genteel fans and "polite supporters."[28] Nonetheless, revolutionary ideas about patriarchy continued to circulate, not least among the working classes, thanks to feminist comrades of the utopian co-operativist Robert Owen, such as Anna Wheeler, an Anglo-Irish activist who wanted "a national system of equal education for the Infants of both sexes"[29] and who translated the ideas of Fourier and his fellow Frenchman, Henri Saint-Simon—"free love" and family abolition—into English.

Conversely, right through to the 1830s and beyond, well-to-do British ladies in the pro-imperial mainstream of the abolition movement actively nurtured an ethos of condescension toward non-white women and men at the center of their pro-woman thought. This was not a simple failure of inclusion but, rather, this feminism's core logic: gender emancipation in this context *was* a cult of white maternal pity (and discipline) vis-à-vis the wretched, be they the victims of plantocrats in Antigua or the creatures of sheikhs in the Eastern harems and zenanas of Western fantasy. Male or female, the very existence of the racially downtrodden provided these Western progressives with a rhetorical arsenal (*we rights-deprived females know firsthand what they suffer!* or *only we women can understand their shame!*) as well as a philanthropic purpose, to wit, to save them. Deep listening played no part in this. Although the self-described "West Indian slave" Mary Prince traveled to England in 1828, and stayed for at least five years, "she was never accepted as an anti-slavery campaigner by white women," concludes Midgley. Prince's autobiography was published in London in 1831, but imperial feminists could only see and use raw transcripts of slave suffering, it seems. They could not view *The History of Mary Prince, Written by Herself* as a book—a political book—by a woman.

Wollstonecraft's heirs imagined themselves universalists, but painted pictures of black and brown women's progress that looked very different from their hopes for themselves. It is superbly ironic, given that the domestic sphere was just what ladies wanted to empower themselves to enlarge or transgress, that the destiny they conceived for freedwomen (and oriental maidens) centered on the traditional home. As feminist historian Louise Newman contends, that irony was, as it were, baked in. The European feminists' "critique of the cult of domesticity—as too restrictive and oppressive when applied to themselves—went hand in hand with their defense of domesticity as necessary for the 'advancement' of 'primitive' women."[30] It was thought, for example, that black women had to evolve up to the condition of private cisheteropatriarchal gender, before they moved onto anything else. The feminist novelist and eugenicist Charlotte Perkins Gilman detested the gender division of spheres when it came to white people, but also believed, on the basis of new evolutionary science that the housewife-breadwinner dyad was the highest ambition befitting all "primitives."

If the goal behind politicizing the "bloodstain'd" commodity of sugar was to bend the gendered ideology of separate spheres—public versus private—then early imperial feminists also contrived to shore up that very dyad by pushing black women precisely into the ideal of marriage they themselves were exiting. If they demonstrated that the domestic world was not an insignificant void disconnected from the callous world of imperial commerce, they refused to perceive that the connection runs both ways, that economic logics also permeate the family. Feminist sugar abstainers never considered that they themselves might share responsibility with the men of their "race" for empire and its atrocities, from exploiting to enslaving. Compassionate and kind, the modern-mannered Englishwoman only attenuates these ills. Worse, a narrowly domestic gender needs to be imposed on the less fortunate races, so as to free up (white) womanhood for civic work. This new woman possessed "the power to make the nation virtuous," Midgley explains. "Moralising the Empire, she transforms imperialism into a *legitimate* source of prosperity and civilisation."[31] On social media, two centuries later, whenever a campaign to decolonize this or that British institution is ruffling feathers, one can still readily spot this vision—hard-dying in a latter-day empire's soul—of women as removers and mitigators of colonizer violence.

The truth is that the new models of English womanhood, crafted during and after the sugar boycotts, fit to cleanse and uplift various masculinist bloodbaths of their era, were instruments of empire from the beginning. And if their first iterations were thoroughly saccharine—based on an essentialist notion of tearful feminine sympathy for the oppressed—they also rapidly became more arrogant. One of the early feminist reform initiatives directed at colonial India, for instance, was the evangelical campaign against so-called widow burning, or *sati*. (This Sanskrit word for the self-immolating widow herself was used in English to refer instead to the practice, which was rare, even in the early nineteenth century.) The rite was not a strictly religious one, as feminist attorney Rafia Zakaria notes in *Against White Feminism*. Nevertheless, she writes, "in the 'sati' of British colonial imagination, Hindus were . . . hypnotized by Brahmanic texts and hence incapable of disobeying them."[32] Stories of male pagan "Hindoos" forcing sobbing teens onto the funeral pyres of their ugly old husbands circulated sensationally in the UK periodicals of the 1800s, leading dozens of ladies' associations to send petitions to the superintendents of the Raj, beseeching them to intervene against "suttee."

The anti-sati campaign kicked off in earnest with the missionary incursion into India in 1813. It positioned white women (sometimes more so than white men) as the key to saving brown women from brown men. While Indian groups had long been organizing against poverty, caste apartheid, femicide, and rape, it apparently never occurred to the Europeans at the helm of this new single-issue crusade that Indian widows should be self-determining within—let alone leading—the campaign. As Gayatri Spivak highlighted in her field-defining 1988 essay "Can the Subaltern Speak?," the figure of the sati, as a sexed "subaltern" or sub-political entity, was thus caught between white and brown patriarchies, hopeless of having her real social and economic concerns heard.[33] Her subalternity was key to European feminist evangelicals' excited new proposition that Indian women were *the white woman's burden*. In feminist historian Antoinette Burton's phrase, Indian women represented "a reformable clientele" for feminism, while at the same time being "the colonial subjects in whose name British women's political authority in the imperial nation-state was justified."[34]

Increasingly, Western feminists and missionaries coalesced around the idea that Indian women were transhistorically feminism-less, while white Christian women were mostly already free, actually. "Is it not manifest," asked one Baptist missionary in 1820, "that the Ladies in Britain are the natural guardians of these unhappy Widows and Orphans in British India?"[35] Oddly enough, much earlier in the 1780s, a fair few English writers like Eliza Fay, Elizabeth Hamilton, and Phebe Gibbes had treated the subject of sati with somewhat more respect for the widows' agency, even drawing parallels between the Hindu patriarchate's stigmatizing treatment of single women, and British patriarchy's treatment of *them*. But by the time the missionary campaign won its aim, in 1830—when William Bentinck, the governor-general of India, issued a sati ban—it had become unusual to equate the positions of British and Indian women.[36] When Jane scoffingly invokes suttee at the end of *Jane Eyre* (1847), it is as a foil to her own proto-feminist individualism and desire to be a missionary in her own right.[37] The British Empire needs emancipated Englishwomen, Eyre reminds us—not mere missionary's wives.

Charlotte Brontë's famous heroine was representing the state's interests well. In 1851, the census found that fully 43 percent of Britain's women were single, and Harriet Martineau—a suffragist and abolitionist—called for educated British maidens at risk of becoming old maids to emigrate en masse to Australia, "converting a crowd of pining daughters of England into rejoicing Australian matrons, the mothers of a new race."[38] Concurrently, a group of somewhat bolder bourgeois feminists got together in Langham Place, in London, to create a paper, *The English Woman's Journal*, dedicated to boosting middle-class women's emigration. Leaving aside Martineau's emphasis on "imperious maternity" (marriage and childbearing), which they insisted was optional for the ambitious colonial woman, the Langham Place Group took up the chaste imperial allegory of Britannia, decreased its sweetness further, and reworked it to make a hip "new model" of womanhood in the 1850s. This neo-Britannia was independent, unconfined, and self-sufficient: a well-bred *lady* and yet, possibly, a *wage-earner* (how modern!). She was still massively racist.

Maybe, come to think of it, she should have a name—a brand—of her own? The time for grand performances of selflessness, as in sugar boycotting, was drawing to a close. As it happened, in the patriotic women's press, there already existed "Mrs. John Bull": an old, no-nonsense female counterpart to the stout, jolly, politically nonpartisan male figure of "John Bull" (Britain's equivalent of America's Uncle Sam). Mrs. Bull was a frugal, hospitable matron who, like her husband, embodied the myth of a well-fed, timeless, prosperous Englishness, and hearkened nostalgically back to preindustrial scenes before the industrial invasion of "dark satanic mills" began polluting green and pleasant land. This was the metaverse to which Langham Place ladies ingeniously added a feminist. Their idea was that Mr. and Mrs. Bull have an Amazonian daughter: Jane Bull. And so, in the opening article of *The English Woman's Journal*, readers were introduced to the era's new it-girl, *Miss Bull*.[39] Energetic yet feminine, middle-class, Protestant, and hands-on, Jane was fashionable and futuristic but still rooted in this archaic gender-progressive "shield-maiden"-esque Anglo-Saxon past. Lads, this capable English rose was born ready to sally forth and clean up the colonies!

As the "new model Englishwoman," Miss Bull was of course bolstered by the unbeatable feminist authority of that real-life Britannia and ultimate girlboss, Queen Victoria. Tailored to the eugenic anxieties of the age, she also bore the complexion of a patriot and came freighted with assurances that olde Anglo racial purity would not be compromised one jot by all this newfangled female independence. Between 1858 and 1862, *The English Woman's Journal* sought to use its new girly avatar to inspire a small army of well-educated Miss Bulls to sign on for imperial service.[40] Instead of languishing as underpaid or unemployed governesses in the overpopulated, sooty confines of the metropole, they could be abroad, galloping across wide open spaces on horseback, enjoying exercise, and experiencing self-sufficiency and respect (on account of the "dignity" supposedly afforded in the colonies to the hardworking white single woman). Even as these appeals enthralled some readers, the propaganda was also much mocked in the press for its inaccuracy. Counter-accounts proliferated of ex-governesses' thoroughly miserable experiences in the "bush," the prairie, and the jungle. What was worse, arguments for shipping off burdensome "surplus" females to the antipodes were circulating freely, in parallel, in the mainstream newspapers, for literally opposite—antifeminist—reasons.

Slowly, a feminist consensus did emerge in London that emigration could only help a small number of women. Although the Female Middle Class Emigration Society hung on for a few decades, early British feminists' preoccupation with emigration as a mass, structural solution to women's confinement and anomie proved, ultimately, short-lived. Nevertheless, the new prototype of privileged womanhood had been invented: an adventuress who needs to travel around in order to stretch her freedom-loving limbs. You might think that figures like the Crimean War heroine Mary Seacole, a "doctress" and businesswoman who thought of herself as a new type of middle-class Englishwoman—that is, a proud black colonial from Jamaica yearning for emigration—would precisely fit the bill, but you would be wrong. While Mrs. Seacole's white peers Caroline Chisholm and Florence Nightingale were feminist icons, Midgley writes, "Seacole was not celebrated by Langham Place feminists as an exemplar."[41]

What can one say, but that this school of feminism was an ethnonationalist endeavor—it was openly eugenic and nationalist? In the 1860s, *The English Woman* routinely scaremongered about moral catastrophes that would occur in the New World "unless an emigration of white women from Great Britain took place."[42] White, here, meant: not Irish (Irish girls are wild and fast) and not Scottish (Scots are unskilled, indecent, half-savage, fit only to cut peat). For Langham Place women like Maria Rye, Barbara Bodichon, Matilda

Hays, Bessie Parkes, and Emily Davies, it had to be well-mannered Anglo-Saxon Englishwomen sailing from the core to the periphery, even if they weren't going to procreate. They worried that, already, Irish, Scottish, "half-breed" and non-white girls had caused some of Britain's colonies to degenerate—both morally and materially. With reference to British Columbia, *The English Woman* warned that "religion and morality would be altogether ruined" before long, because of the racial "miscegenation" bound to occur wherever male British settlers were mostly single. By disseminating the "right" genetic stock in the form of swarms of can-do Miss Bulls, though, feminist emigration advocates were going to inspire the settlers of the commonwealth to govern more effectively. This would include, for example, not allowing events like the 1857–8 Indian Rebellion to happen again, in which white women's bodies had been threatened (as the non-feminist and feminist press supposed together, racistly) by violent Southeast Asian men.

While they reserved the most dehumanizing rhetorical treatment for brown men, metropolitan feminists of the imperial persuasion also frequently criticized male English colonists' disappointing lack of patriotic virtue abroad insofar as they were dishonoring, abusing, and (worse?) breeding with the natives. Their willingness to bash "their own" did not extend, however, to imagining the *brown woman* as warranting feminist defense against the colonial officer. In 1880s editions of the Langham group's journal, whenever articles like "An Opening for Women in the Colonies" beseeched readers to offer their services to Indian women whose plights should be a "special and deserving object of feminist concern," it was not the women's treatment at *Englishmen's* hands that the feminists had in mind. Rather, in a manner we've seen echoed time again in the voting patterns of affluent white women in the West, racial and colonial class loyalties firmly trumped sisterhood. Biological as well as cultural whiteness was thought to be imperiled all over the world, and the feminist "twist" was that it was men's fundamentally un-Anglo-Saxon tyranny, at home, in excluding women from public life, that was to blame.

I have no investment in claiming that Mary Wollstonecraft invented imperial feminism, but she supplied certain templates for feminist reasoning—by analogy to race, with macho reference to national interest, and through the posit of "our" children's need for mother's moral authority—that have contributed heavily to the genre. Today, Western feminists owe it to the rest of the world to take a hard look at the echoes between the antiquated program of sending the "enslaved" Englishwoman overseas, which built indirectly on Wollstonecraft to promote well-educated women as ideal colonists, and the Islamophobic "femonationalisms" and feminist "enlightened fundamentalisms" of our era, which romanticize "empowered" saviorists and aid volunteers, or trumpet women's suffering under Islamist regimes, only to ban women from wearing the hijab on European beaches. Sour as it may feel to dwell on: early European advocacy for expanding women's sphere of action—from sugar-shunning consumer advocacy to colonial missionary work—was, at the same time, feminism and white supremacism, both empowering a sex, and charging eugenically at a perceived cultural crisis eroding the empire.

TWO

The Anti-Antiracist Abolitionist

Thank God the Black man was freed! I wish for him all possible happiness and all possible progress, but not in encroachments upon the holy of holies of the Anglo-Saxon race.

—BELLE KEARNEY (Woman's Christian Temperance Union superintendent and future Democratic senator), address to National American Woman Suffrage Association, 1903[1]

While the flaxen-haired Jane Bull was flexing her Anglo-Saxon muscles, many American women had "created freedom for themselves" (in the historian Stephanie Jones-Rogers's words) on the other side of the Atlantic by owning and trading slaves.[2] Right from the beginning of New World colonization, female settlers had participated in the slave economy despite being, themselves, legal nonentities or "femes covert," meaning that, as wives, their legal being was subsumed under their husbands, along with their property. Margaret Hardenbroeck was one such slave-trading Dutch burgher in what is now New York—formerly New Amsterdam. Hardenbroeck receives semi-apologistic treatment, as a pipe-smoking business whiz, in a recent feminist monograph by the "mother of lesbian history" Lillian Faderman, *Woman: The American History of an Idea* (2022). The feminist historian calls her "the first woman in America to build herself an empire," "as ruthless as the male shipowners," and so on.[3] Faderman is hardly an outlier. When I googled "Margaret Hardenbroeck," the top result was from a website called Boss-Babe: "15 Badass Entrepreneurial Women Who Shaped History."[4] Besides slaving, Hardenbroeck's boss-babe badassery consists of her insistence on signing a prenup to ensure that her daughter would inherit her husband's wealth, human chattel and all.

American women—especially members of the Southern plantocracy—regularly inherited, purchased, and exchanged human beings throughout the eighteenth and well into the nineteenth centuries. "For them," Jones-Rogers reflects, "slavery was their freedom."[5] Owning slaves was a neat way to mitigate or refuse the patriarchal legal doctrine of "coverture." In *They Were Her Property: White Women as Slave Owners in the American South* (2019), Jones-Rogers shows how slave-owning women frequently rejected the strictures of coverture "by devising instruments that protected their personal investments in chattel slavery."[6] Certainly, she acknowledges their investments in the slave economy were "not part of a grand scheme to secure women's rights or gender equality."[7] Nevertheless, they underwrote a gruesome culture of feminine empowerment in the antebellum South, and decades later, some feminists would show themselves ready to defend this legacy as echt feminism.

Even as some women were defying the patriarchy by trading in commodified human beings, others were of course developing their feminism from *within* the condition of enslavement and its wake. Maroon feminism—the everyday anti-patriarchal action of runaway slaves—was far more likely than bourgeois feminism to be a feminism of consistent abolition.[8] After all, it was forged at the "ground zero" of capitalist gender because it embodied the resistance and the freedom dreams of those whom the private American family cast outside of itself (in order to, itself, come together). Defined within the grammar of slavery as antithetical to the institution of motherhood—and therefore *non-women*—captive female Africans could not rely on solidarity from "femes covert" on the plantation. In fact, ladies (feminist or not) not infrequently intensified pregnant slaves' torments, whipped them, and punished them for the very adulterous rapes inflicted by their white male relatives.[9]

But it is not the all-too-obvious villainy of plantation mistresses I am ultimately interested in here. Rather, it is the robust tradition, within US feminism, of *anti-antiracist* abolitionism—in other words, opposition to slavery but not to white supremacy—that this chapter seeks to sketch. This enemy feminism was on the other side of only *some* aisles from the suffragism of slavers and the proto-girl-bossism of slave traders (best embodied by the staunchly feminist first woman senator of the US: white supremacist lynching fanatic Rebecca Latimer Felton).[10] It's a small mystery, in this context, that the most widely canonized contribution to feminism by somebody in and after captivity—namely, that of the preacher-prophet Sojourner Truth—has been subject to a long-standing and persistent misrepresentation in American women's studies. Our whistle-stop tour of suffragist anti-antiracism begins with Truth's friends and allies. Rightly, the visionary freedwoman has been cultivated as an icon, a poster in every women's studies department, and a picture-book role model for little girls. But her very visible story, preserved and handed down the generations by suffragism's grandes dames, is also unfortunately an object lesson in some feminisms' non-solidaritous solidarity; our uncanny reflex to overwrite, ventriloquize, domesticate, and erase sisters of color.

Liberals have canonized Sojourner Truth not so much for her lifelong activism as for a single moment: the challenge she is supposed to have posed to a roomful of suffragists in a speech at the Women's Rights Convention in Akron, Ohio, in 1851, all while baring her naked breast and brandishing her sturdy laborer's bicep. "Ain't I a woman?" she famously asked—or so we're told. Understandably, her rhetorical question and perceived ontological riddle caused the spillage of much philosophical ink. Was she appealing to white women for inclusion within their concept of "woman"? Or was she challenging their concept? No, better to assume she was applying for membership in the ever-widening circle of the liberal progress narrative. *Of course* she was a woman—the Department of Treasury even recently threatened to put her face on the back of the $10 bill in an ultimate gesture of state-sanctioned inclusivity. In the twenty-first century, the "ain't I a woman?" formula, because it was deemed so successful in appealing to the conscience of the powerful, inspired a number of white trans women ("ain't *I* a woman, too?") to riff on it and repeat it.[11] To quote the critical theorist Cameron Awkward-Rich, Truth's immortal question "is a position to be occupied that allows the speaker to extract and use the symbolic power of Black womanhood."[12]

In the 1990s, however, a handful of scholars dug a little deeper into the Sojourner Truth archive and cast serious doubt on the quote. It turned out there were several competing myths and fabrications; some of them might have even been the preacher's own. But one thing is certain: the received version of the famous speech she delivered has an embarrassingly obvious problem. The *ain't*s, *tink*s, and *chillen*s ought really to have tipped scholars off a century prior, because Truth . . . wasn't a Southerner! She was born in New Amsterdam and spoke both low Dutch and Afro-Dutch English. It transpires that Frances Gage, the white suffragist and abolitionist who chaired proceedings at Akron, reconstructed the speech twelve years after the fact "from memory," with every intention of celebrating and supporting a by-then international icon.[13] Astonishingly, Gage simply went ahead and rendered the whole thing in what philosopher Donna Haraway calls the "imagined idiolect of The Slave, the supposedly archetypical Black plantation slave of the South."[14] (It was "not a southern Afro-American English that any linguist, much less actual speaker, would claim," Haraway pointedly adds.) Gage also did her Black comrade the dubious favor of making her remarks four times longer than the plain-English transcript published at the time by the abolitionist minister and editor Marius Robinson in the *Anti-Slavery Bugle*.

It is highly likely, then, that Sojourner Truth never said *ain't I, ar'n't I,* or *am I not a woman.* Not literally, writes the African American studies professor Imani Perry. But "she said it symbolically through her work, through her 'shadows'"—Truth's term for the photographic portraits she sold of herself, as *cartes de visite.* Via these cards, if nowhere else, white women *were* forced to look at and consider Sojourner's gender. For Perry, "The frequency with which she had her shadow made suggests that not only was she arguing for the recognition of her womanhood, but also of her unrecognized beauty."[15] Interestingly, while disseminating this visual (and oral, via her preaching) campaign of insurgent non-ladylike femaleness, Truth was sometimes happy to let false, grandiose tales printed about her stand. She took exception, however—scholars agree—to misrepresentations of her dialect. The most sympathetic reading of the convention chairwoman's presumptuousness is therefore that Gage, despite knowing Truth, calculated that a "standard" idiolect of blackness was non-optional in the 1860s context (put differently: she was trying to maximize her audience). If Truth was going to continue enjoying commercial success as an evangelical, Gage bet, she had to be legible to white readers *as* Black.

So, Gage slotted Truth's gospel of critical difference into a classical humanist figuration—the same one that bourgeois abolitionists tended to fashion out of every ex-enslaved voice—a worldview in which Black women are simply white women *but more so*, oppression-wise. The unilateral stylistic choices inscribed, in Haraway's phrase, a hostile notion of difference: "One that sneaks the masterful unmarked categories in through the back door in the guise of the specific."[16] As a result, every single time Gage's version of Truth's speech is anthologized, white society's "inability to hear"[17] grows more entrenched. Of course, the abolitionist sisterhood's high-handed misuse of Truth is itself a kind of text, a history that contemporary feminists can and should study. To do so doesn't require further romanticization of Sojourner Truth; it is, in fact, the layering of past gestures of violent romanticization that we must unpeel. In her book *Sojourner Truth*, Nell Painter makes a start on this, wading into the weeds of Truth's own oracular fictions about her past while also judiciously puncturing other people's self-serving appropriations, notably Harriet Beecher Stowe's.[18]

In 1863, Stowe, the author of *Uncle Tom's Cabin* (1852), published a long feature in the *Atlantic* magazine entitled "Sojourner Truth, The Libyan Sibyl," chockful of breathless mystifications and plain errors. Incredibly, Stowe said that Truth was dead; actually, she lived for a further twenty years. Furthermore, at different points in her article, Stowe said contradictorily that Truth came from Africa, Egypt, Ethiopia, Libya, and the American South, as though these were somehow synonymous. Most egregiously of all, she wrote that the "sibyl" thought little of feminism, implying that abolition and woman suffrage were unrelated causes in a "race" activist's mind, and therefore that Stowe and Truth could not be fighting the same fight. Sojourner Truth, in reality, was a veteran suffragist. Stowe herself, at this point, was a rather lackluster suffragist in her own right, but world-famous. A best-selling novelist and (clearly) miserably careless journalist, she liked to winter in Rome. Surrounded by other literary stars such as Elizabeth Gaskell, she entertained them by doing impressions of Truth's "baritone" voice.[19]

According to Painter, when "The Libyan Sibyl" came out in the *Atlantic*, Truth only corrected one of Stowe's falsifications: "I never make use of the word honey."[20] It is possible to read a frosty dignity in this statement, but it may also be that Truth saw value in the spin on her identity in the context of the wider cause. What is beyond dispute is that Harriet Beecher Stowe bears much responsibility for the shaping of understandings of Truth that are still taught in US classrooms today. This is because what Stowe emphasized above all was one apocryphal story, in which Truth is supposed to have smacked down Frederick Douglass's proposal that Black people move to armed struggle in the wake of the Fugitive Slave Act, silencing him (and the whole room) with the simple, thunderous question, "*Frederick, is God dead?*" The Black abolitionist on whom Stowe showers so much respect in the *Atlantic* is a pacifist largely of Stowe's own conjuring. Not only is Stowe positioning herself as the "real" feminist of the two (since she is a woman undistracted by any other intersecting axes of concern), but also that, ultimately, it is Stowe who is the real authority on abolitionist strategy, too. Stowe pointedly offers readers a purely nonviolent and all-forgiving Libyan Sibyl, whereas, in reality, as Painter shows, the ex-enslaved preacher had vengeful and caustic moments much as one would expect. Defanging and disarming her subject, Stowe spreads "the gentleness of spiritualism over Truth's own millennial conviction that there surely would come a day of racial judgment."[21] No doubt, this gentler version of the Sybil, full of forgiveness and wedded to nonviolence, has been more palatable to white feminism than the reality. Both Gage and Stowe "hijacked Truth's body as a vehicle for their own words," concludes Kyla Schuller. They turned her "into a colorful caricature who promoted the white feminist agenda."[22]

Stowe's maneuvers—quietly ejecting Sojourner Truth from feminism in the middle of the Civil War—were tellingly elitist. Truth's gender interventions in the suffrage movement were, after all, rooted in her experience of brutally alienated physical labor: an experience to which hundreds of thousands of majority-women industrial and agricultural laborers, "mill girls," and domestic servants in the early nineteenth century could relate a great deal better than could people like Stowe and Gage. In *Women, Race & Class* (1983), Angela Davis stresses the high intensity of gender-class militancy that existed in the US among mill women in the 1820s and '30s. Hundreds of large-scale "turn-outs" and strikes by textile employees protested "the double oppression they suffered as women and as industrial workers"[23] long before the heavily over-mythologized birth of American feminism, the convention at Seneca Falls, 1848, took place.

Tellingly, antebellum woman-suffrage discourse by people like Stowe, Susan Anthony, and Elizabeth Stanton tended to ignore, rather than support, this agitation (even if Anthony later toured the country addressing working women in a pro-suffrage speech cunningly entitled "Women Want Bread, Not the Ballot" to attract attendees prior to flipping them to her cause). At the same time that it ignored working women, this prewar feminism emphasized a common victimhood between bourgeois white women and Black men. But after the war, this too fell away, and many feminist former abolitionists refused to enact solidarity of any kind with ex-slaves (not even committedly woman-suffragist ones like Sojourner Truth and Frederick Douglass).

Prewar, among bourgeois feminists, the two slaveries, that is, slavery and, er, male supremacy, had gone hand in hand. (Incidentally, historians agree that the resolution at Seneca Falls demanding the vote for women only passed thanks to the radical freedman Frederick Douglass's oratorical brilliance.[24]) Admittedly, Stanton, the self-styled first leader of American womanhood, had only been an abolitionist out of political convenience rather than real conviction anyway, or so some historians claim.[25] While synthesizing undeniably new and pathbreaking arguments for sex equality in employment, income, property, custody, and divorce, Stanton was equally devoted, like it or not, to the antidemocratic principles of liberal racism and elitism. As soon as slavery was abolished, indeed, her racist invectives against Blacks and immigrants were expressed far too widely and often to be minimized as mere demagoguery. In the *New York Standard*, for example, Stanton published a truly foul letter to the editor expressing her disgust at the very idea that educated Anglo-Saxon females who campaigned for abolition were now ungratefully being asked to "stand aside and see 'Sambo' walk into the kingdom first"—that is, to support ratification of the Fourteenth and Fifteenth Amendments.

After these amendments *were* ratified anyway, in 1868 and 1870 respectively, without her support, the haloed feminist founder fumed for decades about her sex's humiliation. It was the tragedy of her life, and Susan Anthony's too, that white women were made to wait for the ballot like mere Native Americans, for another half-century, while male immigrants and ex-slaves got down to work "making laws for Lucretia Mott."[26] (Stanton thought it ludicrous that multiethnic hoi polloi would rule democratically over someone as estimable as her friend Mrs. Mott—a feminist abolitionist from Nantucket who was also Benjamin Franklin's first cousin.) Stanton and Anthony, these two grandees, actively opposed universal suffrage—simple as that. They, for example, strongly supported instating an educational suffrage bar (that is, a literacy test) to qualify men and women for the vote. Simultaneously denying that Black women's enfranchisement was a "sex" question at all and refusing to support any further "race" progress as long as white women didn't have the vote, Stanton freely recounts in the *History of Woman Suffrage* (1881) how she told Douglass plainly after the war that she does "not believe in allowing ignorant negroes and foreigners to make laws for her to obey."[27]

Despite not bothering to lie about unedifying incidents such as that one, Stanton and Anthony took care to control the historical record in such a way as to marginalize or exclude outright (except as "race" adversaries) central Black feminist players, notably the poet, abolitionist, and temperance activist Frances Harper. In the baldly revisionist, coauthored *History of Woman Suffrage*, it is the heroic authors themselves (Stanton, Anthony, and Gage)— along with that quite minor meeting at Seneca Falls that only one of them even attended—who stand at the mythical fore. They are conspicuously angry about the fact that, when their movement finally split ignominiously over race in 1869 at the American Equal Rights Association (AERA) annual meeting, both factions wanted Truth's support—and their side lost. They are unashamed of their ex-antiracist stance, and actively opposed to Black enfranchisement if it means that "woman" must "wait." What they don't make clear, conversely, is their adversaries' longtime feminism. These were people like Harper, Douglass, Lucy Stone, and Julia Howe, who recognized that even an exclusively *male* black enfranchisement was a small step toward Reconstruction and an overwhelming priority in the wake of slavery's industrial-scale annihilation of black humanity. "When it is a question of race," said Harper, "I let the lesser question of sex go."[28]

Douglass, Stanton's old ally on the women's vote resolution, concurred. "I do not see how any one can pretend that there is the same urgency in giving the ballot to the woman as to the negro," he said. "With us, the matter is a question of life or death":

> When women, because they are women, are hunted down through the cities of New York and New Orleans; when they are dragged from their houses and hung upon lamp-posts; when their children are torn from their arms, and their brains dashed out upon the pavement . . . then she [the white feminist] will have an urgency to obtain the ballot equal to our own.[29]

Again, this world-historic oratorical power prevailed. Sojourner Truth, like many of her comrades present at the 1869 AERA split, bleakly hated the fact that the state had successfully pitted two facets of herself against each other. But she went, as any anti-elitist must, with Douglass and Harper.

Anthony and Stanton continued to advance white supremacist arguments for women's civil rights right up until their respective deaths: Anthony's in 1906 and Stanton's in 1902. From the 1870s onward, a number of thwarted and resentful suffragists followed their lead in touting white women's racial and cultural superiority to the newly enfranchised male constituencies—black and/or naturalized immigrant men.[30] In fact, well into the twentieth century, the conferences of the National American Woman Suffrage Association (NAWSA) included numerous speeches making the case that, per Mississippi temperance activist Belle Kearney, "the enfranchisement of women would ensure immediate and durable white supremacy."[31] In 1917, the president of NAWSA herself, Carrie Chapman Catt, issued a compilation of demographic papers that aimed to prove that "white supremacy will be strengthened, not weakened, by woman suffrage."[32] One hundred years later, the *New York Times* belittled an antiracist student protest at Iowa State that opposed naming a building after Catt for this reason. "Mrs. Catt made one controversial statement in a losing effort to win ratification in two Southern states of the 19th Amendment," wrote the *Times*, passing off a whole white supremacist treatise as a single "controversial remark."[33]

They wish. From the 1880s on, the burgeoning field of eugenics—meaning the perfectibility of human "stock" through selective breeding, based on ableist notions of perfection—began to present all kinds of new opportunities for the spiritual daughters of Stanton and Anthony to retrofit their white supremacist worldview with scientific ballast. Not only Catt and Kearney, but many suffrage women took up these latest theories of biological evolution as platforms from which to assert their sex's duty to be the natural protectors of uncivilized races.[34] It is partly for this reason, as we shall explore later on, that white supremacist organizations in the early twentieth century—from the Ku Klux Klan to the British Union of Fascists—attracted feminist women in droves. The feminist revaluation of female maternity as creative rather than passive, as powerful rather than incidental to the making of history, did not inherently come with antiracism. On the contrary, many "scientifically backed" feminisms were all about remaking racism anew.

Some of the new eugenic feminisms were even black, and Frances Harper herself (much like the early W. E. B. Du Bois and other voices of racial uplift) increasingly deployed eugenicist arguments as part of what Schuller calls her "black feminist biopolitics," a worldview that maintained distinctions between the "fit" and "unfit" but dismissed the role of race in determining such "fitness" to reproduce.[35] As part of Harper's orientation toward "transcending blackness," she prevailed on her fellow elite feminists not to "class the worthy and worthless together."[36] *Some* black people, she said, had all kinds of respectable, civilized, even civilizing potential in them as a group, just waiting to be unleashed. The innovative feminist tactic here was that she borrowed racial-scientific language to denounce the rape of enslaved or formerly enslaved women by "licentious and exploitative white men (often working class, and therefore uncivilized)." Rather than deny the existence of the "impulsive sensibility for which black women were widely condemned,"[37] in other words, Harper cast the sexually predatory lower orders of white masculinity as the true progenitor of that black sluttishness.

Today, it is painfully obvious that many people who study the black eugenics of this period—for instance, the "baby contests" held by the NAACP (National Association for the Advancement of Colored People, founded in 1909)—want to minimize it, or even defend it as "oppositional eugenics," a form of resistance involving the strategic co-option and turning back of white supremacist power discourse against itself. Clearly, this is a fool's errand, since—as Schuller notes—any attempt "to improve the racial stock and challenge white supremacy by limiting the birth rate of the poor and celebrating the rising fitness of the race" can only be "oppositional in a very limited sense."[38] White supremacy has always been flexible enough to include visions of non-white evolutionary progress (up, up toward a less black blackness) within its shifting accounts of racial hierarchy. Far from threatening whiteness, even the most cunning versions of black feminist eugenics could only ever affirm it.

Black women were frequently the "other abolitionists" of white feminism—the feminists who refused to put white ladies first. *And* at the same time, several black clubwomen lay down, now and then, with the enemy, putting respectability and whiteness, in the guise of ladyhood, first. Thus, until we resolve it, a persistent inheritance of pseudo-abolitionism—that is, abolitionism without antiracism and even *against* antiracism—will continue to flow from the core of Western feminism. (I call this "pseudo-abolition" because the real meaning of "abolition" is akin to unraveling a ball of wool as big as the whole world. In order to get to the bottom of one un-freedom, we have to keep tugging until all the other unfreedoms, which aren't "other" at all, come undone.) To be sure, it hurts to sit with the anti-antiracist element of enemy feminism, this ableist and anti-poor eliminationism, that coexists with the other, liberatory forms of feminism in the black abolition archive. Yet there's no way around it; to paraphrase philosopher Sara Ahmed, if talking about eugenics in feminism gets in the way of feminist happiness, we need to get in the way of feminist happiness.[39]

THREE

The Civilizer

*Of course one can't condone the (alleged) behaviour of
Oxfam staff in Haiti and elsewhere. But I do wonder
how hard it must be to sustain "civilised" values in a
disaster zone. And overall I still respect those who go
in to help out, where most of us wd not tread.*

—MARY BEARD, author, professor of Classics, feminist, 2018[1]

What was feminism when it was forged, quite literally, on safari?
Between March and May of 1891, a wealthy American suffragist by
the name of May French Sheldon, who believed that "on the status
of women depends the progress of nations,"[2] led a long caravan expedition through Kenya and Tanzania, ostensibly to collect ethno-
graphic impressions for the advancement of science, but also simply
to prove that a woman could do it. This daring feminist celebrity
was in the company of over 150 hired Africans. She was still reported in the Western press to be traveling "alone and unescorted."[3]

In 2013 (the same year *White Queen*, a period drama, aired on
Netflix), the general chatter about season three of HBO's *Game of
Thrones* often described the pale, white-haired conqueror Daenerys
Targaryen in the same way—as a single heroic traveler charting a
luminous path. Throughout that season, as the army of the *khaleesi*
made its civilizing progress through the fictional oriental continent

of Essos, the story went that she single-handedly uplifted the un-differentiated barbarian hordes. A key episode ended with her held aloft in gratitude, clad in virginal blue, by a sea of faceless oppressed people of color. By season five, Targaryen's liberating mission had reached Slaver's Bay, where she was hailed as *mhysa*—Mother—by all the freed slaves.[4] She promoted one castrated Black man and one Black girl to be her advisers.

In 2016, millions of Democratic voters shared a meme of Hillary Clinton photoshopped as "Dany"—baby dragon on one shoulder, emerging from the flames—not because they were imperialists, so magazines like *Vox* happily explained, but because they were fem-inists.[5] In an essay that hasn't aged well given that the Mother of Dragons ended up effecting a holocaust and throwing a visually Nazi-esque victory rally, the 2020 presidential runner Liz Warren extolled Daenerys as a democratizer. Warren felt that the drag-on-wielding blonde sought "to win with the people," progressively, in contrast to the other blonde queen, Cersei, the tyrant who "ex-pects to win in spite of them." For Warren, Dany symbolized the belief that people "rise up together to win."[6] This was a ludicrous claim to make, even at the beginning of season eight, about a blue-eyed, blue-blooded "Valyrian" fan favorite who is quite straight-forwardly a ruthless humanitarian imperialist. Yet it belonged to a visual and aesthetic Anglo-American tradition that is over one hundred years old: of celebrating feminism through the figure of a "white queen" whose purity and splendor are visually offset by grateful brown or Black populations, and who concludes a long career of feminist adventuring by participating in genocide.

In 1891, when Mrs. Sheldon set off from New York for her three-month-long adventure safari in East Africa, leaving her banker hus-band behind, she packed a huge spun-silver sequined ball gown, a ceremonial sword inlaid with jewels, a tiara, a set of dangling chains and brooches, and a blonde wig longer than Daenerys's. The *New York Times* reported that the Parisian fashion brand, House of Worth, had "made this dress for the express purpose of furnish-ing the wearer with an irresistible means of conquest." In Sheldon's own words, the outfit was "a well-devised plan" to exploit "the penchant of savage and semi-barbarous persons for finery in dress and ornaments"[7] (a femmephobic racial stereotype Wollstonecraft had already expounded at length in 1792). The effect of all this sumptuary cunning on the part of 1891's number one macho high femme must have been spectacular. While trekking, or being carried in a litter, from Zanzibar to Mount Kilimanjaro and back, Sheldon flew a US flag over her retinue, as well as a kind of chivalric banner attached to her walking stick, blazoning the Latin phrase *noli me tangere*: touch me not. Everyone back home wanted to know, did her male escorts heed the banner? Did the warriors and sultans whom she met along the way—or, God forbid, her porters—try to touch her? The sexual frisson of May's "unescorted" status was irresistibly magnetic. This cosplaying "queen" knew exactly what she was doing in terms of media strategy.

In 1893, a reporter called Fannie Williams fannishly reported that "the White Queen" had been holding court in the ethnological section of the Woman's Building at the Chicago World's Fair, where Sheldon's palanquin, tent, and food storage equipment were also on magnificent display. "She told me the story," wrote Fannie, "of her fright one morning on waking, to discover a huge python wound around the corner of [the palanquin]." Yet Sheldon had been unafraid! Positively swooning, Williams relays how, everywhere she went, Africans "would crowd around to see her . . . entreating her to remain and rule over them."[8] As fans like this already knew from the White Queen's own post-safari publications and lectures, upon arriving in Mombasa, she had found that porters were in short supply. Irritatingly, Mrs. Sheldon therefore had to go to Zanzibar to find staff sufficient for her thirteen-week trip. There she spent large sums hiring porters as well as soldiers, interpreters, female attendants, and litter bearers for the huge wicker "conveyance" she'd commissioned.

In Sheldon's telling of these preparations, we encounter her at one point walking nervously to see the sultan of Zanzibar to get clearance for this mass hire, "sandwiched between two marked dragomen, with all the Black people gazing."[9] The worry she felt in this moment concerned being perceived as a prostitute. No sooner has this unthinkable crossed her mind, however, than she demonstrates, for all the wannabe girlbosses back home, how one prevails over such situations—regaining one's composure through sheer force of will:

> The thought came flashing into my brain that even these wretched blacks, in their debasement, imagined the very worst thing possible about the white woman, and I felt choked with self-indignation that a freeborn American woman should have sought the opportunity to conspicuously place herself in such a questionable position; then the absolutism of my one determination asserted itself, and the humiliation was from thence a mere detail, albeit keen and uncomfortable.[10]

The "very worst thing" here self-evidently is to be a white whore offering herself up (not, um, to extractively abuse Africa). Sheldon performs cringing inwardly, and then shrewdly silences those critics who might "question" the sexual decorum of her choices (that is, accuse her of "asking for it"). Following momentary doubt, she adopts a resoluteness of *racial* mission so intense it *proves* the rightness of what she is doing. A similar movement of temporary reverie and distress, followed by steely self-possession, recurs throughout Sheldon's travel memoir, *Sultan to Sultan: Adventures Among the Masai and Other Tribes of East Africa* (1892). The text, in this sense, only ever engages in shadow play, extrapolating confidently from dialogues she has only had in her head. (One could argue that May French Sheldon never traveled one single inch.)

Her small army assembled at last, on the first day of the three-month itinerary, the White Queen "looked with amazement over all these strange Black and every shade of brown faces, with much brutality imprinted thereupon, and marveled if I should always be able to control them and make them subservient to my commands."[11] Her doubts, she quickly adds here, instantly dissipated. Of *course* she could! Evolutionary science practically guarantees that everyone in this primitive zone will respond intuitively to the edifying influence of her womanly whiteness, rather like extras in Essos turning, sunflower-like, toward the radiance of *mhysa*, Dany Targaryen. The fraternal kindness and virtue embodied in the "freeborn" feminist's person are by themselves enough, in this fantasy, to make the mob "subservient to my commands." She is a beneficent, serene imperialist. But soon enough—as we are about to see—old-fashioned, murderous methods reveal themselves to be the backup in this picture, the truth that hovered behind that snowy dress all along. Under the old-world imperial silhouette? A modern settler-colonist.

Although a southerner from Texas, Sheldon styled herself an "English Traveller." At key moments along her route, she would whip out her jewel-festooned costume and dress up as Britannia, the maidenly avatar of Saxon civilization so beloved of the ladies' emigration advocates at the *English Woman's Journal*.[12] Every day she dedicated considerable time to chronicling, in her diary—for the sake of her subsequent bestseller *Sultan to Sultan*—the effects of this racial gender armor upon the natives. While her eccentric antics were not much to the taste of British journalists that spring, who decided they found the whole circus vulgarly American, in the US, newspapers were in raptures over what Sheldon herself termed the "White Queen" expedition.[13] No wonder: every time this faux-royal decked out in glittering, sword-toting, silvery white met African potentates, she was clearly mugging for the cameras back home. Much like Mae West, who surrounded the characters she played in movies with submissive mammy figures played by Black actors, Sheldon created star-spangled, iconic images of herself surrounded by abject, tyrannized, and degraded Africans and Arabs. As the historian Tracey Boisseau contends, this was designed to "throw her triumph over subjugation into relief."[14] It was all about constructing a feminist alternative to conventional male imperialism—one that effected power through moral education rather than colonial violence.

Born into a wealthy Texan family of plantation owners, Sheldon was steeped from childhood in the myth of the grateful African slave. "They called me Bébé Bwana," she declared dreamily upon returning to New York, citing a dubious Kiswahili compound title she claimed means both Woman Master and White Queen.[15] She signed her published work "Bébé Bwana" quite frequently, and even referred to herself as such in private. Journalists obligingly followed suit. "Many hundred years ago," offered one rave review of *Sultan to Sultan*, "Ethiopia was invaded by an Assyrian queen. In these modern days the invasion was by an American queen . . . Bébé Bwana."[16] Reporter Fannie Williams went further: until now, "Woman has made herself famous in every sphere" *except* in the exploration "of undiscovered and remote regions"—but hark! "an American heroine has appeared" who "shines equally well as hostess at an intellectual social function in her own drawing room, or as sole leader and commander of a caravan of Black men in the wilds of Africa."[17] The salacious reader is informed how, down in darkest Africa with only her small army of porters and bodyguards, Mrs. Sheldon had

> no protection, save the constant and evident assertion of her will, from men of a barbarous nation only one remove from brutes. Only the unconscious influence over these rude savages of the refinement of her deportment and manners; and above all, a certain commanding dignity, saved her from danger.[18]

Indeed, Sheldon recounts in *Sultan to Sultan* that dozens of "sultans" proposed to her that spring. Not being like the other girls, in each instance, she didn't blink, but agreed to pledge, instead, a blood pact of fraternal trust with them, explaining that white queens take only one single husband.

Insofar as these proposals all transpired, which seems doubtful, Sheldon's performances of queenliness for her African encounters, hosts, and travel companions were always simultaneously performances *of* a performance. Her "well-devised" expedition was one long proof of concept of a new feminine colonial method that might guide interfaces between the West and "the primitive" in the future. This is not to say that Sheldon didn't strike, shoot at, humiliate, or threaten East Africans: as British writer Dea Birkett notes in her book *Spinsters Abroad*, "she flogged her porters with her kibosh."[19] But the point was she didn't have to *kill* anyone. In lieu of routine fatal physical force, in the Bébé Bwana school of foreign relations, emancipated white ladies can use the suasion of their *moral impressions* upon unruly people. They can govern, open up markets, or do ethnography that way. Far from a mere jaunt, in other words, the White Queen expedition was a (race) science enterprise—recognized as such by the Royal Geographic Society— and a diplomatic experiment in soft power aimed at the elite.

It was also a domestic sexual ethics intervention; and here, Sheldon used racism, interestingly, *against* white men. This particular aspect of Sheldon's feminism was unaggressive and nonconfrontational. Albeit subtle, there was an inference against male Americans to be drawn from the condescending concepts of Black indigenes she projected in her post-safari lectures (as superficially volatile and brutish but also, to the expert handler, childlike and innocent, depending on ethnic type). In the first place, "Mrs. Sheldon thinks the tribes of Eastern Africa differ widely from those of the Congo," recorded *The Chautauquan*, "the moral nature of this people is as pure as that of a child, and their only vice is drunkenness." Sheldon's white audiences likely thought of all African men as "sexual beasts" prior to learning about these made-up tribal distinctions, Louise Newman notes. Mrs. Sheldon, however, both exploited *and* challenged what Angela Davis later called "the myth of the Black rapist"[20] in her tall tales of Tanzanian courtship overtures. Contrary to appearances, she was really talking about white men. Her implicit question was: How did her audience's husbands, beaux, and male associates generally, compare? Pushing all of America's racial sex-titillation buttons in her scholarly theatrics and self-promotions, she nevertheless "always insisted in the end that she had never been treated more chivalrously by men anywhere in the world than she had been by the so-called savages of Africa."[21]

This wasn't antiracism so much as it "put white men on notice," Newman elucidates. "To prove their superiority to the African, they would have to treat the white woman with the same respect and deference that she claimed to have received" in the bush.[22] From her numerous pulpits, Sheldon desired white women to demand better conduct from white men (first and foremost in their treatment of white women). But rather than suggest *all* women are capable of inspiring respect, she based this demand on her exceptional self: "On the grounds that she was a competent ruler of African savages known to resist and disobey white male rulers."[23] Even when she was physically in the Maasai steppe, standing on top of crouching porters (yes, really) because there were no boulders nearby and she made a point of always looking down on her caravan when addressing them, the real targets of Sheldon's strategic self-fashioning were pretty much always her colonial and woman-suffragist US audiences. Bébé Bwana would sometimes don her White Queen costume back at home, too, "to deliver lectures on the 'inner lives' of Africans and the 'proper method' of colonizing them."[24]

With the force of her regalia and her personality as a kind of present physical proof of her claims, Sheldon gave testimony that the thousands of Africans she met had all interpreted her costume and her manner in perfect conformance with her intentions. Of course, we have no way now of verifying that claim, as Boisseau archly remarks. What we can tell is that the knowledge the elegant adventuress wished to bring back, and *did* bring back, was this: wherever legendary male explorers like Henry Morton Stanley would have run into Maasai hostilities, she herself was welcome, having

> withered African resistance to her free-wheeling access to their land and their "inner lives," with nothing more than the fact of her racial superiority, manifested by her costume, confirmed by her exhibition of impeccable bourgeois manners, and declared by the iron-clad logic her race and class hubris put at her disposal.[25]

The conclusion to draw was that the womanly virtue of a (soi-disant) Englishwoman emanates from her white presence and automatically exerts eugenic effects upon the darker races.

One of the many ironies here is the fact, already mentioned, and documented by Sheldon herself, of Sheldon's eye-watering physical violence during the caravan's travels. For her, "it was not contradictory to denounce the slave trade in East Africa while flogging porters, some of whom may have been slaves," as cultural historian Robert Burroughs reflects.[26] Thus Sheldon carried two pistols at all times, as well as a whip, and as her caravan progressed, she arrogated a veritable mountain of collectibles for display in Europe—crowns, spears, ornaments, amulets, garments, and utensils—never taking "no" (as she proudly avows) for an answer. Sheldon bartered and acquired more or less everything she laid her eyes on, even if, as is the case with jewelry that is fixed on in childhood, it was literally embedded in the flesh of a living person and had to be cut out.[27] At one point she amputates the legs of a female corpse so as to obtain the anklets that adorn them. Dead or alive, in her narrative, the Maasai are always *surrendering*—not giving freely or selling—their ornaments to her.

The special scientific value of Sheldon's bourgeois gender, as a new breed of hands-on traveler-explorer-ethnographer-redeemer modeled consciously on the Britannia avatar Jane Bull, was that she would "see, and calmly report on what had been, in earlier missionaries' reticent ethnographies, tantalizingly omitted (but spotlighted) as 'practices too disgusting to mention.'"[28] Sheldon delicately cataloged all the indelicate details of polygamy, adulteress burning, nudity, and harem interiors—things a man would not be able to write about so honorably. Her probing self-insertion into Africa wanted to prove something about the rights and uses of imperial femininity, and the poet Edwin Arnold was clearly drawing the intended conclusions when he wrote of her safari that "her sex gave her evidently vast advantages."[29] Her journey, gushed the news editor Thomas Knox, "did not require the taking of a single human life"—in sharp contrast to the masculine method of colonization employed by a German explorer in the same year, which had been "a tour of slaughter from beginning to end."[30] Let a lady do the job!

Female whiteness is working here like a speculum to open up wild Africa: "In consequence of her sex," Knox marveled, much ethnological information was made sensible about African women "which by no possibility could ever reach the eyes or ears of a male traveler."[31] Clayton McMichael, another newspaperman, concurred. Her wondrous results were not only racial—that is, the result of a "heritage of staunch and honest blood" plus "that indescribable power of control which is born, not made"[32]—but sexual, he opined in *Arena* magazine. Sheldon "burned" with "the woman's will to know, the woman's generous desire to communicate, the woman's indomitable bravery to master, the home laws and habits of the aboriginal Africans, at the thresholds of whose dwelling-places every previous explorer had been turned away uninformed."[33] Likewise, a preacher, Thomas Swing, mused that Africa had hitherto only been explored "by means of gun and lash, and it seemed time for the same Africa to be explored by a woman": lo and behold, with her firm, sometimes ironhanded gentleness, Sheldon has "robbed Africa of its terrors."[34] Not so much an "everywoman" as the ultimate role model for women, in these gentlemen's opinion, Bébé Bwana was a feminist *star*. Judging by their reviews, they didn't mind, or even clock, her negative insinuations about white gentlemanhood at all.

Sheldon goes mostly unremembered by feminists in the twenty-first century. Yet at the turn of the twentieth, she was no less than the "foremother of the modern American woman and normative feminism,"[35] according to Boisseau. (Although Olive Schreiner's feminist novel of South African settler-colonialism—*Story of an African Farm*—predated Sheldon's trek by a few years; it had appeared under a male pseudonym.) Indeed, without Sheldon's example, it's hard to imagine the fame of Karen Blixen, that Danish baroness who authored *Out of Africa*—a 1937 memoir of British Kenya later embodied in memorable style by Meryl Streep. The "White Queen" example felt earth-shattering to neophyte feminists in the 1890s. Bébé Bwana felt, to her often lovestruck fans, like "a living story—a historical artifact—of how feminism in America had come to be."[36] *How do you birth feminism? By posing in front of various unenlightened mobs and taming a new frontier (while looking extravagantly fabulous), of course.*

No doubt about it, Sheldon's history, like feminism's, is deeply improbable. Between the 1890s and 1930s, this eccentric Victorian traveler's biography comprises a charmed existence as a frontierswoman, a career as an Amazon pinup for progressives, and a leisurely spell as a world-renowned *salonnière*, hobnobbing with figures like Stanley and Henry Wellcome (she was sometimes even dubbed "the Lady Stanley"). After her husband prematurely died, her life featured a forty-five-year intimate cohabitation or "Boston marriage" with Nellie Butler, a spinster. It included the above-described East African safari, but also a second and third trip to Central Africa in 1903 and 1905, plus decades-long celebrity as a motivational speaker at women's colleges. The carving out of an "emotional" place in the gruff world of scientific ethnography was her legacy. She was granted membership in London's Royal Geographical Society, and a post, in old age, at the Wellcome Museum's African department. In 1915, she was cheerleading nativist immigration restrictions in the US. In the 1920s, she became a women's rights champion, with real-life damsel-in-the-desert experience in the context of the craze for Hollywood star Rudolph Valentino's schlocky "sheik abduction" romances.[37] Most significantly for our purposes, she attempted to start a profit-making firm: the Americo-Liberian Company.

Could the US be the enlightened colonizer of the Dark Continent? The enthusiastic journalist Fannie Williams had intuited the potential significance of the White Queen's pioneering accomplishment for American capitalism's global ascendancy back in 1893. She reported how regressive it was that

> The English Parliament sat in judgment upon her apparently impracticable scheme, and did all in their power to prevent "that crazy woman" from starting out into the wilds of Africa. The German authorities also tried to interfere; but being an American, born in this land of freedom, she remained untrammeled by any preventive laws, and could follow her own sweet will.[38]

Of course, it was precisely the "untrammeledness" of individual white American entrepreneurs that helped make several of the vast European bloodbaths in Africa profitable over the centuries, from the transatlantic slave trade to what—between 1890 and 1910—has often been called "King Leopold's holocaust of the Congolese people,"[39] in other words, the Rubber Terror, a genocide in which American companies played a central role. It was very much in this ignoble capitalist tradition that Sheldon followed her "sweet" will back to Africa in 1903, finding that neither foreign national nor supranational authorities existed to thwart or "trammel" her.

The Congo Free State was a state-controlled concessionaire economy in Central Africa, privately owned by Belgium and ruled as an absolute monarchy. In the 1880s, various European and US firms set up shop there and began indiscriminately mining resources like ivory, copal, and rubber. Leopold II of Belgium's sovereign rule over this vast portion of the Congo River basin enjoyed warm support from the colonial powers of Europe and the US in that early period. The king declared his mission in the Congo to be overarchingly "moral": all about protecting the region's indigenous population, bringing religion to them, and generously opening up the fertile land to international trade. In reality, he created a state-run militia for the purpose of marshaling unpaid labor from the hundreds of ethnic groups living within the arbitrary borders of this new colonial realm (unpaid, because in theory, it was being levied against the cost of generously building all that civilizing industrial infrastructure).

By the 1890s, rumors abounded of the European militiamen and plantation foremen waging untold terrors, committing mass murder, and, to mention just one brutal example, levying baskets of severed Congolese hands. Colonial powers began to feel embarrassed enough to think about withdrawing.[40] Here, however—surprise!—the erstwhile beatific advocate for the "feminine" nonviolent colonial method stepped in. Sheldon, writes Burroughs, "was one of a handful of travelers to the Congo Free State who denied the accuracy of other travelers' reports of widespread atrocities in the colony."[41] This handful of "experts," by rationalizing European crimes and running interference on humanitarian media coverage of the same, essentially served as holocaust apologists. For over a decade, their revisionist reports on what was going on in the Congo were very useful for stalling action in the councils of Europe to stop the genocidaires. It wasn't until 1908, a year before Leopold's death, that the corporate "free" state was wrested from his grasp, renamed the Belgian Congo, and annexed as a traditional colony of Belgium under government control. In return for her services in laundering and downplaying his crimes, Sheldon's third expedition to Africa was even sponsored by the king himself.

Amazingly enough, it was the opposite team—the Western activists trying to halt the carnage in the Congo Free State—who sent Sheldon to the Congo in the first place. Or so they thought. Given her critique of outmoded colonial practices and her track record of sympathy for the *reformable* aboriginal, the British press mogul W. T. Stead solicited and commissioned Sheldon (for £500) to harvest data toward articles that might inform the international campaign to halt the Rubber Terror. The job she accepted specified that she should discover the extent to which Congolese were being compelled to collect rubber in the *Domaine Privé,* Leopold's personal fiefdom, under threat of murder, torture, or other force, and to "determine whether the forced labor Leopold would admit to amounted to the same thing as enslavement."[42] However, before the end of the year, the anti-slavery campaigner E. D. Morel was claiming in private letters to Stead that Sheldon had conned them both ("she is a put-up job"). As one newspaper reported in 1903, Mrs. Sheldon seemed to have been dispatched to the Congo simultaneously by Sir Alfred Jones, King Leopold's consul in Liverpool. Was she getting paid twice, once by each side? Stead and Morel's fears were certainly well-founded. A Baptist missionary who met Sheldon in the Baringa provinces of the Upper Congo in July 1904 wrote:

> Although posing as an absolutely unprincipled and independent visitor she is here as the "King's guest" & travels exclusively by State steamers. Her father was [a] Southern States' planter & slave owner, & she is herself (she is 56 years of age) quite "Southern" in her sympathies. However, she poses as a great advocate of the rights of women.[43]

Was the missionary saying he could see through Sheldon's feminism—which anyway did not address itself to native women—as a veneer covering ordinary colonial greed? Or was he saying that, on women's rights, one had to at least concede this point to her? I leave it to you to decide.

The articles Sheldon provided to Stead in fulfillment of her contract with him, upon her return, were apologetic puff pieces, quite "useless for the anti-Congo campaign."[44] In December 1904, a gaggle of journalists attended her disembarkation at the port of Southampton, "having spent fourteen months investigating the alleged atrocities in the Congo Free State." The atrocities in question had newly surfaced via a detailed report by Irish anti-colonial revolutionary Roger Casement, commissioned by the UK government. Were they real? No, said Sheldon. In a flat dismissal of Casement, reported in the *Times*, she declared, "[I've] seen more atrocities in London streets than in the Congo."[45] Could her fans, who so lavishly praised the bloodlessness of her earlier safari, have predicted it? This time, she was exiting the so-called dark continent not with trinkets stolen from East Africans whose morality is "as pure as a child," but—on the contrary—laden with apologias for the dismemberment of "pygmies," whose hand severing was their own "fetish," she said, and whose skin was too thick to be harmed by harsh lashing anyway.

Sheldon had networked and prospected for twelve months in the ghoulishly named Free State. Now, she was emerging not only to sing the praises of the Belgian government's blood-soaked concession economy, but also to set in motion new plans to become a plantation owner in her own right. All forgotten, seemingly, was the kind maternal alternative to male imperialist exploitation in Africa. Having lent colonialism a girlbossish spin before, she now did the same for the "red rubber" capitalism busy underdeveloping Africa. It was time to use her feminist credentials to whitewash the armed wing of the imperial state.

After she had made the rest of the trip home, across the Atlantic to New York, Sheldon was once again interviewed in major publications just as she had been in London. Amazingly, the double-crossed W. T. Stead himself still published an interview with her in the June 1905 edition of his journal, notwithstanding her participation in the counterpropaganda campaign stymying his "Congo reform" campaign. In this interview, Sheldon states that the colonial government in the Congo is just, and that compulsory labor there is necessary. In response to Stead's query about the status of women in the colony, she says she regards it as a poetic justice that Congolese men are forced to labor, since the women of their society are kept in "slavery" by their husbands.[46]

Male slavery to alleviate female slavery, again? Across the Western press, Sheldon explained that it was the "white woman's burden" to ensure the slow and gradual moral and eugenic improvement of all backward races "up" toward Christianity. She consistently framed the West's possible course of action in the Congo in terms of a false binary: either military takeover by Europe, or capitalist "development." Guess what? The latter was the better and more feminist route, or so she argued (leaving the Congo alone, somehow, was not an option). But perhaps the obscenest fact of Sheldon's life is that her year in the Congo basin inspired her to develop a scheme—the aforementioned Americo-Liberian Co.—for exploiting the timberlands of Liberia for rubber "using the labor of African Americans, whom she intended to 'repatriate' to Africa for this purpose."[47] That scheme ultimately came to nothing, because negotiations between Sheldon and the Liberian authorities were unsuccessful. Nonetheless, as we learn toward the end of Boisseau's book *White Queen: May French-Sheldon and the Imperial Origins of American Feminist Identity* (2004), Sheldon ended up a lifelong apologist for the Belgian holocaust. King Leopold II's royal successor, Albert, awarded her a knighthood for her civilizing efforts in Africa and services to Belgium (the "Chevalier de l'Ordre de la Couronne").

As the Baptist missionary likely understood, Sheldon's progressivism on white gender relations, as well as her prior experience as an "unescorted lady" in Africa and feminist record of ethnological sympathy for *some* African tribes, all functioned to obscure the reality of her underlying "Southern" attitudes from the public eye. White feminism magnified Bébé Bwana's obstruction of the struggle to shut down the Congo Free State. Consequently, the "civilizing" White Queen was a formidable enemy of the anti-colonial movement of the period. Today, it's incumbent on all anti-colonial leftists to spot and disarm her inheritors, not only in fiction, but in reality: from Laura Bush in Afghanistan in 2001, to Gal Gadot, Hollywood actress, in Palestine. When popular British expert on antiquity Mary Beard—to give another example—denounces decolonial efforts like the student-led "Rhodes Must Fall" campaign, and makes apologies for the "civilized" violence of Oxfam staff's sex exploitation crimes in Haiti, we owe it to each other to understand the history and draw connections.[48] Why does the rape of Haitians and Palestinians pass without fanfare? Palestinian women's agency, in relation to their experiences of patriarchy, features in the Zionist iteration of White Queen feminism no more than did Congolese women's feminism for May French-Sheldon.

Recall how, as soon as Benjamin Netanyahu and other fascist representatives of Israel alleged—on trumped-up evidence—that Gazan fugitives and "terrorists" had "systematically" raped settlers on October 7, 2023, Zionist feminists sprang into action, attempting to distract from the accelerated genocide of reprisal (commenced on October 8) and even to apologize for it outright.[49] Often dressed up in a Bébé Bwana–esque iconography of feminine purity, armored courage, and radiant whiteness, feminist Zionism has cheered the elimination, via starvation or bombs, of millions of people from the Gaza Strip, well over a year.[50] Celebrated in the pages of the *New York Times* and *Daily Mail* as "lionesses of the desert,"[51] the colonizing queens in the Israeli army—self-styled as enlightened rape avengers—have proven indispensable in the smearing of the global pro-Palestine movement as antisemitic and antifeminist. Gal Gadot purposively blurs the line between herself and Wonder Woman (the feminist superheroine role she popularized) in her public support of Israel's all-female tank battalions in their righteous civilizational struggle against the sexual barbarism supposedly represented by the armed national liberation party Hamas.[52]

This is why we must unlearn the cult of the white queen: for as we've seen in the aftermath of October 7, it is not only on *Game of Thrones* that the feminism of the "civilizer" ends in mass slaughter. In the real world, too, historically unprecedented quantities of hellfire rain on open-air prisons in the name of keeping women safe, and amputated limbs signal woman's contribution to science and commerce. Genocide is sometimes feminist.

FOUR

The Prohibitionist

*"This country must be purged of petty vice before it can
be fit to rule the world," cried Eugenia. She . . . galloped
away. "That's a fine girl," said Jasper. "If she had been born
twenty years sooner she would have been a suffragette."*

—NANCY MITFORD, *Wigs on the Green*, 1934[1]

It was in 1869 that the legendary English liberal Josephine Butler first got wind of the fact that the British state, in a number of
military towns, was openly regulating prostitution. Despite being
an illegal industry, sex work was openly under state management
in many ports and garrisons, Butler learned—basically, wherever
the British Crown desired army and navy officers to keep free of
venereal disease. The legal regime governing this was called "the
Contagious Diseases Acts." The laws empowered police officers to
detain any woman or girl on the street, and hand her over to local
magistrates, who would in turn order a medical examination of her
genitals. Then, if found to be diseased, the suspected sex worker
would be warehoused against her will either in a "lock hospital" or
in a workhouse. On discovering all this, Mrs. Butler, a flawed but
often genuinely subversive feminist who had backed the Union and
the abolition of slavery, flew into a rage. She dug deeper and discovered, to her disgust, that similar regulations were on the books

in many foreign countries: rules amounting to governmental pimping, plain and simple. Coercive medical treatment and extralegal detention of working-class women were, she learned, endemic.

Butler gathered her resources. Under the banner of the Ladies National Association for Repeal of the Contagious Diseases Acts (LNA), she embarked on a self-styled "holy war" against the state-as-pimp. While leading the repeal campaign for the next three decades, she also tended—in her own home—to many sex workers on their deathbeds. Butler's organization became a hugely influential international lobby to repeal all Contagious Disease–style legislation, as well as a movement to transform the character of "women's work and women's culture"[2] by building routes out of survival sex.

The wave of activism Butler catalyzed—even her critic Judith Walkowitz, the historian, concedes—included "brilliant organizing drives that successfully aroused female anger, stimulated grassroots organizations, and mobilized women not previously brought into the political arena."[3] Britain repealed the acts in 1886. At this point, Butler opened up her grand "second chapter"—aiming at the colonies—and duplicated the LNA's success in British India. Laws under the "Raj" were nearly identical to the ones in the metropole, with a set of military "cantonment rules" defining colonial garrisons as under "venereal disease control."[4] The main difference between the two "chapters" of LNA was that, while the domestic campaign focused on the figure of the profligate aristocrat as a seducer of penniless girls, when it came to the Indian crusade, the object of feminist anger became the UK officer class.[5] (In phase two, in short, the aim was to save brown prostitutes from the lust of the British army.[6]) Butlerism did not survive its transatlantic dissemination among vice fighters, as we shall see. But in the absence of working-class Indian or English sex workers in the leaderships of either campaign, repeal politics' descent into moralism and double standards was surely inevitable.

In both the UK and the Indian setting, Butler referred to all laws regulating prostitutes' lives as "slave codes." Despite this confusing rhetoric, she also believed in respecting (while not supporting) these so-called slaves' decisions to sell sex—a recognition of agency women retain even when overwhelmed by patriarchal and capitalist constraints. In this sense, paternalistic as her thinking often was, Butler did differ from many of her imperial-feminist peers. She exhorted Europeans to "cultivate a truly international . . . spirit of sympathy, not only for those of your own race . . . but with the whole human race, more especially for the native women under the conquering races everywhere."[7] As we are about to see, however, she wholly lost control of what might have become an internationalist movement for sex work decriminalization. Her campaigns tragically gave way to a massive movement toward criminalizing prostitutes, working-class teenagers, and immigrants, in the name of stamping out sexual exploitation. One particularly hard-hit population was sexually active children: experimental masturbators, same-age lovers, or juvenile sex workers for example (all of whom were pathologized, in this feminism, as deviants in need of rescue via punishment—and systematically institutionalized in insane asylums).

Perhaps Butler should not be held responsible for the organized racism, ableism, and class hatred that would follow in the name of the "abolition" of state-run prostitution she kick-started. In itself, though, the fact that she christened her campaign "the new abolitionism" bears a fair share of the blame for the confusion that still prevails, one and a half centuries later, around what it means to abolish something. I can think of few words so misused as the word "abolition."[8] Contrary to what is often implied, the criminalization of the transatlantic slave trade and thereafter of chattel slavery by Western nations in the nineteenth century did not by itself realize the goal of unmaking the society that had enslaved—that could enslave—human beings. Yet the latter is what abolition requires: a rebirthing of the world such that the "humanism" embodied in the slave economy is at once turned inside out, destroyed, transformed, and realized for the first time.[9] The struggle is ongoing. It is a struggle not only to get rid of—let's say—prisons, as to get rid of the world that could think of prisons as a way of meeting humanity's need for justice.[10] Abolition will have been realized when a system of real justice is operative. Thus, if Butler truly wanted to abolish the sex-caste system, she needed to stoke the world's appetite for a revolution in the very gender division of labor. To give another example, dear to my heart, the horizon of care deprivatization known as "abolition of the family" only destroys care in the way that slave emancipation destroyed humanism: it flips it by universalizing and overhauling it, thereby realizing its promise, such that a form of kinship uncoerced by economics becomes possible at last.[11] As Ruth Wilson Gilmore puts it, the task is to "change one thing: everything."[12]

At the same time, the confusion of criminalization with liberation has been happening for centuries. People have been substituting prohibition and criminalization for abolition for as long as the latter concept (also called positive supersession, or *Aufhebung*, in German) has been around. Many of the original "abolitionists," as we saw, were themselves committed racists who had no desire to see abolition all the way through once slavery had been illegalized. In the 1870s, instead of committing to the long haul of Reconstruction, many of these veteran abolitionists turned around and began applying the word "abolition" to a new rubric entirely. This time, they were going to abolish not a mode of production like slavery, but rather a single sector of the wage economy: the sex industry.

A key source of inspiration for this about-face was the radicalism of that British feminist across the pond, Josephine Butler, who in 1871 accused governments that regulate and sponsor sex work of conspiring to "reduce women to a slavery more complete than any which the earth has ever seen."[13] The growing commitment to this new "abolitionist" cause, especially among US anti-slavery's more respectable set, culminated in the Progressive Era with the passage of the federal Mann Act in 1910, which prohibited the "transportation of any woman or girl for the purpose of prostitution or debauchery, or for any immoral purpose." James Mann, the congressman who introduced the legislation, might have been quoting Butler when he called the traffic in women "much more horrible than any black-slave traffic ever was in the history of the world."[14]

Slavery of the "old" kind was not by any stretch of the imagination less bad than what the feminist repealers were talking about, nor was it by any means abolished from the earth, as May French-Sheldon was discovering in the Belgian Congo. For that matter, the institutionalized forced labor of Black Americans hadn't ended. Nevertheless, suffragists and Progressives of many stripes were impatient to move on to something else. Combining elements of the savior ethos of Jane Bull and the White Queen with elements of solipsistic piteousness that simultaneously (if contradictorily) inspired imperial feminists to paint white women as a race of suffering slaves, the New Abolitionists took over the rhetorical force of abolition and channeled it into the cause of Woman, which is to say, the white slave. In 1875, Congress accordingly passed the Page Act, mounting a defense of vulnerable womanhood and a vindication of female dignity, and banning the "importation into the United States of women for the purposes of prostitution."

The Page Act was the very first law limiting who could come and inhabit the settler-colonial republic, and it was a feminist law. Critical legal theorist Lorelei Lee recounts how quickly and inevitably this politics fused with xenophobic white nationalism:

> Even as the Black Codes and subsequent Jim Crow laws reinstituted a racialized system of forced labor that continues to this day, white Americans told themselves that the country had entered a new age of freedom that was now under threat from Chinese immigration. Chinese women who worked in gold rush-era brothels in California were, claimed one reformer, "infusing a poison into the Anglo-Saxon Blood."[15]

The hunch that nativist and eugenic motivations were firmly on top here is confirmed by the Chinese Exclusion Act of 1882, which banned all Chinese people from coming in (again on the pretext of ending "yellow slavery").

Three years later, in London, tens of thousands of people gathered in Hyde Park to demand an end to the "slavery" of white girls in direct response to one of the most popular pieces of scandal journalism ever published. "The Maiden Tribute of Modern Babylon" (1885) was a lurid exposé in the *Pall Mall Gazette* about foreign pimps "selling" the "daughters of the people" for £5 a fuck to old aristocratic rakes. It painted a picture of English damsels "snared, trapped and outraged either when under the influence of drugs or after prolonged struggle in a locked room,"[16] and inspired instant protest demonstrations. The sex panic helped secure passage of the first of two Criminal Law Amendment Acts, which prohibited the "debauching" of any female who is not "a common prostitute"[17] (a category never defined). Several whole organizations even sprang up, such as the International Bureau for the Suppression of the White Slave Traffic. Concurrently, in the US, the Woman's Christian Temperance Union (WCTU) was fleshing out the same rhetorical arsenal about modern slavery being not just as bad as but worse than the "old" slavery.

A very particular construct of womanhood was kicking into overdrive here. The ideal had been conceptually perfected within slavery and colonization, where it was tied to the privilege of owning one's "legitimate" offspring. The womanhood in question, then, belonged to a proprietary system of class and racial reproduction. It was a gender defined in opposition to an un-gender ascribed to many native and/or unmarried mothers, sex-working mothers, and enslaved mothers—the ensemble of females whose access to patriarchal motherhood (understood as ownership) could be denied. In short, the white slave feminist constituency was a formidable racist and cissexist weapon. In the hands of many of the "purity" workers who flocked to join the LNA's repeal campaign, it became a mechanism for criminalizing non-respectable poverty and proletarian deviance.

Some of that "deviance," without doubt, consisted of real violence committed by men against women. But much of it was simply nonreproductive sexuality.[18] Within the frame of "modern Babylon," sex work, extramarital sex, intoxication, porn, rape, child abuse, queer cruising, and pregnancy out of wedlock all came to seem like gender evils more or less of a piece.[19] Organized British and American womanhood had always figured prominently in anti-prostitution efforts.[20] But in the half-century between 1871 and 1921, a nexus of specifically feminist forces coalesced around the "slavery" of waged, extrafamilial sexual labor. In the Chinatowns of the New World's

West Coast, suffragists like Rose Livingston mounted vast saviorist enterprises to "rescue" Chinese women from their jobs in brothels.[21] Two Woman's Christian Temperance Union stalwarts declared in 1907, confusingly, that "practically all the Chinese prostitutes in the United States are literal slaves. Some are willing slaves, some unwilling."[22]

As this slippery elision implies, the not-always-white so-called white slavery epidemic was a phantom social emergency in which untold numbers of girls (newly economically active, vulnerable, and virginal) were pictured squirming in foreign men's lecherous hands—ruined, debauched, and somehow "lost." In the initial years of the Butlerite antiregulation campaign, there were times when more liberatory feminist discourses than this "were able to dominate and structure discourse on sex,"[23] or so Walkowitz contends. When Butler's anti-state rage was on top, cops, politicians, judges, doctors, and the army took a lot of the heat for women's collective unfreedom and poverty. But, notes Walkowitz, "this anger was easily diverted into repressive campaigns against male vice and sexual variation." In short order, Butlerism was declawed.

Related devolutions were occurring everywhere. According to the scholars Ellen DuBois and Linda Gordon, the campaign to raise the sexual age of consent "had a radical moment: it communicated an accurate critique of the limitations of 'consent' by women in a male-dominated society."[24] Yet by the end of the century, age-of-consent legislation denied women the right to heterosexual activity until they were either adults or married (which, by the way, they could be at any age). Feminists had actively fostered hostility to the sex lives of girls. In so doing, they had helped create a new class of female offender, who soon filled the reformatories: the juvenile (pre- or post-pubescent) sex delinquent.

Once unleashed, the central term of prohibitionist feminism, white slavery, functioned like a potted moral panic in twelve little letters, evoking a (somehow previously unnoticed) unseen epidemic of abductees who were overwhelmingly—unlike yesterday's captives—Anglo-Saxon girls. The gender historian Jessica Pliley notes that the term first appeared in conjunction with prostitution "when a London doctor wrote about Jewish pimps as 'white-slave dealers' who trepan [ensnare] young girls in their dens of iniquity"[25]—an unpromising beginning. Regrettably, it was the French novelist Victor Hugo who introduced the phrase (*la traite des blanches*) to feminists when he wrote, in a letter to Mrs. Butler in 1870, that "the slavery of Black women is abolished in America, but the slavery of white women continues in Europe."[26]

Hugo didn't mean wives. Just as temperance allowed women to blame something (booze) for male violence other than marriage and the institution of the private nuclear household, the focus on prostitution, too, was a focus on extrafamilial evil. As such, even the least carceral neo-abolitionists' obsession with the victimization of the prostitute was, in the end, conservative, and unable to transcend the sexual morality bifurcating women into the groups "respectable" and "fallen." Even the best of them failed to understand that many prostitutes wanted to be neither rescued nor rehabilitated. They "clung fast to the idea that some kinds of sex were inherently criminal," DuBois and Gordon conclude, "and they were confounded by the existence of unrepentant whores."[27]

The New Abolitionists were all also undeniably switching focus with amazing speed away from Black oppression—under the pretense that that was now pretty much solved—over to the racially unmarked (that is, tacitly white) female subjugation they located in the sphere of sex crimes (where Black women once again didn't really exist as victims). This maneuver didn't really "de-race" prostitution—the word "white" was there from the jump—so much as de-sex chattel slavery, implicitly rewriting the history of the plantation as an experience of simple labor rather than one involving forced breeding and rape. A moral panic about non-white procurers and traffickers, merging with fears of miscegenation and white genocide, spread like a rash.

Some leftist voices in the WCTU tried in vain to change the terminology to "the women's slave traffic,"[28] to reflect the larger numbers of non-white sex "slaves." But by the time the Mann Act (or White-Slave Traffic Act) was passed, it was too late. It didn't help that, in the WCTU pamphlet *Traffic in Young Girls* (1899), white slavers were "human gorillas" committing crimes "worse than murder"—a rhetorical excess that feels eerily reminiscent of the war on terror and the widespread Zionist-feminist claim, in late 2023, that Hamas perpetrated sex crimes on Israelis "worse than the Holocaust."[29] Apparently, "worse than any race-slavery is the slavery of the brothel, into which thousands of our loveliest girls are mercilessly thrust."[30] Clearly few in the WCTU imagined that "our" loveliest girls might have suffered race slavery too.

By 1900, there were multiple interrelated prohibition platforms in circulation, all aiming to liberate the "mothers of the race" from their "shackles." Myriad non-feminist campaigners drove this frenzy, including straightforward antifeminists, old-school moral zealots, and common-or-garden variety puritans. The US purity movement's 1870s surge had in fact been what led many states to ban abortion and contraception for the first time, and it was only after that surge and legislation that the new "vigilance" groups diversified and started campaigning for sobriety, suffrage, female police matrons, gender segregation in prisons, censorship of obscenity, and the prosecution and "reformation" of prostitutes. Many if not most had no particular emancipatory hopes for women, perhaps fearing and hating commercial sex more than anything else (for "tempting" half of all married men into making a mockery of the patriarchal family). Non-feminist fears probably helped more than feminist ones to stoke the xenophobic frenzies and paranoid social attitudes that congealed in criminal legislation and immigration restrictions in this period. Yet it is undeniable that many who contributed to this cauldron of Progressive Era vice busting were bona fide feminists—and even feminist radicals.

Neo-abolitionism included the trailblazing social worker Jane Addams and the free love activist Victoria Woodhull. It boasted giants of the Anglo-American establishment like Elizabeth Blackwell (the first US woman doctor), Millicent Garrett Fawcett (president of the UK National Union of Women's Suffrage Societies), and Barbara Bodichon, one of the women of Langham Place who also cofounded Girton College, Cambridge. Dr. Blackwell, it's worth mentioning, objected to the prostitution of white and non-white women for different reasons: in the case of Britain's sponsorship of brothels in its colonies, her problem was that it was resulting in the "gravest form of racial injury"—by which she meant the human consequences of interracial sex.[31] At the same time, these feminists often argued powerfully against the sexual double standard and the stigma on "fallen" females. Addams, certainly, argued that the "blame" for prostitution lay with capitalism, or at least low wages.[32] Still, whenever and insofar as they exceptionalized voluntary sex work, rather than bring married and unmarried women and whores and ladies together in common struggle, theirs was a family-values endeavor. Conversely, the anarchist Emma Goldman and her prostitute comrades were, at this time, perfectly able to formulate a proletarian feminism opposed to both marriage and the market.[33]

There was no stopping the terms *white slavery* and *white slave traffic* once they'd crossed the Atlantic. A century and a half before "Pizzagate," US tabloids pruriently detailed the plight of unthinkable numbers of young Americans Literally Enslaved for Sex in graphic tall tales of naïve small-town virgins drugged, kidnapped, and transported to the big city to be pedophilically consumed.[34] No evidence ever emerged that a criminal cabal devoted to this human traffic existed at any scale (indeed, no more than a few incidences of abduction were ever recorded). Yet the discourse proved elastic, as though thriving, QAnon-style, on its own slippages: whenever required, the white-slave panic could shrink to focus on an immigrant subgroup, or swell to encompass unforced, noncommercial, merely extramarital, and/or (especially) interracial sex.[35] All the while, it ignored real victimization suffered by Black people or by whites inside "good" families.

To be sure, on its face, the new slavery was a gender-based slavery, and the new abolition therefore a gender- instead of race-related abolition. But this was a misnomer. The cause was still racial—an anti-antiracist counterrevolution linked to eugenics, to be precise. The feminist task, here, was not only to define the sympathetic woman citizen, but crucially to define her opposites: the un-American loose woman and the race-defiling male pimp. Easily tied to a burgeoning southern White Redeemer discourse machine, white slavery helped reformers across the political spectrum build the counterrevolutionary regime known as Jim Crow.[36] It became an elastic many-headed Hydra of social impurity, bundling prostitution, perversion, adultery, violence, child abuse, booze, and race mixing. It was all to be vanquished by votes for women or Prohibition—and at this point, these seemed to many like synonyms.

While I have suggested that anti-prostitution neo-abolition ought better to be called prohibition, Prohibition in the US context of course refers specifically to the anti-alcohol campaigns that culminated in the fourteen-year tenure of the Eighteenth Amendment, prohibiting the "manufacture, sale, or transportation of intoxicating liquors," starting in 1919. Bourgeois feminism was tightly linked with the passage of this amendment. When Carrie Catt addressed the "World's WCTU" convention in 1913, she told the assembled delegates that the temperance pledge was "the first vow I took in this world." Many if not most suffragists supported Prohibition, and the liquor lobby, in return, campaigned against woman suffrage. The temperance suffragists were top players in the anti-liquor crusade, alongside the Prohibition Party and the Anti-Saloon League. All three groups brought together a motley mix of reform-minded progressives, radical feminists, Klansmen, Klanswomen, anti-Catholics, nativists, white nationalists, xenophobes, and religious revivalists. In the received narrative about Prohibition, the story goes that the enlightened partisans of temperance were opportunistically used and overwhelmed by nightmarish bigoted interests. But the problem with this is that, to quote Kelefa Sanneh, writing in the *New Yorker* in 2015, "In many cases, the high-minded Progressives and anti-'alien' sloganeers weren't merely awkward allies but the same people."[37]

One such hybrid, Mrs. Catt, told the convention that "the greatest enemy today to the enfranchisement of women is not ignorance, is not stubbornness, is not prejudice, but the legalized government-protected saloon system."[38] True enough, the saloons of 1910s America were mobbed up and corporate-run, with huge numbers of clubwomen, both Black and white, opposing them and decrying the role of men's alcoholism in the miseries of wives and children. On the other hand, Catt and her ilk also dog-whistled about saloons—rather than fighting ruling-class boozing—because they were sites of Black sociality and immigrant labor union coordination. So, if anti-prostitution and woman suffrage often expressed themselves, through people like Catt, as xenophobia and white supremacy, so did anti-liquor vigilance, which in turn was also a feminism. It was the view of Frances Willard, the ardently suffragist WCTU president (from 1879 until her death in 1898), that "alien illiterates rule our cities today. The saloon is their palace; the toddy stick their scepter. . . .Better whiskey and more of it has been the rallying cry of the great dark-faced mobs in the Southern localities."[39] Frances Willard, feminist icon.

Willard was an amazingly charismatic leader and populist pundit. Unlike Butler's, but like Catt's, her feminism was fundamentally a "feminism of fear."[40] Her success as the face of the WCTU flowed from the intoxicating image she projected of the traditional "home" as the only safe place amid a sea of savage dangers—what historian Ian Tyrrell dubbed "the home against the harem."[41] Willard bolstered southern lynch logic while heading up a titanic international nonprofit, and Jane-Bull-ishly called on women to "Do Everything" (her famous motto), painting pictures of her purity-pledge troops as conquerors of heathen lands. Despite publicly abhorring homosexuality, her own domestic partnerships were with women, and she liked her inner circle to call her "Beloved Chieftain" or "Frank," as she did "the rougher work" around the house. Not least because the moral badge of the war on liquor helped legitimate certain such discreet forms of lesbian community life and passionate female friendship behind the scenes—for the very women propounding queerphobic morality in public—vice hunting carved out powerful niches for bourgeois women. Meanwhile, Willard's/Frank's politics were self-described as Christian socialism, a pointedly anticommunist ideology that did not treat class conflict as central (the aim was rather to bring workers and capitalists together in cooperation). Bosses and proles together would put down the bottle and listen to their mothers, redefining woman suffrage as "home protection" and the Nineteenth Amendment as the "home protection ballot."

Despite recent efforts to reclaim her as a queer ancestor, Willard's maternalist feminism amounted to repression for thee, and liberation for me. Sure, there were "positive" elements.[42] Some temperance women created shelters and group houses for destitute or battered families fleeing alcoholic men. Some slammed their non-feminist peers for over-romanticizing the Christian forbearance that wives were supposed to show to drunk, brutish husbands, developing instead a sisterly self-help discourse—just leave him!—that understandably remains popular today. One famous and particularly startling part of the feminist history of temperance is the large number of saloon razings that were carried out by hatchet-wielding, hymn-singing mobs of religious fanatics (Carrie Nation is merely the best remembered of these). Some have claimed that vigilante tavern destruction was righteous given that the ballot was "closed against" women, "the law-making power" denied. A few historians even feel that purity women were mounting "a physical attack on the gendered order that they could not combat legally."[43] I'm unimpressed by these claims, attempting to justify pogroms on sex-working and working-class life. Sometimes, property destruction is reactionary. Riots are sometimes white riots— including feminist ones.

The Black American anti-lynching activist Ida B. Wells was visiting London in the fall of 1890. By coincidence, so was Frances Willard, who was staying at the house of her bestie in London, one of the richest women in Britain: Isabella Somerset, aka Lady Henry, the president of both the British Women's Temperance Association and the international branch of the WCTU.[44] Isabella was a feminist aristocrat who dedicated her life to the cause of temperance, as well as a self-described socialist and major English slumlord. In 1895, she was said to have one hundred thousand tenants, of whom most lived, despite her reputation as a benevolent reformer, in her vast slum properties in East London.[45] Like any good philanthrocapitalist, the landlady founded a "home for inebriate women" in Surrey that same year. She started paying Bible-reading visits to a selection of her tenants, while giving instructional classes on eugenic motherhood at her castle in Hertfordshire to local women of the lower orders. Awkwardly, several of her properties in the working-class district of Somers Town carried liquor licenses. She seems to have made some face-saving attempts to have these premises closed down and turned over to uses more befitting a world-famous abstinence warrior. Nonetheless, the rents drawn from these pubs, and from all her other properties, provided the temperance movement with resources for decades.

It was in London that Willard and Somerset began a bitter four-year public fight with Ida B. Wells, despite the fact that Wells, a feminist, also opposed alcohol.[46] It began when Willard gave an eye-wateringly anti-black interview to the *New York Voice* on the subject of southern lynching in October 1890. Far from condemning lynching, Willard depicted "the colored man" as a swarming, "locust"-like threat to white women's purity in the South. Miss Wells swiftly responded, quoting and refuting Willard in *Fraternity* magazine. Lady Henry was not going to let a Negro speak to the WCTU president that way. Cossie and Frank (as they called each other) took to the pages of the *Westminster Gazette* together to, in their own words, "guard Miss Willard's reputation" by belittling Miss Wells.[47] "So far as I know, I have not an atom of race prejudice,"[48] Willard confessed. Wells hit back decisively, revealing that the WCTU practiced segregation in the South. "There is not a single colored woman admitted . . . but still Miss Willard blames the negro for the defeat of prohibition in the South!"[49]

The enmity raged on in various periodicals. Wells published *Southern Horrors*, her pamphlet explaining that "white men lynch the offending Afro-American, not because he is a despoiler of virtue, but because he succumbs to the smiles of white women," in 1892.[50] Horrified at the very idea that white women were capable of voluntarily fornicating with Black men, Willard attacked her at the 1894 WCTU convention, hoping—as Vron Ware writes— "to silence her on this issue once and for all."[51] The convention did not adopt Wells's anti-lynching resolution, resolving instead, despicably, to condemn both lynchings and their imagined causes (i.e., miscegenational rapes by Black men, which constitute an even worse "outrage"—worse than death!).[52] While the WCTU's Beloved Chieftain did eventually come around and oppose lynching, she never revised her belief that white women never voluntarily put their racial purity at risk by sleeping with non-white men. For far too many temperance women under her motherly, covertly transmasculine wing, the anti-Catholic prejudice of cross-burning Protestantism and the sociobiology of militant white supremacy would soon become usable tools in their crusade.

Prohibition, in Willard's hands, became an instrument of white nationalism, both in terms of temperance supporters' account of the "races" that are most susceptible to alcoholism, and in terms of the populations—working class and of color—who were disproportionately hit by anti-alcohol enforcement. Frank's so-called White Ribbon Army embraced social Darwinist doctrines about the superiority of Anglo-Saxon stock, and even followed the openly anti-black self-appointed mothers of American feminism in advocating for educational voter bars. The huge overlap between the constituencies of (brothel) abolitionism and temperance (with the latter wishing additionally to "abolish" liquor, drugs, gambling, and other vices marring Christian civilization) has to be understood in terms of the coalition's perceived utility for preserving white rule.[53] Prohibition did reflect a misandrist understanding of white slaving as just one more form of demonic, chauvinistic consumption by men. But the men in question—who in the British version had been aristocrats—were here coded as proletarian and non-white (in fact, the slightly longer phrase "Black traffic in white slaves"[54] was popular). It was non-white workers' appetites, specifically, that white feminists wished to curb first.

Willard felt that "only Christian countries treat women kindly,"[55] and that the "lower" classes and ethnic or racial orders around the world were more susceptible than were Christian whites to drunkenness and loss of sexual self-control. What Catt called the "saloon system"—the brothel system, aka white slavery—was as such inherently racialized. It effectively constituted the new non-white plantocracy for feminists to boycott as their foremothers had boycotted the sugar planters of yesteryear. Seen in this light, the British suffragette Christabel Pankhurst's progress from the slogan "Votes for Women, Chastity for Men" circa 1913 to Second Adventist evangelism in Canada by the 1920s begins to make a bit more sense.[56] Criminalization was an evangelical tide painting the map "white" (in the WCTU's terms) and turning it "dry" with womanly love. The nativist ontology of these feminists, Tyrrell writes, prevented even "good Indians" and other temperate but non-white "races" from being included in the White Ribboners' ranks; it "barred their acceptance as fully human."[57]

How did prohibition manage to crush everything positive about neo-abolition, while also stealing its name? We know that "the attraction of the social purity cause for women was not peripheral but fundamental," as Gordon unhappily insists. ("The closer we look," she writes, "the harder it is to distinguish social purity groups from feminist ones."[58]) This convergence persists to this day. Save Our Eyes is the name of a campaign against the "managed prostitution area" in the city of Leeds, England. The feminist campaigners' demand, sighs Alison Phipps, boils down to: "keep the 'undesirables' out, 'our' eyes will be saved by moving sex workers back into criminalization."[59]

Even back then, it was clear to some that bourgeois moralists were simply romanticizing white ladies as the nation's spiritual daddies, imagining a caste of strong, clean moms whose vote was needed to bring in universal sobriety (although, as it turned out, it wasn't). Freethinkers like the Michigan-born anarchist Voltairine de Cleyre and the aforementioned labor organizer Emma Goldman typically viewed the Thirteenth Amendment as liberatory, the Eighteenth as carceral, and the Nineteenth as bourgeois but not unwelcome. In their essays in *Mother Earth* magazine, these women insisted that (to quote Goldman) "governmental suppression and moral crusades accomplish nothing save driving the evil into secret channels, multiplying its dangers to society."[60] Pioneering what would now be called the "harm reduction" approach to substance abuse and sexual exploitation, such feminist analysis viewed "the visionless and leaden elements of the WCTUs, Purity Leagues, and the Prohibition Party . . . [as] the grave diggers of American art and culture."[61]

A feminist moralist can still issue a powerful rebuke to prevailing hypocrisies of the age. WCTU feminists sometimes boldly slammed the norms that dehumanized prostitutes as irredeemable or condemned them to hell. For example, Katharine Bushnell, the national evangelist for the WCTU's social purity department, traveled widely as a Christian-feminist theologian and missionary in China and India, conducted reportage on women in Wisconsin lumber camps, and excoriated the prevailing form of whore stigma in polite society as highly specious—"pharisaical."[62] In her temperance pamphlet *The Woman Condemned* (1887), Bushnell denounces ladies who think of themselves as inherently different to fallen women, for committing the heresy of thinking that anyone (even a lady) is untouchably pure and securely immured against moral ruin. Much like Butler, Bushnell insisted on whores' returnability to the human condition, provided of course that they cooperate with the Salvation Army and the law.

We would do well to study this blackmail, not least because of the carceral tenor of much feminist anti-prostitution thought today. Today's "sex-worker exclusionary radical feminists" display a markedly prohibitionist bent—epitomized by their so-called "Nordic model" policy, which nominally criminalizes only the buyers of sex, while pushing sex workers ever deeper underground and coercing them into government-run "exit" programs. This presents a striking contrast to the anti-statism of the surprisingly left-libertarian Josephine Butler, who wanted the police, the medical authorities, and the state generally out of women's lives. Although she did call sex work worse than slavery a mere six years after the American Civil War, Butler at least wrote in explicit opposition to all patriarchal control of women: in marriage and in courts, jails, and hospitals. It is bittersweet that Butler grew increasingly horrified at the repressive and punitive policies that some of her fellow feminists were prepared to endorse in the name of the "Great Crusade" she had started. For all her flaws, she opposed the coercion, harassment, and detention of all women (who weren't overtly "indecent"). "My principle," as she put it in 1894, "has always been to let individuals alone, not to pursue them by any outward punishments, not to drive them out of any place, so long as they behave decently—but to attack organised prostitution, that is, when a third party . . . sets up a house in which women are sold to men."[63]

It is—amazingly enough—explicitly for this reason that anti-prostitution feminists of the last fifty years criticize this particular first waver's "sexual liberalism." In *The Prostitution of Sexuality* (1995), feminist Kathleen Barry—cofounder of the Coalition Against Trafficking in Women—regrets that Butler drew a "false distinction between free and forced prostitution." She criticized her, moreover, for giving "implicit acceptance to prostitution that is not imposed by a third party." This means that, far from being a prostitution abolitionist—yes!— "Butler accepted prostitution. This was the fundamental weakness of her new campaign."[64]

By accepting some women's refusal to be saved, according to Barry, the Butlerite strategy actively "set the stage for the modern formulation of prostitution as 'sex between consenting adults'" (a formulation she considers evil).[65] Similarly, in *The Idea of Prostitution*, the self-described revolutionary feminist Sheila Jeffreys agrees: Butler made a "tactical mistake" in concentrating on "forced prostitution," because this implies that there is an unforced kind.[66] For the neo-abolitionists of today—and we will deal further with Jeffreys in the context of anti-trans feminism—Josephine is in league with the enemy because she was too focused on coercion.

In *The Spinster and her Enemies*, Jeffreys celebrates purity campaigners, such as Ellice Hopkins, Elizabeth Wolstenholme-Elmy, Lucy Re-Bartlett, and Frances Swiney, who feared and loathed independent female sexuality.[67] Worse, these late-Victorian lobbyists and charitable grandees were quite willing to use coercion to stamp that sexuality out. Walkowitz, in her historical work, persuasively claims that they simply shared the "repugnance" and "feelings of anxiety over youthful female sexuality" of non-feminist members of their class. Their desire to protect girls masked an impulse, simply, to control and repress young female sex lives. In her 1887 treatise

The Purchase of Women, the eugenicist Dr. Blackwell—a prominent member of the National Vigilance Association—bemoaned a "growing army of shameless women."[68]

In the neo-abolition playbook, feminism became a respectability mission. The condition that anti-porn activists today still call "female sexual slavery" was bound up, for purity feminists, not with the systems of marriage and private property, but with the scourge of male intemperance. As an answer to rape, they advanced the "Anglo-Saxon dominion" of good manners over the inferior "races." And despite the appeals of women's purity groups for an end to the double standard in the enforcement of anti-vice laws, in the end, they supported state violence against working-class women's lives and livelihoods, such as police sweeps of brothels and red-light districts. Whereas sex-worker liberation theorists and feminist organizers in the sex industry have always built platforms from the "workers' inquiry" up (a perspective some call "sex workers against work"[69]), Jeffreys, on the contrary, suggests sex workers have nothing to offer feminism. "Studying prostitutes to explain prostitution," she writes, "is as useful as examining the motives of factory workers to explain the existence of capitalism."[70] Quite useful, then?!

People like Frances Willard and Lady Henry positioned themselves in their anti-prostitution work as so many Sister Abraham Lincolns rescuing a categorically lowlier class of "sister" from a condition of racially determined debasement. The members of this temperance nobility didn't place their own genders on the same plane as the ones they were "purifying" by battling vice. In an 1895 article in the *London Evening Dispatch*, the movement leaders' understanding of themselves as a species apart was mocked mercilessly: "A self-advertising coterie of Anglo-American ladies" whose "routine" consists of "writing each other's biographies, telling beautiful stories of one another, and publishing each other's photographs."[71] Racist, elitist, self-regarding, and reactionary as they were, the purity vanguard were nonetheless trying to expand (some) women's sphere of opportunity. They gauged the value of a civilization by its degree of female emancipation and derived this measurement, in turn, from colonial Christianity.

It makes no sense to exclude the prohibitionists from feminism, even as we emphasize that their essential feminism was shared, not only by the pro-emigration *English Woman's Journal*, as we saw, but also by the great feminist bishop of the KKK—a story to which we now turn. Can it be a coincidence that Lulu Markwell, the first Imperial Commander of the Women's KKK, was the longest-serving chapter president of the WCTU?[72] The Klan was an organization thoroughly legitimated by Willard's White Ribbon Army; and let's face it, the logic of the sisterhood checks out.[73] Willard made excuses for lynching while championing white motherhood, the sanctity of the marital home, and the moral authority of eugenic maternalism. Like Charlotte Perkins Gilman, she fought white slavery in the name of the home even though she escaped homeliness herself and theoretically "agreed with those feminists who found contemporary patriarchal marriage relations as little different from prostitution."[74] Rather than grapple with patriarchy as a system propped up, at times, by almost all of us, her feminism of fear constructed a villainous underclass. Only a deeply undemocratic worldview can explain why, while eschewing the slavery of patriarchy for herself, the prohibitionist evangelized it as the path to grace for others.

FIVE

The KKK Feminist

God made men and women equal. Smith &
Wesson makes damn sure they stay that way.

—Texas gun manufacturer's bumper sticker[1]

"Where are our women senators," thundered Alma Bridwell White in 1924 at the New Jersey launch of her periodical *Woman's Chains*, "where are our women judges, where are our women jurors?"[2] Oddly enough, this person does not feature in any of the listicles of pathbreaking female industry pioneers that I can find on the internet, although she was the first woman to be ordained a bishop in the US. She founded a church, a publishing house, a magazine in support of the National Woman's Party, and a radio station. "Those who would discriminate between the sexes and rob women of their God-given rights," she preached, are ignorant "of God's plan for the redemption of the world."[3] So far, so commemorable—add the first American bishop to the feminist listicles! Between her sanctification in 1893 and death in 1946, White worked zealously as an evangelical, and one of her favored sermon topics in the 1920s was gender equality and woman suffrage, views she published in *Woman's Chains* with illustrations of a woman "scaling the heights," overtaking various male politicians on a mountain and reaching for the summit, the White House.[4] Her periodical even reprinted Elizabeth Cady Stanton's famous "Declaration of Sentiments" from the 1848 suffrage convention at Seneca Falls. As one would expect, then, White championed the 1923 Equal Rights Amendment (ERA). In fact, her Pentecostal Union, the Pillar of Fire, was the *only* American religious group to support the ERA from the start.

So: Why haven't you heard of her? Well, as the *New York Times* puts it delicately in a 2017 feature on her congregation's New Jersey campus—now enjoying a membership boom—Zarephath Christian Church has a "complicated, ugly past." The *Times* insists on giving credit where it's due, but unfortunately Alma's "positive legacy of feminism was complicated in the 1920s by her ardent embrace of the Ku Klux Klan."[5] Is "complicated" really the right word? The only religious group to endorse the ERA from its inception was also the only one to publicly endorse the KKK during its roaring 1920s revival.

Alma Bridwell was born into a large working-class leather-tanner's family in Kentucky in 1862. She decided to become a preacher when she was sixteen, threw herself into the Holiness movement, and at twenty-five married a Methodist Episcopalian, Kent White, with whom she raised two sons—Arthur and Ray—in Denver. These children served her devotedly all their lives, but her husband soon felt embarrassed by Alma's leadership ambitions. So, after she received her first independent mission, she broke with Kent's denomination on account of its refusal to ordain women. She still paid public lip service to the idea that her spouse was lord and master of her home, but she materially defied heavy opposition from him (as well as many other Methodists) in a yearslong quest to gain sole control over a ministry and Bible school of her own.

She could find no scriptural grounds for prohibiting women from leadership in the church. She fiercely denied that her feminism constituted a scriptural "modernization" of any kind (modernization was actually a trend she fervently opposed). Her strategy was to call her sectarianism "fundamentalism." At the top of her list of foes was "popery" (Catholicism). Alcohol ranked a close second. She wrote no less than three pro-Prohibition morality plays in which men are turned into feminist allies by joining the Dry Legion Crusaders at Alma Temple, the hall of worship she named after herself. Alma Temple stands in Denver to this day.

At long last, in 1902, having figured out which Pentecostalists would sign her ordination, she went ahead and incorporated the Pillar of Fire. Her revival-tent services in Denver started featuring "holy jumping," ecstasies of acrobatic hopping up and down, and "joyful leaping" so noisy that adjacent residents and business owners petitioned the mayor to have her permit revoked. He declined. In 1903, though, cops arrested fifteen of her followers for "disturbing the peace" in an impromptu drum parade that gave vent, according to the police report, "to unearthly screeches of no articulate form."[6] Alma was then increasingly attracting press and touring the country with an evangelical network called the Burning Bush, which went so far as to bring her, Kent, Arthur, and Ray to London in 1904. Once back in the US, fearing that Kent was trying to seize control of the Pillar of Fire brand, she filed unsuccessfully for divorce. Kent and Alma separated, ambivalently, and continued to fight, while sometimes trying to reunite, for many years. In 1908, White began to transfer her base of operations to a farm in New Jersey, donated to her by one of her fanatical followers. This became "Zarephath," the site featured in the recent "ugly, complicated" *Times* article. Bishop Alma White's franchise began to blow up.

People who moved to Zarephath to live in Alma's "model community" of utopian "holiness communalism"—which soon boasted its own state-of-the-art printing press and broadcasting studio—relinquished all their money. They wore a weird-looking handsewn blue Pillar of Fire uniform, slept little, fasted constantly, and accepted Alma's total authority on all matters including bathing, exercise, diet (vegetarian), praying, choice of spouse, sex, shoe care, and personal journaling. The camp gained instant notoriety as a woman-led, woman-suffragist outfit years before women had the right to vote. Soon, it started eating up the surrounding district, such that, by 1920, Zarephath was a whole 1,200-acre zip code with a fire station, power plant, farm conglomerate, cemetery, and

Bible college. The leader of the Holy Jumpers was only formally consecrated as a bishop in 1918, but she controlled every aspect of an ever-expanding property portfolio, with churches in California, Florida, and Ohio long before then. (The blurb on her biography calls her "a brilliant businesswoman."[7])

Even her apologists can't deny that White's hundreds of workers nationwide were tightly surveilled and required to obey their cult leader's every syllable. They worked the land, evangelized, staffed the schools, and dropped everything to fundraise, conduct "prayer sieges," or sell copies of Pillar of Fire's journals (all edited, written, and/or overseen by Alma herself). According to theologian Priscilla Pope-Levison, she "micromanaged every detail" and treated her workers "like commodities."[8] Helen Swarth, a woman who lived in the colony for fifteen years, vouchsafed in an exposé, "My Life in a Religious Commune" (published much later), that Alma sought to absorb devotees into herself, "leaving nothing but a shell devoid of originality or initiative."[9] At times, the shells mobilized for the National Woman's Party. At other times, they wore pointy white hoods.

White was never a card-carrying Klanswoman herself, but circa 1914 her revivals began to stage cross burnings, and the KKK directly funded her acquisitions of colleges and resorts, such as Belleview in Colorado and Alma White College in New Jersey. There's no question that her fervent support helped swell the white supremacist terror group's membership to an estimated six million by the end of the 1920s. After all, the "Second Klan," as the original nineteenth-century organization's 1914–44 iteration was called, routinely used her churches and auditoriums for rallies. She sermonized all over the country that "our heroes in the white robes" are "a tree of God's own planting," and rejoiced that "God has raised up this great patriotic organization to unmask popery."[10] Three books extolling the cross burners—*Heroes of the Fiery Cross* (1925), *Klansmen: Guardians of our Liberty* (1926), and *The Ku Klux Klan in Prophecy* (1928)—were penned and published by Bishop White, complete with illustrations by a fellow Klan fan and Zarephath colonist, Reverend Branford Clarke.[11]

White concurred with the KKK that slavery was good, that the Fifteenth Amendment must be repealed, and that the "Sons of Ham" (Black people) weren't capable of suffering much anyway, being happiest living as servants of the "Sons of Japheth" (whites) as God intended.[12] Alma's favorite conspiracy theory was that a "class of cultured Negroes" had "organized societies to promote mixing of white and colored blood," the members of which were "oath-bound to marry none but white women."[13] Race mixing and "social and political equality"[14] disgusted her almost as much as the glossolalia—speaking in tongues—that her heretical husband had decided he believed in. And the solution to these threats to white America, she felt, was the kind of feminism the Klan stood for: *Klan feminism*. Alma White expected the Klan to deliver the final victory of the crusade begun by Stanton and Anthony.

From her pulpits, she routinely called the Nineteenth Amendment "the triumph of the Cross in the liberation of women who in their inequality with the opposite sex had worn the chains of oppression"[15] and, in the same breath, endorsed the KKK for its past suffragism and ongoing commitment to equal rights. Startling as it might sound, she had a point: part of the Klan's appeal to Protestant women who had previously been active in suffrage and temperance was, in the 1920s, its vocal quest for sex equality. Take the Atlanta-based Klan paper *Searchlight*, which printed its principles with the item: "The Klan believes in the EQUALITY of the sexes without hesitation."[16] According to historian Nancy MacLean, "The order even asserted on occasion that some of the world's problems resulted from the exclusion of women from power."[17]

Few nonexpert people today would guess that many organs of the KKK affirmed—in historian Kathleen Blee's words—"the need for women to have equal power with men in marriage, to be free to stay unmarried, and to be treated as equals in political and economic life."[18] To be sure, these white supremacists were only talking about white Protestant women, a massive caveat. But it is difficult to deny that a feminist structure of desire guided their insistence on both votes for women and equal wages for female workers within the bounds of the purified ethnostate (sans Jews, Catholics, Blacks, communists, and anarcho-syndicalist Wobbly-organizer types) they fantasized was just around the corner.

Not all Klanswomen (or Klansmen) were feminists. However, a glance in the archive confirms that historian Linda Gordon's phrase "KKK feminism" is amply justified. Blee documents "the ideological merger of women's rights with racism and nativism"[19] that took place in the Second Klan. For example, one of the questions in the "Ku Klux Katechism" required Klan recruits to reply, when quizzed about the Klan's attitude toward women, that "The Klan believes in the purity of womanhood and in the fullest measure of freedom compatible with the highest type of womanhood including the suffrage."[20] It is instructive to notice the tension between belief in the purity of womanhood generally and the caveat, in the same sentence, that only the "highest type of womanhood"—no doubt maternal, Protestant, and white—is deserving of freedom. Without trying to straighten out its contradictions, we must understand Klan feminism as a haunting of the WASPish mind by the logic of colonial evolutionism: "our women" (advanced, powerful, but also chaste and threatened) versus "their women" (passive, oppressed by their men, though somehow also conniving and degenerate). When the Klan newspaper *The Fiery Cross* reported favorably on the launch of a campaign for congresswomen by Alice Paul's National Women's Party,[21] the core Klan-feminist view that Anglo-Saxon women "already were emancipated"[22] would seem to stand contradicted. But the tone of respect the KKK consistently evinced for white women of a militantly maternal bent clearly won the hate group some feminist adherents.

Alma shepherded their conversion. Evangelical Christianity of the fiery kind was a gospel of women's liberation, she proposed. The brand, as summarized by her, was "emancipation for women and ultra-fundamentalist doctrine."[23] Simultaneously, without blinking, she defied fundamentalist opposition to divorce, affirming a woman's right to it in cases of infidelity or unsafety. In addition, Alma called for sanctions against wife beaters and championed equal rights of property, inheritance, and independent legal domicile for wives. She denounced the practice of granting child custody to men—which was important, as Linda Gordon points out, "because the risk of losing children was by far the most important factor keeping women in abusive marriages."[24] Unlike most mainstream feminist leaders, Alma concurred with Alice Paul that the fight for gender justice had just begun in 1920. Hence, Susie Stanley, White's biographer, firmly positions her as a "radical feminist" even in the "marginal minority" of pro-ERA feminists.[25]

By all accounts, the bishop's feminism was full frontal: this was a woman who challenged men's power ferociously every day before breakfast. The press liked to call her a despotic "Cromwell in skirts"[26] (a "mannish-voiced gynotheocrat"[27]) while quipping that, for a temperancer, she sure had an intemperate personality—ha, ha. She shouted by turns about Black men's threat to white women and children, and about the satanic Catholic church—the latter being the major global force, in her opinion, obstructing women's liberation.[28] I can almost see her stern face as she jumps "joyfully," with cymbal accompaniment, at the front of a procession in Zarephath, praying for the death of the "purple woman of Babylon," i.e., New York City (to this day a hive of popery, boozing, card playing, sex, existing while Black, and other antifeminist vices).[29]

Two decades before she published her book *Woman's Chains* (1943), Alma founded her magazine of the same name, which reminded readers that Alice Paul and her comrades had suffered prison and police brutality for the sake of women's freedom. "The least women could do now was to exercise the hard-won right to vote."[30] What, though, should grateful daughters in Zarephath use their "hard-won" vote to accomplish? Why, restoring the sanctity of the color line established via slavery, of course. In *Behind the Mask of Chivalry: The Making of the Second Ku Klux Klan*, Nancy MacLean makes the feminist appeal of white supremacist views like these, via the sexual logic of lynch rule, just about discernible. Klansmen's chivalrous insistence on an honor code compelling them to "protect" white Protestant women—notably by maiming and murdering Black and vagrant men—gained a certain amount of credibility from the reality that women in the 1920s *were* "vulnerable, as those who knew unmarried or deserted mothers could see,"[31] albeit vulnerable for reasons to do with the privatization of care in the unwaged marital household, and not, primarily, with strange men.

Besides its racist certainty that "strange" men were much more dangerous than husbands and dads, perhaps the key defining characteristic of Klan feminism was its separatism. While internal gender politics in the KKK were "complicated,"[32] as Blee stresses (that word again!), the Klan press routinely celebrated female enfranchisement and spoke in its circulars of the need for "women's economic freedom."[33] When some women, such as Elizabeth Tyler of Atlanta, rose to the highest echelons of the KKK, many men and women in the organization responded with discomfort, by hurrying along the inauguration of a separate women-only Klan. Tyler was colloquially known as the "First Lady" of the Klan and coheaded its PR firm. Now, she received a mandate to oversee a new women's Klan. Instantly the press was keen to know: What shape was the new separatist women's Klan going to take? Whatever it is, it "will be on par with that of the men," declared Tyler to the *Times*; "we plan that all women who join us shall have equal rights with that of the men"—the women's Klan "will not be in any sense a dependent auxiliary."[34] Tyler boasted about being swamped with inquiries. The piece concludes simply by quoting her calling on all Protestant white ladies over eighteen to sign up and join the Klan, since the KKK "stands for all the things women hold most dear."

The national and southern local newspapers continued to report vaguely on these feminist Klan-spinoff plans until 1923. Finally, three contenders emerged: the "Ladies of the Invisible Empire," "the Kamelia"[35] and "Women of the KKK."[36] The *New York Times* article "Join 'Invisible Empire'" (indistinguishable from an advert) copied out the stated objectives of Ladies of the Invisible Empire in full. To quote five of the seventeen points:

> The bringing together of the Protestant women of America; to cleanse and purify the civil, political and ecclesiastical atmosphere of our country; . . . to advocate more stringent immigration laws; . . . to oppose the efforts of certain groups in this country to teach the doctrines of social equality of all races; to oppose intermarriage

between members of white, black, yellow and brown races; . . . to make America so intensely American that no room will be left for un-American ideals, religious or political.[37]

After a messy tussle between the three factions, the Women's Ku Klux Klan (WKKK) proposal won, and its leaders proceeded to open headquarters, hundreds of miles away from the male Klan's headquarters. The WKKK also anointed its own first Imperial Commander: the temperance activist, suffragist, loyal Democrat, and Presbyterian Mrs. Lulu Markwell of Arkansas.

What is scariest about the Klan of this era is its banality. "The good people *all* belonged to the Klan," reminisces one lady from Indiana: "Store owners, teachers, farmers. They were going to clean up the government."[38] Bishop White listed the occupations of Klan members in one of her books: "Ministers of the gospel, United States senators, congressmen, governors, and other federal and state officials, judges, lawyers, doctors, college professors, school teachers, bankers, manufacturers, businessmen of all classes, and clean-living level-headed men from the rank and file of our citizenry."[39] Indeed, feminists in the WKKK fused their anti-vice, racial-purity maternalism with a message of national motherhood no different from myriad other Progressive Era eugenics-tinged movements that similarly promoted temperance and anti-corruption measures intended "to cleanse America of perceived ills—everything from violence to divorce to Marxism" (to quote the author of *Sisters in Hate*, Seyward Darby).[40] Gordon concurs: "In much of their agenda," unpleasant as it sounds, "Klanswomen were indistinguishable from many other clubwomen, including Catholics, Jews, and African Americans."[41] In many ways, the KKK was just another organization—albeit one that did terrorism—historically married to the Democratic Party and teeming with middle-class philanthropists bent on forcibly rescuing prostitutes, purging the land of drink, sterilizing the unfit, and censoring smut.

The Klan was also a co-ed mafia with sophisticated and sinister mom-led strategies for winning elections. Daisy Douglas Barr was a woman suffragist and ex-Quaker who served in the WCTU in Indiana, steered the WKKK, and was crowned "Imperial Empress" of the Klan-affiliated group "Queens of the Golden Mask." According to Gordon's history *The Second Coming of the KKK*, Empress Daisy elaborated a Black psywar strategy to get Klan politicians elected a hundred years before QAnon attempted something similar. Barr established the "poison squad": a statewide women's network whose agents spread false, malicious, and violent rumors pretending to be *from* Catholics or Jews.[42] The psyop was designed to make the ostensible sources seem horrific, thus driving popular support for the Klan's political candidates.

The Klan roiled with embezzlement scandals and internal power grabs and mini-coups. Lulu Markwell was ousted before she'd served one year in command, in a nepotistic affair that resulted in the Arkansas Grand Dragon's fiancée, Robbie Gill, being crowned leader of the WKKK. But Queen Robbie, if anything, was an even more committed feminist than Lulu. In a 1924 address to the Imperial Klonvokation in Kansas City, entitled "American Women" and frequently reprinted in the Klan press, Mrs. Gill copied Mary Wollstonecraft, appropriating an ethnonationalist pride in Christianity to support a feminist agenda: "It has never been the purpose of God," she cried, "that woman should be the slave of man."[43] But don't worry! "We" Protestant "native"-born European Americans needn't feel ashamed for our gender shortcomings, because women's subordination is only the legacy of "primitive" theologies!

In her pamphlet, *The Equality of Woman*, Gill lays out a strategy on "organization and the feminist movement" and defends the accomplishments of Anglo-Saxon feminism. After all, "It is the pagan religions . . . that have oppressed and repressed women." Not unlike May French-Sheldon in her lectures, digressing about male African chivalry, Mrs. Gill cunningly pivots from praising Klansmen for their feminism to berating them for being insufficiently feminist, noting, "Many are the readjustments yet to be made." Since both equal sexes are "necessary in the economy of the race," she reasons, and since the race cannot develop properly if one sex is stymied, the white supremacist Klan *must* abolish "the selfish man who insists that woman's only place is in the home, to manage the household and to bear and raise children," in order to achieve its aims.[44] The argument was absurd. How could "primitives" have bequeathed patriarchy to Westerners and at the same time fail to conform to patriarchal domesticity?

Gill may well have been paraphrasing Charlotte Perkins Gilman when she unspooled this paradoxical gender eschatology. In tracts such as *Women and Economics* (1898), *The Home* (1903), and *Man-Made World* (1911), as well as in her famous novels, Gilman had theorized that patriarchy was an evil invention of the racial savage.[45] The sharp bifurcation between white femininity and white masculinity was, for her, the result of racial evolution having occurred for many centuries on that erroneous track. Non-white races, on the other hand, didn't have as much sex differentiation, in her view, because they didn't like to labor and so had not evolved as much of that very gender hierarchy that their primitiveness is responsible for. Yes: for white supremacists like Gill and Gilman, the non-white world is somehow both insufficiently sex differentiated *and* the source of a (bad) sex differentiation suffered by whites. Men's enslavement of women in the home has got to stop if whiteness is to fulfill its destiny, something that can only happen if "the mother of the race is free."[46]

Bishop White echoed all the main points of Gilman's maternalist racial nationalism, including those that patently let white men off the hook. Although far harsher than Gill in her self-presentation, White gladly allowed (for example) that the fact that white women are stymied and confined to the domestic sphere is a kind of evolutionary glitch, much more so than it is husbands' fault per se. Additionally, "the apparent lag in gender equality in a Christian nation," explains Kathleen Blee, could be explained away by KKK feminists by reinterpreting US history "to emphasize women's hidden power."[47] And if that still didn't feel satisfying enough, people like Gill and White would always emphasize that *both* paid female employment and Christianity were necessary for women to achieve full equality, because the feminist gospel of Jesus was unable to liberate women while they languished in economic bondage to men.

Seen in this light, the lucrative and aggressive entrepreneurship of Klan boosters like Alma, public relations moguls like Tyler, and "kluckeresses" like the Indiana WCTU heavyweight Daisy Barr was fulfilling a millenarian destiny. But if the cross-burning girl-boss is theoretically breaking racial-evolutionary shackles in order to inspire others of her sex to do the same, it is curious that Pillar of Fire records show no sign of Alma lifting others as she climbed by ordaining women. "Evidence of women serving as ministers proves to be elusive," puzzles Pope-Levison, "even though current members claim they did." It seems it took three generations for a woman to assume leadership within White's outfit (when she did, it was White's granddaughter, Arlene). A bastion of sisterhood and female solidarity Zarephath was not.

No doubt, the WASPs-only prophecy of feminist sovereignty that Alma embodied in her formidable person was easier to fantasize, for most people, within a situation of artificial segregation from men. That's presumably why, when the one or two million-odd kluckeresses went independent in 1923, they set up an independent judicial system for themselves, explaining that *ladies of the invisible empire*, as Klanswomen in various suborganizations liked to call themselves, know how to check and discipline each other better than men can. Sometimes, at Bishop White's direct urging, these outwardly prim suburban ladies devoted a decade or more of their lives to playing dress-up in anonymous white satin, conspiracy mongering, and running the "klaverns" of a clandestine anti-black, anti-immigrant terror mob. They conceived of themselves as an ever-whiter caste of millenarian mother-amazons defending a god-given "empire" visible only to them.

These women's "combination of feminism and bigotry may be disturbing to today's feminists," writes Gordon, "but it is important to feminism's history."[48] On this note, it is worth noting that some people were radicalized as feminists only once they were inside the Klan. For instance, they may initially have interpreted social reform work and political activism as *female responsibilities,* but then, as Gordon notes, "once active, they often came to resent men's attempts to control them and even challenged men's power."[49] In

1924, Colorado governor Morley (who was elected in the Republican/Ku Klux Klan landslide of that year) ordered all Klan members in the state legislature to support a minimum-wage bill for women, no doubt under the bishop's influence. In Colorado, Pillar of Fire members flocked in especially large numbers to the local KKK and WKKK, and Klan feminists there actually went considerably further than the bishop—controversially promoting the dissemination of birth control information and the manufacture and sale of contraceptives.[50] Birth control was definitely a bridge too far for Alma White's "sexual abstinence" style of radical feminism.

Still, Klan feminists, like their male counterparts, hyped the ideal of "chivalric" protection of women by men. By now, though, we are no longer surprised by the proposition of *feminism for patriarchy*. Speaking out of one side of her mouth for the arming of southern women with pistols to deter Black bogeymen, and out of the other in favor of the robed-and-hooded brotherhood who defend the empire's maidens, a Klan feminist's bottom line was that there was no such thing as white extrajudicial violence. White violence is always legitimate violence because, in America, it *is* the police. Lynching is feminism and feminism is the armed wing of the state, because, as White observed, "women have always been the greater sufferers under the violation of law; and those who stand for law-enforcement are the espousers of woman's cause."[51]

In reality, despite what lynch mobs began to say after Reconstruction about their sublime pro-woman motivations, lynching had nothing to do with helping women. As Davis analyzes in *Women, Race & Class* (1983), the practice had actually begun much earlier, as a terror campaign against white and Black abolitionists. "The cry of rape emerged as the major justification for lynching" only later.[52] Lynching did not improve white women's lives one iota, but lying to oneself about the real source of one's vulnerability can be an attractive panacea. A woman swallows her own conspiracist and pseudoscientific bullshit about Black men's savage lasciviousness, even though it bears no or little resemblance to her lived experience or empirical reality, because it's easier than indicting her own husband, uncle, priest, dad, or the family form itself. She looks to the Klan as a para-governmental force for disciplining violent men, nonsensically, by inciting any or all of the violent men in her kinship network *to* vigilante violence (against pre-dehumanized male others).

This only "works" in the way a suicide vest works, because the vigilantism of the lynching of the "Black rapist" enacts the lynchers' ownership of female sexuality almost as much as it expresses their anti-blackness. That, in a nutshell, is the logic of white supremacist patriarchal feminism: the illusion of honor and protection for "her" belies the sharply felt, radically disavowed disposability she actually shares with "him" (the non-white rapist) in the event of her race treachery or unchastity.

But while this cultural script was pervasive and powerful, it is quite wrong to imagine that white women had little agency in the matter. Plenty of white women, such as the Texan suffragist Jessie Daniel Ames, didn't just eschew these suicide-vest gestures but organized bravely and effectively against them, banding together in the Association of Southern Women for the Prevention of Lynching. Conversely, other white women participated actively in the lynch mobs, and many spectated. When the cultural feminist Susan Brownmiller wrote, in her 1975 classic *Against Our Will: Men, Women, and Rape*, that the lynching of Emmett Till was "indefensible overkill," "but we must also accept" that his whistle at Mrs. Bryant was "just short of physical assault," she was channeling KKK feminism.[53]

At the turn of the twenty-first century, some years before the resurrection of Alma White's church was documented in the *Times*, Kristin Kandt, a feminist lawyer, argued in a journal of law and social policy that White was "a trailblazer in her advocacy of equality for women in both the religious and secular spheres"—even though she "was not a trailblazer on the issue of race" (admittedly a "profound limitation").[54] The lawyer painstakingly separates White's feminism and white supremacism, framing the latter as a mere matter of being "aligned with this majority on racism." The bishop's antisemitism and anti-blackness were terrible, Kandt vaguely indicates several times; but hey, at least it was nonviolent: "Alma White sincerely believed that the Klan was opposed to lynching."[55] The level of apologism here rivals that of White's biographer Susie Stanley, who, in *Feminist Pillar of Fire: The Life of Alma White* (1993), insists that anti-Catholicism and feminism alone were what attracted an *actually antiracist* Alma White to the Klan; and that, moreover, her premillennialist Christian Zionism clears her of the charge of antisemitism. (White accused Jews of funding popery, controlling the media, waylaying Protestant girls, and spreading porn, but these are just "statements critical of activities engaged in by Jews," and not "necessarily" bigoted, Stanley protests.[56])

Kandt notes that White deemed the "liquor curse" an effort to "enslave women and children" under drunkard men and suggests she may have supported the Klan primarily because she "construed their support of Prohibition as a sign of their kinship to women."[57] It's true, as Nancy MacLean reminds us, that "Klansmen viewed female suffrage as the best defense for Prohibition." Yet this isn't the intimation of Klan feminism's insincerity Kandt seems to think it is. As we have seen, temperance itself was a gender ideology. Seemingly unperturbed by the close collaborations of the WCTU and the KKK, Kandt boldly states that "Alma White's insights regarding alcohol support [the] revisionist view of temperance workers" laid out by eco-radical theologian Mary Daly—a 1960s cultural feminist whose transmisogyny we will explore later. The view in question is a view of temperance supporters as real feminists rather than moralists—as though one couldn't be both—and is exemplified in the 1983 tract *Pure Lust*, where Daly slams "man-made [male or patriarchal] caricatures of the Women's Christian Temperance Union,"[58] and claims the famous hatchet wielder Carrie Nation as an anti-rape activist comrade.

This kind of recuperation is hardly unique in an era in which politicians sometimes described as "Christian feminists," such as Michele Bachmann, publicly point out the supposed upside to slavery.[59] Ethnonationalist, feminist politicians are currently prevalent in Europe, and tend to mix praise of "tradwives" with Islamophobic formulations of girlbossery: think of Giorgia Meloni, Frauke

Petry, Alice Weidel, Siv Jensen, and Pia Kjaersgaard.[60] In the US, comparable alt-right figures like Marjorie Taylor Greene, Lauren Boebert, Ayla Stewart, Lana Lokteff, and Lauren Southern—who are every bit as Islamophobic—typically frame themselves instead as *antifeminist*s, evangelizing racial honor, the "trad" life, and women's return to the domestic sphere. At the same time, it is not uncommon for these "white baby challenge"-touting "wives with a purpose" to claim feminism as a good whenever doing so feels strategic: "When will we learn that pushing women into the workforce at the expense of our kids is NOT feminist?" and so on.[61]

It certainly feels incongruent to view the latter set as KKK-feminism revivalists, given that 1920s Klan feminists aligned themselves with the radical fringe of the women's movement of their day, the Woman's Party, in support of the Equal Rights Amendment. Nonetheless, the fingerprints of Pillar of Fire–style "pro-woman" religion are all over the contemporary Christian-nationalist "Save Our Children" right.

To what end might one shine a light on the connection? The Zarephath Christian Church's resurrectors in New Jersey in 2017 see "no reason to discuss her"—and, pointedly, they don't. "But with the amnesia about Bishop White," worries the *Times*, "also comes the loss of the example of an early feminist leader within conservative Christianity."[62] (Presumably it was this amnesia that caused the *Times* not to mention White's Klan commitments in their obituary.[63]) Personally, I would go out of my way to celebrate such a loss, because early feminist leaders like Bishop White, or the first female US senator, Rebecca Felton—a woman suffragist pro-lynching fanatic—can, in the end, only be ignored. They cannot actually be excised from feminist history, since they were ideological wellsprings of feminisms that still live and breathe.

From the 1930s on, White's extremist temperance zealotry and, perhaps less so, her eliminationist screeds against Blacks, Jews, and Catholics, helped seal the commune's decline and collapse. Nonetheless, her very "sincere belief" that Christian nationalists only use weapons in justified self-defense lives on in the form of twenty-first-century gun-lobby front groups like

"EmPOWERed, "a movement made of and for women on college campuses across the USA who feel empowered exercising their second amendment rights."[64]

Antonia Okafor, a figurehead for "EmPOWERed" and national spokesperson for Gun Owners of America, positions herself as a Texan, feminist, African immigrant, and sexual assault survivor. She frames the self-reliance and safety that come with "concealed carry" laws as "real feminism." Her moral touchstone and constant refrain is the trope of "the most vulnerable and defenseless human beings," in whose service Christian gun rights become "the true meaning of the feminism movement."[65] It is perfectly clear, however, from her ambassadorship for the fascist group Turning Point USA, that the "self-defensive" firepower she is championing is to be placed in the hands of a nationalist sexual elite and used on depraved racialized others.

Undeterred, the Canadian self-described "radical feminist" Meghan Murphy invited Okafor to be a podcast guest on the platform Feminist Current. The "Second Amendment feminist" surreally proceeded to invoke Ida B. Wells, the Black Panthers, and bell hooks—as well as the fact that the KKK fought against *Black* gun rights—to bolster her fascist-funded concealed-carry advocacy. Murphy, a trans-exclusionary and sex-worker-exclusionary (neo-abolitionist) radical feminist, clearly welcomed Okafor's alt-right politics, reflecting that she herself had once upon a time "identified as a Marxist," while, at one point, agreeing that armed self-defense is clearly, if we're being realistic, a must for women in a world of endemic gender violence. Okafor is Nigerian American, but her enshrinement of universal female precarity in an ideology of hyperpatriotic armed citizenship centered around the tribal defense of select feminine honor is perfectly Klannish.[66] Like the National Rifle Association spokeswoman Dana Loesch, whose rageful YouTube videos threaten "every rapist, domestic abuser, violent, criminal thug, and every other monster who preys upon women"[67] with imminent (and preemptive), bloody retribution, Okafor conjures a spectral, ignoble male figure with one hand and brandishes a holy automatic at him with the other.

This is, as we learn from Caroline Light, author of *Stand Your Ground: A History of America's Love Affair with Lethal Self-Defense*, the through line connecting post-Reconstruction "anti-rape" lynching ideology to both mainstream and radical feminist self-defense pedagogies that center on racial concepts of stranger danger.[68] It is how someone comes to believe, with Okafor and her ilk, that "gun rights are women's rights," and, as the evangelical Christian president of Turning Point USA Charlie Kirk likes to say, that the Second Amendment did more for women than feminism ever did. A 2016 Turning Point USA publication, with Rosie the Riveter on its cover, includes a section resolving that "Girls Just Want to Have Guns"—full of cooked statistics on increased incidences of rape in foreign countries in the wake of handgun bans. It opens with the observation: "God made men and women, but Sam Colt made them equal."[69]

The offer that the feminism of lynchers makes to white women is a devil's bargain, drawing us into the rewards of whiteness as property if we sign away our solidarity—a wicked compensation for our lack of ownership of other forms of property in capitalist societies.[70] Seductive as it may seem when we are hopeless, unsafe, and resentful, it is, and has always been, possible to just say no. Jessie Daniels, the author of *Nice White Ladies* (2021) and *White Lies* (1997), grew up in Texas with a version of that Sam Colt one-liner, though the gun manufacturer named was different. Jessie's name—which she gave herself—is a tribute to the Southern Women for the Prevention of Lynching cofounder Jessie Daniel Ames. Nowadays, Daniels teaches at Hunter College, New York, while continuing to write extensively on the "gender-only feminism" she was raised into down South (intriguingly, of course, the rise of Antonia Okafor suggests that "nice white ladies" can sometimes be Black). The feminism in question was Christian-nationalist and racist. But instead of espousing this ladyhood, Daniels turned queer "race traitor."[71]

While researching her first book in the 1990s, Daniels found herself racked by nightmares in which she was alternately a pregnant Black woman facing street abuse from a mob of white women, and a Black man, desperately fleeing, hiding in a ditch from torch-bearing Klansmen on horseback who are pursuing "him."[72] She had accidentally discovered that her paternal grandfather was briefly a member of the 1920s KKK. Prevarication followed, for Daniels, about the role of this discovery in her scholarship. "Should I go on to reveal that he was the very same grandfather that molested me as a child?" she debated. "I think not." And yet, as the preface to *White Lies* relates, "this Klan member and child-molester raised my father, who was most certainly not abusive and who, for his generation, held astonishingly egalitarian views of gender."[73] Klan feminism, after all, is structurally compatible with child sexual abuse even while rhetorically condemning it, since its figuration of sexual threat shores up the sanctity of the familial unit as a stronghold against stranger danger.

Daniels makes no bones about her feminist father's intense anti-blackness and antisemitism. She notes, though, that "when I was growing up, my father was more of a feminist, in his Texas-styled way, than my mother was." His feminism—gender only—was a doctrine well encapsulated by a bumper sticker slogan that touts guns as the preserver of sex equality. He gifted Jessie a gun for her seventeenth birthday, "to protect me from sexual assault and other dangers," and for several years she "believed in" this justification for carrying arms. Then, one day, a man stalked her and tried to break into her home. Shooting him was an option she considered. But suddenly, Daniels saw that if she shot him, she would "never be able to unknow him."[74] It was then, she writes, that she perceived the fundamental poverty of carceral gender justice, and its irremediable racism. "It was then, I think, that I outgrew my father's Smith & Wesson feminism."

SIX

The Blackshirt

*Fascism alone will complete the work begun by
the militant women from 1906 to 1914.*

— NORAH ELAM, former WSPU general secretary, 1935[1]

Ugly things happen in cults, and yet more ugly things happen when
cult leaders betray their followers. In 1920, the cult of Emmeline
Pankhurst was in total disarray. Mrs. Pankhurst's passionate army
of suffragettes had fought a guerrilla war against the UK government between 1906 and 1914. But as soon as World War I broke
out, their dear general had called it off. To the rage and disgust of
many suffragettes, including her own communist daughter Sylvia,
Emmeline turned her troops around to work for the British state
instead of against it, patriotically supporting what turned out to be
the wholesale decimation of Europe's male proletariats by the capitalist political class. Some five million British men were enlisted in
the British army over the course of the war, many of them, after the
state introduced conscription, against their will.

In this period, to risk stating the obvious, British women with
heroic inclinations were even less able than usual to get recognition

for their heroism—except as nurses—since the War Office was in the habit of telling ladies keen to sign on to "go home and sit still."[2] What is less well-known is that the unprecedented scale of the human devastation unleashed in the trenches, as the Central Powers and Allies battled it out interminably, wiped away the UK population's memory of the yearslong domestic campaign of political violence the Women's Social and Political Union (WSPU) had waged. To this day, remarkably few people talk about the British bombing and arson campaign for women's votes, which detonated as many bombs between 1912–13 as the Irish Republican Army did during its 1939–40 "S-Plan."

The reason for this is partly also that Pankhurst herself decided to memory-hole her terrorism campaign. After June 1914, rather than bombing cabinet members' homes, the autocratic head of the WSPU was penning broadsides against conscientious objectors, excoriating cultural treason and scaremongering about German "enemy blood." Together with her eldest, Christabel, Emmeline tried to redirect (in the opposite direction) all the energies her foot soldiers had previously poured into disobedience. The government was now the suffragettes' master, not their enemy. The WSPU's newsletter *Suffragette* got rebranded—patriotically—to *Britannia*. Politicians the women had previously assaulted on the street were suddenly, in a sense, the boss. "I won't pretend we liked it," one of the decommissioned militants, Mary Allen, said of this about-face: "We were heart and soul in our fight to gain recognition for women."[3] Regardless, the WSPU was disbanded and turned into the law-abiding Women's Party. At the close of the war, as though in patronizing recognition of the ladies' service to the Crown, a hollow victory was handed down. But the only women to gain the vote in 1918 were property owners over thirty. Before long it seemed clear to many feminists that the radical change promised to them probably wasn't reachable via Parliament. Had they sacrificed so much for a false cause?

Meanwhile, in Italy, the antisemitic ex-socialist Benito Mussolini was building the National Fascist Party, paving the way for a redirection for our suffragettes. The so-called Duce's demagoguery played on feelings among petty-bourgeois Italians of having been set up by "democratic elites," during the war, for colossal betrayal and bloodshed. In the wake of the armistice—and limited enfranchisement—a substantial number of women in Britain felt similarly. Some had hoped to return to their great adventure on the streets postwar, and now felt disoriented, defrauded, used, betrayed, and abandoned by Mrs. Pankhurst. For them, at this juncture, Mussolini's rants offered one possible explanation for what had happened to them: a liberal elite double-cross. Additionally, the "fascisti" worldview afforded the intoxicating pleasures of a new radicalization spiral, allowing women to fight Parliament again—this time not as bomb throwers for votes but as anti-democratic and anti-immigrant "squadristi" in a struggle that was presented to them as deeply feminist—the violent struggle for a "corporate state."

In 1922, Mussolini's paramilitary Blackshirts secured power in Rome (with secret assistance from the British government), and, that same year, black-shirted Duce supporters used Westminster Abbey for a military remembrance.[4] "Fascisti" fan clubs formed all over Britain (the first of which—The British Fascisti—was founded in 1923 by a woman, Rotha Lintorn-Orman). Among the fans, one celebrity couple, Oswald and Cynthia "Cimmie" Mosley, stood out sharply. These were Labour politicians who loved fascism and were literal aristocrats (a marquess and a baronet). They nonetheless gained some radical women's and trade-unionists' trust, especially in the city of Birmingham, during the 1926 General Strike, by supporting striking workers against the government, the riot police, and vigilante strikebreakers.[5] A feminist-fascist estuary formed in the crater generated by Mrs. Pankhurst's pivot from lawbreaking insurgency to conformist cheerleading. Oswald Mosley, a playboy, became more than a pinup: he became the new Mrs. "My movement has been largely built up by the fanaticism of women," Mosley said. "Without the women I could not have got a quarter of the way."[6] He founded the British Union of Fascists (BUF) in 1932.

"We have to emphasize that only three former suffragettes joined the Blackshirts," insists the historian Julie Gottlieb in the preface of *Feminine Fascism: Women in Britain's Fascist Movement*,

1923-1945. "They were aberrations."[7] Why exactly is it important to emphasize that only Mary Allen, Norah Elam, and Mary Richardson crossed over from the WSPU to the BUF? Would it be bad if readers asked further questions about compatibilities between liberal feminism and fascism? For one thing, the figure of "only three" doesn't square with the who's who of Britain's interwar fascist milieu at the end of *Feminine Fascism*, which lists several more suffragettes who embraced the movement of British fascists, including Lucy Houston, Mercedes Barrington, and Nina Boyle. There were also others who don't get a mention, including Iveigh Nisbett and Isobel Goldingham. Regardless, what is the threshold number of suffragettes turned right-extremists above which we worry about some feminisms' convergence with fringe fascist agitation?

The suffragette army and the BUF both depended, Gottlieb mentions, on "the leadership principle, hero-worship, quasi-spiritual inspiration, palingenetic imagery, and Romantic longings for national regeneration."[8] Both organizations "aestheticized politics" and were "accused by rivals," rightly or wrongly, "of criminality, lunacy, fanaticism and tyranny." Both also encouraged, she says, "the development of women's skills for self-defense, and gave vent to female aggression and rebelliousness" by training ladies in ju-jitsu. According to one of the converts from the one personality cult to the other, the two alike were "conducted under strict discipline," and each was a "remarkable and determined manifestation for ordered change."[9] The latter one, some thought, restated the feminist mission of the former. It clearly causes discomfort to many of us today to characterize the WSPU "as a dictatorship," but Gottlieb notes that some people do—and even that "traces of proto-fascism have been identified in the suffragette movement."[10] Luckily, we can "reassure" ourselves that most ex-suffragettes didn't support Mussolini. If we concentrate on framing such support as an aberration, we don't have to ruminate on overlaps between liberal feminist and fascist mediations of race, class, and empire.

Well, I am curious what happens if we do consider the possibility that feminism can and did express itself fascistically. To be clear, I do not consider terrorism inherently fascistic, nor do I feel compelled to condemn or denounce the terrorism of the nonconstitutional wing of the woman suffrage movement in Britain. My concern is that the liberal erasure of the suffragettes' thousand-odd bombing and arson attacks from the historical record smacks of an inability to understand the WSPU—a profoundly autocratic single-issue militia—as the paramilitary cult of personality it really was.

This denial began with the suffragettes themselves, a small core group of whom, not unlike Stanton and Anthony, wrote revisionist patriotic histories of their own movement and its relation to other woman suffrage organizations in its immediate aftermath. Members like Annie Kenney, Constance Lytton, Emmeline Pethick-Lawrence, Edith How-Martyn, and Christabel and Emmeline themselves created what one scholar calls "a highly stylized story of their participation in the Edwardian suffrage campaign that equated militancy with service to the nation during the First World War."[11] In order to curate this bowdlerized legacy and burnish its pantheon (while eclipsing the contributions of the anti-war and leftist wings of suffragism in Britain), a club called the Suffragette Fellowship was set up in 1926.

In a letter to this fellowship in the 1930s, Edith Mansell-Moullin, a Welsh suffragette, explains that she is planning a biography of the group's one martyr, Emily Wilding Davison—the WSPU militant who likely bombed the house of future prime minister David Lloyd George, and then died shortly after subsequently intercepting the king's horse at the Epsom derby. The question troubling Mrs. Mansell-Moullin? Whether or not she should continue to "leave out the bombs."[12] Leaving out the bombs, of course, is exactly what our standard narratives of the suffragettes, from *Mary Poppins* (1964) to *Suffragette* (2015), do. Even those histories specifically focused on the role of British women in the BUF do not make links between the fascist movements' tactics of intimidation and stochastic violence and British women's earlier role in injuring postal workers by pouring acid into postboxes, or injuring rail workers by bombing train carriages and stations, or risking mass civilian injury by planting nitroglycerin bombs and potassium-nitrate bombs at busy street intersections, sporting grounds, cathedrals, pavilions, and in politicians' houses full of sleeping servants.

We might start countering this avoidant tendency by asking, simply, what happens to a feminism (or indeed any social movement) when it relies too heavily on terrorism. I'd submit that the answer is always: it lurches inexorably to the right. This question is quite distinct from the justifiably unending debate over whether the suffragettes' terrorism worked or, on the contrary, delayed the passage of the parliamentary vote for propertied ladies over the age of thirty in 1918. In that debate, scholars typically weigh the role played by the behind-the-scenes continuation of suffragism in the anti-war women's labor movement, the role played by the labor of millions of women in munitions factories in reshaping society and swaying statesmen, and the effect of the WSPU's immediate cease-fire at the war's outset (a heel turn that was followed by consistent bootlicking thereafter). The consensus view is—to quote one historian's melodramatic formula—that women "earned" their limited franchise "not by throwing bombs but by making them; not by raising children but by sending them to die."[13]

We do not have to pronounce ourselves on one side or the other of that "terrorism efficacy" debate, though, to understand that planting bombs for women's votes was not always a liberation struggle so much as it was an early available version of the adventuring life that Blackshirtism later made available to socially suffocated girls. Sometimes, proposes the fascism expert Richard Thurlow, suffragettism was just "one kind of genteel revolt by spirited upper-middle-class women against the stultifying effects of the Victorian ethic of limiting the role of respectable ladies to ornaments in the social round."[14] In retrospect, delusions of grandeur, a degree of sadism, and a martyr complex are traceable in both their suffragettism and their fascism. We do ourselves a dangerous disservice as feminists today by disappearing, flattening, or equivocating about the huge quantities of state and anti-state political violence that, for good and ill, helped birth what we today call liberal democracy.

From the late nineteenth century on, a number of ladies' vice squads and "vigilance" patrols had attracted Anglo-American feminists seeking the adventure of brothel busting, Freikorps-style (referring to the German paramilitary groups that appeared after World War I). This hobbyistic civic service was typically articulated as racism—a modern spin on the old White Ribboner mold. As late as 1928, a British group called the Imperial Fascist League attempted to gin up a "white slavery" panic, posting stickers around London inciting pogroms in the name of women's rights: "Britons! Do not allow JEWS to tamper with White Girls."[15] Naturally, anti-fascist and fascist women both participated in these street confrontations. Anti-fascist feminists were out in force on October 4, 1936, at the Battle of Cable Street: a series of physical clashes with the BUF's battalions as they attempted to march through London's majority-immigrant and Jewish East End. After Cable Street, dozens of anti-fascist women and two dozen fascist ones were jailed in Holloway Prison, a decade after the suffragettes rotated in and out of there under the infamous law of medical release and rearrest for women on hunger strike, the Cat and Mouse Act. Some feminists had turned to trade unionism in that decade—while for others, the taste for street combat had crossed over from women's enfranchisement to blood-and-soil chauvinism.

While the vital importance of feminism to anti-fascism has been richly argued and studied, the role of feminism in fascism is a neglected counter-thesis that may help us better understand not only fascism in the present, but also ourselves, the inheritors of a liberal-democratic feminist legacy that fascistic women helped bequeath.[16] Contrary to our expectations, there were clearly reasons why a cult of action against antifeminist politicians morphed into a cult of action against degenerates, and reasons why "Votes for Women" became "Britain First" on many British feminists' lips.

"British Fascisti," but also German and Austrian brownshirts, were following Italy's example over the course of the 1920s—capitalizing on popular sentiments of national betrayal all but guaranteed to mushroom upon the onset of the global Great Depression. After the Wall Street crash of 1929, the spores spread. In the early 1930s, all across Europe, Irish Blueshirts, Greek Metaxists, Spanish

Falangists, and sundry other fascist legions surged to prominence. Norah Elam—the antisemitic, very homophobic onetime general secretary of the WSPU—followed these developments closely from London, optimistic about their potential to advance feminist revolution. According to Mrs. Elam's granddaughter, none too few ex-suffragettes believed that women had been "given the vote to shut them up, then shrewdly side-lined and made politically powerless."[17]

They reeled from Mrs. Pankhurst's evident indifference to any further frontiers of women's emancipation after 1918, and the whiplash of seeing her cozily befriend the very politicians she'd once attacked with explosives. This was compounded by the trauma and cognitive dissonance born of a continent-wide massacre. Emmeline, somehow, had applauded the military decimation of the working classes, even calling for the detention in concentration camps of Germans living in Britain. Were Germans really suddenly the enemy? Year after year, Elam brooded on all this, biding her time. Then, when the BUF was launched, she joined it.

From 1933 on, if an erstwhile woman-suffrage soldier was stewing, or simply feeling restless, missing the sisterly camaraderie of the days when she was earning press and medals for her valor, she could pick up a copy of the BUF magazine *Blackshirt* or *Fascist Quarterly* and readily find articles by other ex-suffragettes denouncing parliamentarism as a swindle incapable of delivering real change. Referring to the suffragette years, Elam herself appealed in print to "those women who endured the ordeal of the great struggle of pre-war days," to notice that "there is no freedom either for men or for women under the present antiquated system of democracy."[18] Two courses are left open to women, she proposed, namely fascism and communism. It is fascism that "gives justice and equality for the first time in the history of the Women's struggle."[19] One fan of the suffragettes, Olive Hawks, aged only sixteen, agreed. Hawks joined the party in 1934 and contributed an enthusiastic article: "Youth and Womanhood Turns to Fascism." Several such features extolled the futuristic pro-woman radicalism of the fascist ideology, and publicized the WSPU exploits of new members, painting them "as heroic agitators in a feminist revolution."[20] Mary Richardson, a heavily decorated ex-suffragette, was one such hero.

Miss Richardson hailed originally from Ontario. The child of a bank manager, she had emigrated to Europe at the turn of the century and toured France and Italy. It was in 1913, it seems, that Mary befriended Benito Mussolini,[21] a fellow socialist at that time, as he was editing the left newspaper *Avanti*.[22] As an anglophone cosmopolitan with novel-writing ambitions, however, Mary decided to settle in London, live in Bloomsbury, and join the Labour Party. Then in 1908 she heard Emmeline Pankhurst speak at Albert Hall and fell in love on the spot. Richardson quickly became one of the bolder terrorists in the suffragette army. Adopting the nom de guerre "Polly Dick," she threw herself into the WSPU membership's internal competition of self-sacrifice, to earn the specially minted medals, honors, and favors Emmeline bestowed on her youthful knights.

"Polly" broke windows, assaulted bobbies (British police), and jumped onto the running board of the king's carriage to thrust a "Votes for Women" petition into His Majesty's hands. She was arrested nine times and forcibly fed "to the point of death" (according to one protesting doctor) before being released "on the pretext that it is only because an operation for appendix trouble is required." In her WSPU leaflet, "A Personal Experience of Torture," Mary writes: "Forcible feeding is an immoral assault as well as a painful physical one, and to remain passive under it would give one the feeling of sin; the sin of concurrence."[23]

In 1914, Mary "Dick" additionally earned herself the title "Slasher" when she took a small meat cleaver to a painting of a nude woman by Diego de Velázquez in London's National Gallery as a protest against the imprisonment of Mrs. Pankhurst. The *Times* published Richardson's statement about the "Venus" she'd hacked in five places: "I have tried to destroy the picture of the most beautiful woman in mythological history as a protest against the Government for destroying Mrs. Pankhurst, who is the most beautiful character in modern history." All five blows landed on the Velázquez nude's back and buttocks. It helped, as Mary later reflected, that she "disliked the painting." (In a radio interview decades later, the Slasher explained that it had infuriated her how men "gawped"; in her opinion, the painting was "sensuous," that is, pornographic.) Between late 1912 and early 1914, she coordinated secret WSPU operatives collectively carried out up to twenty incidents a month of property destruction in Mrs. Pankhurst's name.[24] Richardson considered herself to love women, but when it comes to this particular suffragette—as Asa Seresin contends in his essay "Lesbian Fascists on TERF Island"—her "sex-negative" love for women was already inextricable in 1914 from "her brewing fascist inclinations."[25]

A fierce dissenter from institutional power, Richardson was a socialist before she joined the BUF. In her Labour candidacies, she notably displayed all the classic hallmarks of "the socialism of fools," not just the feminism of fools. Describing the problem of capitalism as though it were equivalent to bankers, foreign monopolies, and middlemen, she denounced food production "rings" and lamented their "corruption" of nature and health, pledging, in environmentalist and eugenic language, to restore the agricultural economy intended by "evolution," so as to provide wholesome food, "pure" milk, and "healthy" lives to all Britons.[26] Markets, she implied, could be definancialized—curbed, rather than abolished—by bringing them under "socialist" national control. Alas, Richardson was not remotely unique in defecting from this area of the left to fascism. A fair few red-brown converts came both from Labour and the Communist Party–affiliated Independent Labour Party (ILP) (itself still affiliated with Labour). Mosley himself had made this same journey.[27] Still, according to anti-fascist researcher Jeffrey Wallder, Richardson was still sufficiently removed from fascism in 1922 to send Mussolini "a stinging letter accusing him of betraying all his principles" upon learning that his National Fascist Party had marched on Rome.[28] Mussolini's reply to his suffragette comrade was chillingly prescient, as the story goes. He dispatched a telegram with just four words: "Someday you will understand."

It took nine years in the wilderness, but eventually Mary "understood." In the immediate aftermath of the suffragette war, she found herself desperate for purpose, so, like several of her former

WSPU comrades, she ran an unsuccessful campaign to become an MP for the Labour Party. She then ran again—again unsuccessfully—as Independent Labour before switching back to Labour to lose a third parliamentary candidacy in 1931. It was at this juncture that she and others like her gravitated to the BUF due to its apparent feminism and (in her own words) imperialism. "I feel certain," she told the magazine *Fascist Week*, "that woman will play a large part in establishing fascism in this country."[29]

When Richardson wrote in the *Blackshirt* or spoke to *Fascist Week*, she never brought up her long spell of service for Labour. What she did expound, however, was her glorious past as a feminist. Mary was always (according to veteran fascists) spinning yarns about her WSPU days. But then, too, fascism spat her out. Aged seventy when she wrote her autobiography, *Laugh a Defiance*, the Slasher made no mention of her BUF phase at all.[30] The project she presented as her life's exclusive work was sacred service under Emmeline.

To be sure, Oswald didn't cut it for Richardson, in the end, as a replacement or surrogate goddess to whom she could transfer devotion as an acolyte. The Slasher was kicked out of the ostensibly feminist BUF in 1935—and the reason was, undeniably, her feminism. She had joined in 1933 and promptly taken over the women's section. For two years, she had sung the praises of the BUF as feminism's great hope. But then she was expelled, in her own aggrieved words, for "daring, with other women, to put forward demands to the great Mosley, whereby women would receive some measure of fair play."[31] Anti-fascists who were active in 2017 will remember, here, the similar case of white supremacist Lauren Southern complaining about sexism in her movement.[32] I dare say the phenomenon of feminists in neo-Nazi movements suffering misogyny at their comrades' hands is difficult to document without mirth and schadenfreude. Yet it isn't quite proof enough that feminism and fascism are mutually exclusive substances.

The feminism of Mosleyites in the early 1930s was often, it must be said, materially enacted via acts of comradely solidarity. For instance, one fascist organizer in North London, Mrs. H. Carrington

Wood, spoke to the press about her and others' resignation from the BUF in solidarity with Richardson's ouster. Wood herself had "fought unavailingly for the equality of women within the Blackshirt movement,"[33] according to the *Star*, and in a memo to Mosley, she'd warned that if he axed Richardson, it would break fascism's feminist promise. She at first refused to believe that Mosley would expel the women's section leader for convening a meeting on the gender pay gap within his organization.[34] Fascism, Mrs. Wood felt, was meant to represent the women who "naturally do not want to risk going back to where they were before the days of the Suffragettes!" "All the best women left with me," Richardson noted, smugly.[35] She and Wood immediately gave an indignant speech at a meeting of the Six Point Group, a radical women's rights think tank, on the "antifeminist trend"[36] in fascism. Imagine that.

In 1997, a veteran fascist from Lancaster, Robert Row, reflected that the BUF had been "on the side of true feminism." The fascist vision, as paraphrased by Mr. Row, was that "working women [will be] protected against exploitation and receive the same high pay as men" in "as many" occupations, "but also that the care of mothers and children becomes a special duty of the State."[37] More so than their liberal and socialist counterparts, it was the fascists, in this view, who knew how to celebrate "a generation of women who have turned from the ties of Victorianism to the wider world of business."[38] One of Mosley's top lieutenants, Anne Brock-Griggs, hammered out this position in the pamphlet *Women and Fascism*, which vindicates "the need for more women in such professions as medicine, architecture, engineering, nursing, law and domestic science," and paints a utopian picture in which "women architects and engineers will help in planning the homes and cities of the future."[39] Fantasizing that the ancient Anglo-Saxon past had enjoyed great relations between the sexes, just like their contemporaries in the Women's KKK and foremothers in Langham Place, British fascists like Griggs trumpeted a true feminism that was palingenetic, that is, achieved through civilizational rebirth. Above all, this was a feminism not like the other feminisms, oriented by Mosley's motto (which also happens to sound like a line from a recent trans-exclusionary radical feminist screed): "We want men who are men, and women who are women."[40]

Bizarre as it might seem today, the Nazi Party itself had feminists in its ranks in the 1920s. In early 1926, the National Socialist party paper published articles in its women's supplement advancing the position that women are the equals of men in all respects. The argument was that sex equality, far from being an alien ideology, is autochthonous to Germany (sound familiar?). It was "the order that prevailed in ancient German society. Indeed, it was foreign values that had infected German society with belief in women's inferiority."[41] Consequently, feminism was a restorative project, as it had been for imperial feminists a century earlier. In this case, the Nazi in question, Emma Hadlich, declared that a fascist post-democratic "state, based on merit, should recognize women's right to lead as much as men's."[42] Her argument very much wasn't the one that won the day in the Nazi Party, whose "cult of motherhood"–style antifeminism was of course firmly established by the time Hitler came to power. However, in the UK, fascists developed similar ideas, often romanticizing, in their case, a pre-parliamentary era— the "Golden Age of Tudor Government"—wherein, according to their fantasy, women's accomplishments were celebrated by everyone, only for everything to be ruined in the seventeenth century by Puritanism, democracy, and . . . sexism.[43] As late as 1937, a Nazi, Anne Seelig-Thomann, was defending the gender record of Nazism in *British Union Quarterly*.

If having confidence in the Blackshirt baronet's gender liberation bona fides seems improbable, it is worth recognizing that gender progressives of Griggs's, Wood's, and Richardson's persuasion didn't pluck it entirely out of thin air. They were responding to an explicit promise that a futuristic fascist "return" to "corporatism" would "give women greater privileges than they enjoyed under democracy."[44] Mosleyite propaganda was to some extent sincere, as well as strategic, in presenting fascism to women as a system that would ensure equal pay for equal work, abolish restrictions on married women's employment, and prioritize material support to mothers and children. Blackshirts certainly sold these policies explicitly as superior to the fake feminism of anyone who still put faith in the gerontocratic mainstream parties.

Thus, especially in the period when he was crossing over from the Conservative Party to the Independent Labour Party, Sir Oswald impressed many people with his promise of a radical shake-up of British life. Astonishingly, in both 1922 and 1923, his voting record inspired the Six Point Group to single him out as the best feminist candidate.[45] Campaigning for gender equality in six areas—political, occupational, moral, social, economic, and legal—the Six Point Group was set up in 1921 by ex-suffragettes, businesswomen, magazine editors, League of Nations lobbyists, and the lesbian couple of Margaret Haig Thomas, a viscountess, and Helen Archdale. Other lobbyists in their group included the well-regarded socialist feminists Vera Brittain and Winifred Holtby. I cannot excuse them. It grieves and alarms me that the Six Point Group was taken in by a totalitarian gang of sharply dressed believers in the cult of "me no frego," Mussolini's pogrom-ready catchphrase, meaning: I don't give a damn. Naturally I thought of these fascist-enabling progressive feminists from a prior century when, in 2018, liberals deemed the "f-word" hysterical even as First Lady Melania Trump wore a military green jacket emblazoned with the words "I really don't care, do u?" while visiting a migrant detention center full of undocumented children separated from their kin. (In 2024, a few weeks after her husband claimed that immigrants "poison the blood" of America, Melania wore the same jacket again.[46])

One early embodiment of me no frego was Rotha Lintorn-Orman, a chronic host of wild, house-trashing parties on her parents' stately property—and the the aforementioned woman who founded the British Fascisti in 1923. Except that, when someone pointed out that a patriotic group shouldn't have a foreign appellation, she changed the name to "British Fascists" (BF). Poor Lintorn-Orman: a cross-dressing army auxiliary, she was routinely assumed by the police to be an ex-suffragette. In reality, Rotha was too young to have served in the Pankhursts' guerrilla operation, and she never was a woman-suffragist of any stripe. As a tomboy, she had instead spent the 1910s pretending to be a Boy Scout (settling instead for being one of the first-ever Girl Guides). But Rotha did take notice of feminism when the interwar Italian fascist movement she so admired adopted a platform promoting women's suffrage, and women's right to hold office—the same platform that had helped spur two thousand women to join Mussolini's party on its founding in November 1921. At that time, the Italian fascist party paper in Bologna was referring to "fascist feminism" in its articles on local militants.[47]

In 1931, the BF, which was full of aristocrats, debated whether they should allow themselves to be subsumed into Oswald Mosley's "New Party" (the precursor to the BUF). Believe it or not, Lintorn-Orman hesitated to agree to the merger because she worried that the Blackshirts were insufficiently right wing. They might be too soft on the threat of communism, worried the OG British donna fascista—hadn't Mosley, after all, been with the ILP once upon a time? On the other hand, his gender progressivism was encouraging. Lintorn-Orman didn't call herself a feminist, but the cops' assumption that she was an ex-suffragette was grounded in a real trend. In her exclamation mark–studded essay "Women's Loyalty," published in the journal *British Fascism*, Rotha articulates a romantic idea of fascism's ennoblement of the nation's females:

> Women have political power! Let them use it for the country! Women have almost equality with men in business! Let them think of the future welfare to the coming generation by teaching children that British Business is best! Women have superiority in the most essential thing of life—the Home! Let them insist on the purchase of British goods only.[48]

Here, Lintorn-Orman echoes aspects of the philosophical tradition of sugar boycotting (although for a xenophobic rather than humanitarian cause). Let's face it: in the aftermath of partial women's suffrage, Blackshirtism was making white British feminists a serious offer.

It is in the examples of "Slasher" Richardson and "Commandant" Mary Allen—the subject of the next chapter—that one can

most readily find documentation of suffragette fascism in interwar
Britain. But dozens of similarly feminist, equally far-right "sisters"
swirl around them in the archival shadows. Instead of greeting this
history with panicked rationalization, perhaps we can let ourselves
be guided by a spirit of anti-fascist intelligence gathering. What can
we learn from the switch some WSPU heavyweights effected when
they swore fealty first to a women's rights firebrand, then to a jack-
booted blood-and-soil strongman? Championing women was available as a macho, hard-hearted, death-romanticizing sport, both in
purple, white, and green, and in black. Some women, not long ago,
saw no contradiction between the two, remaining, in their minds,
not only feminists but truer feminists than their erstwhile fellow
hunger strikers.[49] Our movements, today, need this knowledge.

It is typically Adela Pankhurst, the youngest daughter of Emmeline, whom people think of as the "black sheep of the Pankhurst
family."[50] Intriguingly, Adela was the only member of the family to
work as a paid organizer for WSPU. Despite her rowdy contributions to suffragette militancy in Scotland (slapping a Dundee police officer, throwing "missiles," occupying a building), Christabel
and Emmeline disliked Adela because she was a socialist. In 1914,
therefore, they pushed her to emigrate to Australia—and never saw
her again.

After the long boat trip, Adela joined the anti-conscription
Women's Peace Army in Melbourne, opposing the very war for
which her mom and sister were beating the drum. An undercover
cop reported that her charisma as a speaker transfixed crowds.
In 1920, she nominally veered even further left, cofounding the
Communist Party of Australia (though she expressed her eugenicist
sympathies in an essay entitled "Communism and Social Purity").
This spurred her mother back in England to telegram the Australian prime minister to disown her, but it also meant that she could
write to her communist sister Sylvia and say, "This is the life."[51]

However, six years later, Adela about-faced again and founded
the Australian Women's Guild of Empire, an outfit devoted precisely to fighting communism. Bitterly estranged now from Sylvia,

it was to her imperialist mother that Adela could now turn, explaining via mail that she had changed her mind. Just before her death, Emmeline replied to say that she was delighted, and "full of regret for the long rift." Henceforward, Adela devoted herself to strikebreaking and right-wing pamphleteering. She denounced—to quote the Australian socialist Jeff Sparrow—"contraception, abortion and even nursery schools as detrimental to the maternal values she identified as the key legacy of suffragism."[52] Applauding the Nazis and Imperial Japan, she joined the antisemitic and fascist Australia First party in 1940.

To my mind, it is the revolutionary left-communist feminist Sylvia who is the real black sheep in this family of Blackshirts and ultranationalists. Sylvia is the one whose lifelong anti-colonial anti-fascism, from Ireland to Ethiopia, was radically informed by her firsthand experience of her kin succumbing to the socialism of fools. She devoted herself to the WSPU for eight years, but Christabel expelled her in 1914 because her working-class East London Federation of Suffragettes was open to men and trade unionists. After organizing in the labor movement against the war for five more years, she came to reject parliamentary politics; for example, you may be unaware that Lenin's 1920 tract *Left-Wing Communism: An Infantile Disorder* is an admonishment addressed largely to her. Emmeline herself all but disowned Sylvia for having a baby at the age of forty-five, out of wedlock. Troublingly, Sylvia called the baby "eugenic," explaining that what she meant by this was "wanted." She was otherwise a deeply anti-eugenic thinker, proclaiming: "We do not call for limitation of births, for penurious thrift, and self-denial." By posing for the media with her "bastard" baby and calling it eugenic, she may have been trolling the fascistic, ableist racists in the eugenics movement. It was of course the latter people's claim on eugenics that would win out in the 1930s—the underlying truth of the scientific field in question being revealed in the concentration and extermination camps of the Third Reich.

In June 1934, Sylvia spoke in Trafalgar Square in an attempt to dissuade the "spirited upper-middle-class women" and men of England from joining the fascist movement. Ten thousand people had just attended an immensely violent Mosley rally in London's Olympia stadium (to which the *Daily Mail*, incidentally, gave out free tickets, while cheerleading, "Hurrah for the Blackshirts!" in its tabloid every day in the lead-up). While denouncing the rally and calling for fascists to be detained, the antifa comrade Pankhurst argued that Mussolini's rule in Italy was terrible for women (among others): regardless of what he'd initially done for women, Italian wives and children were desperately subordinated to their husbands in the household. Anyone who supported fascism was making themself an enemy of all women, she said, including middle-class women, as well as the women of Ethiopia—a country increasingly threatened by fascistic invasion—and of working-class and immigrant life all over the world. Swiftly, Mary Richardson, Sylvia's erstwhile WSPU colleague, took to the pages of the *Blackshirt* to publish "My Reply to Sylvia Pankhurst."[53]

The comparison of British fascism's future with the fascism of a "Latin" culture was invidious, Mary claimed, since Italian women did not even yet have the vote. Had Sylvia forgotten? It was while campaigning for the vote that Sylvia and Mary had been arrested together in the East End in 1913. Now Sylvia the soi-disant feminist was calling for her arrest—some sisterhood. "As for pretending that fascism has degraded women by lowering their status in the eye of the law, this is unjust and utterly false," Richardson wrote, with some justification. "I was first attracted to the Blackshirts because I saw in them the courage, the action, the loyalty, the gift of service, and the ability to serve which I had known in the suffrage movement." (Remember honor, you backstabber?) As for the violence at the Olympia rally: real feminists who experienced the bloody assault by the police on suffragettes at the Houses of Parliament on Black Friday in 1910 ought to understand what unprovoked violence is. "When I discovered that Blackshirts were attacked for no visible cause or reason, I admired them the more when they hit back, and hit hard." The Blackshirts, in a way, were the new suffragettes, Richardson implied. They were a bit like women, righteously standing up to men. I heard echoes of this rhetoric in 2020, in Donald

Trump's apologias for the "self-defensive" actions of murderous white-power vigilante Kyle Rittenhouse and the Proud Boys.

"Anti-gender" and nativist attacks on feminism are on the increase—including attacks on the suffragette legacy from the right—and it is understandable in this context that someone might want to place guardrails on her own inquiry into women's attraction to fascism in the aftermath of a massive suffragist movement that included both constitutionalist and terrorist factions. The conclusions that could arise from such an inquiry are perhaps too discomfiting not to settle in advance. Thus, the explicit assumption of feminist scholars of Julie Gottlieb's school is that, despite the interwar BUF's claims to the contrary, "no such doctrinal position as fascist feminism was, or is, possible."[54] This strikes me as wishful thinking, yet I understand the impulse to reject, out of hand, any association between feminism's historic record and actual fascism. Women who simply stand against sexism still get called ballbusters, censors, or feminazis every day. Even now, I feel echoes of the fierce protective twinge I've felt in the suffragettes' regard ever since I first watched the suffragette scene in Mary Poppins and, gleefully, learned the anthem by heart: "We're really soldiers in petticoats / Fearless crusaders for women's votes." As an undergraduate, I frequently said that I felt "so grateful to the suffragettes."

I harbor no desire to purge myself of that gratitude. But if we imagine that no true socialists or feminists labored for fascism during and between the world wars, we are falling prey to a post-Hitler revisionism that posits socialism and fascism, feminism and fascism, as necessary opposites. The temptation is strong to assert these antinomies as pure, since contemporary mainstream discourse so often grossly posits left and right revolutionary poles as functionally identical. Nonsense, we radical feminists say: we cannot cross-pollinate. But our inability to countenance the possibility of elective affinities between feminism and fascism makes us more vulnerable to the Brownshirts' seductions of us and our comrades. It weakens our ability to fight back against red-brown rhetoric when we see it in cases like Tucker Carlson's appeals to working-class anti-work sentiment—for women only—when he bewails that Democratic bosses force abortion on employees while the average professional workplace (this part is true) still barely tolerates pregnancy.

Conversely, when we ask uncomfortable questions about our inheritances, expose our political ancestors' collusions, and lay some of them bare as "bad kin," we do not disrespect those who once walked under the same banner, "FEMINISM," even as they fought fascism tooth and nail in the name of a classless, decolonized society of gender freedom. Quite the opposite. I would rather honor the history of feminist anti-fascism even as I—because I—attend to the non-synonymity of feminism and anti-fascism. This, to me, seems like the best way to strengthen the arts by which we do turn feminism and anti-fascism into synonyms, via struggle, contingently.

SEVEN

The Policewoman

The time to end the feminist-police alliance is now.

—Aya Gruber, 2020[1]

If I told you that one of Emmeline Pankhurst's core terrorism campaign coordinators went on to invent "women's policing" and made it go global, would you believe me? Or perhaps you already intuited a deep link of this nature between Anglo-feminism and literal carceralism. After all, cop feminism is the air we breathe in the age of Kamala Harris ("California's top cop"), former Chicago mayor Lori Lightfoot (former president of the Chicago police board), and London Metropolitan Police Commissioner Cressida Dick. During the anti-police uprising of 2020, a slew of op-eds, from *Ms.* magazine to CNN, called for police departments to hire more women.[2] "Let's add women and stir" has been pleaded for as an alternative to abolishing the police in America since the near lynching of Rodney King by cops in 1991. The feminism of cops itself, though, goes back over a century. In her book *Why Would Feminists Trust the Police?*, Leah Cowan tells its history in relation to a fantasy of "policing by consent."[3] It's a vision of unpatriotic masculinity soothed into submission by uniformed womanhood—at least, womanhood with a badge. The colonial vision of social work it conjures is armed, yet *sensitive.*

Our culture is saturated with these social workers: weary, gun-toting heroines of carceral gender progress, glamorous avatars of the thin blue line. From *Charlie's Angels* to *Cagney & Lacey*, from *Decoy* to *The Silence of the Lambs*, not to mention *Prime Suspect*, *Top of the Lake*, *Killing Eve*, *Jessica Jones*, *The Fall*, *Mare of Easttown*, and literally hundreds more dramas and procedurals featuring various kinds of armed female civil servants, we are conscripted in our millions every day to pay our respects to the lady cop.[4] She is allowed to be "imperfect." (Sociologists have found that, in real life, policewomen often employ emotionally flat, macho, dehumanizing speech patterns in their dealings with civilian women.[5]) Feminism means cutting the lady cop some slack. Even if she's "an imperfect protagonist," the trail of women's empowerment she's on is blazed by weapons with state-backed legitimacy. Her feminism is a disciplinary saviorism, a fantasy of a benevolently undemocratic route to sisterhood. Feminist progress, for the cop feminist, is something she can impose from above, compassionately, but also, if need be, coercively. What is she here for? To rescue all of society, and sometimes (especially) to use her womanly instincts to rescue other women—even from themselves.

In the past, as we shall see, feminist Freikorps were often a bit of a laughingstock and became something of a nuisance to the government. Nowadays, in contrast, the cop feminist typically treads the hallways of Harvard, the International Criminal Court, NYU, Columbia, Yale, Stanford, or the American Philosophical Society. Her arguments come in new and sophisticated flavors of self-described radicalism. And yet, cop feminism is sometimes part of a self-described revolutionary politics. A cop feminist may even understand on some level that the prison-industrial complex is a vast support system for white capitalist patriarchy, and yet nevertheless believe that female police officers don't serve the interests of class power in quite the same way male cops do. For her, the sheer feminist force of the woman with a gun is not fatally diminished by the gun in question's tie to the armed wing of the state. She feels pretty confident that women cops don't murder unarmed Black people; that women cops don't harass sexually active women on the street, nor post vile comments on police union message boards; that they have a positive effect on the community; that they serve as little girls' best defense against sex traffickers and other predators; that they're just what the police needs in these trying times, what with public trust in the institution being so eroded; that they simply care more; or that they look good in a uniform.

"The woman police officer in uniform will be a lighthouse, preventing in some cases the wrecking of a life," rhapsodized the editor of the *British Journal of Nursing* in 1914.[6] Glossed recently in *Women's History Review* as "the redoubtable Ethel Bedford Fenwick, outspoken feminist," the suffragist powerhouse Mrs. Fenwick was the very antisemitic hospital matron who championed UK nurses' registration.[7] Still celebrated today, Fenwick banged the drum, crucially, not just for nurse feminism, but for cop feminism, as advanced by policies of mandatory arrest, surveillance, deportation, and detention. Already, she enviously noted in 1914, in Germany "the women police have the entire supervision of prostitutes."[8] She tried hard over the next two decades to gain the same kind of coercive medical control over all sex workers in Britain that Josephine Butler had specifically set out to abolish in principle.

In 1933, Mrs. Fenwick concentrated briefly on advertising a proposed "vigilante reserve" initiative—again in her high-circulation nursing journal—whereby women would fight communism and foreign "subversives." They would do so—learning to pilot planes, patrol vice, and use gas masks or firearms—under the wing of the world's leading policewoman—a known fascist and former suffragette by the name of Mary Sophia Allen.

Allow me to pause here and ask: Can one call Allen a "police officer" if, despite being hailed internationally as a pioneer of the women's police, she was fined for impersonating a member of the Metropolitan Police of London, and then "erased" by the Met from their history of women's policing?[9] To my mind, the answer is straightforward. The history of the police is the history of Freikorps gangs, vigilante slave patrols, and volunteer militias getting folded into the state.[10] You fake it 'til you make it, and through the 1920s and '30s, Mary Allen traveled internationally to be a "women's police" consultant, in Germany, the US, Czechoslovakia, Egypt, Greece, Brazil, Uruguay, Scandinavia and Palestine, where she was typically misrecognized, to her delight, as a real emissary of the British Crown. In the end, there was no official absorption or legitimation of her fake police force by the British state. But there was emulation. The official force known as the Metropolitan Women Police Patrols—which Britain's government consolidated shortly after the Second World War—even copied Allen's uniform.

While Fenwick's sympathy for an unsubtle fascist never perhaps amounted to fascist sympathizing per se, if one dips into the archive of the *British Journal of Nursing*, it quickly becomes clear that the category of "nurses" encrypts, in Fenwick's mind, a class- and race-marked womanhood—an aspiration to being "the better class of person," and, above all, a state of non-Jewishness, since "Jewish women in England have shown little interest in nursing the sick, as the majority dislike strenuous domestic work of any kind."[11] (Self-) protection, in the form of women's militias with wartime powers of arrest, is vital, then, to defeat the enemy within: the "subversive forces," white slavers, rapists, and race poisoners of all genders. "We can't arrest our way to feminist utopia," notes the feminist labor journalist Melissa Gira Grant, "but that has not stopped influential women's rights organizations from demanding that we try."[12]

Allen ran her Women's Auxiliary Service like a military squadron, across many parts of England, with several municipalities' active permission, for over a decade. Although banned from operating in the London area, she never, and with good reason, entirely abandoned her hope for an office of state. However, in the context of her interwar hobnobbing with fascist leaders like Eoin O'Duffy, Oswald Mosley, Francisco Franco, Benito Mussolini, and Hermann Göring, not to mention her disquietingly overt lesbianism and history of imprisonment as a suffragette, Allen was too unpopular in Westminster (or just deemed too much a wild card) to make the cut.

With her hair cropped like a man's, she required patrolwomen to call her "Sir" and "the Commandant" while, among intimates, she went by "Robert." I am using she/her pronouns here, in keeping with the obsessive, albeit anxious, self-location within womanhood that "Commandant" Robert/Mary performed. (Her autobiographies bear the remarkably gendered titles *The Pioneer Policewoman* (1925), *Woman at the Cross Roads* (1934), and *Lady in Blue* (1936).) Regardless of her gender, this suffragist "of leisure," fanatical police cosplayer, and, later, British Union of Fascists organizer, was without question one of the first cop feminists.

From the moment Mrs. Pankhurst declared her ceasefire vis-à-vis the cabinet in 1914, Allen switched her energies from burning down buildings in the name of suffrage to LARPing as a police lieutenant and future wartime reserve commander. She made this switch without ever changing her mission of "social purity" or "women's protection" in the slightest. She also befriended Hitler.

The "Commandant" may have first heard of the Women Police when, in 1914, the Women's Freedom League suffragette Nina Boyle appealed to all suffragettes in the pages of *The Vote*: "We want women police, women gaolers, women inspectors, and women in more and more departments of police life."[13] (It would seem that Nina's league stood only for some women's freedom.) Her appeal was cunningly well-timed. The abandonment of the WSPU by Allen's first great love, Mrs. Pankhurst, had meant that Allen would no longer receive medals of honor for hunger striking and coordinating bomb attacks. The craving for a new drastically hierarchical, militaristic cult of personality pressed upon hundreds if not thousands of whiplashed militants. In the case of Norah Elam, Mary Richardson, and others, Oswald Mosley's organization directly replaced the WSPU. In Allen's case, there was more circumspection.

According to the current website of the Metropolitan Women Police Association in England, Boyle formed the Women Police Volunteers (WPV) in August 1914, and was "joined in September" by a fellow well-bred lady from "the Chelsea Head of Transport (they had been rescuing Belgium [*sic*] women and girl refugees from white-slavers at the railway stations)."[14] Dawson and Boyle, like others in the Belgian Traffic Committee and National Vigilance

Association, had indeed been stalking around in plainclothes on a miniature crusade to save wayward girls from a "white slavery" traffic they thought was operated by foreigners across England's railways. According to Allen's biographer, "white slavery became an obsession with Mary" too.[15]

Others in this exact milieu, it should be noted, were less susceptible to conspiracism. The Women's Freedom Leaguer Teresa Billington-Greig—who conducted an inquiry into "white slave traffic" and concluded that it categorically did not exist—thought the feminist frenzy against "white slavers" was absolutely bananas. While the twenty-first century Met Women Police website clearly sees fit to represent Dawson's and Boyle's white-slavery fighting activities as real, for Billington-Greig, this was simply a pernicious case of "women on the rampage against evils they knew nothing of, for remedies they knew nothing about."[16]

Despite having no purchase on reality, the WPV founders' human-trafficking vigilantism seems to have led inexorably to their decision to get into uniform. Allen's feelings about uniforms and their magical powers became quasi-religious when she joined the WPV, and never faltered from that day forth. Fenwick fawningly told her nurses:

> The uniform consists of a long double-breasted blue overcoat, a blue beret, and a colored silk scarf. London detachments will wear buttercup-yellow scarves. Green is the color chosen for Sheffield. Commandant [Mary Sophia] Allen said her ambition was to have every woman and girl trained along some lines which might be useful to either State departments or municipal authorities in the event of war or civil emergency. They also wished to counteract subversive forces.[17]

Until her death, Allen never shut up about the civilizing influence of uniformed femaleness on the body politic. "It was evident to all those closely concerned with the maintenance of order," she wrote in *The Pioneer Policewoman*, "that the uniform was itself a deterrent, an actual weapon of defense, and that it had also a prompt moral effect."[18] Morality, here, signified order: the uplift-ingly eugenic influence of a "pure," well-bred, patrician lesbian in class armor.

"One great weakness they all had, it must be admitted," muses the narrator of *The Well of Loneliness*—the infamous novel about posh lesbians by the fascism-curious society butch, Radclyffe Hall, which stood at the heart of a 1928 obscenity trial—"and this was for uniforms—yet why not?"[19] Sexologists had already identified among upper-class "female inverts" of the early twentieth century a marked penchant for uniforms.[20] One simple and sympathetic explanation for this, implied by Hall, was that well-educated, ho-mosexual English women gravitated toward employment sectors where they could "cross-dress" with cultural impunity within a homophobic society. Nevertheless, according to Hall's lesbian protagonist "Stephen Gordon," this adaptive survival mechanism typically coincided with an intense erotic charge. "Yet why not?" One good reason why not is the sum of Mary Allen's ideolog-ical output over her lifetime, which amounts to one long fascist philosophy of the uniform. For example, it was Allen's view that "all laxity, or looseness of morals, militates against women as a whole."[21] Uniforms, in contrast, symbolized feminist tautness. The antidote, for her, was uniformity.

Nina Boyd's biography, *From Suffragette to Fascist: The Many Lives of Mary Sophia Allen* (2013), is no less confused and repulsed by its subject's fascist feminism than was Julie Gottlieb in *Femi-nine Fascism* (2000)—and similarly nervous. Allen and her fellow suffragettes were, surely, not "typical" in fighting for fascism, Boyd hopes. Their transition was "perhaps indicative more of their own personality types than of a natural progression from one cause to the other."[22] The Commandant, in particular, "was a woman of whom it would be impossible for any liberal-minded reader to ap-prove, but at the same time she inspired deep affection and loy-alty from friends and family throughout her long and eventful life."[23] Implicitly, there can be no particular explanation for why, in Gottlieb's terms, "the progress from women in blue to women in black was not a grand leap."[24] She was simply, as Boyd offers piti-fully, "a woman of contradictions."[25]

Boyd is perfectly able, at specific points in her narration, to re-proach Allen unequivocally, writing for instance, of her "enthusi-asm for the work of strikebreaking," that her "fear of Communism was widespread, and her xenophobia triumphed over her human-ity." She even vouchsafes that "the virulence of Mary's hatred of foreigners and Communists (which were more or less synonymous in her mind) was extraordinary."[26] Nevertheless, and notwithstand-ing her devotion to Adolf Hitler ("she finds him utterly without fault,"[27] writes Boyd), it is apparently "hard to decide whether Mary Allen was mad or bad; or both."[28] Surely, not all that hard!

Apparently yes—there are things we have to hand to Allen. "For all her obsessions, follies and misdeeds, she earns at least some praise for her unflagging energy and loyalty, even if they were sometimes misplaced." Of course, Boyd doesn't say explicitly whom Allen "earns" this praise from—who feels compelled to bestow on Allen this credit for loyal and energetic service to "sometimes mis-placed" causes like the British equivalent of the Third Reich. Boyd reflects in her introductory note, in which she deems Mary an "un-sung hero of policing," that "I cannot hope to rescue the reputation that Mary lost by her own wilfulness and folly. But I do believe that this opinionated, infuriating woman should not be entirely forgotten."[29] Willfulness and folly is certainly one way of putting it.

Listen: Allen cannot be forgotten. She was not quite a national treasure, but she was an eccentric and divisive household name who played a major role in the rise of British fascism in the 1920s. C. S. Lewis, the author of the *Narnia* series, almost certainly had her in mind when he wrote the clearly lesbian character of Fairy Hardcas-tle, the head of police at the evil totalitarian organization N.I.C.E.—National Institute of Co-ordinated Experiments—in his 1945 novel *That Hideous Strength: A Modern Fairy-Tale for Grown-Ups*:

> It would be misleading to say that he liked her. She had indeed excited in him all the distaste which a young man feels at the prox-imity of something rankly, even insolently sexed, and at the same time wholly unattractive. . . . She had told him a good many smok-

ing-room stories. . . . She knew from both ends what a police force could do and what it could not, and there were in her opinion very few things it could not do. . . . Soon anyone who had ever been in the hands of the police at all would come under the control of the N.I.C.E.; in the end, every citizen.[30]

Lewis's "Fairy" is an ideologue of the total police state. The novelist understands well the class logic of her feminism: "smoking-room stories" for me, and vice-busting anti-profanity for thee. What he misses about the fascism of her real-life counterpart is only its alignment with an imperial-capitalist pro-corporatism, its grifty narcissism, and its intense aesthetic corniness—which is in no way to trivialize its annihilationist undertow.

Allen *was* unbelievably corny, though. In an era when monocle-wearing was a universally recognized part of the symbolic visual language used by labor organizers, communists, and anarchists to depict factory owners, bankers, cops, and other forces of the ruling class, she always wore a monocle ("Monocled Lady Cop in New York," blared the press when she disembarked a boat in 1924). She was also, by all accounts, never not in uniform after 1914: an absurd affectation.[31] This, combined with her habit of writing (unsigned) hagiographical reviews of her own books and all-around grandiosity, rendered her a figure of ridicule outside her following.[32] She was the butt of jokes in music halls. Boyd includes examples of satirical, sometimes leftist, always sexist, open letters to Allen in print: articles demanding to know on what authority she and her girls were constantly marching around in uniform, trying to usurp men's jobs. A mocking piece in the *Evening News* pretends to celebrate the fact that more of the scowling, hypermasculine ladies in jackboots will be on patrol: "As a keen lover of beauty I rejoice to learn [this]. . . . A few of these daringly clad sylphs at every corner would . . . encourage susceptible law-breakers to give themselves up without any invitation."[33] (Allen exultantly quoted this article in the *Policewoman's Review*—"one of the many examples," winces Boyd, "of Mary's blindness to mockery."[34])

However, her chivalric regalia really did captivate and seduce some people. The novelist Naomi Jacob wrote in *Me and the Swans*

(1963) of "Commander Mary Allen O.B.E.," that "her uniform, a severe military 'frock coat' in dark blue, which fell just below her knees, breeches and riding boots, with a field service hat with a gold band round the peak, was both dignified and arresting. Her boots alone could have demanded respect."[35] Allen's post-suffragette career was, after all, a success story: a narrative of ultranationalist paternalistic feminism whose devotion to class hierarchy and "sex" hygiene (meaning: "racial" purity) was applied practically, on a police beat.[36] Her attempt to sanitize her lesbianism, via the bourgeois authority of her uniform, imperfectly concealed the homoeroticism of her cult affiliations past and present, or for that matter her desire for fascist insurgency. This placed her in a mutually frustrating, uneasy, oscillating insider-outsider relationship with the superintendents of the British Empire. But it was a relationship only terminated after twenty-six years. For a quarter century, the state leaned on her knowledge while disavowing her.

In 1914, Mary Allen set aside her flame for Emmeline and fell in love with Margaret Damer Dawson, a posh—in Allen's phrase, "delicately bred"—blonde stepdaughter of a baron, and fellow ex-WSPU member. Margaret campaigned against animal vivisection and "white slavery," owned two homes, and liked to go by the titles of "Sir" and "the Chief." It was Dawson's ship onto which Allen jumped at the dawn of World War I, because Dawson, together with another aristocrat, Nina Boyle—a Women's Freedom League ex-suffragette and future ultranationalist—had founded the WPV. In the fall of 1914, the newly besotted Mary and Margaret posed for a photo together, both wearing their sui generis police uniforms and polished jackboots, their field-hatted hair in buzz cuts, quiet smiles playing on their faces. They look like proto-Nazi Prussian field officers. Boyle would barely last another year in the force before splitting. Dawson remained commander. "The Chief," don't you know, saw "protection of women from their own folly, and from the predations of men, as key elements in the emancipation of women."[37]

The Great War was a great opportunity for this kind of feminism. Margaret was thrilled when the army enlisted her to furnish it with two women for the purposes of policing Grantham, a small garrison town whose population had doubled with the stationing of twenty thousand troops deemed at risk of venereal disease because of all the loose women in the area. The lady cops Dawson sent to Grantham were Ellen Harburn (a friend of Mrs. Pankhurst's) and Mary Allen. Historians are generally in agreement that the wartime activities of these feminists were a disturbing case of "women controlling women" and "poacher turned gamekeeper"[38]—former women's freedom fighters, in other words, enlisted by the army in the cause of destroying women's freedom.

Under the Defence of the Realm Act (DORA), as the British scholar Lucy Bland notes, "women began to be subjected to the most extraordinary and oppressive regulations."[39] In Grantham, under the direction of Brigadier-General Hammersley, Allen and Harburn willingly enforced a de facto "emergency" reintroduction of the Contagious Diseases Act. They enjoyed the right to enter any house, building, or land "within a six-mile radius of the Army Post Office," and did not demur when asked to help impose Hammersley's 6 p.m.–7 a.m. curfew—just for women. The Women's Police Service (WPS) declared in its official report that, in Grantham alone in the period of 1916–17, it had "cautioned" one hundred "wayward girls," helped picture houses "blacklist" ten "frivolous" types, "assisted" eighteen "respectable girls," proceeded against one hundred "prostitutes and disorderly houses," arrested sixteen "drunks, women," intervened in twenty-four "illegitimate baby cases" (often removing the babies into the care of the state), and reported ten "dirty houses" to the Society for the Protection of Cruelty to Children, or the Sanitary Authority.[40]

One of Allen's constables in Grantham, Edith Smith, granted dozens of "interviews to the public" and recorded that many of these involved tacit agreement to spy on women on men's behalf: "Husbands placing their wives under observance during their absence" and "husbands inquiring as to the reported misconduct of their wives."[41] While it isn't clear how much marital detective work the WPS actually undertook, these entries indicate willingness on Allen's part to at least consider cooperating with husbands' demands for surveillance of local women. They weren't even paid by the military—rather, their salary came from a donor, Lady Thorold. So, in choosing to do Allen's bidding, the police volunteers were morally rather than criminally terrorizing women.

Back in London, Nina Boyle couldn't believe what she was hearing. The Women's Freedom League did not want to "be associated with any work, no matter how useful, which meant the coercion of women and girls, and depriving them of their liberty to make things easier for commanding officers, constables and recruits."[42] Allen boasted that Hammersley had praised her and Harburn's work as "a great safeguard to the moral welfare of young girls in the town"; in response, Boyle called for Dawson's resignation in the pages of *The Vote*, so disgusted was she that her comrades "should be so ready to drop their principles for the sake of a little police favour and temporary official countenance."[43]

When the Ministry of Munitions asked for WPV/WPS policewomen to start policing munitions factories, Sylvia Pankhurst—who was, after all, organizing a communist movement in these factories—openly jeered at Dawson, Boyle, and Allen, explaining in the periodical *Home Front* how, "under the aegis of these ladies, thousands of women patrols were introduced whose efforts to control the behavior of their sex were not seldom the subject of irritation . . . and also of mirth."[44] Outright hatred and physical self-defense would have been equally justified, in my opinion. By its own admission, the feminist police service spent a lot of time "inspecting lodging-houses," driving men out of them, separating women "from the company of soldiers,"[45] and reprimanding couples for reclining in "suggestive attitudes"[46] in parks. Allen personally compiled dossiers on women she suspected of performing illegal abortions and spoke of women who had extramarital sex, whom she called "prostitutes"—as well as actual prostitutes—as either foolish, or evil, or both.

In her three memoirs, Allen makes clear that she considers the working-class women of Grantham as a species quite separate from her own. Describing her suffragette days, she calls the few working-class women in the WSPU stupid and violent, even as she wrote sentences like "I was actively—and shall I admit it, delightedly—planning some further burnings of empty houses."[47] Meanwhile, in the munitions factories during the war, she felt that workers who earned their own money "sank, during the four years of their freedom from all supervision, to a terrible and often scarcely human condition" due to sex, drink, and, above all, independence. She has no qualms about confiscating their children, outing their affairs to their husbands, vilifying their queerness, and generally treating them much the way Bishop Alma White treated her acolytes. Their "frequently appallingly coarse" and "profane language" was best targeted, she felt, with "continued remonstrances, grave but kindly," such that "the whole tone of the factory was raised."[48]

At this stage, it will hardly surprise you to learn that Allen praises Nazi Germany in 1933 for taking action against nudism—yes, nudism—describing it as "a new form of slavery . . . a deeply laid scheme to undermine the natural cleanly and normal outlook of our youth."[49] Disrobing in a context of high-jinks on the Lintorn-Orman estate would clearly be another matter. But proletarianism, in her mind, is a kind of infantile quasi-racial condition, not unlike "primitive" nakedness. Working-class women ought to aspire to sobriety and service, striving to earn the honor of swathing their bodies in the heavy uniform that bestows eugenic class power. But they can only get so far: it's the women of delicate breeding who lead.

By the spring of 1920, Dawson was dead at the age of forty-six, following a heart attack. But Mary—long since returned from Grantham—didn't have to move out of her soulmate's house, much to her relief. Margaret had already bequeathed both her properties, including one in Lympne (Kent), to "the Commandant." (Handily, nine years on, Allen's subsequent wealthy girlfriend and full-time aide, Helen Tagart, also bequeathed everything she owned, in a will, to her hypermasculine commander.) Some months before Dawson's death, Allen had taken over command of the WPS following the acrimonious split between Boyle and Dawson (Dawson and Allen were happy to do "moral" policing, while Boyle, ultimately, was not). After the war, Dawson and Allen—unlike Boyle, who quit in disgust—were awarded Orders of the British Empire by the king and fêted alongside other representatives of the "women's war services" at a royal garden party at Buckingham Palace.

What, then, triggered Margaret's premature heart attack? According to *Lady in Blue*, it was "undoubtedly . . . hastened by her bitter disappointment at the treatment she received after the war."[50] After the garden party, to the couple's dismay, the "Chief" was not announced as the head of the new London Metropolitan Women's Police Patrols (MWPP). On the contrary, the "Women Police Service" (formerly Women Police Volunteers) was told to stop calling itself that immediately, and, in fact, to stand down altogether. Under the aegis of a government inquiry into women's policing—the Baird Committee—police commissioners William Horwood and Nevil Macready accused the Women Police Service of "cross-dressing" (this was one charge Allen and Dawson couldn't deny) and deception. Furthermore, they threatened their troops with fines of £10 apiece for "masquerading" as members of the MW[51] This, as Allen points out in her memoirs, was grossly unfair: the uniform had been theirs first. Allen refused to stand down. Dawson, apparently astonished by their betrayal at the hands of the ungrateful generals they had served, began succumbing to ill-health.

It appears that it was only now that Allen and Dawson came to question the male-centered police hierarchy their ex-friend Nina Boyle had rejected. Although Dawson had clashed with Boyle over the very question of cooperation with male power, she now clashed with the gentlemen of the Baird Committee over their framing of policing as a matter of protecting men from female disease. Too late, she stepped up to defend sexual women and sex workers: "They talk," she wrote, "as if men were innocent angels helpless in the hands of wicked women!"[52] Finally, the "Chief" tried to subject the deputation to a full-frontal display of aristocratic class power: "We have enough funds to equip a small standing army of policewomen," she warned.[53] But even this approach didn't work. Nevil Macready, who "hated lesbians" (according to Nina Boyd), unapologetically told the committee that he had overlooked the WPS when putting together the MWPP "because its leaders were mostly former militant suffragettes."[54] Despite holding "no official standing"—in the Home Office's exasperated phrase—Allen's once again rebranded Women's Auxiliary Service continued to operate, long after Dawson's death, in many cities, including British-occupied Dublin.

In 1921, the "Commandant" campaigned unsuccessfully for a seat on the London County Council with the National Union of Women Teachers. In 1922, she failed again as a Liberal parliamentary candidate in Westminster. Then, luckily for her, in 1923, the secretary of state for war hired her to police occupied Cologne. At this point, Allen started addressing conventions, such as the American National League of Women Voters (founded by Carrie Chapman Catt), the International Police Exhibition and Congress in Karlsruhe, and the League of Nations Conference on the Traffic in Women, in Geneva. But Allen's most ecstatic hour arrived when the general strike was organized in Britain on May Day in 1926. For the duration of this small civil war, the Commandant was permitted to raise an emergency corps in order to break the strike and purge the land for good—or so she hoped—of communists, foreigners, and communist foreigners. (On this occasion, as we've seen, a couple of notable fascists stood cannily with the opposite side.) Emmeline Pankhurst herself reported for duty in the strike-breaking counterinsurgency, taking orders from the arsonist she'd herself commanded two decades prior.

Following the bloody defeat of the left that spring, Allen once again felt deflated, wishing for a permanent state of emergency, and refusing to stand down. She learned how to fly planes and tried to set up the aforementioned Women's Reserve, a trained militia that would stand ready at all times, chomping at the bit, for the next world war. To popularize this idea and the idea of uniformed women's patrols in general, between 1927 and 1937, she founded, edited, managed, and—according to Boyd—mostly wrote an international periodical, the *Policewoman's Review*. However, again, the secretary for war turned her reserve proposal down. In fact, a Home Office intelligence dossier on her activities was opened in July 1927.

In the 1930s, Allen visited Spain and Germany via private plane multiple times. She attended the Nazi Olympic Games and lectured at pro-Franco meetings in England. Immediately after the burning of the Reichstag, as she recounts in *Lady in Blue*, "for two and a half hours I sat absolutely entranced beside the Chancellor [Hitler]'s charming sister, listening to the great Dictator. . . . [His] hypnotic gestures, his passionate, forceful voice and his visionary eyes held me spellbound."[55] In turns secretive and open, erratically in denial and proud about her fascism, she nevertheless often lauded Hitler in print—in the *Policewoman's Review*—as above. Nor was she lacking feminist allies, even now; praise for the *Policewoman's Review* appeared, for example, in a sister periodical, the *Woman Teacher*, in 1936, in between a book review section on Mary Wollstonecraft and a radical feminist critique of traditional marriage.[56] While Allen's "rumored secret visits to Germany at the invitation of SS Chief Heinrich Himmler"[57] are difficult to prove, and she testified that she was "waving to the pilot"[58] (not throwing the Sieg Heil) when deplaning, she finally went public with her BUF affiliation in 1939.

In his monograph *Feminist Freikorps*, Raymond Douglas notes that "in January 1934 [Allen] was already a person of sufficient stature to merit an invitation to Germany to meet the leaders of the Nazi government":

> The manner of her reception also suggests that her hosts regarded her as someone worth taking seriously. She was escorted around Berlin by "Putzi" Hanfstaengl, attended a Hitler rally in the company of the Chancellor's sister Paula, and obtained a private interview afterwards with the dictator at the Wilhelmstrasse. . . . She was also introduced to Goering, who likewise aroused her admiration as the head of a police force "which has set itself to exterminate the enemies of the country"[59] and who, she was gratified to learn, shared her opinion on the importance of policewomen wearing uniform.[60]

As historian Martin Pugh notes in *Hurrah for the Blackshirts!*, "fascist sympathizers" and outright fascists like Allen, instead of being condemned or ostracized, "continued to penetrate the British establishment" well into World War II.[61] It fell to the public to raise objections and demand Allen's dismissal from the Women's Volunteer Service in 1940.

Civilians had been sounding the alarm for years. A tourist who crossed paths with Allen in 1938, in Switzerland, wrote to the Home Secretary: "She stated on many occasions that she was a personal friend of Hitler's," "discussed Hitler at dinner time every evening," and "spoke fluent German."[62] Similarly, a journalist alerted the state to the fact that "Miss Allen had expressed her admiration for the Gestapo and Himmler and had more or less said that she would help the Germans if they came here." Yet another journalist—reporting from the Spanish Civil War—said he had seen a dossier on "Commandant Mary Allen" kept by the prominent Spanish Republican socialist Julio Álvarez del Vayo. Whenever Allen visited Spain, she was "always promptly received by the Caudillo [Franco] himself," reported del Vayo. She went "on a mission which Franco himself entrusted to her" at least once. All in all, "this lady was Franco's most dangerous agent in Great Britain . . . unquestionably a political character and . . . the most classic example possible of a 'Fifth Columnist.'"[63] A fifth column is a presence within a country at war that is working for its enemies, and—like most fifth columnists—Mary Allen fervently believed herself to be working not for Britain's real enemies but against them, for Britain, Crown, and empire.

While opposed to fighting Nazi Germany (and hence, like all BUF activists, somewhat of a "peace" activist after 1939), Allen yearned for imperial war in the manner of all fascists, the core imperative of fascism being Lebensraum. Her imperial war, moreover, was going to be feminist because of its destruction of un-British diseases, like nudity and working-class laziness, that insult womanhood. In her "Call to Women" of November 1933, Allen denies that she is beating the drum for war, but appeals to all women to "enroll for service" because "the steady undermining of the 'Will to serve' is the ultimate aim of the enemies in our midst." (By the latter, she means strikers and communists with their "poisonous doctrines" and "subversive teachings," a bunch of generally "disruptive forces"—likely Jews.) In the face of accusations of belonging to a fifth column, fascism, or warmongering, patriotic Englishwomen will, she hopes, obey a higher law. "We should be ready calmly and quietly to state that, whether in peace or war, we are willing and able to uphold the ideals of those who made our Empire."[64] Defending herself and the BUF (that woman-driven movement, pace Mosley) against accusations of treachery in 1940, Allen stated: "The British Union [of Fascists] was and is for the British Empire."[65]

Though her reputation, like that of many other Nazis, never recovered after World War II, and the Metropolitan Police now refuses to remember her at all, it bears repeating that, especially prior to 1927, Allen enjoyed a mutualistic rapport with the UK political establishment as a whole. She was intermittently threatened with prosecution by the police commissioner for masquerading as a police officer, and, given her criminal record as a key coordinator of suffragette terrorism, most politicians kept her at arm's length, to be sure. Yet she also benefited from royal honors and received protection throughout the 1920s from Home Secretary (and fascist sympathizer) William Joynson-Hicks. The latter—a viscount—shielded her at least twice from Metropolitan Police prosecution. Furthermore, as Boyd notes, the government asked Allen to advise them on policing the postwar British occupation of the Rhineland in 1923, "long after she had been instructed by the same government to disband her police force."[66] While her fascist party membership was unseemly, her zeal for strikebreaking and passion for the empire were appreciated. This, if nothing else, has much to tell us about the likeliest permutations, alliances, and priorities of cop feminism in the present day.

As of 2023, Mary Allen's picture appears—very misleadingly—on the cover of a new "feminist" book about the NYPD by Mari Eder, a retired major general of the US Army (its snappy title is *The Girls Who Fought Crime: The Untold True Story of the Country's First Female Investigator and Her Crime-Fighting Squad*). I doubt the cover designer knew about Allen's Britishness, let alone her Nazism, but it's all grist for the copaganda mill. Similarly, in 2021, magazines like *Salon* and *Bust* praised the feminism of the outer-Philadelphia police detective played by Kate Winslet in *Mare of Easttown*, despite the fact that the character of "Mare" plants drugs in the car of a substance-addicted woman "with a history of prostitution" to facilitate the woman's forcible separation from her child. Mare, apparently, represented "crucial progress"[67] in gender representation because she was "honest," and because of Winslet's inspiring willingness, in scenes featuring a belly "bulge" and no makeup, to "embrace her unaltered body on TV."[68]

Back in the UK, on March 21, 2023, the celebrity feminist Caitlin Moran mused that the 2022 mass protest and vigil for Sarah Everard, a civilian who was raped and murdered by Met Police Officer Wayne Couzens, would not have been brutalized by the police if the officers on duty had all been female. Tweeted Moran:

> I recently had a long chat with a couple of female Met officers, who said, of the Sarah Everard memorial fuck-up. "It should have just been policed by female officers. We all knew it. And every female officer in the UK would have come down for it." Imagine the difference.[69]

We don't have to imagine it, as hundreds of abolition feminists immediately pointed out. Women officers had actively participated in the indiscriminate beatdowns of mourners. One month later, in Minneapolis, the white police officer Kim Potter was released after she'd served just sixteen months in prison for murdering the Black Minnesotan man Daunte Wright during a traffic stop.[70] In Moran's hometown, women officers had strip-searched and brutalized the anti-police activist Koshka Duff,[71] as well as the fifteen-year-old Londoner "Child Q,"[72] despite knowing the latter was on her period. In the cases of Dalian Atkinson[73] and Olaseni Lewis,[74] two Black Britons who died in police custody in recent memory, it was also lady cops who restrained them.

To apply the logic of "let women do it" to the police is simply to ensure more violence by women, or so anti-violence abolition feminists insist.[75] Under the regime of the posh lesbian police commissioner Dame Cressida Dick, Janey Starling notes, "this mawkish fantasy of sisterhood between the police and the public is punctured by the reality that it was, in fact, a woman who instigated the brutality against women protesting that night."[76] To be sure, for those of us socially and economically assigned to the "white" domain of womanhood, policing does often represent protection, not oppression, as Ali Phipps discusses. For us, criminal punishment can be

> the colonial master's intervention, the "empathy" of Angry Dad. It is also the indirect demonstration of our own will to power. (Mostly) lacking legitimate authority and economic power in a still-patriarchal world, we "take back control" by ceding control to the punitive technologies of the state. (And we really do cede control: survivors have been arrested and prosecuted for refusing to testify or otherwise cooperate with carceral agendas.)[77]

Nothing good can come from calling the (feminist) cops, but this is doubly true if you're a sex worker. Contrary to what cops often say, sex-working women are the last women police move to protect, and in this sense, feminist lawyers' opposition to the decriminalization of sex work, no less than *Brooklyn Nine-Nine*, is cop feminism too.

In a 2010 speech bewailing sex work decriminalization, the decorated lawyer Catharine MacKinnon—a central subject of our next chapter—conceded that "not being arrested" is "in general a real improvement" for sex workers, but, she suggested, on the other hand, detention can be "a respite from the pimps and the street."[78] (A Florida Supreme Court advisor opined that "jail is the closest thing many women in prostitution have to a battered women's shelter."[79] A Colorado lawyer concurs: "Jail provides a temporary safe haven from johns, pimps and drugs."[80]) Can a cop feminist even hear a sex worker who tells them different? In 1993, the sex-worker union organizer and feminist Carol Leigh went to hear MacKinnon speak in San Francisco, hoping against hope for a dialogue. "I'm sure you don't want women controlled by police," pleaded Leigh, sister to feminist sister, to no avail. "MacKinnon told me that she had nothing to discuss with women like me, that we are too far apart."[81] As a self-described "unrepentant whore," Leigh, perhaps, simply stands outside the charmed circle of women capable of appreciating that police work done right—done by women—safeguards, helps, and benefits women.

The writer Sarah Mesle watched *Mare of Easttown* as a critical, yet also powerfully seduced, quasi-fan. In her essay "Mare's Hair," she articulates the solace of cop feminism—as embodied by Winslet—as follows: "Maybe I could be the special version of copaganda this show offers, which is where the gap in power between police and white women collapses, and one woman, Mare, or me, holds the weapons of both. Maybe, just as Kate is, I could be the one who could keep the other white women safe."[82]

There are more and less contemptuous versions of this desire, and Mare's is represented as "community"-minded and almost horizontal, rather than top-down. Mary Allen's was at the other pole of that spectrum. Nonetheless, the feminism of cops is a fast track to fascism. It's a place where subaltern solidarity dies an instantaneous death.

EIGHT

The Pornophobe

The women who hate me hate
their insistent desires, their fat lusts
swallowed and hidden, disciplined to nothing
narrowed to bone and dry hot dreams.

—DOROTHY ALLISON, 1983[1]

I want you to take a leap with me, now, from the 1940s in Britain, all the way to the late '70s women's liberation milieu in the US, where we will encounter our next enemy feminism. But it's not such a leap at all because policing and pornophobia—the hatred of whores—go hand in glove; and, while the earlier feminism that expressed itself in voluntary moral policing and vigilante vice patrols openly revered masculinity in a way that the later feminism generally didn't, both feminisms had a "uniform" (that is, "sturdy shoes, dungarees, work shirt and back pack," in the '70s).[2] If the effort to preserve the division between good women and fallen ones was at the heart of Mary Allen's persecution of "dirty houses," loose girls, unfaithful wives, and frivolous mothers in the name of women's rights in Grantham, the same can be said of the American group founded in 1976, Women Against Pornography (WAP) (whose leaders would not even deign to *debate* sex workers).

However, the world within which WAP's pornophobia emerged looks completely different from the one we left, due to the transformations wrought by World War II, the civil rights struggle, McCarthyism, the second "sexual revolution," and the proto-revolutionary convulsions of the 1960s, including the extraordinary Third World, women's, and gay liberation movements. Between 1967 and 1973, the US saw an efflorescence of leftist radical feminisms, from which campaigns like WAP's totally departed, just as Frances Willard's did from Josephine Butler's, and Mary Richardson's did from Sylvia Pankhurst's.

The fake British policewoman we have just contemplated belonged to a backlash conservatively resisting the sexual revolution and new queer freedoms of the 1920s (emblematized by sexology, cross-dressing, psychoanalysis, birth control advocacy, and speakeasies). The Commandant's nasty fascist story ended in her arrest in 1940; but in the '30s, she had celebrated Hitler's crackdowns on porn, prostitution, perversion, and, of all things, nudity. Even earlier as a suffragette, Allen had been passionate about covering and disciplining the pure, emancipated female body in immaculately turned-out uniformity. She linked up with North American women on her speaking tour during Prohibition, influencing social purity and temperance feminists in the National League of Women Voters, the American Social Hygiene Association, and the New York Anti-Vice Society. Ironically, half a century later, the US feminists who started a new campaign against "pornocracy" were— unlike Allen—fervently opposed to Nazism, which they constantly cited as pornography's root logic. In other respects, however, their approach was not as different from the pioneer policewoman's as one might hope. In fact, the drastically different world of the '70s was full of echoes of the bitter end of the first wave.

Once upon a time, I myself felt the overlap between the new anti-porn feminism and the much older tradition of feminist policing. I remember well the feeling of yelling inside a crowd of "strong women" taking a glorious stand against the sacrifice of young girls, white slavery style, to the male god of "sexual gratification." The very first street-feminist event I ever attended was a Take Back the Night picket organized in 2007 by the British group Object outside a proposed lap dancing club. As I recall, I was very envious of my university roommate's homemade placard, which just said, with suave succinctness, "Nope." But at nineteen, truth be told, I hadn't given much thought to lap dancing and was no more informed about Object (it was founded in 2003, I now know, by the CEO of Not Buying It, another anti-porn organization). Strip clubs were bad, though, probably. Right? Rich men groping working-class girls? And certainly the phrase "take back the night" rang a bell freighted with a doubtless noble history, legitimated by untold legions of veterans of sisterly marching. I wanted to be part of such a feminism in movement, a feminism of the streets. Here, surely, was my chance.

Yet over the course of the picket, I started to doubt. Why were none of the strippers present at this protest? Weren't we fundraising for them or something? Was our protest messing with their earnings? I asked a couple of women, but they didn't know either. Then it dawned on me that no one had even mentioned the dancers over the megaphone. In fact, the more I listened, the more it seemed that we were saying it wasn't them who were harmed by the club so much as us—the women of the town whose dancing wasn't on sale. Our message to the lewd business operation was pretty much just "not in our back yard," I realized. If patrons got lap dances there, they'd feel encouraged to treat all of womankind here "like whores" (apparently, respectful treatment of a sex worker was a contradiction in terms). Strippers themselves, we inevitably implied, were antifeminist—walking pornography—liabilities we didn't want to have to see unless, of course, they agreed to be hurt victims in need of rescue. "We object," we chanted, "to ob-ject-ification just for sexual grat-ification." I decided that I hated the dreary chant. The suspicion was creeping up on me that "objectification" within sex isn't always or necessarily bad, and that even when it is, it still isn't the central thing about capitalist gender.

In 1981, the New York–based feminist group Women Against Pornography expressed its zero-tolerance stance vis-à-vis "lesbian sadomasochism" by pressuring the publisher of *Big Apple Dyke News* to withdraw from printing "Esther's Story," an erotic fiction by the working-class Jewish socialist Joan Nestle. WAP deemed the short story objectifying and anti-woman. Their problem was that Nestle

had recounted her narrator "Joan" enjoying a butch/femme sex relationship with a male-passing Puerto Rican taxi driver ("Esther")
"whose lover was a prostitute." Worse, Nestle had included brief
mention of a dildo. The feminists objected to the following (ostensibly vile and misogynist) sentences:

> With extreme tenderness she laid me down. . . . I was trying so
> hard to be good for her . . . I turned to touch her, but she took
> my hand away from her breast. "Be a good girl," she said. I knew
> I would have to work many months before Esther would allow
> me to find her wetness as she had found mine. The words, the
> language of my people, floated through my head—untouchable,
> stone butch.[3]

I can scarcely believe that any "sisterhood" would seek to deplat-
form this text, which describes a transmasculine dyke with "hands
like butterflies shaking with respect and need," for misogyny. Yet
in this period, anti-porn feminists "fought really dirty," or so the
leather-community feminist veteran Patrick Califia recalls. "They
attacked anybody who argued with them as an advocate of violence
against women, a child molester, or (gasp) a sadomasochist. They
weren't above calling employers, publishers, or dissertation com-
mittees to inform them of the 'perverts' in their midst."[4] Nestle
received a call to let her know "that if I write about butch-femme
relationships in the past, I am O.K., but if I am writing about them
now in any positive way, I am on the 'enemy list' . . . a 'reactionary,'
'heterosexually-identified Lesbian,' 'believer in patriarchal sex.'"[5]

How had it come to this? When did "radical" sisters ditch solidarity with lusty freaks and other sexual minorities, and start
thinking of objectification rather than, say, property, the gender division of labor, the state, or the private nuclear family, as the root of
capitalist gender oppression? "How has it come to pass," asked Alice
Echols in 1984, another lesbian feminist, "that some lesbians are in
the forefront of a movement which has resurrected terms like 'sexual deviance' and 'perversion?'"[6] Amber Hollibaugh, a communist
organizer and self-defined "sex-radical, incest survivor, poor-white-
trash, high femme dyke," likewise could not believe her eyes. "The

borders are shrinking," she wrote somberly in a contribution to the legendary *Pleasure and Danger* anthology. There, Hollibaugh's and Echols's are but two among many like-minded voices collected by feminist scholar Carol Vance, preserving the real content of the unforgettable "sex conference" Vance helped organize in 1982.

Held at Barnard College, the conference, "The Scholar and the Feminist IX: Towards a Politics of Sexuality," featured workshops on everything from disability and fatness to abortion, taboo, and psychoanalysis. Yet, infamously, Women Against Pornography activists, clad in "AGAINST S/M" T-shirts, painted the proceedings (on the basis of sex workers' and kinksters' involvement) as one big woman-hating celebration of sadomasochism that should be shut down. Picketing and leafleting at the gates, WAP accused the conference of abetting rapists, pedophiles, and pimps.[7]

Moral panic had clearly set in. Queer liberation's light, Amber realized, was dwindling pitifully. The media had institutionalized the feminist anti-porn lawyer Catharine MacKinnon as the spokeswoman for a women's struggle that she'd barely even participated in. But to some street radicals, MacKinnon's partner in crime fighting, Andrea Dworkin—a legit 1960s veteran whose once-utopian politics, like so many of her peers', veered rightward in the mid-'70s—lent a degree of street credibility to the anti-abolitionist idea that "squads of women police formed to handle all rape cases are crucial,"[8] and that, in domestic violence cases, "arrest needs to be mandatory."[9] In other words, Dworkin's unkempt, poetic, nonacademic rhetorical rainstorms were laundering the legal professor's immaculate attaché-case-carrying straightness for the left. Amber wanted none of it. The rise of Women Against Pornography was a despairing and reactionary development.

Yet there were not simply two sides—pornophobia vs. whorephilia—to the sex wars, as is sometimes popularly assumed. Outside of the feminist frame, a great number of non-feminist actors in society (not to mention actively antifeminist ones, both religious and commercial) fought their own vast battles in the courts and the press over the censorship of "obscenity" (or: protection of the family) and deregulation of visual media (or: the liberal principle of free speech). Within the frame of the feminist-on-feminist "porn war," too, the field was bisected along multiple axes. Some belligerents were civil libertarians; others overlapped in their critiques of sexual liberalism—the idea that individuals can pull themselves up by their self-actualizing erotic bootstraps—while disagreeing above all on "what is to be done." On the feminist left, sex radicalism made a mockery of the idea of a "pro" side (vs. "anti") in the matter of pornography. Whereas radical, post-left feminist pornophobes focused on fighting objectification in media and law, and liberal feminists continued to endlessly reinvent sex positivity, sex radicals stayed with the trouble, criticizing porn and arguing for seizing the means of human libido production.

One thing is for sure, writes Hollibaugh: "We cannot afford to build a political movement that engraves the sexual reactions of nineteenth-century bourgeois women onto a twentieth-century struggle."[10] The denunciations and purges triggered a much less distant historical association in some older queers' minds. "I will never forget the words, 'Are you now or have you ever been . . .'?"[11] shudders Nestle. "I remember the fifties in tones and gestures, in cadences of accusation." Between 1958 and 1962, Joan marched for abortion and against nukes, attended college in New York, and was active in mobilizations against the Red Scare led by Senator McCarthy. Never did it occur to her, though, that there would be a "second McCarthy period in my life."

The comparison may appear hyperbolic, but the more I come to know about the sex-radical movement's destruction by pornophobia, the more I am willing to lend it credence. The inquisitorial tactics of certain feminists in 1981 clearly conjured for some the rageful and traumatic association of sitting in on the House Un-American Activities hearings (the chair of the committee called Nestle and her friends "the scum of the earth"). Writing for her community of aging commies, bar lesbians, sex workers, and leather kin, Joan describes a bitter and crazy new reality: "Lesbian-feminists will turn us in and feel they have made the world safer for women by doing so." Clearly both historical analogies—the Red Scare and the purity drives—are illuminating. Nestle uses both: "I almost think I have lived too long when I see Lesbians become members of the new vice squad."[12]

Not for nothing, then, is this episode of feminist history called the sex wars, rather than the sex conversations. To privileged philosophical onlookers it often appears as though reconciliation between belligerents might be possible, or at least desirable; whereas, for the sex-working and otherwise criminalized groups who are targeted by pornophobic lawyering, the effort to impose a "feminist sexuality" (as the other side of the WAP picket T-shirt proposed) is typically experienced as a bourgeois bid to flush away sex work and clean proletarian public pleasures off the map, pushing both offending realities out of sight. People like Nestle, Echols, Hollibaugh, and Califia realized that radical feminism (as they understood it) had been thoroughly beaten out of the communities where utopianism once thrived. The new ideology sure called itself "radical" feminism, but it was really something quite different—female cultural nationalism might be a better phrase. You could tell just by looking at the old counterculture zine racks. As the feminist, Brooke Williams, noted at the time, whereas movement journals used to be called things like *off our backs*, *Tooth 'n' Nail*, and *No More Fun and Games*, now they were called, for example, *Amazon Quarterly*, *13th Moon*, *Womanspirit*, and *Chrysalis*.[13]

The prevailing politics was no longer centrally about defying the state or smashing the institutions of motherhood, private property, or the wage. The focus instead was almost exclusively on prostitution, porn, and sexualization. In addition, quite unlike the "old" radical feminism, cultural feminism positioned itself in opposition to the left. It organized itself ideologically around feminine supremacy and virtue, and conceptualized objectification as the source (rather than merely one mediating mechanism) of the danger women face. Strikingly, it even repudiated the terrain of politics proper—the task of unmaking patriarchy at the level of homes, workplaces, and institutions. Instead, its strategy was one of spiritual transformation, a sea change that was going to be led by an unstoppable separatist "woman's culture" (kickstarted by local networks of women's publishers, women's businesses, and women's banks). All in all, the consequences of this coup, over the course of the '80s, were severe. Echols argues that cultural feminism "brought about feminism's reconciliation with the market, religion, and, most important, the state"—"the very components of 'the system' which the movement had once opposed."[14]

If, when I was recounting my Take Back the Night debut earlier, the idea of treating the workplace of local sex workers like prime terrain for a white middle-class "porn abolitionist" safari made you wince, then you will be discomfited to learn that radical feminists in New York for several years led guided tours of the inside of live strip shows, sex emporia, and adult stores and porno booths around Times Square. As a member of the public, you first "donated" five dollars to Women Against Pornography, then you viewed a slide show, prior to stepping out with your trusty feminist guide into what WAP cofounder Dolores Alexander called the "alien, scary, enemy territory of the sex supermarkets."[15] Thousands of people took the tour. Naturally, the "live sex show" workers did not take kindly to the middle-class women who invaded their place of business, scaring away the johns. After all, they pointed out, they "did not show up at the feminists' places of business, clucking over their exploitation as women."[16] To top it all, WAP had literally displaced the population of queens and trans women, largely of color, from the soul food eatery that used to occupy the WAP office premises. Get this: the City of New York evicted the storefront and handed it rent-free to the radical feminist anti-pornography crusaders.

Amazingly, this act of state-mandated feminist gentrification— blatantly harmful to the very population of sex work "victims" WAP purported to care about—wasn't something writer Susan Brownmiller (another cofounder of WAP) particularly bothered to hide. In Brownmiller's tour script, she praises Mayor Ed Koch's Midtown Enforcement Project as "a city agency that we have a good working relationship with," explaining, according to one historian, that "its efforts to clean up Times Square were hindered by confusion over the definition of obscenity in the U.S. courts."[17] While composing packets for her tour guides, the author of *Against*

Our Will (1975) plotted the itinerary using data supplied by Midtown Enforcement and by Carl Weisbrod, president of the 42nd Street Development Corporation. Before long, a local women's shelter organizer—Margaret Hunt—noticed "the willingness of some radical feminists to assist vice squads in rounding up prostitutes."[18] Leafing through the magazine *West Side Spirit* one day, Joan Nestle found to her horror that one Captain Jerome Piazzo of the Manhattan South Public Morals Division was quoting data on call girls he said had been provided to him by WAP. In short, collaborating with cops and mayors conducting mass arrests and displacing sex workers was not a problem for Ms. Brownmiller and her crew.[19] Internal whistleblowers protested, of course. The gay leftist and erstwhile Women Against Violence Against Women ally John D'Emilio wrote publicly about how angry WAP made him: "Angry because I am witnessing another 'clean up Times Square' effort, an anti-sex movement, a new social purity campaign, masquerading under the guise of something that's been profoundly important in my life: feminism."[20]

Undeterred, WAP published its anthology *Take Back the Night: Women on Pornography* in 1980. The collection makes clear that all strategies of female "self-defense" against the penis, including repression, incarceration, and militarism, are justified under the current circumstances. Porn is "gynocide." Thus, "if my assessment is correct," writes Judith Reisman—a conspiracist and homophobe soon to be appointed by Ronald Reagan to study porn—"it is a time of war."[21] In the piece, she uses her nom de plume, Judith Bat-Ada, in a conversation with the volume's editor, Laura Lederer, who for her part went on to work for George W. Bush as a born-again anti-trafficking expert. End times are near: "The *Playboy* ethic," they affirm, is "a threat to our very lives as human and humane beings." Verily "we are up against a powerful media industry which encourages pornography in order to fulfill its own present and future interests."[22]

The tone of the above interview is far from unique to the anthology. The existence of static and moving images of women captured in the act of holding erect cocks in their mouths, cunts, and anuses (and liking it), is shamelessly equated, throughout, with chattel slavery and the Holocaust. Essay after essay analogizes the class- and race-undifferentiated condition of 1970s femaleness in "pornified" America to Jewishness in Nazi Germany. And that's if it's not being equated to Black enslavement—but most often, it's both. Psychic permission to place racially unmarked female-ness—metaphorically—in the gas chambers and the cotton fields was provided to the *Take Back the Night* cohort by literary star An-drea Dworkin. Back in 1976, Dworkin had narrated how chattel slavery related to sexed "slavery": the latter came first and served as the former's model. In heterosexual marriage and sex, "the woman does literally give herself to the man," she claimed: "He does liter-ally take and possess her" (implying, I take it, that slaves somehow gave themselves).[23] We've seen several instances of eighteenth and nineteenth-century feminists theorizing that the legal condition of middle-class European women was "slavery." Here, astonishingly, Dworkin extended the same analysis to fully enfranchised US cit-izens. That wasn't all: she further contended that colonizers knew to enslave Africans because they had already enslaved their wives. "The whip, used to cut the backs of white women to ribbons, was now wielded against Black flesh as well."[24]

Goebbels, Hitler, and the slave auction undergird the group's diagnosis of "anti-woman propaganda,"[25] and are invoked blithely and incessantly across *Take Back the Night*. Roughly halfway through, we encounter Gloria Steinem's incredible 1969 bon mot: "A woman who has *Playboy* in the house is like a Jew who has *Mein Kampf* on the table."[26] This time, in fairness, Steinem's own contribution more modestly avers that pornography's "message is violence, dominance, and conquest,"[27] but at other points we learn that the Nazis "flooded the Polish bookstores with pornography" when they invaded Poland, to "socially castrate" the population.[28] Even as it castrates us all, "pornography, like rape, is a male inven-tion"—this last is from an excerpt of *Against Our Will*—and specif-ically gets "designed to dehumanize women."[29] Bat-Ada feels that *Playboy* "makes woman the 'other' just as the nazis made the Jews the 'other.'"[30] She warns the US: "We can be said to be breeding a nation of whores." A bad thing!

"Pornography is about slavery," states Adrienne Rich, finally. "The enslavement of women as women has traditionally gone almost unrecognized."[31] How do I put this? White women are not and have never been enslaved. As we've seen numerous times, however, the titillating possibility of a traffic in "us"—so-called white slavery—is hardly something that has "gone unrecognized." On the contrary, a narrative about "the enslavement of women" drove the creation of a swath of what we nowadays know as the prison-industrial complex, as Judith Walkowitz and others were loudly documenting even at the time that Rich, Dworkin, and others were saying these things.[32] We are still thoroughly haunted by the vice policing and social-purity politicking that took shape in the nineteenth and early twentieth centuries in the name of ending the "white slave traffic."

Much as I hate to flatly contradict Rich—after all, she recanted her anti-porn position shortly afterward—porn isn't "about" slavery unless, you know, it is about slavery explicitly, which, certainly, it sometimes is.[33] In her book *The Black Body in Ecstasy: Reading Race, Reading Pornography* (2014), the feminist scholar Jennifer Nash discusses porno magazines and movies involving KKK and plantation scenarios. Distasteful as it may seem to many of us, even here, unexpected pleasures may arise for both porn workers and viewers, since "Black pleasures can include sexual and erotic pleasures in racialization," and "Blackness is a site of pain and a locus of pleasure."[34] To playact rape is not the same as rape, even if and even when the reasons people enjoy playacting it, and watching others playact it, stem from the influence of the real thing on our desires as they are presently constituted—real desire to harm, and real traumatized repetition compulsion. To be exploited is not to be thingified. The double freedom of capitalist wage labor is always "wage slavery": there's no excuse for the purity flex of exceptionalizing porn labor.

The context for pornophobia's ascendancy was the rightward conversion of many erstwhile communists of the New Left under Reaganism. In her 1989 book *Daring to Be Bad: Radical Feminism in America 1967-1975*, Echols makes this analogy plain, offering ample evidence to understand cultural feminism, quite simply, as women's lib's counterrevolution. As I see it, *Daring to Be Bad* narrates how the counterrevolutionary movement first took root in radical feminism's brutal betrayals by the "male" left, grew tall on the comforts of revanchism, truncated analysis, and failures of accountability, and eventually became a conspiracy theory, a veritable feminism of fools.

Heartbreakingly, in the process of getting the left (as much as it had injured and disrespected them) off their backs, radical feminists separated their movement "from the very social radicalism out of which it had formed."[35] Defeat and depression was compounded, in 1976, when the anti-abortion Hyde Amendment passed. As the Hulu show *Mrs. America* (starring Cate Blanchett as antifeminism warrior Phyllis Schlafly) depicts, opposition to the ERA perversely grew in various state legislatures in the late '70s. To top it all, a bunch of ex–New Left types like Kit Lasch, Michael Lerner, and Tom Hayden were suddenly all pushing out the basest pro-family ideology.[36] No different to their male counterparts in this sense, once feminists decided they owed no allegiance to the left, their politics became downright scary.

The originator of the phrase "the future is female," Sally Gearhart, thought that the "proportion of men must be reduced to and maintained at approximately 10% of the human race."[37] Protecting the flock by culling the wolves (in other words, committing androcide) probably sounds reasonable if, like Susan Brownmiller, you are willing to make the claim that "anatomical fiat" decrees human females "natural prey" and human males "the predator," based on the "inescapable construction" of "genital organs."[38] Among post-left feminists, having a vagina became a kind of badge of cosmic unsafety, requiring, perhaps, a Zionist solution ("womyn's land"). Heavyweight pornophobes Robin Morgan and Kathleen Barry started outright "assailing" feminists who wanted to explore questions of class, race, and sexual preference. Gynonationalism, like any nationalism, cannot brook difference, as Echols tracks. At the 1973 West Coast Women's Studies Conference, Morgan suppressed discussion of the differences between women, while Barry "denounced the women who raised issues of class, race, and imperialism as saboteurs who 'must be treated as the enemy from within' the movement."[39] Barry, who wrote *Female Sexual Slavery*, claimed later that feminist opposition to pornophobia was a plot to enable "male leftists to continue their sexual abuse of women without fear of censure." Lesbian S/M was "a leftist strategy" for splitting feminism, "attempting to annihilate it."[40]

The point of no return in the schism between US radical and cultural feminisms was likely the creation of the Circle of Support for Jane Alpert. A former Weather Underground member, Alpert's defection from the left and alleged collaboration with the FBI (upon being captured) came alongside a conversion to eco-cultural feminism. In her "Letter from the Underground," circulated widely between 1972–4, Alpert presented a "new feminist theory" to the world called Mother Right, a screed that had been copiously edited and shaped by the aforementioned cultural-feminist honcho (and arch-transphobe) Robin Morgan.

The "new" theory, in a nutshell, was the exceedingly defeatist, conservative, biologically determinist, and anti-utopian view that "nature" unites all women via their cellular potential for motherhood. Unsurprisingly, while laying this out, Alpert called feminism and leftism incompatible. In her memoir *Growing Up Underground*, Alpert freely admits, "Robin and her version of feminism were leading me back to my family, to the friendships I'd formed in college, and to the world of middle-class values I had violently rejected in 1969."[41] So committed was Jane to bridge burning, bourgeois rehabilitation, cultural feminism, and Robin Morgan, she did not stop at blaming her ex-lover Sam Melville for everything she stood accused of, but even callously disavowed the prisoners killed while protesting the murder of George Jackson in the Attica Prison Rebellion of 1971. "I will mourn the deaths of 42 male supremacists no longer," Alpert wrote—and was born again.[42]

The feminist attack on sexual "perversion" looked very similar, historians Ellen DuBois and Linda Gordon argued in their 1984 anthology *Pleasure and Danger*, to "a conservative and anti-feminist version of social purity, the Moral Majority and 'family protection movement.'"[43] In 1983, for instance, when MacKinnon and Dworkin drafted a civil ordinance for the City of Minneapolis defining porn as a rights violation, half of the ordinance's supporters didn't even know that feminism was involved.[44] I cannot ignore the misogyny and femmephobia in Dworkin and MacKinnon's vague definition of graphic sexually explicit female subordination:

> Pornography is the graphic sexually explicit subordination of women, whether in pictures or in words, that also includes one or more of the following: (i) women are presented dehumanized as sexual objects, things or commodities; or (ii) women are presented as sexual objects who enjoy pain or humiliation; or (iii) women are presented as sexual objects who experience sexual pleasure in being raped; or (iv) women are presented as sexual objects tied up or cut up or mutilated or bruised or physically hurt; or (v) women are presented in postures of sexual submission, servility or display; or (vi) women's body parts . . . are exhibited, such that women are reduced to those parts; or (vii) women are presented as whores by nature; or (viii) women are presented being penetrated by objects or animals; or (ix) women are presented in scenarios of degradation, injury, torture, shown as filthy or inferior, bleeding, bruised, or hurt in a context that makes these conditions sexual.[45]

I doubt that even MacKinnon and Dworkin themselves know whether "whores by nature," here, means desirous of getting fucked hard, or temperamentally well-suited to the sale of sexual labor. Either way, the idea that being a whore by nature is impossible (that is, a misogynist myth) or else a state of real false consciousness (representable but dehumanizing) is what leads to Joan Nestle getting censored when she writes about being a "good girl" for Esther. As one would expect, then, radical—sex-radical—feminists fought back against this totalitarian theory of visual semiotics. In their book *Sex Wars*, two queer anti-censorship socialists, Lisa Duggan and Nan Hunter, note that "underlying virtually every section of the proposed laws there is an assumption that sexuality is a realm of unremitting, unequaled victimization for women. Pornography appears as the monster that made this so."[46]

In her 1984 cultural-feminist tome *The Anatomy of Freedom*, Robin Morgan has the gall to speak of "painfully-arrived-at unity among feminists on this issue."[47] It's more accurate to say: the "MacDworkinites" sought to impose their analysis by putting state power behind it. The Dworkin-MacKinnon legislation was passed by Minneapolis City Council, then swiftly vetoed as unconstitutional by the mayor. The cat, however, was out of the bag. In 1985, an identical ordinance was adopted by the City of Indianapolis.[48] The law, once again, did not survive scrutiny by the Supreme Court. The model law also "flunked out"[49] in Wisconsin and California, as Califia, the author of *Public Sex*, noted with relish.

Eventually, though, a version of the law stuck. In 1992, when the Canadian Supreme Court decided to take a MacKinnonite approach to obscenity statutes, authorities moved to suppress all kinds of queer work, such as *Bad Attitude*, the lesbian magazine.[50] Besides putting a chill on gay publishing, one tragicomic consequence of Canada's judicial feminism was that texts by Dworkin herself were refused entry into the country.[51] One can imagine the ominous opening paragraph of *Only Words* by MacKinnon leading to problems at customs too: "Your husband ties you to the bed and drips hot wax on your nipples and brings in other men to watch and makes you smile through it. Your doctor will not give you drugs he has addicted you to unless you suck his penis . . ." and so on.[52]

In her 1985 "Cyborg Manifesto," the socialist-feminist biologist Donna Haraway railed against the institutionalization of MacKinnon's "rewriting" of radical feminism's history, calling the brewing *Only Words* version of feminism "a kind of apocalypse for all revolutionary standpoints."[53] The lawyer's analogization of her own theory to "Marxism" was especially troubling for Haraway, who saw the anti-porn feminism in question as radically un-Marxist. The analogy drawn between sexual objectification and alienated labor, for example, was completely untenable ("To be constituted by another's desire is not the same thing as to be alienated in the violent separation of the laborer from his product"). Hence, "A Cyborg Manifesto" argues that, quite unlike Marx's approach to proletarian unity, MacKinnon's feminism "achieves its end—the unity of women—by enforcing the experience of and testimony to radical non-being." What MacKinnon does is construct "a non-subject," a "self-who-is-not." She thereby does "what Western patriarchy itself never succeeded in doing," namely, manufacturing "feminists' consciousness of the non-existence of women, except as products of men's desire."[54] I agree, and I consider Haraway's theorization of women's cyborgicity, which is to say, our deep entanglements in systemic sources of both pleasure and danger, one of the soundest heuristics I know for thinking about the struggle ahead toward a sensuous "post-gender" world.

The "Cyborg Manifesto" offers an admittedly demanding theory—asking us to commit to the unceasing collective feminist coding and recoding of the world. In MacKinnon's oeuvre, in contrast, one central contention is that women must do less reading of the culture because, simply, there is nothing to read. Porn is everywhere, yet it is not ideas or speech so much as it is death itself, an illocutionary act (like "saying 'kill' to a trained attack dog"[55]). The single command it encrypts, or so MacKinnon believes, is gynocidal: "Addressed directly to the penis, delivered through an erection, and taken out on women in the real world." Women don't exist in this diagram except as prey. The command is apparently "'get her,' pointing at all women,"[56] making penis havers a species of trained predators. Women, meanwhile, are nothing. We don't do any getting, and getting "got" is psychic murder. Bottom line: porn weaponizes the dogs/dicks and nonmetaphorically violates "us" with them every minute of every day. It's a hard-on holocaust.

This approach to cultural interpretation is mechanistic to the point of absurdity.[57] It is also deeply consolatory in its confidence that women have played no part in building our hell world, which, as we've seen, couldn't be further from the truth. When a woman in an image wears a collar, womanhood itself dies a little bit, end of story. It's hard to respond to these claims without sounding as hyperbolic as them, and I suspect that's by design. At minimum, one might say, with Echols, that anti-porn feminism's "insistence upon the incorrigibility of male sexuality suggests that it is concerned with something other than its reformation."[58]

I will grit my teeth and try to say more. Human penises, you know, are only intermittently hard muscles, and even when hard, they are sensitive, springy, dribbly, and vulnerable. Everyone knows that cocks are fragile—everyone, because, whatever your genitalia, genitals are clearly all made of the same contractile and erectile stuff that just gets torqued around in varying styles in different bodies. Further, as anyone who has ever encircled or enveloped a cock knows, there is nothing "active," inherently, about a cock. There is nothing inherently "passive" about a cunt, an asshole, a mouth, or a cupped hand. Both roles (and neither) are quite available to all the above body parts. For example, just as vaginas aren't "sheaths," nor are they bolts, boa constrictors, vises, vacuums, or maws. Maybe MacKinnon is confused, but when we liken our penises (or clits) to swords, ploughs, pens, quills, guns, trains, and so on, we are obviously indulging an adorable fantasy. Come on! The groin is one of the first places one aims to kick a putative attacker. Our phallic fantasies about genitals enthrall us because our genitals are, self-evidently, so very vulnerable. Part of the awfulness of sexual violence is the humiliating character of the fact that one can feel so reduced, in the semiotic and material context of layered male-supremacist history, by a weaponized tube of flesh. MacKinnon, though, treats this humiliation as objective. To read MacKinnon, you'd think strings of cum on a tongue were, transhistorically, bullets to the soul.

Luckily, up here in the real world, "penetration" is only one name for a process that is always also "circlusion."[59] Coined by Bini Adamczak, this term is the antonym of penetration, that is, the same process, only it's understood from the standpoint of the mouth, not the finger. Our organs don't objectively plough, engulf, "circlude," or drill anything. Rather, they come to do these things discursively—"rail me," "ride me," "let's dick each other down simultaneously with this two-way dildo"—thanks to relational descriptions, which can always be modified or reversed. Notwithstanding the epidemic instrumentalization of penises of flesh and of silicone in acts of rape that are themselves part of the structure of violent gender, it is a horrible mistake to take seriously the notion that a muscle is somehow in and of itself dangerous. It is especially backward to do so in the name of feminism. Sex domination doesn't flow from the penis. Besides, penises are big sources of joy and gender euphoria. Many women love their own cocks and each other's very well. Many more—greedily, skillfully—just love cock.

Andrea Dworkin, in a dark, violent way, was one of them. In her novel-memoir *Ice and Fire* (1986), reminiscing about the year 1968, she effuses about the "lush," "dissolved" way that women look "when they've been fucked hard and long, coming and coming," women "fucked out, creamy and swollen."[60] She calls her girlfriend Ricki Abrams, whom she calls "N" here, "easy to love, devotedly," specifically because "she fucks like a gang of boys." Together, *Ice and Fire*'s protagonist and N do a lot of sex work and have a lot of penetrative sex. They "fuck for capsules of mescaline. We fuck for loose change. We fuck for fun. We fuck for adventure. . . . We sleep and fuck [each other] at the same time, not letting go."[61] N is "a rough fuck," gushes Andrea. "She pushes her fingers in. She tears around inside. She thrusts her hips so hard you can't remember who she is or how many of her there are. The first time she tore me apart. I bled and bled."[62]

Unfortunately, this period came to a brutally violent end a couple of years later when Andrea married an anarchist man, Cornelius "Iwan" de Bruin—a virgin—whom she initiated into BDSM sex only for him to begin beating her, nonconsensually, to a pulp. Andrea escaped, barely, with her life, and told a friend "I released a sadistic monster"[63] in Iwan—a man who she later learned was charged with thirty-eight offenses against other women, including "grievous bodily harm" and "malicious wounding," in the 1980s alone. "I had been a hopeful radical. Now I am not," Andrea wrote. "Once I was a child and I dreamed of freedom. Now I am an adult and I see what my dreams have come to: pornography."[64] It was shortly after these experiences that Dworkin decided that "men will have to give up their precious erections," because any real "transformation of the male sexual model under which we now all labor and 'love' begins . . . in a limp penis." Men, she said, "will have to give up their precious erections and begin to make love as women do together."[65] But which women are those? Was Ricki, who clearly didn't need a penis to tear Andrea apart in the best possible way, not a woman? How did Andrea come to the conclusion that something inherently violent can be imputed to nervous erectile tissue?

I freely grant: Dworkin did not say that all heterosexual intercourse is rape. (Though she gets close enough: once, in *Intercourse*, among her characteristic litany of orphic pronunciations comes the claim that men are "supposed to slice us up the middle, leaving us in parts on the bed."[66]) A more interesting question for me is whether she thinks all criticism is. "I use them; I cut and slice into them in order to exhibit them," she promises sadistically in the preface to *Intercourse*, explaining her use of male authors: Leo Tolstoy, Tennessee Williams, D. H. Lawrence, Gustave Flaubert, and so on.[67] Must we use or abuse with the same ruthlessness in order to read Dworkin correctly? When I read Dworkin, I often wonder if she is trying not to activate but to smother all resistant agency (the iciest of dommes). "Women are tortured, whipped, and chained," she writes, more or less, in book after book after book. "Women are bound and gagged, branded and burned, cut with knives and wires; women are pissed on and shit on; red-hot needles are driven into breasts, bones are broken, rectums are torn, mouths are ravaged, cunts are savagely bludgeoned by penis after penis, dildo after dildo."[68] To point out the libidinal charge in this compulsively prolific litany of horror almost seems redundant. Dworkin hungered lustily, as literary scholar Leah Claire Allen suggests, after the "pleasures of diagnosing the worst dangers of our culture."[69]

It's because of this lustful intensity, I think, that one of Dworkin's number one public enemies—the sex writer and queer kinkster Susie Bright—sincerely thinks of herself as a "Dworkin-inspired feminist." I find it a movingly anti-fascist gesture, this willingness to claim Dworkin as an unwitting forebear, and to honor her as the mother of a whole hive of femme sickos and hardcore horror fans (including Bright herself). "Every single woman who pioneered the sexual revolution, every erotic-feminist-bad-girl-and-proud-of-it-stiletto-shitkicker was once a fan of Andrea Dworkin," Bright attests. "Until 1984, we all were."[70] I understand this, even though I belong to a later generation. I speculate that Dworkin loved gothic horrors, but couldn't tolerate the enjoyment, and tried therefore, all her life, to kill it. Bright writes: "She was the animator of the ultimate porno horror loop, where the Final Girl never gets a chance to slay the monster, she only dies, dies, dies."[71] The pleasure of a nihilist "loop" is severely limited. Dworkin's disloyal daughters, being less ashamed about kink, swiftly superseded it. Yet the fact remains: Dworkin was one of the first literary critics in the West to take porn seriously. Feminist porn studies scholars and feminist porn practitioners themselves are all Dworkin-inspired. "She was," Bright says, "the one who got us looking at porn with a critical eye."

I greatly enjoy the erotic utopianism of early Dworkin. The Dworkin of *Woman Hating* (1974) calls for an end to the incest taboo, an end to the nuclear family, and a recognition that everybody's bodies have a version of the same sexual components—beautifully, diversely, she says, humanity is a "multi-sexed species."[72] In a passage that remains hotly contested among Dworkinites to this day—the final chapter—Dworkin affirms the sexual rights of children, theorizes transsexuality as resistance, and asks that we, every one of us, "develop our pansexuality to its limits" by engaging in revolutionary erotic transvestism and multispecies androgynous "fucking."[73] In her own words, she also "in effect advocated fucking animals."[74] Bestiality is already universal, she writes, and erotic relationships with animals are "life-affirming and life-enriching" so long as they are "not predatory."[75]

Tellingly, it is not the bestiality or incest-related parts of this infamous chapter, but the pro-trans part that has caused the most stink of late. In 2020, Dworkin's life partner, John Stoltenberg, invoked Dworkin's name against TERFs in the context of the "transgender tipping-point," publishing a piece entitled "Andrea Dworkin Was a Trans Ally" in the *Boston Review*.[76] One year later, Janice Raymond, the arch-TERF, hit back and "set the record straight" in her book *Doublethink*, calling out "an analysis of transsexualism

that Andrea would not have affirmed today." After all, the incensed
Raymond wrote, Dworkin many times "admitted she was wrong in
her last chapter of *Woman Hating*."[77] Quoting Dworkin's 1979 en-
dorsement of her own anti-trans tome *The Transsexual Empire*, and
re-airing her own anti-trans beef with the "otherwise insightful"[78]
Dworkin as she'd registered it in 1977, Raymond now proclaims
with certainty that, "were she alive today," Andrea would denounce
the "denigration of natal women on which the transgender movement is built."[79] I think Dworkin did repudiate her early pro-trans
views, along with her optimism about eros—in other words, her
utopianism. To her credit, meanwhile, MacKinnon has stayed
steadfastly trans affirming—as long as the trans women, it goes
without saying, aren't whores.[80]

Did anybody win the sex wars? It seems to me that feminist radical-
isms both right and left lost, while at the same time, middle-class
pornophobia came joint first—alongside liberalism. Sex-positive liberal feminism, which gave us Madonna's coffee-table book *Sex*, girl
power, the Spice Girls, Naomi Wolf, and Camille Paglia, attained
hegemonic status in the 1990s. Meanwhile, the sexual reactions of
pornophobic lawyers like MacKinnon continue to influence state
policies on trafficking and to animate resurgently popular strains of
"radfem"-inism opposed to the decriminalization of sex work. For
instance, one plinth of MacKinnon's thought that still boomerangs
around our present is her anti-BDSM metaphysics. In the '80s, she
spilled a lot of ink disgustedly quoting the aforementioned pioneer
leather daddy, community builder, and trans man "P. Califia" on
the practices and pleasures of lesbian sadomasochism—"the paradigm of male domination."[81] But decades later, a transnational
radical feminist group called Liberation Collective is still arguing
straight-facedly that "BDSM prevents revolution," and warning
feminists of the problem of Patrick Califia, a 1970s bogeyman responsible for "severely polluting our lesbian communities with intensely patriarchal, male-centric views on sexuality."[82]

The doyenne of smut busting is still kicking. "We are living in the world pornography has made,"[83] she declared in 2021,

melodramatically opening a *New York Times* op-ed at the age of seventy-four. She states unequivocally that it is porn—not television, say, or religion or literature—that "desensitizes consumers to violence and spreads rape myths and other lies about women's sexuality." The "explicit" image-subscription platform OnlyFans is no less than "a pimp," she charges. (OnlyFans does take a 20 percent cut from content creators, about twice what Patreon takes from people who subscribe to my writing. We should all unionize.[84]) In MacKinnon's emotive phrase, pimps are "grooming the culture" with porn, to believe that women are made for one thing: something "degrading." And if we follow MacKinnon in understanding pimps not as bosses, but as owner-jailers who rent out inert, non-laboring bodies, then it should anger us that the term sex worker has gained widespread acceptance. "What is being done to them is neither sex, in the sense of intimacy and mutuality," MacKinnon writes of OnlyFans creators, "nor work, in the sense of productivity and dignity." Leaving aside for one moment the sentimental definition of sex here, this is a deeply sentimental definition of work. From an anti-capitalist proletarian standpoint, productivity is not a virtue. Nor is dignity something one can expect from a job in a class society.

We are, in a way, living in the world that Kitty MacKinnon has made. In 2018, Donald Trump signed into law a couple of "anti-sex-trafficking" acts known as SESTA-FOSTA, which conflate huge swaths of sex work with human trafficking in perfect conformance with MacKinnon's definition (derived from Josephine Butler, who meant well) that "the sine qua non of trafficking is . . . neither border crossing nor severe violence. It is third-party involvement."[85] Sex workers were driven en masse off the advertising website Backpage.[86] MacKinnon wants OnlyFans to be next, and she might get what she wants. In 2023, an inquiry into porn's "role in fueling violence against women and girls" by an all-party parliamentary group in the UK concluded that "all pornography should be treated as commercial sexual exploitation in law and policy."[87] The report drew on prominent MacKinnonites—Robert Jensen and Gail Dines—as two of its main witnesses.[88] Dines celebrates rising feminist interest in "porn abolition" in Britain as "a resurgence of a new national movement to liberate women from misogyny and oppression."[89] Porn workers and their allies are painfully aware that a significant strand of global "neo-abolitionism" on porn (styling itself as "radical feminism") has continued to conference, lobby, and publish against the decriminalization of sex work ever since WAP started allying itself with the carceral state in 1980.[90]

Andrea Dworkin, specifically, has been central in this cultural comeback in Anglo-America. In 2022, the feminist scholar Claire Potter assured the world that "#MeToo activism has opened the door to a long-overdue recognition of Dworkin's contributions," and added that "her prose seizes even a hostile reader by the throat and refuses to let go"—as if this were a good thing.[91] If her recommendations sound cruel, no matter—as Jennifer Szalai explained in her Dworkin encomium in the *New York Times*, "in wartime, no strategy is off the table."[92] A person might protest: Surely it matters most during war that strategies are off the table? But for those who would say that "our" sex is literally under siege—as Lederer and Reisman said, in their crusade against female extinction—the effect is to justify any and all countermeasures.

From inside the war room, those of us who persist in "seeking ecstasy on the battlefield" (as sex radicals Ellen DuBois and Linda Gordon put it in 1983) begin to look a bit like traitors to womankind. We are told it is wrong to imagine that one can taste any joyful, unalienated ways of embodying gender now, before the revolution. Or that, even if feminist heterosex is tastable, there's no excuse for putting political focus there while the corpses of women are piling up. At the very least, one ought to perform heteropessimism, the posture of straight female lamentation Asa Seresin named in 2019.[93] Earnest shamelessness about one's androphilia has become, once again, of late, a feminist faux pas.

"Seemingly all at once," notes the lesbian writer Sarah Fonseca, "Andrea Dworkin is everywhere."[94] Even the now-disgraced elite women's coworking club, The Wing, sold enamel pins of Dworkin's face for a spell. Etsy, too, has been full of Dworkin-branded stickers: "Dump your porn-addicted boyfriend," and so on.[95] In

2020, the New Press published a long and admiring biography of Dworkin by Martin Duberman. The editors of *Last Days at Hot Slit* (2019), a giant collection of Dworkin's writings published by Semiotext(e), even introduce one extinction-phobic screed called "The Coming Gynocide," not as a dangerous, millenarian, con-spiracist phantasm, but as "a harrowing presentation of her predic-tions for the near-future, where male-supremacist logic reaches its logical extreme."[96] *Guardian* opinion writer Moira Donegan wrote in *Bookforum* that Dworkin, her heroine, is "unpopular" and "ridi-culed," mainly because she "requires us to know more than we can stand to know."[97] Lauren Oyler likewise hailed Dworkin as "a lu-cid, scarily persuasive writer" in the *New Yorker*.[98] The film director Pratibha Parmar's hybrid documentary *My Name is Andrea* (2022) was executive coproduced by Abigail Disney, Gloria Steinem, and V (formerly Eve Ensler), while starring Ashley Judd.[99]

Fonseca, who coedited *The New Lesbian Pulp* (2024), watched Parmar's documentary and laments its elisions of Dworkin's col-lusion with right-wing statecraft. She also laments, however, the scrubbing of her lesbian sex life. For Fonseca, the film (ironically) makes a schlocky, gauzy kind of "pornography" out of Dworkin's biography, her copious experiences of male violence and gendered pain—"centering men in a conversation that should be about lov-ing women." After all, Dworkin didn't just villainize certain kinds of women (leatherdykes, sex-worker activists, sex radicals). She also, by her own account, fucked the hell out of women, notably Ricki Abrams, the sex worker who introduced her to feminism. Fonseca regrets the expurgation of this lust from the reverent *I Am Andrea*, even as she firmly allies herself with those of us—"kinky, or en-meshed in sex work"—whom Dworkin called Nazis.[100] Fonseca opposes Dworkin, but protests that the fandom exemplified by Parmar and company "perversely endorses the worst of Dworkin, who has become a totem of a new strain of feminism that is keen on annihilating not only sex workers, but trans people." I am touched by Fonseca's ability to be Dworkin's opponent even while defend-ing her against distortions imposed by champions.

Sometimes, however, I feel more aligned with Joan Nestle's pure enmity and fury in response to the moralism and totalitarianism of MacDworkinism. In 1981, with over two decades of left organizing experience under her belt, Nestle sat and listened to Dworkin denouncing "the penis" in a New York auditorium, then went home and typed a timeless response: the widely anthologized short statement "My Mother Liked to Fuck." The piece ends with an imagined speech by the cigarette-toting Regina:

> I never allowed anyone to bully me out of my sexual needs. Just like you, Joan, when in the fifties . . . they called you a freak, and they never stopped you either. They called you freak and me whore and maybe they always will, but we fight them best when we keep on doing what they say we should not want or need for the joy we find in doing it. I fucked because I liked it, and Joan, the ugly ones, the ones who beat me or fucked me too hard, they didn't run me out of town, and neither can the women who don't walk my streets of loneliness or need. Don't scream penis at me, but help to change the world so no woman feels shame or fear because she likes to fuck.[101]

What can we do, pending revolution, but seek ecstasy on the battlefield? And why, as Fonseca asks, "is everyone so obsessed with showcasing and inventorying feminine pain when pleasure is right there, ready to be fought for?"[102] "My mother," Nestle insists, "was a working woman who liked to fuck, who believed she had the right to have a penis inside of her if she liked it."[103] This solidarity between queer daughter and slut mother fills me with me tears, and love, and hope.

NINE

The Girlboss

*I have bought a lot of real estate cause I believe we gotta
get our money straight. Girl, get your money straight.*

—BELL HOOKS, 2015[1]

People began writing obituaries for the girlboss when she was just
six years old. The *Atlantic* declared her demise a couple of months
into the first US coronavirus lockdown in 2020, and *Wired*, *CNN*,
Business Insider, *Elle*, and the *Cut* soon followed suit.[2] The British
magazine *i-D* called the girlboss "retrospectively cheugy" (uncool
and dated),[3] and the meme "gaslight, gatekeep, girlboss," a parody
of the bossbabely wellness gospel "eat, pray, love," reigned supreme
on the internet.[4] The subcultural enjoyment of anti-girlboss memes
(for example, "no more girlbossing, only girlsleeping!") stays consistently popular. It is a truth universally acknowledged, certainly
on TikTok, that the girlboss "girlbossed too close to the sun."[5]

Yet the funeral for "trickle-down feminism," eerily, keeps repeating itself, suggesting that, every time we report that the girlboss is
dead, we're being wishful. We seem to have a case of *the girlboss
is dead, long live the girlboss* on our hands. Or, as *Forbes* put it,
"girlboss may be over, but the woman founder is here to stay."[6]
As is, for now, the celebration of people like the "Iron Lady of Israel," genocidal prime minister Golda Meir (in a biopic starring

Helen Mirren), and Ruth Handler, the inventor of a highly salable doll (in the hit movie *Barbie*). After all, how could it be otherwise? How could the aspiration to own the means of production instead of alienating your labor possibly "die" in the absence of a mass movement against capitalism? Even the tradwife, despite her avowed commitment to wagelessness, is typically a self-optimizing influencer, firmly still in the formal economy.[7]

The girlboss was born in a conversion-redemption story. "I entered adulthood believing that capitalism was a scam," the term's key popularizer Sophia Amoruso wrote in her memoir *#Girlboss* (2014), "but I've instead found that it's a kind of alchemy. You combine hard work, creativity, and self-determination, and things start to happen."[8] Funnily enough, Marx also called capitalism a kind of alchemy, albeit his take was that—to be a capitalist—you combine *other* people's work with something you own. Still, as Amoruso herself implicitly recognized, the girlboss was no more an innovation than was the girldebtor, girljob, girldictator, girlsergeant, girlspy, or indeed, girlsploitation. She actually isn't six years old at all—more like four hundred, if we remember Margaret Hardenbroeck. Or, if you like, fifty. In 1973, clerical workers in Boston set up a labor group, 9to5, which soon boasted thirteen chapters nationwide with ten thousand members (subsequently, they created a union: District 925 of the Service Employees International Union).[9] While the founders of 9to5 were New Left radicals, the group soon split into two strands—managerial versus mass activism—when the leadership allowed a gulf to form internally between its rank and file and subgroups like Women in Publishing. While the former prioritized "pulling together," the latter's priority was shattering glass ceilings.

It was here that the betrayal of pink-collar workers by their aspirational white-collar "sisters" began, or so the professor of business Allison Elias argues in *The Rise of Corporate Feminism* (2022). Within 9to5, blurring the lines between employees and managerial wannabe bosses, for example, by letting managers join unions, meant that, slowly but surely, to quote Jess Bergman, "bosses ate feminism" in the pink-collar sector. The counterinsurgent how-to guide *Games Mother Never Taught You: Corporate Gamesmanship for Women*, by Betty Lehan Harragan of NOW, was published in 1977 and sold over a million copies. People like Harragan "were disdainful," as Bergman attests, "of working women who set their sights any lower than CEO."[10] Worse, Harragan's guide to female upward mobility—which foreshadowed Sheryl Sandberg's *Lean In* manual of 2013—was only the most successful of a glut of professional similar self-help titles—for example, *The Right Moves: Succeeding in a Man's World Without a Harvard MBA* (by Charlene Mitchell, 1985) and *Feminine Leadership: Or How to Succeed in Business Without Being One of the Boys* (Marilyn Loden, also 1985). In the late socialist Barbara Ehrenreich's opinion, it was books like these that transformed the "bra-less" 1970s image of the liberated woman into "a tidy executive who carries an attaché case and is skilled in discussing market shares and leveraged buy-outs."[11]

The whole post-2013 girlboss cultural trend, in short, is *Games Mother Never Taught You* rebooted—yassified. It is merely the cult of the entrepreneur, cynically using the latest signifiers of un-privilege (*intersectional*, and *girl*, in place of the *working woman* of yesteryear) to self-arrogate strategic innocence while anointing profit seeking with the elixir of progressivism. To state the obvious: a wannabe boss, of any gender, espouses the hope of one day being an owner and a dominator instead of a hustler, let alone a comrade. Deep down, we know this; we know the matter is not actually remotely complicated, and that, as journalist Nicole Froio sums it up, "all girlbosses are bastards."[12] Most of us will remain girlproles until we either overthrow class society or, individually, escape into the bossing class. Could it be *me*? Alongside Cinderella (marriage) plots, tales of professional ascent, entrepreneurial gratification, and upward class mobility such as *Working Girl, Joy, I Care A Lot, Legally Blonde, The Devil Wears Prada, Self-Made, Shrill, Survival of the Thickest*, and *The Intern* saturate our culture.[13]

It is for this reason, pure and simple, that *#Girlboss* made such a splash. Our collective ears pricked up when we were told how, once upon a time, a pantsuited executive was a vegan freegan, into "petty thievery," psilocybin, and Earth First meets. Amoruso spilled the tea in retrospective disbelief:

> I refused to buy new wood; too angry with capitalism's disregard for sustainability, I furnished my places with a mix of sidewalk freebies and lifted merch instead. I dumpster-dived at Krispy Kreme, dated a guy who lived in a tree-house, and had hair upon my legs.[14]

Thank God, the "fashion empire" builder's road-to-Damascus moment came just sixteen pages later:

> I got sick of listening to my friends whine about living in poverty while refusing to get a job. Compromise is just part of life. We all, at some point, find ourselves either directly or indirectly supporting something we disagree with. There are ways to avoid this, but it generally includes eating roadkill and making tampons out of socks.[15]

Amoruso used to have principles. But then she realized: this is no way to live. Cut to the image of a new and reformed Sophia. She has renounced shoplifting and hitchhiking and is crying "tears of joy" because she now pays help to clean her house: "Yesterday's underwear is clean and folded."[16]

Who folded it? No doubt the ghosts of the well-heeled Harriet Beecher Stowe, May French Sheldon, and Emmeline Pankhurst would all, in their own way, reproach me for asking such an undermining question. (I suspect even Alma White, the big business bishop, and Frances Willard, the "do-everything" temperance mogul, might give this clean-panties-wearing go-getter a hallelujah. *Doing everything* was always about foisting unromantic aspects of daily social reproduction onto the working classes anyway.) Does an ambitious woman not deserve to exploit the wage relation, procuring herself a housekeeper, thereby freeing herself up for public feminist accomplishments? Why should the onus *not* to do so fall particularly on women, who are already at a disadvantage? Remember that Anglo-feminism, in its earliest days, promised middle-class women economic freedom in the form of emigration to a land where servants were "cheap." In this way, it was imperial feminists claiming racial exceptionalism that paved the way for capitalist feminists claiming moral exceptionalism.

Another extensive employer of domestic help—and boss of recent note—is Ivanka Trump. In contrast to Amoruso, this particular businesswoman is very much to the manor born and never hated capitalism. Wouldn't you know, though, that the feminism she preaches is the same? It's actually very difficult, as Catherine Rottenberg, the author of *The Rise of Neoliberal Feminism*, points out, to distinguish between all the *New York Times* bestsellers in the feminist self-help genre, even though their authors are on different sides of the party/political aisle.[17] Whether it's Amoruso's *#Girlboss* or Trump's "how-to-succeed guide" *Women Who Work*, or Fox News anchor Megyn Kelly's *Settle for More*, or even the extended liberal think piece *Unfinished Business* by former Princeton dean Anne-Marie Slaughter, the advice is always mainly that women should work—yes, just *work*, more—on all facets of their life.[18] The emphases change from text to text, but the bottom line is mostly, to quote financial coach Glinda Bridgforth, "girl, get your money straight."[19]

The gospel of feminist capitalism is hard to resist. None other than bell hooks, the Black feminist philosopher, refers to Bridgforth's book *Girl, Get Your Money Straight: A Sister's Guide to Healing Your Bank Account and Funding Your Dreams in 7 Simple Steps* as a "manifesto" she "believes in." Ironically, hooks herself is one of the most-quoted critics of the "lean in feminism" of Sheryl Sandberg, the now billionaire, hailed by Gloria Steinem as "feminism's new boss," who was chief operating officer at Facebook between 2008 and 2022.[20] While *Forbes* in 2013 proclaimed Sandberg the fifth-most influential woman in the world, and *Time* ranked her as one of the world's one hundred "leaders," hooks decried Sandberg's brand as "faux feminism" and a "whites-only proposition." Surveying Sandberg's 2010 TED Talk ("Why We Have Too Few Women Leaders") and her mega-bestseller *Lean In: Women, Work, and the Will to Lead*, hooks saw not feminism, but a "corporate infusion of gender equality."[21] Sandberg's inability to name white supremacy, or even racial difference, rightly struck hooks as racist. Quoting Sandberg's 2011 commencement speech at Barnard—"I hope that you have the ambition to lean in to your career and run the world, because the world needs you to change it"—hooks heard "a call to support and perpetuate first world imperialism."

The iconic author of *All About Love* and *Feminism Is for Everybody* was absolutely right to mock Sandberg's claim, in *Lean In*, that "conditions for all women will improve when there are more women in leadership roles giving strong and powerful voice to their needs and concerns."[22] This is the kind of fantasy of cross-class solidarity that doomed the 1970s clerical workers' movement. Ironically, however, not long after she published her broadside against the white feminist corporate executive's bestseller, bell hooks boasted at an event at the New School in New York about being a landlord *for feminist reasons*.[23] Criticism of this, at the time, stayed in the back channels. But as political scientist Sophie Smith insists, "Honoring hooks doesn't require deifying her."[24] Implicit in hooks's "get your money" speeches, disappointingly, is the idea that the power garnered by extracting rents from commodified housing is good when the deed owners are Black women.[25]

Still, it was thanks in large part to hooks's widely referenced 2013 critique of *Lean In* that when a bevy of reviewers later lambasted the shallowness of both *#Girlboss* and—to a far greater extent—*Women Who Work*, they were shooting fish in a barrel.[26] In addition to hooks, a small army of comedians and leftists had clamored loudly against boss feminism. At CNN, Sandberg allies bewailed the trashing of a successful woman.[27] Undeterred, Ali Wong said she didn't want to lean in, she wanted to *lie down*.[28] Two authors published books called *Lean Out*, and three leading socialists penned a counter-manifesto, *Feminism for the 99%*.[29]

It worked—somewhat. *Lean In* received flack for being elitist in the *Times*, the *Washington Post*, and on NPR. By 2018, amid brewing criminal investigations into Facebook over data misuse, even celebrities knew to avoid uncritical Sandbergism.[30] No less than "Mom-in-Chief" Michelle Obama threw shade: "It's not enough to *lean in* because that shit don't work all the time."[31] The cover of *Time* pleaded with us not to "hate her because she's successful." Few and far between were those cultural pundits who hadn't heard, by 2018, that you basically had to be rich to "have it all" in the manner recommended by Sandberg.

The antifeminist "trashers," as well as comradely feminist killjoys and comedians, did undoubtedly do damage to the credibility of lean-in-ism.[32] At the same time, the self-styled "feminist companies" dulled the ideology's sheen all by themselves. In 2015, Amoruso got sued for firing three workers from Nasty Gal™, her start-up, just before they were scheduled to go on maternity leave. Netflix accordingly canceled *Girlboss*, a show based on her life, and the ex-freegan "She-E-O" had to file for bankruptcy.[33] Meanwhile, the technology behind biomedical girlboss Elizabeth Holmes's start-up Theranos™ was exposed as a complete sham.[34] Miki Agrawal, the founder of Thinx™, a "vag-tastic," wellness-oriented, period-underwear brand, was revealed to preside over a culture of fear, sexual harassment, and ageism, in which members of the mostly female, twentysomething staff were routinely referred to as "children," while the few employees in their thirties were "nannies."[35] Accusations of sinister labor practices among "female-founded" firms became common. The public heard of the "jarring mismatch between feminist mission and lived reality" at, for example, Babeland™, the woman and queer-owned sex toy store where workers unionized in 2016.

Former Babeland employee Lena Solow testified:

> Customers experience Babeland as a welcoming and fun place to learn about their bodies and celebrate pleasure. But for workers, the experience was far from a feminist ideal. It wasn't until we bargained our first contract that we secured basic safety protections from workplace harassment, job security, and higher wages for the mostly queer and trans workplace.[36]

In short order, Steph Korey (of the luggage brand Away™), Audrey Gelman (of the women-only coworking space The Wing™), Leandra Cohen (Man Repeller™), Jen Gotch (Ban.do™), Christene Barberich (*Refinery29*), Anna Wintour (*Vogue*™), and Emily Weiss (Glossier™) were all forced to step down and/or apologize for their racist management styles.[37] And as they fell from grace, girlboss companies were disproportionately shamed in the press for their unremarkable corporate nefariousness.[38]

Sexism *was* prevalent in the public commentary on the hardly surprising news that an industry self-defined as liberatory for "women" (as though an industry could ever be collectively liberatory) had failed to make good. For journalist Moira Donegan, it was clear that girlbossery "attracted contempt far out of proportion to its actual numbers or influence."[39] Yet, too, it was the capitalist women who made the claim to moral exceptionalism (by virtue of their "female founded"-ness) in the first place. When they turned out to be the same as the old bosses, and we held them to a higher standard, it is fair to say that that standard was of their own making in the first place. But ultimately, bosses have more to fear than unduly harsh, even sexist, popular judgment. In 2009, all across France, militant factory workers revived the common 1968-era tactic of "bossnapping," that is, taking bosses hostage. On the plus side for them, in some cases the hostages were served *moules-frites*.[40] Were a group of Nasty Gal employees to bossnap Ms. Amoruso, they could serve vegan lentils and dumpstered donuts.

A steady trickle of girlboss disgraces colored the 2010s and early 2020s, accompanied by a constant loop of pro-girlboss, anti-girlboss, and anti-anti-girlboss opinionating on the part of the commentariat.[41] Some leftist "anti-work" critique, as I have suggested, penetrated the zeitgeist, including in the form of "girlresting, girlnapping" memes.[42] "Anti-girlboss memes are an invitation," Froio writes, "to imagine a world that is not structured by capital, wealth accumulation and exploitation—an invitation to imagine a world where our time really belongs to us rather than to our employers and our patriarchs."[43] The crimes of manbosses still outnumbered the girlboss scandal sheet, but a certain "a plague on both your houses" sentiment gained ground among Generation Z.

Unfortunately, when it comes to middle-class millennial Americans, those who are aware that there is an "opposite" feminist view to *Lean In* are likely to think that it consists of Anne-Marie Slaughter's one. Slaughter's *Unfinished Business*, in reality, is nearly identical, and simply spends a little more time "revaluing" the time a woman spends at home. "If family comes first, work does not come second."[44] Thus, Michelle Obama's line about leaning in— "that shit don't work"—was widely read to be "Team Slaughter." (Perhaps relevantly, Slaughter directed policy planning under President Barack Obama.) Slaughter made noises about universal childcare provision, and stressed that "workplaces, not women, need to change."[45] But Sandberg and Slaughter fundamentally agreed that the elusive key to "work-family balance" is mostly attitudinal.

While the media insisted on pitting Slaughter and Sandberg against one another, "both women's fundamental assumptions— that achieving a balance constitutes liberation and progress for women—are virtually indistinguishable" trickle-down ideologies, as Rottenberg notes:

> Sandberg focuses on changing women's attitudes about work and self, exhorting them to "lean in" to their careers. Slaughter focuses on legitimating women's "natural" commitment toward families, while urging social institutions to make room for these attitudes. In both cases there is a deeply held conviction that if high-potential women undertake the task of revaluing their ambition (Sandberg) or the normative expectation that work comes first (Slaughter), then all women will be empowered and will be able to carve out their own felicitous work-family balance.[46]

The First Lady may have dissed the girlboss, in other words, but she did not state the obvious—that both shattering glass ceilings at Fortune 500 firms (à la Sandberg) and *letting family come first* (à la Slaughter) does less than nothing for people scrubbing the floors at both Facebook HQ and the homes of ruling-class politicians.

The terms *lean in* and *girlboss* have come to seem like low-hanging fruit, unworthy of inclusion in, say, a discussion of fascisant dynamics within feminism. It is lurching along, undead. But as the journalist Rafia Zakaria sees it, girlbosses haven't so much lost ground as changed their costumes: "All of them are still there, wearing intersectional masks that fall off whenever they see a brown feminist stepping out of line."[47] Secretly, perhaps, even these wounded egos sense the truth: that the girlboss mirage—the desire that "a visionary woman can be single-handedly responsible for creating an empire and fatally wounding sexism in the process," as scholar Sarah Arkebauer puts it—cannot but drag itself down in the end. "When these empires falter, the retreat from the top hits similar notes as the rise; the girlboss can't be culpable—women are judged too harshly, she was trying her best, how could she have known."[48] The boss form lives, as does the violently weaponizable innocence its feminine avatars afford.

In 2019, Liz Truss wore kitten heels while talking about inflicting austerity on the poor and food-insecure people of Britain. "I am a 'Destiny's Child' feminist," she said, clearly seeing this as compatible with slashing services for victims of domestic violence.[49] I should pause here in case you do not know who I mean. Truss was the UK Conservative politician and Thatcher cosplayer who served as prime minister for just six weeks in 2022. Her brand of feminism was a reference to the girlband that, back in the 2000s, used to contain Beyoncé. Destiny's Child was celebrated widely for its proto-girlboss anthems—songs like "Independent Women" (about being affluent), "Survivor" (being a self-managerial subject), and "Bills, Bills, Bills" (being fiscally responsible, unlike your mooching boyfriend). Neoliberal feminists adored these elements. They still do.[50] The historian Elizabeth Cobbs, author of *Fearless Women: Feminist Patriots from Abigail Adams to Beyoncé* (2023), admits as much on the New Books Network podcast.[51] Beyoncé's music isn't to her taste, but she loves its message: "If I'm a single lady and you don't put a ring on it, I have other guys, and by the way, I pay my own bills!"[52]

For Cobbs—and no doubt for Sandberg (another Beyoncé stan), and perhaps even for the non-American Liz Truss—Queen Bey is the latest, perhaps *last*, rung on a ladder of patriotic progress toward "having it all," first erected in 1776.[53] This ladder of bourgeois feminism grows whiggishly by incrementally adding rights. (Cobbs: "You can't skip a rung!") First, in the Cobbsean account of history, "feminists patriots" establish their "right to learn" in the founding moments of the American republic. Then, their daughters and granddaughters and great-granddaughters go on to deliver the right to *speak*, the right to *lobby*, the right to *vote*, the right to *earn*, the right to *equal treatment*, the right to *compete*, and finally, in the era of #MeToo, the right to *physical safety*. The best part? Now that these rights have been hammered into the constitutional commonsense of the American people, there's no need any longer for feminism to be "political."

The idea that feminism is left wing and patriotism right wing is "dumb," argues Cobbs.[54] The US today has to accept that patriotism itself *is* feminism, so let's focus on what "we" all have in common. (Apparently, what "we" all have in common in 2023 is a love of the national economy and *feminism*.) If Thomas Jefferson said, in his inaugural presidential speech, that "we are all federalists, we are all republicans," then the US motto today is "we are all federalists, we are all republicans, we are all feminists," Cobbs affirms.

Are we? It's a bold contention in the aftermath of the *Dobbs* ruling striking down *Roe v. Wade*, but indeed, as we shall see in a future chapter, feminists helped strike it down, so Cobbs may have a point. Cobbs herself supports a right to "reproductive choice," yet this right—the right not to be pregnant—somehow isn't one of her "rungs." It is deeply unclear, in fact, where, for her, in a post-political account of the feminist present, abortion belongs. (While we're at it, can we look forward to a feminist right to have back one's stolen land, a right to a world without fossil fuels, a right to shelter, a right to define one's own sex? Is it not—since we're busy inventing "rungs"—human beings' birthright to live in a world of abundant free healthcare, without landlords, and without police?) Self-evidently, any definition of feminism *as* American patriotism will crash against the limits imposed on that formula by a settler-capitalist state. There will never be republican or federalist consensus on abolition. There can be no bipartisan support for decolonization. The kind of thing that patriots *can* enshrine, and have, on the basis of entitlement to equal treatment (or: "right to compete"), is a feminist prerogative to serve in the military, a feminist prerogative to exploit labor and natural resources, and a feminist prerogative to wage war—the focus of Cobbs's 2017 book on "America's first women soldiers."[55] Cobbs doesn't like hip-hop,

but she'd presumably be pleased that soldiers in uniform, twirl-
ing their weapons in time to the beat, were incorporated into Beyoncé, Kelly, and Michelle's big-stadium performances of "Soldier"
(2004), a song about "needing a soldier" often paradoxically paired
with "Independent Woman" ("I depend on me") in a cocktail of
American triumphalism befitting the 2003 invasion of Iraq.

In the same vein, around the same time the shortest-serving UK
prime minister ever started saying "I am a 'Destiny's Child' feminist," *Politico* in the US ran the item "How Women Took Over
the Military-Industrial Complex." The story, such as it was, simply
consisted of the femaleness of the CEOs of Northrop Grumman,
Lockheed Martin, General Dynamics, and the defense arm of Boe-
ing. The reader was given to understand that increased female executive-level representation in the military has a positive effect on
the ability of the US to remain the police(wo)man of planet earth.
All these fine American capitalists, we were told, share not only a
sex but also the belief that sex affords *different perspectives* on the art
of designing, deploying, and selling freedom-enhancing weaponry:
"They all contend the nation needs these different perspectives to
confront a host of highly complex global challenges on the horizon."[56] Luckily, one could only conclude, what the nation needed, it
got. The *Daily Beast* breathlessly described how a drone operator at
Creech Air Force Base named Sparkle "pulls her chestnut hair into
a bun" every day, serves her president (Barack Obama), and "kills
people from 7,850 miles away" in Afghanistan.[57]

Sparkle, according to the *Daily Beast* article's standfirst, is "sick
of whiny boys" and "perfectly OK with dealing out death."[58] On
average, American men would probably have qualms about per-
petrating extralegal ultraviolence against racialized enemies of the
homeland. But women like Sparkle, the author implied, have the
instincts it takes. Perhaps Sparkle's tender—eugenic?—womanhood contributes to her gut-deep knowledge of what male enemy
combatants are capable of doing to *children*. In any case, for the
sake of American families, Sparkle doesn't pussyfoot around wor-
rying about war crimes and racism. No: Sparkle presses the button.
So, if "women" are "taking over" the war machine, as both of the

aforementioned journalists reported, then we really ought to rejoice alongside them. Power to the Sparkles! They are both more, and less, prudential, by virtue of their sex, depending on what we need them to be. The nation "needs their perspective." Female Americans—and sure, this might seem like a coincidence, since they're the ones historically excluded from oval offices and missile control bunkers—are the very organisms that can change those centers of power for the better if given access. *Who runs the world? Girls.*

Simply place the levers and triggers of military power and statecraft in women's hands, the twenty-first-century liberal news media suggests, and good things are practically guaranteed to follow. Listen, what kind of person would scoff at this? A person who has some kind of problem with women in power, that's who. Why be persnickety and demand to know: Of what, exactly, does Sparkle's, or for that matter Lockheed Martin CEO Marillyn Hewson's, *different perspective* consist? Only a jerk would notice that there is nothing in the *Politico* article that concretely explains what it is that makes this "takeover" indeed a takeover (a word that implies people acting in concert toward a specific end) rather than, say, a reshuffle. Why not focus on the cute distractions? There are, above all, extensive quotations from Karen Panetta, an engineering professor at Tufts. One of Panetta's favorite talking points is an anecdote about "soldiers in the desert using pantyhose to keep sand out of sensitive equipment." This is triumphally followed up with the rhetorical question "Do you think a guy thought of that?"[59] (We are meant to say, *no, a* guy *would never think of that, men don't know about pantyhose.*)

Panetta is the author of a feminist empowerment manual, *Count Girls In: Empowering Girls to Combine Any Interests with STEM to Open Up a World of Opportunity* (2018). In it, Panetta argued—in a probably conscious paraphrase of Anne-Marie Slaughter—that "girls don't have to change who they are" to become arms dealers and military officers.[60] Rather, the war machine must change for *us.* And which female "us" is that? The writer and journalist Rania Khalek once sardonically declared that, in American geopolitics, "all that actually matters is breaking glass ceilings, even if that means breaking the actual ceilings of women in Yemen."[61] Real events bore out Khalek's observation with spine-tingling crudeness when, in 2019, the weapons manufacturer Raytheon (responsible for many lethal drone bombings of Yemenis) wrote a check to the Girl Scouts of the USA, after which the two organizations cosponsored a series of "Cyber Challenges" themed around juvenile females' career advancement. Smiling cadettes learned code and received "mentorship," all courtesy of the "defense" megalith that ongoingly profits from selling bombs to Saudi Arabia, which end up obliterating Yemeni school buses.[62]

Raytheon's feminist Cyber Challenge events were intended to encourage Girl Scouts to grow up to become "women in STEM," based on the insight that "Raytheon's vision about making the world a safer place and the Girl Scouts vision of making the world a better place couldn't be more well suited as partners."[63] It is unpleasant to reflect (especially for a former Girl Guide like myself) that this hilarious assertion isn't entirely wrong in light of the history of feminist youth clubs—such as the junior partners of Mary Allen's militias—enrolling in patriotic militarism.[64] Today, Girl Guides and Brownies don't, as far as I'm aware, sew navy uniforms or go around shaming conscientious objectors by handing them white feathers. But a story about girls possessing special powers to uplift, heal, soothe, and generally morally edify the nation and, by extension, the economy, lives on. Today, instead of leading "auxiliary" volunteer services on the home front, Girl Scouts are encouraged to use their special girlpowers as Pentagon commanders, which is a perfectly feminist goal if you believe that, to quote erstwhile National Organization for Women president Eleanor Smeal, "peace is not a feminist issue."[65]

The hymn sheet of the nineteenth-century White Ribbon Army can be heard today, alive and well, in places like the *Yale Journal of Law and Feminism* whenever it runs articles on themes like "Women Could Save the World, If Only We Would Let Them."[66] Such articles typically urge readers to "celebrate extraordinary women" (even if said individuals are responsible for the death and suffering of millions). For example, it was once the delusion of the *Washington Post* that "the kids" think Madeleine Albright is "amaaazing," "a badass," a "girlpower icon," and "the epitome of KWEEN."[67] The geopolitical commentariat never seems to lose its appetite for profiles of "strong women" who project what one ambassador has called a "nice mixture of liberal interventionism and Realpolitik."[68] In this vein, journalists endlessly reported on an endlessly repeated proposition by Christine Lagarde, former president of the International Monetary Fund, that, had it been "Lehmann Sisters" instead of "Lehmann Brothers," proper regulatory interventions would have occurred and the 2007 financial crisis would never have happened.[69] (The pseudoscience behind this has to do with women being socialized not to gamble or take risks. Banks can stay, we just need to put moms in charge of them.)

Samantha Power, former US ambassador to the United Nations, channels Christine Lagarde's "Lehmann Sisters" creed in the "security" field. Almost Sophia Amoruso–esque in her trajectory from antiestablishmentarian to imperial stooge, Power was once a Pulitzer-winning critic of US empire. But she now believes—according to her fulsome recantation in her nomination hearing at the UN—"that we are a great, a great and strong and powerful country, and the most powerful country in the history of the world. Also, the most inspirational."[70] (Henry Kissinger himself confessed, after a Yankees game he attended with Power, that "when she analyzed contemporary problems, she and I didn't differ all that much."[71])

Straddling the political aisle, Power channels a modern version of the "sensible" maternalist standpoint perfected in the nineteenth century, blending patriotism with no-nonsense anti-utopianism. Femininity legitimizes her authority, she routinely implies: as a mom, she is compassionately tuned in to the interests of the national family and unconcerned, for that reason (that is, willingness to do anything for her kids), with "political correctness." Heather Wilson, the former air force secretary of the US, asks "everyone in this room to think about the most protective person you know in your life," and then declares that half the people "think about their moms" because "we are the protectors, and that's what the military does . . . [it's] a very natural place for a woman to be."[72] Power, a Mom who Bombs on the other side of the aisle, clearly concurs.

Power—looking back with regret (in a series of half-assed mea culpas)[73]—wrongfully backed the disastrous Obama intervention (using Raytheon bombs) in Yemen; and, later, she successfully pushed for another Obama administration bloodbath in Libya alongside Hillary Clinton and Susan Rice, a detail that prompted unimaginative news(wo)men to report relentlessly on a "troika" of "warrior women" or, especially, "Valkyries."[74] (The so-called "Hillary Doctrine" framed all this slaughter as empowering of women—not only the bombers but also the women under bombardment—and therefore all the more patriotic because "the subjugation of women is a threat to national security."[75]) Power became the head of the United States Agency for International Development (USAID) under President Biden, having apparently dodged any consequences for the aforementioned brutalities on her record and burnished it, instead, with novel spins on the notion that US hegemony can be benign.[76] In late 2017, she gave interviews about her reverence for the US flag, detailing the key experiences that "made her a feminist," namely being "the only woman on the UN Security Council."[77]

In Power's book *A Problem from Hell*, she notes that "no US president has ever made genocide prevention a priority."[78] Judging by her actions, she's fine with that. In 2023 and 2024, she has worked uncritically for the administration directly responsible for the US-Israeli genocide in Gaza, only to then release a bleeding-heart humanitarian statement on the rampant famine, six months in. When challenged on her silence regarding the holocaust by protestors from her own staff at USAID, she has spoken vaguely about mass sexual assaults by Hamas.[79] (This, long after that genocide-justifying distraction had been debunked.[80]) But no doubt her feminism lent the missiles she helped launch a sorrowful, gender-emancipatory character, much as Madeleine Albright's feminist bombs on Iraq in the 1990s were, in Albright's solemn phrase, "worth it."[81]

As girlboss militarism illustrates, updates on the capitalist-feminist brand are always in the pipeline, always re-upping the fantasy of the good boss—the boss*babe*. In the wake of the 2020 uprisings, swaths of US business culture entered the discursive era of intersectional feminism sans class, an utter travesty of the original commitments embedded in the term "intersectionality." As Ashley Bohrer's history *Marxism and Intersectionality* lays out, the concept of intersectionality emerged from an anti-identitarian Black struggle against capitalism and imperialism spearheaded by feminist communists from the 1930s into the '70s, from Claudia Jones to Frances Beal. In 2021, I have zero doubt, both Jones and Beal began spinning in their graves, because none other than the CIA—the lethal enemy of communism all over the world—aired a promotional video starring an "intersectional" girlboss of color.

The recruitment clip in question is part of an ad campaign called "Humans of CIA" and, in it, the CIA spotlights a female Latina agent, backed by inspirational muzak, chatting with Vice President Kamala Harris, and proclaiming (nonsensically, given that intersectionality is a heuristic, not a characteristic) that she "is" intersectional.[82] Under her blazer, the agent is wearing a T-shirt with the classic feminist symbol of a fist inside the "female" sign printed on it, as well as the words, "Mija: YOU ARE WORTH IT." In public discussions of the ad, "Mija" (meaning "my daughter" or "honey" in Spanish) has also been treated as the agent's name. Behind her, in one shot, is a children's drawing bearing the motto, "NOBODY CARES: WORK HARDER." (Mussolini meets Frances Willard.)

The voiceover of Mija's CIA prose poetry is worth quoting in full, including its shout-out to the author of *Their Eyes Were Watching God*, conservatives' favorite anticommunist Black woman:

> When I was 17, I quoted Zora Neale Hurston's "How It Feels to Be Colored Me" in my college application essay. The line that spoke to me stated simply, "I am not tragically colored. There is no great sorrow dammed up in my soul, nor lurking behind my eyes. I do not mind at all."

I imagine forgiveness and an absence of racial rage are helpful if one is going to work for the CIA.

> At 17, I had no idea what life would bring, but that sentiment articulated so beautifully how I felt as a daughter of immigrants, then and now. Nothing about me is tragic.

On the other hand, making bloodbaths of social movements and installing right-wing dictators across the Global South is surely not un-tragic. To say nothing of the tragically individualistic anti-whining maxim "nobody cares, work harder!"

> I am perfectly made. I can wax eloquent on complex legal issues in English while also belting "Guayaquil de Mis Amores" in Spanish.

OK, but why is the "complexity" of being an Anglo spook here being contrasted with the putatively less civilized simplicity of singing Ecuadorian pasillos?

> I can change a diaper with one hand and console a crying toddler with the other. I'm a woman of color. I'm a mom. I'm a cisgender millennial who's been diagnosed with generalized anxiety disorder. I am intersectional. But my existence is not a box-checking exercise. I'm a walking declaration, a woman whose inflection does not rise at the end of her sentences suggesting that a question has been asked.

Mija's maneuver here involves using femmephobia (in the denigration of uptalk) as the foil for her professional-imperial maternalism. Flashing liberals the badge of "relatable" obstacles (POC, millennial, mom, anxiety), she performs a macho, self-responsible refusal to whinge about oppression. Next up is a salute to American meritocracy:

> I did not sneak into the CIA. My employment was not and is not the result of a fluke or slipped through the cracks. I earned my way in, and I earned my way *up* the ranks of this organization. I am educated, qualified, and competent. And sometimes I struggle! I struggle feeling I could do more—*be* more—to my two sons, and I struggle leaving the office when I feel there's so much more to do.

One way she does not struggle at *all* is apparently against discrimination within the CIA (who needs diversity, equity, and inclusion [DEI] in such a great workplace?). Here, the Intersectional Girlboss of Color combines liberal antiracism with a canny synthesis of the "Sandberg" and "Slaughter" positions as popularly construed. One senses she is about to quote Sandberg's "Ban Bossy" campaign (which seeks an end to that word's application to assertive girls) and follow it up with a Slaughter quote about "fitting care and career together."[83]

> I used to struggle with imposter syndrome but, at thirty-six, I refuse to internalize misguided patriarchal ideas about what a woman can or should be. I am tired of feeling like I'm supposed to apologize for the space I occupy, rather than intoxicate people with my effort, my brilliance. I am proud of me. My parents left everything they knew and loved to expose me to opportunities they never had. Because of them, I stand here today, a proud, first-generation Latina, and officer at CIA.

Of course, if the family emigrated north from Guatemala, Chile, Ecuador, Argentina, Bolivia, Colombia, El Salvador, Honduras, Nicaragua, or Panama, they might have been fleeing the CIA.

> I am unapologetically me. I want *you* to be unapologetically *you*, whoever you are, whether you work at CIA, or anywhere else in the world. Command your space. Mija, you are worth it.[84]

The appropriation of a "without apology" stance by people who frankly *should* apologize (as a bare minimum) for all manner of executive-level ruthlessness—or in this case, the quite literal command of extralegal death squads—is my least favorite rhetorical aspect of the doctrine of girlbossismo. It is helpful, though, to see so many strands of the ideology come together in one CIA recruitment video. Even though there is no "brown feminist" per se in the ad (if anything, Mija is it), the "Mija" spotlight in "Humans of CIA" aptly illustrates the slipping of "the intersectional mask" ("whenever a brown feminist steps out of line") that Zakaria pinpointed. With its preemptive repudiations of affirmative action and box ticking, Mija's speech is constantly addressing a left-antiracist

Other—someone who just doesn't work hard enough, complains, and has a negative attitude. Even as she draws attention to her "color," in other words, Mija's leaning in is proudly served up as no more racially marked than Sandberg's own. Mija is a brown white queen on the lecture stand: the "post-racial" imperium's Jane Bull.

Girlbosses are never themselves children but, like manbosses—indeed, bosses of all genders—they do cause the death of a great deal of actual girls (even when they aren't in the FBI or USAID or the military). As Sophia Amoruso once knew, the acquisition of capitalist power automatically entails the despoliation of the biosphere, the desecration of indigenous knowledges, and the extraction of life support from colonized, proletarianized, and feminized human beings. Diplomatically, one might offer, with theorist Janet Halley, that "any force as powerful as feminism must find itself occasionally looking down at its own bloody hands."[85] Still, the fact that the bloodletting *is feminism* hardly lets the girlbosses who instigated it off the hook. We should lay to rest the question of whether the girlboss lives or is dead. She was never exactly alive in the first place. So long as capital rules over earthly social relations, the girlboss shall forever remain undead. After all, as Marx contends, "capital is dead labor, which, vampire-like, lives only by sucking living labor, and lives the more, the more labor it sucks."[86] If we really want to bury the girlboss, we might consider beginning with a general girlstrike.

TEN

The Femonationalist

ERIC ANDRÉ: Do you think Margaret Thatcher had girl power?
SPICE GIRL MEL B: Yes, of course!
ERIC ANDRÉ: Do you think she effectively utilized girl power by funneling money to illegal paramilitary death squads in Northern Ireland?
SPICE GIRL MEL B: I . . . I don't know about that.

—*The Eric André Show*, 2013[1]

In February 2021, the prestigious publishing house HarperCollins released a book entitled *Prey: Immigration, Islam, and the Erosion of Women's Rights*, a salvo against the much-vaunted threat of Muslim migrants' ultra-misogynist violence. The blurb promised to blow the lid off a problem that "few people" dare mention and "no one in a position of power wants to admit."[2] The author of the book in question, although a scion of the neoconservative think tank American Enterprise Institute (AEI), is a self-described "classical liberal" and a feminist. *Prey* is her sixth book. At the Zoom release party, arranged by the Commonwealth Club ("the nation's biggest public affairs forum"), the proudly "canceled" journalist Bari Weiss nodded along while the star of the show talked about an "epidemic" of male Muslim violence currently sweeping European cities. The disease in question was the cause, said the celebrated author, of a mass exodus out of Europe, currently underway, of women and of Jews.[3] Immigration to the US is such a "success story," she said (relative to the Islamized mess in which Europe apparently finds itself), because those individuals who made it "all the way" over the ocean to America historically were, by definition, the fittest and the strongest among humanity.[4] Who *was* this neo-eugenicist luminary? The answer, of course, is Ayaan Hirsi Ali.

Hirsi Ali's foundation is called the Ayaan Hirsi Ali Foundation ("AHA"—as in, *eureka!*), which fights for the "liberty to challenge the ideology of Islamism." Her previous hits—which also address, without exception, the inherent violence of Islam—all bear titles like *Infidel: My Life*, *The Caged Virgin: A Muslim Woman's Cry for Reason*, and *Heretic: Why Islam Needs a Reformation Now*. In monotonous and shamelessly overlapping vignettes, these books argue that "Western civilization" urgently needs to be defended against Muslim barbarity in its myriad forms. It has now been over two decades since a Dutch feminist magazine, *Opzij*, midwifed Hirsi Ali's entry into global politics.[5] Since then, she has gained a regular column in the *Wall Street Journal* and is routinely hailed by the likes of "new atheist" celebrity Sam Harris as "one of the most poised, intelligent and compassionate advocates of freedom of speech and conscience alive today."[6]

Unfortunately, another fan of hers is the incarcerated far-right 2011 Norwegian mass shooter Anders Behring Breivik. In his manifesto exposing the Muslim plot to conquer Christendom, Breivik demanded, "Give the Nobel Peace Prize to Ayaan Hirsi Ali." Astonishingly, Hirsi Ali returned the compliment (in a manner of speaking), lending validity to Breivik's reasons for massacring socialist teenagers, during a prize-acceptance speech in Berlin:

> That one man who killed seventy-seven people in Norway, because he fears that Europe will be overrun by Islam, may have cited the work of those who speak and write against political Islam in Europe and America—myself among them—but he does not say that it was these people who inspired him to kill. He says very clearly that it was the advocates of silence. Because all outlets to express

his views were censored, he says, he had no other choice but to use violence.[7]

Who is Ayaan Hirsi Ali? To answer this question without fueling at least some elements of the lurid mythmaking that is @Ayaan—and burnishing that brand's mystique—may prove impossible. I suspect I will inevitably end up shoring up some aspects of Ayaan™: the personality cult, the feminist institution, the exotic mascot, the free speech warrior, the all-American poster child of Third World anticommunism, the symbol of escape from "savagery," the imperial-humanitarian romance.

Hirsi Ali is a professor at the Hoover Institution at Stanford University. Her spouse is Niall Ferguson, a British historian whose pro-colonial jingoism is unparalleled. She is, additionally, a fan of several other canonically Western-supremacist thinkers, notably Bernard Lewis (a fellow AEI scholar), Friedrich von Hayek, and Samuel Huntington. She presents unironically as a "daughter of the Enlightenment"[8] and a "combatant in the clash of civilizations"[9] (the latter being a reference to the Huntingtonian worldview that depicts the world, *Lord of the Rings* style, as a battle between oriental darkness and occidental light). Pointing out the overlaps between this woman's worldview and that of an Islamophobic mass shooter ought not to feel like a hysterical move, given, you know, her own apologia for him. Yet it does. In a 2010 *New York Times* interview, simply entitled "The Feminist," Hirsi Ali responds to the question, "Do you see yourself as a conservative?" with the words, "No. I see myself as a liberal, a classical liberal."[10] This isn't a recognized terrorist—it's a senior fellow at Harvard's Kennedy School! Yet she's never retracted her characterization of Islam, in 2007, as "a destructive nihilistic cult of death." Interviewed for *Reason* magazine, she stated that Islam must be "crushed."[11] "Don't you mean *radical* Islam?" expostulated the interviewer. "No. Islam, period," she replied. *But, but* . . . "Crush the world's 1.5 billion Muslims under our boot?" A pregnant pause. "I think we are at war with Islam. . . . There comes a moment when you crush your enemy."

None of this genocidal invective has prevented "AHA" from receiving the Lantos Human Rights Prize—also awarded to Holocaust survivor and writer Elie Wiesel—or various other prizes for defending "women's rights." Like so many of the self-proclaimed "canceled," she seems uncancelable. When Muslim feminists in Australia mount a petition protesting her views, she makes headlines denouncing them for "carrying water" for "the terrorists."[12] When, under pressure from student protestors, Brandeis University reverses its decision to grant her an honorary degree, it's a great opportunity for Ayaan™ to bemoan liberals' pusillanimity for not standing up for her, and to team up with Republican politicians like Bill Kristol, who has seized on the decision as "an example of a war on women."[13] When all this behavior gets her listed in a "Field Guide to Anti-Muslim Extremists" published by the hate-group watchdog Southern Poverty Law Center, she is (as usual) offered an op-ed in the *New York Times*—"Why Is the Southern Poverty Law Center Targeting Liberals?"—which she uses to complain about the disproportionate attention being afforded to the minor matter of white supremacists having murdered a woman in Charlottesville.[14] People should care more about *Islamist* violence, chides Hirsi Ali. Feminists should care *only* about Islamist violence.

Hirsi Ali's biography begins with her birth in Mogadishu; her devout grandmother's illiteracy; her subjection, at age five, at grandma's hands, to clitoral excision (carried out against her imprisoned father's wishes); and her education by strict Shia teachers in Nairobi including in a youth group affiliated with the Muslim Brotherhood. The story continues with her decision in 1992 not to travel to Canada for an arranged marriage but instead to flee, seeking asylum in the Netherlands—and subsequently she undergoes even deeper alienation from her biological family. At this juncture, she studies politics at Leiden University and serves briefly in a Dutch Labor Party think tank as an immigration researcher. But upon receipt of Dutch citizenship, she defects to the right-wing People's Party for Freedom and Democracy and gets elected as a minister in 2003. Here, she authors the screenplay for an eleven-minute anti-Islam movie called *Submission (Part 1)*, broadcast on Dutch public television in 2004. The director of the movie, Theo van Gogh, is promptly shot and half-decapitated in the street by a Muslim man who uses a knife to pin, to the still-warm corpse, a letter full of death threats addressed to "Mrs. Hirshi-Ali." The government of the Netherlands beefs up her state-appointed security detail. However, two years later, they order her to leave her governmental safe house because neighbors feel unsafe. Threats erupt within her own (racist) right-wing party to strip her of Dutch citizenship, based on revelations that she slightly falsified her surname and birth date on her original asylum form. Finally, she moves to the US, where, once again, she is promptly recruited by the right.

Ever since the brutal assassination of filmmaker Theo van Gogh on November 2, 2004, Hirsi Ali has refused to put so much as a hair's breadth between her name and that particular "free speech martyr."[15] His demise is a tale she's invoked in almost all of her speeches and publications since the day itself. The story has provided the drumbeat, patterning her every narration of her transformation—from Nairobi to The Hague, from Somali to American citizenship, from Islam to enlightenment, and from mutilated fugitive to internationally acclaimed Ivy League fellow. Her ceaseless repetition of the facts of the man's death is transfixing, libidinized, as congealed trauma often is. Audiences are rapt, picturing Mr. van Gogh expiring under a hail of bullets and a pair of hacking blades, using his dying breath (according to eyewitnesses) to ask his assailant the immortal humanist question: "Can't we talk about this?"[16] Strangely intimate with the details of the terrorist butchery, she recounts: "Then he took out one of his butcher knives and sawed into Theo's throat. With the other knife, he stabbed a five-page letter onto Theo's chest." At this point, Hirsi Ali tends to leave a space, open a new paragraph, and dramatically disclose: "The letter was addressed to me."

The personal shock that clearly propels Hirsi Ali's public repetitions of the details of her friend's bloody death at the hands of the militant Dutch "Hofstad Network"—a killing that was framed as a communiqué *to her*—is nothing if not understandable. Empathy with her traumatic experience should not prevent any of us, however, from calling out the cravenness of her weaponization of said trauma to bloodthirsty, militaristic ends. Think of any Islam-related imbroglio of recent memory; you already know what she is going to say. Responding to anger at the cartoon *South Park*'s depiction of Islam's sacred prophet, she floats the idea of disseminating "stories of Muhammad where his image is shown *as much as possible*" so as to "confront hypersensitive Muslims with more targets than they can possibly contend with."[17] When Obama fails to sufficiently "associate Islam with extremism" (her words) in his speeches, she calls him a pussy.[18] Clearly nostalgic for the Bush-era ethos of overt crusade, she insists, in the *Wall Street Journal*, that Islam and America are "at war."[19] Since coming to the US, Ayaan has continued to imply she is in danger (of becoming a free speech martyr like Theo). She has, however, accrued great wealth and acquired a fan club and a famous husband. She's as secure as the next ruling-class shock jock. It is her suite of manufactured "cancellation" scandals about herself—perfectly pitched to the anti-"woke" media, who eat every nugget up—that suggest otherwise.

Like many, I hoped that Hirsi Ali's brand of anti-Muslim, imperial feminism had peaked back in the early 2000s, in that ghoulish moment when Laura Bush, and later Cherie Blair, declared the invasion of Afghanistan a war of women's liberation ("lift the veil!").[20] In retrospect, it seems silly to have imagined this would have been possible in the absence of a process of thoroughgoing decolonization around the world. "Already extinct" is surely far too optimistic a prognosis for Hirsi Ali's politics, which retains real popularity in the form of contemporary figures like Irshad Manji, Taslima Nasrin, and Seyran Ateş. Ayaan™ is merely the best-known vessel for a deft quilting of imperial pro-femaleness and "free speech" that ensures, with every generation, the rise of these glittering new monsters, these liberal intellectuals for border brutality, these celebrity feminists for George W. Bush and Donald Trump and Ron DeSantis. The brand now boasts new standard-bearers such as Sarah Haider, who runs the organization Ex-Muslims of America.[21] Speaking of which, in November 2023, Hirsi Ali publicly converted to Christianity in a Western civilizationist gesture of solidarity with the

US-backed destruction of Palestine.[22] "God Bless Ayaan Hirsi Ali," gushed the headline of the *National Review*.

Before Hirsi Ali even came to America, a researcher asked the Dutch philosopher Rosi Braidotti: "Who is Ayaan Hirsi Ali?" "A right-wing anti-Islam feminist," Rosi replied.[23] By any standard, this description remains true today. Hirsi Ali has always denied that she is right wing, but the American Enterprise Institute is not exactly secretive about its stances. This is one "classical liberal," then, who compares Black Lives Matter to ISIL[24] and complains when Trump "loses focus" by delaying implementation of the "Muslim ban" (the "extreme vetting" scheme targeting Arab immigrants and visitors to the US).[25] A regular on Fox News, she is the darling of platforms such as *Breitbart* and the *Federalist*. Former Fox host Tucker Carlson contrasts her with the left-leaning congresswoman Ilhan Omar: "Two Somali immigrants, one among the most impressive people in America. The other, among the least!"[26] It is, then, the third element of Braidotti's definition—"feminist"—that seems the most tenuous. I mean, what kind of feminist tweets, in September 2018, "Confirm Brett Kavanaugh"?[27] Well, a *femonationalist*, that's who.

The term "femonationalism" was coined by the sociologist Sara Farris to describe putatively gender-progressive occidentalist attitudes like the ones on display in Hirsi Ali's *Nomad: From Islam to America: A Personal Journey Through the Clash of Civilizations* (2010). "Femonationalism," Farris writes, "refers both to the exploitation of feminist themes by nationalists and neoliberals in anti-Islam (but also anti-immigration) campaigns and to the participation of certain feminists and femocrats in the stigmatization of Muslim men under the banner of gender equality."[28] Be they public intellectuals like Ayaan, or far-right politicians like Britain's Priti Patel and France's Marine Le Pen, or veterans of 1960s left radicalism like Germany's second-wave feminist icon Alice Schwarzer, femonationalists vindicate an ideal of female dignity, freedom, and integrity in order to mount an "enlightened" yet maternally muscular defense of the national economy against foreign threats, which they paint as misogynistically backward.

This is how xenophobic nationalist politics become synonymous with women's rights. It means that female migrants, for example, are loaded down on arrival with "How to Live in the Netherlands" starter packs that presume—especially on the male migrants' part—a regressive, sexist starting point that needs to be "enlightened" with a womanly touch (even as the feminist host society enrolls female arrivals in hyper-traditionally "sexed" forms of low-paid work). A Syrian woman may find herself feministly welcomed to Europe, but only on condition that she toil in janitorial or eldercare facilities and commit to preaching the gospel of assimilation to her menfolk.

In the Name of Women's Rights: The Rise of Femonationalism is Farris's landmark account of a nasty new European policy turn that systematically channels non-Western women into shitty, precarious jobs within highly gendered industries such as nursing and sanitation, and—incredibly—does this in the name of gender equality. Various EU countries, Farris demonstrates, have also been tasking non-white migrant women with the propagation of Western national values in their households, as a way of defending "civilized" womanhood from the bodily threat posed by unassimilated males.

The idea, here, is essentially that the (typically Muslim) woman, properly trained in feminism, will create a non-terrorist husband and raise productive male and female workers who will serve, rather than attack, the European state. Put differently, non-Western migrant women have been constructed as a useful and beneficial "regular army of labor," even as their brothers, sons, nephews, and spouses are figured as an unwanted "reserve." There are two interrelated phobic constructs of the male Muslim here working in tandem: even if he can be rendered non-terrorist by his well-trained wife, he remains an insurgent surplus that threatens the national economy.

Femonationalism, in practical terms, is how neoliberals, feminist agencies, and right-wing populists come together to bring us burqa bans, pronatalist welfare packages, civic integration schemes, and xenophobic two-tier "workfare" policies.[29] It is also visible in Hirsi Ali's articulation of the American nation-state's prerogative to remake (or "structurally readjust") foreign regimes, by force, in the name of women's rights. Take this suggestion in the introduction of Hirsi Ali's book *Nomad*: "Western feminists should take on the plight of the Muslim woman and make it their own cause."[30] Or this, from the end of *Infidel* (2006):

> I wanted Muslim women to become more aware of just how bad, and how unacceptable, their suffering was. I was inspired by Mary Wollstonecraft. . . . Even after she published *Vindication of the Rights of Women*, it took more than a century before the suffragettes marched for the vote. I knew that freeing Muslim women from their mental cage would take time, too. I didn't expect immediate waves of organized support among Muslim women. People who are conditioned to meekness, almost to the point where they have no mind of their own, sadly have no ability to organize, or will to express their opinion.[31]

Ayaan neatly demonstrates how an occidentalist civilizational crusade, underwritten by a universalist definition of sexed suffering, can become the rallying cry of liberal democracy's paladins.

"Crusade" actually is a justified choice of word, because secular-Christian fundamentalists like Hirsi Ali sometimes sincerely advance the notion that, to borrow one reviewer's phrase, "atheists and agnostics should join forces with the Vatican in a religious war."[32] Speaking to the *London Evening Standard*, Hirsi Ali says that Westerners are the victims of a "great deception" that leads us to believe that Muslims are moderate, when, in fact, "Islam is the new fascism."[33] In *Nomad,* she writes:

> [T]he children of the Enlightenment are hopelessly fragmented in their views about how to deal with Islam. . . . [I]n time of war, internal feuding in the ranks—between atheists and agnostics, Christians and Jews, Protestants and Catholics—serves only to weaken the West. . . . We should bury the hatchet, rearrange our priorities, and fight together against a much more dangerous common enemy. . . . The West urgently needs to compete with the jihadis, the proponents of a holy war, for the hearts and minds of its own Muslim immigrant populations. It needs to provide

education directed at breaking the spell of the infallible Prophet, to protect women from the oppressive dictates of the Quran. . . .[34]

Die-hard Ayaan fanboys will tell you, at this point, that she changed her mind and adopted (albeit vacillatingly) a *reformist* rather than an eliminationist approach to Islam in subsequent years. But it is her pro-reform writings' shoddy historiography and calls for an Islamic "Reformation" that have earned Ayaan her most entertainingly obliterating press—for instance, the review by journalist Mehdi Hasan that contemplates, for the sake of argument, what a "Muslim Martin Luther" would look like (Hasan concludes: "Isis leader Abu Bakr al-Baghdadi").[35] Anyone remember the sixteenth-century Saint Bartholomew's Day massacre?

Today, twenty years after Islamists' assassination of an Islamophobic filmmaker in Amsterdam, there can be relatively few people alive who dedicate as much of their time as does Ayaan Hirsi Ali to beating the war drum for Pentagon-led invasions and praising the sacred republic of the US for its culture of enlightenment, goodwill, and freedom (which she sees as bolstered by the peaceful Christian "God of love"). Hirsi Ali tells the feminist Cathy Young that "the best place to be a woman in the world is in the US. The best place to be Black in the world is in the US."[36] So why, oh why, are people who call themselves "liberals," as she calls herself, so ungrateful and unpatriotic, she asks? Why can't feminists in the US stop complaining about minor distractions like gendered Islamophobia and systemic misogynoir, get their priorities straight, count their blessings (being free from the compulsion to wear the hijab or get their clitorises chopped off), and focus on the most important thing ever to have happened in living memory: namely, the "Mrs. Hirshi-Ali" letter pinned to a Dutchman's corpse? Hello? "My friend and collaborator Theo van Gogh was murdered in broad daylight," she exasperatedly reminds the world for the thousandth time in the aforementioned 2017 *New York Times* op-ed. "Yet the S.P.L.C. has the audacity to label me an 'extremist.'"

Actually, a more precise term for Hirsi Ali and her ilk—coined by the director of the Institute of Race Relations (IRR) in the UK,

Liz Fekete—is "enlightened fundamentalist."[37] As the IRR has painstakingly tracked for two decades, the camp of enlightened fundamentalism, born with the war on terror, consists largely of a stack of paradoxes: censors against censorship, jihadists against jihad, ragings against rage, multiculturalists against multiculturalism. For example, feminists like Ayaan™ focus on the plight of Muslim women even while they ignore most Muslim women's speech. They stand for "free speech" even while calling for the criminalization of Muslim anger. They condemn intolerance while demanding that a religion be crushed. And their paradoxical sentiments can be found everywhere: from the mouths of Nikki Haley and Hillary Clinton; in the platforms of the "pro-woman" neofascist National Rally in France (formerly *Front National*) or Northern League in Italy; and in the German media, where pundits speculate about the parenting failures responsible for Muslim perpetrators of urban sexual harassment.[38] They can be found, too, in academia, where the accursed question, "Is multiculturalism bad for women?"[39] resurfaces every few years.

The idea that multiculturalism "has failed" women and girls in Europe flows from the lips of formidable blondes Alice Schwarzer (Germany's number-one radical feminist elder) and Marine Le Pen (French fascist party leader and daughter of Holocaust-denier Jean-Marie) alike. Here, the two figures merge. Le Pen has said, for example, that immigrant neighborhoods are the only reason why France has a sexism problem. Similarly, as a reporter for *New York Times Magazine* found to his astonishment in 2016, some German neo-Nazis are unabashed exponents of feminism when it comes to keeping brown people out of Germany. "With us, men and women are equal," explained a retired Bavarian metalworker and *Lederhosen* folklorist, contrasting his own Prussian gender-liberated culture to that of the Syrian refugees he felt were threatening to crowd out his village. Too many migrants coming over the border is the reason "why the Germans will get nasty again," said another villager, flashing a Nazi salute in order to drive his point home.[40]

The magazine feature in question was part of a global wave of curiosity about upheavals in German society taking place in the

wake of a mass incident of sexual violence on the very final day
of 2015—a year that had, itself, been dominated continuously by
narratives of a so-called "migrant crisis." The incident was seized on
as the final nail in the coffin of Europe's "multiculturalism experiment." It became known simply as "Cologne."

It seems that, on New Year's Eve, a number of men committed
a rash of petty robberies and open-air sexual assaults on the plaza
between Cologne's cathedral and the central station. The victims
were almost exclusively women, and the crimes were attributed to
a "small multitude" of North African and Middle Eastern youths,
thought to be asylum seekers. To quote *New York Times Magazine*:
"By mid-March, 1,139 criminal complaints had been filed; 485 of
them involved sexual offenses, ranging from sexual insults to groping and rape. The police response was widely viewed as a cover-up,
and the outrage was widespread." Headlines imbued with much
the same sentiments expressed by the fascist-feminist Bavarians became commonplace throughout Germany: "Tolerance for religious
worldviews ends in violence and murder"; [41] "These young men [the
Arab migrants] are bringing with them a culture of violence"; [42]
"Such patriarchal men cannot be integrated."[43]

A mere four days after the New Year's Eve incidents in Cologne,
Alice Schwarzer published her first statement—a widely republished essay entitled "The Consequences of False Tolerance." Already, her completely unevidenced framework for apprehending
"that fateful night" was entirely in place: "These sexual assaults
were coordinated, [and] the perpetrators were Islamists."[44] Further,
she (somehow) was able to divulge:

> The terrorism did not involve Kalashnikovs or suicide-bomber
> vests; rather, it rained down in the form of firework-launchers and
> whizzcrackers, and above all, men's groping hands. They're just
> boys, for now . . . they are still just practicing.[45]

To be clear: there has never emerged any data whatsoever to suggest any level of coordination, let alone any *Islamist* logic or purpose, behind the horrible cluster of sexual street violence meted out
on "Silvesternacht" (New Year's Eve). But Alice only escalated, from

here, her carceral, belligerent claims. Two weeks later, in an interview in *Der Spiegel*, she recalled a conversation that, supposedly, laid bare the liberal establishment's calculated suppression of what German policemen had long known. "Once, about 20 years ago, a police officer in Cologne told me, 'Ms. Schwarzer, 70 to 80 percent of the rapists in Cologne are Turkish.'"[46] In her telling, no one listened to the boys in blue, and the result was that hundreds of women had been assaulted. In a way, the police "were themselves victims."[47]

The media circus around "Cologne" was so comprehensive, and the reverberations in government policy so stark, that two German philosophers were moved to focus an entire book, *The Future of Difference*, on the historical meaning and racist ramifications of the event.[48] Sabine Hark and Paula-Irene Villa argue that Cologne was no less than "a tectonic shift in Germany's social fabric."[49] The very word, they note dryly, became a kind of "quilting-point" in the national conversation: Cologne "seems to have secured a far greater degree of cultural receptivity to feminist concerns" even as it coupled that receptivity to a racist logic of carceralism and established "the need for comprehensive CCTV surveillance." Women required vigilance patrols to protect them from the brutal alien enemies who had infiltrated the land. The feminism born in Cologne, in other words, was more or less of the ultranationalist ex-suffragette Commandant Mary Allen's school.

Femonationalists like Alice Schwarzer, the founder of Germany's answer to *Ms.* magazine—*EMMA*—experienced Cologne as a long-awaited watershed, to the point that they were sometimes at pains not to betray their glee about it. In February 2016, not even two full months after Cologne, the German government adjusted its refugee policy, "Asylum Package II," and barred asylum applications from Morocco, Algeria, and Tunisia (this, luckily, was later challenged). Then, in July, it finally passed certain reforms to Germany's criminal law on sexual violence—the law known as §177—that feminist activists, Schwarzer among them, had been fruitlessly demanding for decades. (In 1981, for instance, *EMMA* published its founding editor's strikingly Andrea Dworkin–esque denunciation of a German court justice's exoneration verdict in a rape case, based on §177: "A declaration of war on all women."[50])

Most of the actions reported by the survivors of Cologne, pre-§177 reforms, were not yet prosecutable offences under German law at the time. But this did not prevent the encroachment of a decidedly conspiratorial strain in the German public conversation. Something sinister, some kind of woke cabal, rumor had it, was protecting the "young men of North African and Middle Eastern appearance." Popular fury grew greater and greater over police failures to prosecute the suspects. At one point, even many formerly antiracist voices were referring to the suspects as "Nafris," which is the North Rhine/Westphalia Police Department's internal acronym and radio shorthand for *Nordafrikanische Intensivtäter*—literally, "North African repeat offenders." Also, denunciations of male chauvinism were suddenly everywhere. "Absence of consent" was established for the first time in Germany as "the central factor in criminal liability for sexual violence."[51] A small handful of celebrity liberals and "radical feminist" right wingers—notably the nation's "feminist in chief" Ms. Schwarzer—became near-permanent features of the national TV news, newspaper op-eds, and talk-show circuits. But in Germany's new zeal to become what Hark and Villa skeptically call "a feminist nation,"[52] a number of bitter ironies soon emerged. Notably, the women who had actually been harmed and groped, far from being centered in Germany's response, disappeared from public view, just as their assailants did. They were largely rendered unreal, two-dimensional, and voiceless.

Magazine covers ran cartoon images of naked white female bodies menaced from all sides by dark, groping hands (a tactic much repeated after October 7, 2023, to illustrate comparable narratives about Hamas militants' brutal assaults on Israeli women). They posed the ominous question, "What REALLY happened that night?" and speculated about whether, on a national level, tolerance had perhaps been taken too far. "Have we gone blind?" one popular German magazine pointedly asked. The overall message was unmistakable: your nation, your culture, is in peril.

As is often the case in such sex panics, the overall reality was closer to the reverse. Already before Cologne, attacks on Muslims had been steadily increasing across Europe and North America. After Cologne, they continued to rise.[53] Pew surveys of non-Muslims in the US and Western Europe now suggest that about half think Islam is not a part of mainstream (that is, gender equal!) society; while a similar number (44 percent) say there is "a natural conflict between Islam and democracy."[54] In 2017, an Australian senator called Islam a "disease" that children should be vaccinated against.[55] Soon after, armed Islamophobes carried out attacks in Christchurch, New Zealand, and Hanau, Germany. Under Donald Trump, there was going to be "a total and complete shutdown of Muslims entering the United States"—the "ban" applauded by Ayaan Hirsi Ali.

Cologne was not the last, and it was hardly the first time "Muslim sexism" became the premise for uniting non-Muslim metropoles under women's rights qua civilizational standard. Hundreds of years of narratives about the supposed virulence of oriental misogyny inflected the twenty-first-century coinage of "rapefugees"— that is, asylum-seeking rapists surging into weak and feminized Western lands whose overly "compassionate" border regimes require muscular reinforcement by race-realist strongmen.[56] Cologne was primed to happen. There was practically a pre-written script ready to go. In cultural studies terms, it was "overdetermined." Before any survivors could even speak, matters automatically clicked into place as the latest in a long chain of outrages against white womanhood. The events, before they were understood or even thinly evidenced, were, as Hark and Villa note in *The Future of Difference*, made to "stand for the assertion that certain migrants cannot be integrated—*they do not want to integrate*—simply because, in the end, there are insuperable differences between the cultures in question."[57]

Schwarzer's book on Cologne came out just five months after Cologne. It was entitled "Der Schock" (*The Shock: Cologne on New Year's Eve 2015*), and according to the publisher's blurb, Schwarzer "draws parallels between Cologne's central station, Tahrir Square, and Iran under Khomeini." She calls for an end to the so-called "Culture of Welcome" (*Willkommenskultur*) that was implemented by overly kindhearted Germans, under the advisement of the nefarious chancellor Angela Merkel, during the great "summer of migrants" of 2015. By opening their hearts and doors to Muslim refugees, she argues, Germans have "naïvely imported male violence, sexism and anti-Semitism." Citizens have "really been taken for a ride." Naturally, in 2016, far-right parties like the AfD, völkisch pundits like the family-values traditionalist Birgit Kelle, and neofascist networks like Pegida likewise seized on the "shock" of Cologne to remake German reality and the German state. Albeit ostensibly a lefty, Alice Schwarzer was deeply useful to these other players with her claims that the national policies of "tolerance" and "multiculturalism" had died a death at the hands of those Arab men, among those infernal fireworks. To their delight, assorted nationalists, white supremacists, alt-right populists, and more or less covert Nazis now found that their talking points were being consistently aired in the public arena by a septuagenarian lady who—to quote political scientist Ina Kerner—"sees the world exclusively through sex/gender goggles."[58] The lenses are "race blind," which is to say, white supremacist.

Do the racisms and feminisms here collude, then, or do they merge? Are they making opportunistic alliances and instrumentalizing one another, or are they impossible to disentangle? The more years I spend on this question, the more I want to say that racism *is* a patriarchal form of feminism. By uniting under the banner of women's rights, racist women and racist men offer one another a mandate to be patriarchal toward backward "civilizations." After all, their own societies are superior *because* they are feminist, even if this means that calling attention to gender injustices between and among themselves becomes difficult to do without seeming unpatriotic. Rather than air dirty laundry, racist women are often more than willing to prioritize racial over sexed solidarity, and racist men, in turn, are sometimes happy to fight for racist women's limited equalities. As Josie, one of my students, phrased it in a discussion of the "white woman's burden" in history: "This entire topic is basically the times when *feminism and racism were the same thing.*"[59]

Alice Schwarzer originally became famous for palling around on Paris's Left Bank with Simone de Beauvoir, and for replicating in Germany the famous French "manifesto of the 343," in which many celebrities signed a petition declaring, in 1971, that they had had an abortion. Albeit linked to these socialist-feminist origins, Schwarzer has been a fountainhead of nativist bigotry at least ever since her journalistic stint in Tehran in mid-March of 1979, during the Iranian Revolution.[60] Over the years that followed, she aligned herself unambiguously with CDU/CSU, the center-right "Christian-democratic" duo of political parties that adopted the motto "Germany is not a country for foreigners" in its 1998 election platform. Emilia Müller, head of the women's division of the conservative CSU of Bavaria, hailed Schwarzer in 2010 as "our pioneer and champion . . . our feminist foremother."[61]

According to her own 2002 memoir *Alice in MrLand: An Interim Appraisal by Alice Schwarzer,* she is a lone titan of "emancipation" who has been making inroads for her sisters in a world of men ever since the 1960s.[62] Although often analogized to the mainstream American figure Betty Friedan, Schwarzer likes to style herself as somewhat edgier than that. She cites, as her influences, the more "radical" Americans from the prohibitionist side of the sex wars: Susan Brownmiller, Catharine MacKinnon, and Andrea Dworkin. Mixing all these influences into a Manichaean, civilizationist, patriotic brew, Schwarzer—according to journalist Alena Schröder—"understands feminism as a kind of hereditary monarchy in which she is the infallible and uncriticizable queen."[63]

Besides editing *EMMA* and appearing on numerous TV cooking shows, the queen supreme is the founder of the Alice Schwarzer Stiftung, a think tank dedicated to criminalizing prostitution and banning porn (Por*NO* is the name of the latter campaign).[64] She also created, with public funds, a nonprofit archive of feminist history, which is housed in a medieval turret in Cologne's old city center: the "FrauenMediaTurm" (Women Media Tower).[65] Nonetheless,

Schwarzer's clear predilection is for fighting other women—she does not, as a rule, publicly debate men. In 1975, half the country watched her do battle with the antifeminist writer Esther Vilar on live TV. That was the year she founded *EMMA* and forsook the leftist publisher Suhrkamp in favor of the mainstream Fischer Verlag in order to publish her bestseller, *The Little Difference and Its Big Consequences*. A quarter century later, Germans everywhere tuned in again for an even more bigoted showdown ("the Body vs. the Brain") between Alice Schwarzer and Miss Germany, the beauty pageant model Verona Feldbusch. Upon being charged by Schwarzer with hurting women's image, Ms. Feldbusch pointed out that Schwarzer was, astutely, wearing lipstick and mascara too. More recently, her antagonists for big, ugly public fights have included the neoconservative star CDU politician and family minister, Kristina Schröder,[66] and Judith Butler.[67] For Schwarzer, who echoes here the hybrid—Catholic, fascist, and "gender-critical"— European "anti-gender" movement, the Berkeley philosopher is no less than the demon who brought the world postmodernism and critical race theory, thus betraying *all women*.[68]

In the past decade, the more Schwarzer has shown herself willing to appear in the very sexist tabloids she mounted boycotts against back in the 1980s, the more she has risen to new heights of notoriety. All publicity is good publicity: in 2014, it came out that, for many years, she had hidden large sums of money in a Swiss bank account, so as to evade taxation.[69] Elsewhere it was reported that she had donated her winnings from a million-dollar quiz show to a Berlin emergency aid organization—but instead of helping Turkish migrant women fleeing domestic violence, as promised, the NGO's managers had "bought a luxury car."[70] In 2015, she obtained a court injunction that temporarily stopped the sale of her ex-girlfriend Waltraud Schade's book *Memories of Alice Schwarzer*, in which Schade allegedly details abusive behavior.[71] Moreover, to many of her former fans' acute embarrassment, Schwarzer started giving interviews "accusing feminists who do not share her views on the hijab or prostitution of *jealousy*, of matricidal impulses, and of being duped by men."[72] She recently called for International Women's

Day to be banned (too socialist!), and opined that "if you're for the hijab, you're for prostitution."[73] In a review of Schwarzer's autobiography, *Lebenslauf* ("My c.v."), a journalist for *Le Monde* awards her the rather reverent, tragic title of *"porte-parole d'un mouvement qui n'existe plus"* (spokeswoman of a movement that no longer exists).[74] If only that were the case.

One can rely on the *New York Times* for an entirely uncritical profile of a femonationalist. In *Times* correspondent Alison Smale's 2017 feature, we are introduced to Alice Schwarzer, "firebrand" from Wuppertal with a penchant for Parisian living. Alice, here, is a lone maverick whose fifty-years-long crusade against porn, BDSM, and "the sex trade" remains brave and relentless.[75] "Ms. Schwarzer is still fighting," writes Smale, and "time has not much changed the targets: white men, autocrats and anyone else who wants to decide for a woman what she does with her body, from abortion to shrouding herself in a burqa." Curiously, the *Times* makes no other mention of the grande dame's stance on Islam. How is that possible? Schwarzer "barely seems to have issued one statement on any subject adjacent to migration, immigration or asylum, that is not imbued with anti-migrant and Islamosceptic, not to say Islamophobic sentiment," marvel Villa and Hark. "She has barely published a single text in which she does not contend that migrants should first learn to respect 'democracy and equal rights' before they come 'here' or paint the entirety of Islam as irredeemably impregnated with sexism and patriarchy."[76]

Ina Kerner notes that—much as Marine Le Pen finds misogyny in France exclusively in the banlieues—Schwarzer often implies that Islam is the *only* bastion of male supremacy in the Federal Republic of Germany.[77] It's no surprise, hence, that French philosopher and legal opponent of the hijab Elisabeth Badinter has teamed up with Ms. Schwarzer to tell any newspaper that will listen tall tales of European neighborhoods under sharia law: whole cities where "women no longer sit in cafés" for fear of male Muslim molestation![78] One might ask: What has Alice done for the victims of real sexual violence, exactly? Esra Erdem, a Berlin community researcher, has tried for years to find out if Schwarzer and her ilk have anything to say about "making victim protection services more effective, or about improving immigrant women's access to rape crisis centers, battered women's shelters and counseling." She concludes unhappily:

> They have nothing to say when it comes to . . . promoting the development of robust cross-cultural strategies against domestic, sexual and other forms of gendered violence. Rather, they are single-mindedly focused on using the legal machinery of the border regime to punish and deter migrants who have committed violent acts.[79]

In 2012, the historian Miriam Gebhardt suggested that Schwarzer has been almost *fatal* for feminism in Germany. In her book-length critical analysis *Alice in No-Man's-Land: How the German Women's Movement Lost the Women*, Gebhardt charges that "Alice" starved the women's liberation movement of oxygen, and repelled all manner of leftist, antiracist, and queer youth from feminist organizing.

Actually, though, the reverse seems to be true: Schwarzer has—negatively—*inspired* young feminists to revolt. There is strong local feminist opposition to Schwarzer's femonationalist, racist brand of women's rights, but also, as one would hope, an awful lot of creative grassroots work that simply pays her no mind. In 2015, in the wake of Schwarzer's declaration *"Je suis* Charlie" (following the fatal terror attack on the offices of the racist satirists *Charlie Hebdo* in Paris), the German feminist collective Stoerenfriedas finally broke with the ubiquitous foremother. In their statement, entitled "Who the Fuck is Alice,"[80] the group expresses regret for having bitten their tongues for too long in the name of feminist solidarity. They laid bare Schwarzer's double standard for sexual harassment: cute and easily rebuffed when perpetrated by white men, literal terrorism when perpetrated by brown. And they said goodbye.

In 2019, a group of Muslim feminists protested a conference in Frankfurt at which Schwarzer was pontificating on the headscarf (an item of clothing she has likened to the swastika and Nazism). Footage circulated in which Schwarzer exits the building

and approaches the women, only to wag her finger at them and exclaim—when one of them tells her not to touch her—"I thought it
was only men who aren't allowed to touch you!"[81] Amid the outcry
that followed, *EMMA* responded aggressively, accusing the Muslim women of lying. Students in Austria consequently protested
a Schwarzer lecture scheduled at their university.[82] As is so often
the case, the students know what's up. Unless people like Ayaan
Hirsi Ali and Alice Schwarzer are deplatformed, they will never
stop telling the story of hordes of atavistic male Muslims, armed
with guns and rapacious penises, outraging Western womanhood,
and proving the need for a "war of civilizations."

The bottom line is that, as Azeezah Kanji states, femonationalists evince "enthusiastic complicity with non-Muslim sources of
violence against women."[83] They back Western invasions of Muslim countries in the name of freeing their women, imagining, consciously or unconsciously, that death by drone bomb is better (and
more feminist) for women than life is under sharia law. As such, in
contexts like the war on terror and the ongoing (as of this writing)
war on Gaza, serial autobiographies by Ayaan Hirsi Ali with titles
like *Prey* and *Infidel* function like scrummy, highly calorific fodder
for the US war machine. The *New York Times* eats them up, treating them "as honest and reliable testimonies in spite of the troubling inaccuracies, exaggerated descriptions, blunt neo-orientalist
portrayals, and sweeping generalizations," as one baffled scholar,
Adam Yaghi, notes.[84] But perhaps people are "drawn less to the
ideological position she takes and more to her assertion that she
should be allowed to speak," ventures lawyer Kiran Grewal opti-
mistically.[85] Perhaps, but for anthropologist Saba Mahmood, this
would hardly be any consolation. "Have we lost the capacity," Saba
thundered in 2011, "to hear the voices of Muslim women that do
not come packaged in the form of Ayaan Hirsi Ali, Azar Nafisi, and
Irshad Manji?"[86] She continued:

> Feminist contributions to the vilification of Islam do no service
> either to Muslim women or to the cause of gender justice. Instead
> they re-inscribe the cultural and civilizational divide that has

become the bedrock not only of neoconservative politics but also of liberal politics in this tragic moment in history.[87]

Indeed, there is no reason why people affected by gendered Islamophobia should be expected to cede the right to shape debates about anti-colonialism and religion to people like Ayaan and Alice Schwarzer.

It is often argued by other scholars I respect enormously, such as philosopher Lorna Finlayson, that femonationalism isn't really part of feminist history, and that it is "rather misleading to think of this as a strand of feminism at all—although there are certainly some self-described 'feminists' who argue along these lines."[88] I respectfully disagree. Naturally I wish I could have found out, in my research, that colonial feminism didn't really come from feminism, so much as from colonialism—as Finlayson says—and thus been able to conclude that racist feminism isn't really feminism. But unless we are prepared to say that Mary Wollstonecraft and Emmeline Pankhurst are not part of feminism, then imperial feminism really *does* come from feminism, not least inasmuch as mainstream feminism itself comes from empire.[89] Deleterious to the cause of freedom though it is, today's enlightened fundamentalism is, alas, a feminism, one we must confront as a form of patriarchal orientalism and defeat by making common cause with its victims.

ELEVEN

The Pro-Life Feminist

The demand for abortion is a sell-out to male
values and a capitulation to male lifestyles.

—DAPHNE CLAIR DE JONG, Feminists for Life New Zealand
President, 1978[1]

Of all the forms of feminism that elicits the "that's not actually feminism" response, the so-called *pro-life* variety tops the list. "Pro-life Feminism: An Oxymoron," proposes Senator Joan Bray; "'Pro-Life Feminism' Is an Oxymoron," echoes the *Huffington Post*; "There's No Such Thing As a Pro-Life Feminist," underlines *New York Magazine*.[2] While thousands of twentieth-century feminists have denied that an anti-abortion position and feminism are compatible, a minority, however, has declared with equal consistency that they are—and that, as one such feminist put it on Twitter, "real feminists don't kill preborn babies."[3] Surreal as it might seem, forced-birth feminism is a thing. Consider the slogans that regularly grace the annual March for Life protest in Washington, DC: "Girl power begins at conception." "Both lives matter." "I'm with her" (the arrow points to the T-shirt wearer's abdomen). "Value them *both*."[4] Lately, these anti-abortion activists have talked a lot about an "abortion-industrial complex" that hates women. According to Emily Janakiram, an organizer with New York City for Abortion Rights, they "cast abortion as something which benefits the rich at the expense of the poor." Since the left is so weak, the social justice–oriented rhetoric in the forced-birth movement ends up wooing people.

> When I tell people about clinic defense, they imagine that the forced-birthers outside the clinic are generally white men hurling invectives about sluts. I'm sure this is the case in many places . . . but in my experience, the forced birthers tend to be women. They are often people of color, and they talk about how abortion is a form of violence toward women.[5]

It is of course *true* that the parenthood of the poor is systematically made impossible, while the reproduction of the rich is aided and cherished. Reproductive injustice is a description of US society: ecological collapse in progress, wages stagnant, workers' protections under attack, zero healthcare access for many, two million people locked up—all of which threaten people's ability to care for one another, especially babies and children. Meanwhile, the pathetic mainstream pro-choice establishment has insisted that "reproductive rights" *aren't political*, ignoring the class-conscious leadership of the black-led reproductive justice movement. This mainstream has focused almost exclusively on institutional self-preservation and the law, not on labor movement building and medical defiance, leaving room for forced-birth feminists to enter the political fray and win.

"Open your eyes, pro-life feminists are everywhere," enthused the lawyer Helen Alvaré on CNN in 2018.[6] Indeed. While most of them claim a maternalist, nineteenth-century lineage, some compare themselves instead to the civil disobedience wing of the civil rights movement of the 1950s and '60s. The self-described Catholic "anarchafeminist" Lauren Handy, director of activism at a group called Progressive Anti-Abortion Uprising (or PAAU, dubbed by other activists "The Fetus Thieves"[7] and the "Pro-Life Antifa"[8]), is a case in point. Handy views fetuses as an oppressed minority and intends to dedicate her whole life, on no income, in and out of jail, to the cause of stopping their slaughter. She estimates she's forced her way into a hundred abortion clinics since 2013, and she was among those arrested on federal charges in 2022 for conducting a series of "pink rose rescues," which involved blocking and invading clinics in the Washington, DC area. Recently, Handy "dumpster dived" (her words) 115 fetuses—precisely the gruesome kind of thing that pro-choice organizations have so often stood accused of by pro-life conspiracists. She stored the remains in her fridge with a view to ceremonially burying and mourning them.[9] In this vision, feminism defends "the most vulnerable" of all organisms against the harsh fate meted out to them by a patriarchal, white capitalist culture.

Some proponents of forced life are remarkably well-versed in anti-carceral vocabulary and even appear genuinely committed to social democracy as the only mechanism truly capable of delivering the *real* end of abortion on earth (i.e., instead of the law alone, which they recognize as a limited pathway to reproductive justice as compared to economic reforms). Veteran abortion-access activist Katha Pollitt describes a "lively phone chat" she had in 2017 with the "leftist" pro-life feminist Destiny Herndon-De La Rosa, who opposes the criminalization of abortion, seeking instead—as any good "abolitionist" should—to build a world in which no one will ever need or want the thing in question. "Still," muses Pollitt, "even when it's made by hipsters," the anti-choice argument inevitably demands that we "drop everything" when we become pregnant, "to incubate that egg."[10] Feminists like Herndon-De La Rosa do nonetheless see themselves as waging a rebellion against patriarchy. Besides PAAU, since 2017, several groups have denounced feticide in language designed to resonate with the mass contemporary hatred of the police on the streets: "Stop state-sanctioned violence," cries Rehumanize International, a feminist pro-life and anti–police brutality group.[11] Destiny is the president of New Wave Feminists, a group of self-defined *"Badass. Prolife. Feminists."* bent on "agitating the status quo."[12] Even one of the very oldest groups, Feminists for Life (established in 1972), now coordinates radical-sounding calls to students nationwide to "revolutionize your campus" in life's name.[13] In 2018, a campaign of Catholic anti-abortion feminists called Women Speak For Themselves explained on *CNN* that "capitalism" must "make room for women's ceaselessly expressed preference to do justice to their families first" (for them, evidently, a fetus is always already "family").[14] Here, it is the bosses, the bankers—the enemies of all "interdependent, relational" bonds—who pressure us to get abortions.

Founded in 2021 by the atheist and animal liberationist Terrisa Bukovinac, PAAU's core team's aesthetics are punk adjacent, featuring pins and patches, heavy boots, Black Lives Matter and Trans Lives Matter insignia, goth lipstick, and fishnets. Its slick website outlines its "stances" against capitalism, abortion, and contraception, and *for* feminism. Its communications director, Kristin Turner, informally heads up a band called EmbryoHoez, which now boasts that "the hotties dismantled Roe." Prior to June 2022, they sang "The Hotties Will Dismantle Roe": "They say it's empowerment / They say it's women's rights / But all I see's oppression / And might makes right."[15] According to Turner's prolific, vegan, atheist social media presence, "If you go far enough left you become pro-life."[16] Their struggle continues: notwithstanding Handy's forty-five-day jail sentence, PAAU continued with several direct actions in 2023. These were framed as part of an initiative to #bringbackrescue. This means intervening directly to "save lives," specifically, fetal lives, by preventing abortions from happening, by any means necessary.

It turns out that feminists who are prepared to go to jail for preventing fetus "murder" are working with none other than Randall Terry, the founder of Operation Rescue (now called Operation Save America)—a renowned pro-life terrorist network that was responsible for scores of abortion clinic bombings, arson attacks, and several *actual* murders in the 1980s and '90s.[17] The old-school, non-feminist "rescue" movement's first offensive peaked in 1991, when thousands of activists descended on Wichita, Kansas, to harass George Tiller, one of the few doctors at that time offering abortions in the third trimester of pregnancy. The resultant chaotic blockade was dubbed Operation Rescue's "Summer of Mercy," but the movement mercifully fizzled out soon after, when an activist killed an abortion doctor in Florida (an escalation of violence typical of a movement on the outs). Congress responded by passing the Freedom of Access to Clinic Entrances Act, which made interfering with clinics a crime. This did not, sadly, prevent an anti-abortion activist from shooting Dr. Tiller dead in 2009.[18] Says one PAAU member while invading a clinic in 2023, "We have no moral or ethical obligation to acknowledge the property lines of a business that murders people [*sic*] for profit."[19] Would the Progressive Anti-Abortion Uprising do vigilante *murders*, too, in the name of life?

Anything seems justified in this fascistic, innocence-fetishizing, messianic mindset. In the context of #MeToo, a self-described member of the "new feminist resistance," Lauren Enriquez of the pro-life nonprofit Human Coalition, thundered in the *New York Times* against what she called the peddling of *death* as empowerment; the design of an economy that demands "the sacrifice of a woman's children in exchange for her success"; and the "lie that freedom can be bought with the blood of our preborn children."[20] The following month, her colleague Lori Szala was on the same opinion page, likening abortion seekers to trapped animals gnawing off their own leg.[21] The *Times* hands out bylines to such voices as though its clicks depended on it, and the resultant rhetoric is always like this.[22] It is a wonder no such rhetoric made its way into the very *Dobbs v. Jackson Women's Health* Supreme Court ruling, which struck down *Roe v. Wade*, given that one of the authors of a nail in Roe's coffin—an amicus brief from 240 "pro-life feminist women and organizations," titled *Concerned Women for America*—was a scholar of Mary Wollstonecraft and former Bernie Sanders fan: the feminist pro-lifer Erika Bachiochi.[23]

In her much-trumpeted book *The Rights of Women: Reclaiming a Lost Vision* (2021), Bachiochi makes the absurd claim that, since *Roe*, Americans have had "easy abortion access"—but this access "has not rendered women freer or more equal."[24] Instead, she writes, it has "greatly contributed to the dim view of caregiving." Legal abortion has *harmed* women, Bachiochi claims. In a 2021 op-ed in, you guessed it, the *New York Times*, Bachiochi thanked those who (unlike herself) were willing to hold their noses and vote for Trump *for fetuses' sakes*. "Ending the abortion regime," she wrote, "must be the keystone of standing against the individualistic libertarianism that characterizes our politics."[25] This is because, as she sees it, to give those of us with viable uteruses the option to control what's inside them enshrines the idea that women and men alike are "wombless" individuals, equal instead of different from one another. To accept abortion is, then, in fact, to attempt to turn women into men just to please our corporate bosses and employers. It means that women are "lowering" themselves to men's strings-free, immature, irresponsible level, when we should be requiring men to meet us at our higher level of caring virtue.

On the revolutionary pro-abortion left, we are often every bit as interested as Bachiochi in the history of the definitionally not-pregnant construct of the indivisible ("in-divid-ual") rights-bearing person. But far from endorsing it, the goal—certainly in my book about pregnancy, *Full Surrogacy Now*—is to go beyond it for men too. There is nothing strings-free about the human animal. The flow of caring interdependency between human beings (surrogacy) is coerced, nonconsensual, and drastically asymmetric under patriarchal capitalism—hence the need to abolish the private nuclear household—that is, to deprivatize care, and to actualize a universal mandate (*full* surrogacy) to care for all children everywhere. Yes: people of all genders must mother, at least a little bit. Contra Bachiochi, though, the minimum requirement for a politics that takes life-making care labor seriously is a commitment to not forcing people to labor against their will. A thick web of communal care infrastructures and polymaternal household norms would mean that any one parent could responsibly quit if absolutely necessary. A gestator, too, must be able to stop gestating, or else we are not valuing care labor—we are taking it for granted.[26]

The claim of the "woman-protective anti-abortion argument," writes law professor Reva Siegel, "is that by restricting all women, government can free women to be the mothers they naturally are."[27] "Sometimes there is the argument," adds legal historian Mary Ziegler, "that the law should restrict women's abortion rights in order to protect women from post-abortion regret."[28] But one of the simplest ways to grasp that anti-abortion feminists are indeed feminists is to listen to what their antifeminist peers say about them. When Lila Rose, the leader of the feminist pro-life organization Live Action, publicly recommended that women should not "date or marry a man obsessed with the submission of a woman," she was dogpiled by antifeminists within her own movement, mainly traditionalist-nationalists who *denied* that pro-life politics can be separated from patriarchal familism.[29] In 2022, a self-described "post-liberal" pro-lifer ranted that the pro-life movement was "run mostly by feminist women at this point," as evidenced by the fact that some pro-life women support the use of vasectomy ("men mutilating themselves").[30] At the Catholic website *First Things*, Matthew Schmitz, an editor at *Compact* magazine, conceded that Bachiochi's book is "the most impressive anti-abortion book to appear in years," but criticized her for supporting #MeToo and putting too much blame for the murder of fetuses onto men.[31]

Liberals, conversely, can't get enough. Behold, "'The Pro-Life Generation': Young Women Fight Against Abortion Rights," as the *New York Times* marvels in a long profile of, among others, Kristin Turner, and Students for Life leader Kristan Hawkins. Unlike *other* strains of feminism, the reader learns, this one doesn't "tell" young Americans that they have to end their pregnancies in order to achieve their educational and career goals: no, it goes one better, feminism-wise, and "tells them they can have it all" (girlboss style).[32] All this means in practice is that pro-life feminists will offer some "woman-empowering" services for mommies-to-be—such as factually inaccurate anti-abortion counseling not substantially different from what's provided in non-feminist crisis pregnancy centers (indeed, they benefit from the same enormous donations from antifeminist corporate and religious donors).[33] Feminist pro-life groups may also throw in free or low-cost prenatal care, postpartum doula services, and lactation consultations, and they'll furnish the unwilling future moms with diapers and crayons, for example, and promise to do baby-wellness visits as a kind of "thank you" for not doing the "wrong" thing. Some gesture wistfully toward the structural and substantive goods (for example, automatic state-distributed maternity packages, long-term paid parental leave, socialized healthcare) that still, for now, flow to birthing people in the vestigial European welfare states as a matter of course.

Regardless, the rhetoric never fails to impress the legacy media. In 2013, *Time* magazine ran a veritably effusive piece about the trend, profiling figures like the then twenty-four-year-old Lila Rose as hip, hot nineteenth-century feminist revivalists. The author of the piece, Emily Buchanan, mentioned the activist leaders' youthfulness no less than six times in her effort to paint their movement as woke and futuristic, while at the same time thoughtful, consistent, and ideologically loyal—*heretically* so!—to American feminism's founding mothers. Buchanan throws in an emancipatory godfather for good measure, quoting the incarcerated Martin Luther King Jr. on nonviolence, and extrapolating that mass fetal death is therefore somehow "the civil- and human-rights cause of our day."[34] It should be said that Buchanan is the director of Susan B. Anthony Pro-Life America, a political action committee that donates overwhelmingly to Republicans (even while brandishing the name of a suffragist pioneer who never allied herself, as it happens, with either anti-abortion politics or the Republican Party in her lifetime).[35] Buchanan does not mention her lobby group's investments in the right-wing GOP. On the contrary, she emphasizes that it was "a group of mostly Democratic women" who founded this particular PAC in 1992. She cites Alice Paul's excoriation of abortion as "the ultimate exploitation of women," and cries, "The rights of women cannot be built on the broken backs of unborn children."[36]

This feminism might repudiate the second wave, but in fact, its insistence on female nonviolence, dignity, and civility flows directly from the "cultural feminist" backlash against the utopianism of the early women's liberation movement. In 1973, as we saw in Chapter Eight, erstwhile New Left militants and fugitives like Jane Alpert were reborn as ecofeminist anti-leftists. Alpert's manifesto appeared in *off our backs* before being reproduced in 1974 as a pamphlet. *Mother Right* theorized a feminism of *life*, hailing the capacity for gestation as the source of "the inner power with which many women are beginning to feel in touch":

That source is none other than female biology: the capacity to bear and nurture children. . . . the intrinsic biological connection between mother and embryo or mother and infant gives rise to those psychological qualities which have always been linked with women, both in ancient lore and modern behavioral science. Motherhood must be understood here as a potential which is imprinted in the genes of every woman; as such it makes no difference to this analysis of femaleness whether a woman ever has borne, or ever will bear, a child.

Alpert ends by speculating that "women are beginning to rise in response to the Mother's call to save Her planet," thereby driving "a great rise of interest in psychic and spiritual phenomena."[37] Her and her post-left sisters' thesis, in a nutshell, is that women are "biologically inclined to peacefulness and love."[38]

Fifty years later, Bachiochi is breathing new life (pardon the pun) into this undead, radically cissexist ideology of primally coded maternalism and its pessimistic certainty that only females mother. She opens *The Rights of Women* by juxtaposing two protests that took place over a century apart in Washington, DC: the Woman Suffrage Procession of 1913 (which was "impressively beautiful," guided by the ideals of charity, liberty, justice, peace, and hope), and the Women's March of 2017 (which "extolled 'nasty' women, made generous use of expletives, and engaged in insult, threat, and ad hominem attack on the new president").[39] Bachiochi is appalled that genitals—that is, the pussy hat—were the symbol of the latter march. She considers the whole thing "bereft of noble purpose," emotive, and unreasonable: "Enduring moral principles, which women's rights advocates in earlier days would have employed to make a reasoned critique of the controversial new president, had given way to vulgar irony: 'This pussy grabs back.'"[40] All in all, #MeToo made Bachiochi realize that feminism has "morphed into something that nearly contradicts its original moral vision,"[41] laid out by Mary Wollstonecraft in 1792. The movement, she fumes, was never meant to open up "a life of moral mediocrity, or worse, vulgarity," to women. Damn it, "Wollstonecraft's was a freedom for excellence."[42] Our betrayal of her, says Bachiochi, "took shape the day the modern women's movement wholeheartedly embraced abortion as a remedy, not just for life-threatening risks facing pregnant women, but as the sine qua non of women's freedom and equality."[43]

In this vein, *The Rights of Women: Reclaiming a Lost Vision* even contends that contraception ("the sexual revolution") *stalled* the progress of feminism by trampling on the "republican motherhood" ideals of eighteenth- and nineteenth-century feminists like Mary Wollstonecraft, temperance leader Frances Willard, and factory inspector Florence Kelley. She fallaciously attributes an anti-abortion position to *all* early feminism. This is a classic move for contemporary pro-life feminists, who use this lie to narrate their story, paraphrasing theorist Clare Hemmings, as a tale of "feminist return" to first principles.[44] Obviously, Bachiochi's subtitle, touting "reclamation," is quite open about this desire to go back to the bourgeois, white supremacist, imperialist era of feminism. *The Rights of Woman* argues for a revival of Wollstonecraftian "virtue," meaning that sex belongs inside the sanctity of marriage and is primarily a matter of "voluntary motherhood." Reproductive autonomy is actively bad for women, in this view, because what women want most is babies, and when having them is framed as a "choice" rather than a natural event, then men simply run away from the duty to provide for them.

What women need, apparently, is less freedom, and more marriage, as well as "natural fertility regulation"[45]—not contraceptives—and a culture-wide recognition that "the market is actually parasitic on the work of the home"[46] rather than vice versa. I agree with this last part, but whereas my faction of feminism argues for communizing much of the labor that capitalism relegates to the private nuclear household, Bachiochi treats marriage-based familism as natural law. "In the original edition of *The Feminine Mystique*," she correctly points out, Friedan was not "advocating that women abandon their children or their marriages for careers" any more than Wollstonecraft was.[47] Marriage, concludes Erika, is a pillar of feminism. Rich people know the "value" of marriage, and the inability to "raise the cost of sex" (marry) is why the poor are poor. *The Rights of Woman* now wants to impose marriage on "poor communities"— "enabling and, again, empowering the poor to take seriously the really important work of the home." Generously, she does allow that "it's not just the poor who need self-discipline. It's all of us."[48] Yet, as Bachiochi constantly recalls, the rich and "highly educated" already opt to marry, making it quite clear who she believes requires discipline.[49]

Even before *Dobbs* leaked, the prominent liberal podcaster Ezra Klein hosted Ms. Bachiochi on his show to discuss her book, introducing her, excruciatingly, as a critic of capitalism. "Her view is that abortion and contraception really serve the needs of capital," said Klein, "that contraception and abortion *create* this dominance of market logic."[50] But for the best part of eighty minutes, his guest refused to be pinned down on why gestational autonomy is pro-capitalist. Why would taking away the means to exit pregnancy hurt the culture's libertarian-individualist market logic? Because abortion "takes the attention off the real structural problems in the lives of the poor," said Bachiochi. But she wasn't just saying, "I'm going to join the Bernie Sanders movement," Klein pressed. "You want to close off the option to abort." Yes, admitted Bachiochi, because abortion has become "the privileged solution to poverty." That is nonsense, implied Klein: every single state that has enacted paid family leave laws also has "a firm commitment to abortion rights," meanwhile, not a single hard-line anti-abortion state *does* have paid family leave. Well, flailed Bachiochi, "we don't really know what it is that's pushing women to have those abortions"; so it is good to "restrict abortion more, because then people will take the sexual act more seriously." Yet even if *more serious sex* were desirable, Klein remarked, this punitive wager is not at all empirically supported. (Bans make abortions less safe, not rarer.) *Fine* was the gist of Bachiochi's reply, but "the law" *should* "teach" poor women to "take their place again as gatekeepers of sex." Abortion's very existence is coercive, apparently, since it's an "easier choice."

From the perspective of the "communitarian" forced-birth movement Bachiochi vindicates, bringing an end to neoliberalism's "throwaway culture"[51]—that is, the consumerist culture, based on a Lockean worship of property rights, that makes us feel we can throw away fetuses, nonrecyclable plastics, and so on—must be the first priority of a "life-affirming feminism." Proponents nowadays use the latter term interchangeably with "whole life feminism" or, even more outrageously, "the feminism of care,"[52] in an implicit (and often explicit) characterization of other feminisms as anti-care, unwhole, and broken. In reality, it is indiscriminate vitalism, not unlike capitalism's indiscriminate compulsion to accumulate, that is careless of the wealth that is a life. To my ears, the quantitative rather than qualitative approach to life, banging the drum for more brute life—of whatever quality—rather than showing solicitude for life-in-particular, is fascist.

Pro-life feminists' putatively *caring* feminism doesn't stop at saving America's embryos from the trash can to which women poisoned by individualism consign them. That would be the approach of the non-feminist, non-communitarian wing of the forced-birth movement. Increasingly, groups like Feminists Choosing Life of New York, PAAU, and New Wave Feminists slam that wing as misogynist. Hand in hand with other "pro-woman" communitarian pro-lifers, however, the *feminist* forced-birthers purport to value and support the *whole life* of the children embryos become, including their community and gestator. They try to do so without blaming aborters, in contrast to the patriarchs whose carceral movement they nevertheless, in so doing, bolster and render more appealing.[53]

Some pro-life feminist groups, like PAAU, are secular, while some are "Jesus feminists" called to "'love on' young women facing unplanned pregnancies."[54] Some do direct action; others control sufficient resources to run manipulative and mendacious crisis pregnancy centers. This is called a "consistent life ethic."[55] The goal is a feminist-communitarian world where all lives will be precious and no one will ever *want* abortion, though their vision for that world, like their methods for realizing it, fail to take into account the vast alternative systems—of obstetrics, childrearing, and universal basic income—that would be required before any PAAU "anarchist" or "abolitionist" in good conscience could even think about challenging an abortion seeker's all-too-real desire. In the meantime, criminalizing those who terminate their "preborn" will apparently do.

PAAU openly support a federal ban, even as they say they oppose criminalization.[56] Bachiochi and her fellow Supreme Court brief signatories did not need to wait long. In 2022, the court did their bidding and removed Americans' right to abort.

Bachiochi has been preparing the ground for this result for over twenty years. In 2004, she edited a collection of pro-life feminist essays, *The Cost of Choice: Women Evaluate the Impact of Abortion*, in which she identified herself as "a one-time 'pro-choice' feminist activist, now a full-time mother of two" (unclear whether the latter is supposed to have anything to do with the former).[57] To be honest, it does not surprise me that Bachiochi keeps quiet about *The Cost of Choice* nowadays. In it, she not only platform activists like Serrin Foster (the Feminists for Life president) and all her favorite philosophers (Jean Bethke Elshtain, Mary Ann Glendon, and Elizabeth Fox-Genovese); she also, shamefully, gives space to a medical scholar to speculate about a link (which has been completely debunked[58]) between "induced abortion" and breast cancer.[59]

Quietly, in 2010, she gathered several of the same people again in a different edited volume: *Women, Sex and the Church: A Case for Catholic Teaching*.[60] She followed this up with a paper in the *Harvard Journal of Law and Public Policy* arguing that abortion rights and contraception "actually hinder the equality of women by taking the wombless male body as normative, thereby promoting cultural hostility toward pregnancy and motherhood."[61] (My argument, as we've seen, is conversely that it is the regime of forced gestation that takes the non-"dividual" body as normative.) Leading the charge against *Roe* from within the legal establishment, Bachiochi has made the case that feminists should seek protection for fetuses under the Fourteenth Amendment.[62] For this to be conscionable, she concedes, the people whose bodies produce the fetuses at huge personal risk to themselves must "demand more, far more, from men"—as husbands and dads—as she proposed on CNN in 2015.[63]

The good news is that, once men comply, a world beckons where sexual difference is revered as a "beautiful, wondrous truth," and fertile cis womanhood is treasured. This "dignity of woman" is a far better principle around which to organize feminism than "equality," she wants us to realize. Dignified is she who has no option not to be pregnant. Philosopher Victoria Browne's response is worth quoting in full:

> The first thing to ask, of course, is since when did forcing people to do a thing make that thing more socially valued? But let us accept for a moment this mind-bending argument that state-mandated pregnancy is the way to boost the socio-cultural value of pregnancy and parenting and overturn patriarchal capitalism. What do anti-abortion feminists have to say to those they would deny abortion access? Is the idea that unwillingly pregnant people must take the hit in order to make things better for the pregnant people and parents of the future? Because if they had a legal abortion this would send a signal to the wider society that pregnancy is not to be valued and nothing needs to change? And then, after a period of time has passed, and enough people have endured unwanted pregnancies and births, pregnancy and motherhood will have become so highly valued and economically supported that no one will want abortions anymore?[64]

Believe it, sister! Bachiochi speaks to us from an ex-ally's standpoint: "As a one-time abortion rights supporter, I well know the temptation to see the right to abortion as a representation of women's equality."[65] Simultaneously sacrificial and saviorist, Bachiochi can both insist that, deep down, all women really want to be mothers (such that coercion is really kindness) *and* cast those who do not want to be pregnant as "unwomen" whose disposability is still "pro-woman." Hopefully the latter might mature into the former, she prays. Pro-abortion feminists must acquire "the kind of moral maturity that would regard service to and care of others as life-giving and fulfilling."[66] We might not understand it now, but one day, it will become obvious: pro-child and pro-woman policies are the same thing; abortion is a false techno-fix.

It might surprise you to learn that Bachiochi's rationale chimes with that of the legendary feminist Catharine MacKinnon herself, who does pay lip service to abortion on feminist principle, but who also argued in 1983 that abortion access in the context of patriar-chy simply "removes one substantial legitimized reason that women have had, since Freud, for refusing sex besides the headache."[67] Absent a "sexual critique of gender equality," argued MacKinnon, abortion "promises *men* women on male terms," thereby facilitat-ing "women's heterosexual availability." What's more, she noted with a shudder, "there is also evidence that men eroticize abortion itself."[68] The evidence for this last part mainly consisted of a *Hustler* magazine cartoon of an operating table, punning on the phrase "piece of ass," and Andrea Dworkin's contention that, for the Mar-quis de Sade, "abortion was a sexual act, an act of lust."[69] (Even if it were true, the fact that something turns people on is an odd reason to knock it, in my opinion. But for MacKinnon, nothing could be less feminist, it seems, than the eroticization of pleasure for pleas-ure's sake.) In their views of women's heterosexuality, the anti-porn feminist and the "social-democratic conservative" anti-abortionist radical are not so very far apart. Intercourse, for MacKinnon and Bachiochi, is (under present conditions) mainly a necessity for spe-cies survival.

Shortly after *Roe* was struck down, Bachiochi got to author yet another *Times* op-ed, which she used to reiterate the bizarre an-ti-capitalist framing of her "pro-woman" opposition to gestational autonomy. "Americans have an understanding of property rights, deriving from the philosophy of John Locke, as absolute and un-limited," she wrote. "Today, leftists reject this view of property rights as applied to the economy yet, paradoxically, embrace it as applied to a pregnant woman and her unborn child."[70]

In other words, pro-abortion reds like me hypocritically reject liberalism's property logics *except* when it comes to fetuses, which we happily treat as disposable property. If true, this would be a de-cent point; the only problem is, Marxist and critical race feminists have been grappling with this question since the 1970s.[71] Many of us on feminism's left share her rejection of macho conceptu-alizations of vulnerability as inherently limiting, and of the body as property (I do not find it particularly compelling to affirm the entitlement of the dividual body to dispose of its own intra-uterine property). We don't for that reason have to agree that the fetus's unique kind of vulnerability automatically places a duty to care for it on anyone. It is none but ours to decide which unknowable lives to build—the ones that lie still behind the portal of a pregnancy, or the ones already here.

Quite simply, to force a person to manufacture human life and perform gestational care against her will is a worse dereliction of our collective human duty of care than is a feticide.

In many animal species, large and small, a gestator can discard a pregnancy at will, because she is stressed and has to flee, for example, or because there's suddenly a drought. For us human beings, on the other hand, being pregnant is a condition that locks us down for nearly a year, on account of the hyper-invasive placenta we happen to be saddled with when we gestate. Human pregnancy is absolutely, as Bachiochi says, "natural." But where she is outrageously wrong (especially in a US context, where the "maternal mortality rate" is three times that of the UK) is in saying that "most pregnancies aren't dangerous."[72]

Pregnancy is inherently—naturally—damaging to the body and poses sometimes lethal risks of cardiomyopathy, hemorrhage, eclampsia, diabetes, stroke, and hypertension.[73] Some 287,000 people died in 2020 doing the labor of gestating.[74] Over 1,200 of those were in the US, where that number is on the rise.[75] To my mind, even if these statistics were a fraction as large as they are, the premise that one could ever expect—let alone require—a person to be pregnant against their will for a single minute is, frankly, unconscionable. Nonetheless, the world we inhabit operates uniformly on the principle that it *is* ethically permissible to regulate human gestation in law, as well as morally acceptable to place conditions on the gestator's ability to stop doing what I call "gestational labor."[76]

Whereas women's liberationists fifty years ago fought to "repeal all abortion laws," the best that Planned Parenthood has been able to muster in the twenty-first century is a vision of regulated legality.[77] In the Women's March in 2017, for instance, there was no guarantee that your average marcher could spy a single placard about Medicare for All, free universal 24/7 childcare, or paid parental leave. As recently as a decade ago, "the safest position for a member of the commentariat," to quote Pollitt, was that "you can have your abortion as long as you feel really, really bad about it."[78] The best that American politicians could dream of was that, once embarked upon, stoppages should be—to quote Bill and Hillary Clinton—"safe, legal and rare."[79] Thanks to the grinding efforts of grassroots reproductive justice organizers, "safe, legal and rare" was eventually scrubbed from the progressive vocabulary in favor of the *healthcare* framing (self-evidently, healthcare should not be "legal" or "rare"—rather, it should be patient directed, as safe as possible, accessible, and free).[80]

Pro-life feminists like Erika Bachiochi tend to take offense, on fetuses' behalf, that killing them by scraping them from their environment might be termed "medicine." But of course it is. As fetuses, we are designed to be quite a lot like cancer cells, which is, in a way, badass—but not from our gestational parent's perspective. The placenta exists in part to protect the person inside whom it grows *from* the fetal tissue that is trying its best to devour her; equally, it is there to protect the fetus from the gestator's natural and spontaneous efforts to abort it. The "success" of a process of human gestation goes so much against the grain of what parts of our "nature" intend that, in a sense, every live birth represents a termination of a termination, the failure of a failure. Births are anomalies, miracles. Here's another miracle: thanks largely to thousands of years of herbalism and lay science, it is possible to extricate and disentangle a fetus from a person without doing harm to the latter.[81] Abortion doulas are caregivers who smooth our exits from pregnancy. They often speak of their vocation as sacred.[82] To me, too, it is a sacred matter to be a part of the caring networks that, by enabling a "no," necessarily make the opposite decision—the "yes" to gestating—uncoerced enough to be worth celebrating.

Whereas Erika Bachiochi sees "a new antinatalism"[83] in twenty-first-century America, I see a pervasive logic of antilife pronatalism—"forced life"[84]—and what the critical race theorist Evelyn Nakano Glenn calls "forced care."[85] At present, our care as feminized laborers is ripped from us, in both directly and indirectly market-mediated ways. The care of racialized and colonized populations everywhere is extractively vacuumed up to service the care needs of people in the colonizer classes, locally, and in the Global North.

Care makes the world go around, for better and for worse. Emphasizing this has been extremely important for black and Marxist feminisms since the 1970s—but it often gets mistaken as a celebratory point. (For Bachiochi, forcing life-sustaining care on a fetus is clearly a virtuous act, as is upping the quantity of "life itself" in existence in general.) As so many of us in the "wages against housework" tradition have insisted, the labor of mothering is not only reproductive, but generative—albeit of good things *and* ill. That latter aspect goes missing a lot, in the discussion. As Victoria Browne reflected in 2018,

> One of the aims of promoting the generative maternal paradigm has been to counteract what is viewed as the excessive preoccupation with mortality and death within the patriarchal western philosophical tradition. But this move can obscure the complex intertwinement of life and death within reproduction and the maternal.[86]

Abortions are good for one's health and one's community. They overwhelmingly produce happiness and are overwhelmingly not regretted.[87] At the same time, abortions consist of an act of killing; not of murder, but of violence nonetheless, and my position is that we sabotage ourselves as pro-abortion activists by pretending this isn't the case.[88] After all, the fact that feticide is what achieves a person's desired return to a nonpregnant state is self-evident. It is self-infantilizing for repro-freedom advocates to euphemize it, deny it, or apologize for it. There is self-evidently something there: not a person, but a proto-person, a creature like a squid, a virtual intelligence, with a potential human future. And, like other forms of healthcare—think of the word *antibiotic*—termination of pregnancy stops this organism's life. In my opinion, we should all be as free to kill proto-persons living uninvited in our bodies as we are to kill protozoans and parasites of all kinds. Protozoans will always be around. Similarly, it seems likely that the conditions that necessitate abortions may never be wholly eliminated, even if vasectomies become generalized and care communes replace the dyadic family.

It's worth being explicit here: as long as people are performing pregnancy on this earth, they must be free to change their minds about seeing it through. The adoption industry could be revolutionized and child welfare lavishly subsidized; regardless of the available supports, no one should be pregnant involuntarily. The science of medicine dictates that when foreign organisms inhabit the human body unwelcomely, we tend to eject them.

Lest I be misunderstood as pro-violence, I think killing any creature—even a tapeworm in one's gut—is something (unlike having sex) to take seriously every time. But it can sometimes be necessary that we humans *do* kill: victims of assault sometimes kill in self-defense, targets of persecution sometimes kill for justice—or just to reduce the number of their persecutors—and the colonized sometimes kill for liberation. Mothers living in unspeakable conditions (including chattel slavery) have been documented to kill their children as an act of mercy. Of course, these examples are generated by conditions that we struggle to render extinct. I actually agree when the proponents of forced gestating argue that giving ethical consideration to fetuses is a worthwhile endeavor in an abstract, futuristic sense. But my anti-violence is not nonviolence, nor can any real opposition to violence be nonviolent. It is not possible, currently, to give much ethical consideration to the proto-persons in our bodies. Still, as part of my "critical utopianism," I wonder if we could arrive, one day, at the as-yet-unthinkable place where giving fetuses ethical consideration *has* become practically possible, perhaps thanks to gestator-controlled ectogenetic technologies, advances in obstetric medicine, and a reorganization of life's work beyond the private nuclear household.

When a beloved nonhuman companion is sick and elderly, many pet owners decide not to pay for medical care and opt for euthanasia instead. It is a mark of moral seriousness to acknowledge what it is that we're doing when we butcher a cow, put a pet "to sleep," or, for that matter, euthanize a human relative. According to the philosopher of science Donna Haraway, we must "stay with the trouble" of the violence we inevitably mete out in our attempts to be responsible—or indeed capable of response—to other forms of life, be it at the dinner table, the battlefield, or in the scientific laboratory. Rather than squaring our acts of killing away according to a moral calculus, or pretending that we aren't really killing, multispecies feminists should subscribe, suggests Haraway, to the ethical imperative, "Thou shalt not make killable."[89] This might seem counterintuitive in the context of an argument in favor of abortion as killing, but the distinction between making fetuses killable, and making it easy and stigma-free for people to make the decision to kill a fetus, is significant. The former refers to casting something out of the sphere of the grievable, thanks to a tidy and final verdict on the permissibility of systematically sacrificing its life to a greater cause. People who abort fetuses can and often *do* grieve the proto-person. The "clump of cells" argument is not much to my taste: fetuses should not be rendered flatly "killable" in my view. Expanding access to the means of feticide does not preclude acknowledging the violence. It does not require us to weigh beings in the scales or square death away. It simply means trusting the pregnant.

Bachiochi hopes that feminists like me will one day join her in acquiring "moral maturity."[90] For her, it seems, merely invoking the idea of a woman putting her desires first, killing a conceptus out of self-interest, and repudiating biological motherhood in favor of some other project, is meant to be morally repellent enough to pass for an argument. But many (if not most) of us are simply *not* morally repelled enough to be scared away from abortion by this browbeating, nor even afraid of the premise that embryos or fetuses must die sometimes if gestators are to have bodily autonomy. We feel, indeed, that forcing someone to continue a pregnancy is a form of violence far worse than the violence of abortion. No matter how feminist they are, forced lifers routinely sacrifice the health and happiness of actual persons in defense of the forced survival of potential ones. Idealizing newness and sentimentalizing helplessness, they pit themselves against the care of caregivers, riding roughshod over the delicate and necessary intertwinement of care and autonomy, death and life, and unmaking and making that comprise the collective crafting of any human life in particular. In their minds, it's simple: fetuses deserve every protection, while we actually existing people are morally bound to sacrifice our bodies and labor to make them persons.

It's high time we went on the offensive against this sickening, sacrificial version of vitalism. I don't want to live in a world that valorizes life for its own sake. I want to live in a world that prioritizes the life chosen and wanted.

TWELVE

The Adult Human Female

Eunuchs schemed to obtain political power.

—JANICE RAYMOND, 1979[1]

Just in time for Christmas 2021, the British public intellectual Mary Harrington came out with an essay called "The Feminist Case Against Abortion," rave-reviewing Erika Bachiochi's *The Rights of Women*. "On abortion, I've always been in the 'safe, legal and rare' camp," confessed Harrington, performing her conversion to the pro-life cause. But "Bachiochi makes a persuasive case."[2] The case, as Harrington paraphrases it, is that abortion and contraception turn feminism into a demand that *women become men* (which here means strings-free and aggressive). Full of the zealotry of the newly converted, the Englishwoman pursued this idea in her 2023 book *Feminism Against Progress*. "When individuals of both sexes really can just fuck, with no material consequences," she asked, "what is even the point of going out for dinner first?"[3] (It is the "dark, dangerous" risk of pregnancy, she says, that brings joy to intercourse.)[4] She now claims, as a guest on platforms from *Intelligence Squared* to the Heritage Foundation, that contraception harms aquatic life and perverts womanhood, while "abortion serves as a metaphysical keystone for cyborg theocracy."[5] This phrase is Harrington's catchall for the diabolical anti-naturalism of contemporary non-natalist, trans-inclusive, reproductive-justice feminism. Queer feminists like me (specifically) are "priestesses of cyborg theocracy."

The latter phrase is interchangeable with "Meat Lego Gnosticism": the apparently *evil* idea that bodies aren't ideal essences but rather made up of "meat legos" insofar as they're constantly being remade.[6] What both these fancy terms boil down to is simply the contention that transfeminists, allies, queers, and sex workers *hate* the god-given human form—simply because we do things with it. Abortion, you see, is not Harrington's real focus; "transgenderism" is.[7] She cautions, "I don't wish to make the argument that the only proper starting point for a fightback against this theocracy would be seeking abrupt and radical abortion restrictions. On its own, banning abortion wouldn't heal the dissociative relation we have to ourselves."[8] Forced birth is only part of the "healing" Harrington desires. The counterrevolution she proudly calls "reactionary feminism" hinges on an existential crusade for *sex-based rights*, against trans life. "No more freedom, no more technology," she cries. Feminism must "cissexualize" those "whom the new era is already working to dismember, both culturally and legally"—it must make women *cis* again.[9]

Harrington alleges she used to be a libertarian, and for this, she blames her time at Oxford University, which made her a "less than ideal employee" and sent her "a bit loopy" by giving her "a visceral aversion to hierarchies"[10] albeit "we were all Thatcher's babies."[11] The young, not-yet-saved Mary harbored a "fierce determination to make the world a better place." A true idiot. In the early 2000s, as *Feminism Against Progress* recounts, she "experimented with drugs, with kink, with non-monogamous relationships," she will spare you the horrible details. She worked "slacker jobs" and "hung out among the 'genderqueer' cliques" on lesbian message boards. Thank God, she had a road-to-Damascus moment just before it was too late (in fertility terms) for her to gestate one baby. She now considers the ensuing extremely dangerous birth as the foundation of her communitarian, care-oriented, relational identity as a mother. In other words, she grew up and got real about sexual difference, and so should you: "Take it from someone who has liberalled about as hard as it's possible to liberal: you've been lied to."[12] As she tells it, Harrington experienced her "sex" as violently overpowering during pregnancy, and this turned her against all utopian politics. "Does it really make sense to treat power relations as bad?" she asks. "Why not just accept that they're a fact of life?"[13] After all, the "egalitarian communes" she used to haunt were *fraudulent*, insofar as they weren't free of "power games."

"I changed my name to Sebastian for a while," writes Harrington. "I pondered whether I really was female." She is now firmly cisgender, it's strongly implied. Therefore, so is everyone else. In retrospect, she thinks everyone in her genderfluid dyke tribe was espousing a merely polite approach to people's identities, and never really believed that she was male. For example, according to the logic of their meetups, someone from the message board "who in reality was a pudgy, moon-faced woman with a buzz cut could be a sleek, suave, debonair Oscar Wilde figure, and everyone joyfully played along."[14] (As though Oscar Wilde, rest in power, wasn't moon-faced?) Everyone privately sensed the cruel impossibility of lived trans authenticity, *Feminism Against Progress* assumes. Armed with her new "sex-realist" understanding of gender as an immutable biological matter of "pikes and minnows," Mary sets out to destroy her own former transness as a nonsense, for herself and for everyone else.

"It all felt," as she recalls in bemusement, "thrilling, liberating, revolutionary."[15] Luckily, she went down some algorithmically cursed "research" rabbit holes about biolibertarian transhumanists like Martine Rothblatt,[16] and got wise to the horrors of the "utopian assault on human nature";[17] *et voilà*, a reactionary feminist was born. In her paean to TERFs published in *First Things*, Harrington paints the stakes of trans rights as epochal and civilizational, as deciding the fate of the human race. Pointedly ending the article with the advice to "carry a big stick," she calls for backup in "a bloody and zero-sum fight for dominance of political and cultural institutions," since "it is by no means clear that being on the side of objective reality will be enough to hand victory to the 'TERFs.'"[18]

Harrington was not the only middle-class feminist to be sucked in by the anti-trans right-radicalization vortex circa 2018. The most famous was J. K. Rowling, the richest author in the world, who now says things like "I refuse to bow down to a movement that I believe is doing demonstrable harm in seeking to erode 'woman' as a political and biological class,"[19] and even engages in a form of Holocaust denial—disputing the well-documented facts that the Nazis targeted trans women and burned trans sexological research.[20] Besides Rowling and Harrington, those who had access to trade publishing include: in Canada, Debra Soh (*The End of Gender*, Simon & Schuster, 2021); in the US, Kara Dansky (*The Abolition of Sex*, Bombardier, 2021); and in Britain, Helen Joyce (*Trans*, Oneworld, 2021), Kathleen Stock (*Material Girls*, Hachette, 2021), Julie Burchill (*Welcome to the Woke Trials*, Academica, 2021), Nina Power (*What Do Men Want*, Penguin, 2022), and Louise Perry (*The Case Against the Sexual Revolution*, Polity, 2022). "I used to believe the liberal narrative," writes Perry, who is now a "post-liberal" follower of the self-described "reactionary" G. K. Chesterton.

Perry helps lead the media charge against trans rights in *Unherd*, *Compact*, *Quillette*, the *Daily Mail*, the *Spectator*, the *Critic*, and the *New Statesman*,[21] while her book argues against "easy divorce," porn, abortion, and birth control, and in favor of slut shaming, "chivalry,"[22] marriage, and "sexual repression," all in the name of feminism. Like Harrington, she narrates her departure from liberalism via an anti-utopian question: "What if hierarchy, and viciousness, and violence are baked in?"[23] Marriage may be full of impunity and coercion, she grants, but "where the critics go wrong is in arguing that there is any better system. There isn't."[24] Similarly, she thinks, "male" animals will always rape.[25]

What is remarkable is how comfortably these reactionary newcomers to the anti-trans bandwagon sit alongside a left-feminist old guard. For example, the longtime anti-trans "women's liberationist" Julie Bindel got an anti-trans book deal in this period too (*Feminism for Women*, Little, Brown and Company, 2021), as did the socialist Victoria Smith (*Hags*, Hachette, 2023); and everyone seems to blurb everyone else quite happily, while the *Guardian* obligingly bestows the same warm review on all.[26] Without irony, the whole crew uses the biggest media platforms in existence, year after year, to complain about being silenced. In the *Atlantic*, the establishment left-liberal Helen Lewis celebrated the brave new "feminists insisting that women are built differently" as renegades, bemoaning the fact that American feminists are too afraid even to "engage with any reactionary-feminist arguments" lest they be "tarred as fascists and bigots."[27]

Funnily enough, there is little to distinguish Lewis's piece from Bachiochi's one on the same topic—heralding "Sex-Realist Feminism"—in an American magazine.[28] Meanwhile, two non-feminists in the UK and US—BBC journalist Hannah Barnes and *Wall Street Journal* columnist Abigail Shrier—made similar splashes with their libelous exposés of gender clinics that help trans teenagers.[29] The cover of Shrier's *Irreversible Damage* shows a white child with a hole where her uterus should be, really ramming home the gist of the book's fertility panic. The commercial success of both, despite their eugenicist, queerphobic, mother-blaming bents, benefited from love shown them by North American feminists like Meghan Murphy and gender-critical hubs like *FiLiA*, among other TERF channels.[30] In other words, Helen Lewis need not worry. At the *Times*, the *New Yorker*, and *Slate*, Michelle Goldberg has been legitimizing reactionary-feminist themes, like the debunked, pathologizing "autogynephilia" theory of trans womanhood, for a decade.[31] In May 2023, the former Fox News host Megyn Kelly posted a photo of herself in a baseball hat from the British webstore Adult Human Female: "Make Women Female Again."[32]

The phrase "adult human female" was popularized via billboard campaign, in 2018, by an anti-trans Englishwoman known as Posie Parker, whose real name is Kellie-Jay Keen-Minshull. For years this bleach-blonde suburban mother has been calling for "men with guns" to start using ladies' bathrooms to deter trans women.[33] The now-infamous billboards feature a plain black background and simply say "woman / wʊmən / noun / adult human female." The first of them was erected in Liverpool, where the 2018 Labour Party's annual conference was taking place. It was removed following complaints, but not before Posie, already camera-ready in a black "Woman Definition" T-shirt to match the billboard, purchasable at her webstore, got the publicity she wanted. As the BBC reported, "Ms. Keen-Minshull said the idea that trans women were women was 'preposterous'"; her billboard "was in response to the city's mayor, Joe Anderson, who recently voiced his support for the trans community."[34] The seed was planted. Note that Parker has not called herself a feminist since 2017. Speaking on Louise Perry's YouTube show (alongside episodes with Bachiochi, Harrington, Smith, Joyce, and Power—the whole transphobic gang) Parker cryptically said that, because "most women are *not* feminists and don't want to hear about misogyny or patriarchy, to protect women's rights, we must *abandon* feminism."[35]

I believe Parker when she says she's not a feminist, but the fact remains that until recently, when her associations with outright Nazis turned many TERFs off her at last, her *followers* have overwhelmingly been feminists. Her role in the emergence of this enemy feminism cannot be ignored. Parker's canny grift has long catered to the gender-critical crowd. The slogan "2023 is the Year of the TERF" is the first thing one sees upon clicking on "Standing for Women." And she was right: that year, Prime Minister Rishi Sunak used her core phrases, "adult human female" and "sex matters," to make cissexist arguments in the lead-up to a parliamentary debate on changes to Britain's equality law.[36] Five years after her first billboard, the Posie Parker franchise had gone viral, with partnerships and large pools of funding accruing from organs like the right-wing, US-based Heritage Foundation, alongside hundreds of thousands of followers across various social media platforms. Megyn Kelly is tagging her in social media posts and, at the time of writing, her traveling open mic rally, "Let Women Speak," has just darkened the doorstep of my own hometown of Philadelphia. According to the *Guardian*, the rally in Melbourne, in May 2023, was "attended and supported by white supremacist groups, who marched the streets repeatedly performing the Nazi salute."[37] Remarkably, J. K. Rowling responded to these headlines by condemning not the fascists but the anti-fascist counter-protestors, one of whom had poured tomato juice on the rally leader (this was, according to Rowling, "Kellie-Jay being assaulted").

While some gender-critical groups began disavowing Posie Parker, she had managed to rise to prominence largely through feminist support.[38] Some TERFs will of course plead innocence, but it was on the Radical Feminist podcast *Feminist Current* that the leader of "feminism's Brexit"[39] first praised the leader of the white nationalist English Defence League, Tommy Robinson, in 2019.[40] Clearly, the revolutionary blogger TransGriot, Monica Roberts, had this movement's number back in 2012, when she called them "RadiKKKal feminists" and "Whyte Womyn Gone Wyld."[41] Regardless of the racial position of the TERFs' enemy Other, whenever a cissexist definition of womanhood is being imposed, a colonizing, fertility-disciplining gesture is in play. As the sociologist B Camminga writes, the concerns that inform this feminism are Western and colonial, regardless of its proponents' nationality (the Nigerian writer Chimamanda Ngozi Adichie, for example, joins in).[42] But whence did Parker's, Rowling's, and Harrington's structurally white supremacist formula, that the *truth of gender* is under threat, originate?

"You make a damned good fascist," said Beth Elliott to Robin Morgan in a dream.[43] The year was 1973, and Elliott, the vice president of the San Francisco chapter of the Daughters of Bilitis (a lesbian group), was writing about her dream in the pages of *Lesbian Tide* as part of the general postmortem on the West Coast Lesbian Conference (WCLC). The gigantic gathering had taken place over a weekend that April, at UCLA in Los Angeles. Along with Kate Millett, the poet Robin Morgan (despite being married to a man) had been one of two scheduled keynote speakers. Morgan had gone to bizarre lengths, both in her lecture and in a late-night debrief on a fight she'd started with Beth Elliott the previous night, to justify her own inclusion in the conference. Her vehemence shocked many of the attendees. "I see Robin Morgan as being a very threatened woman," wrote one *Tide* contributor called Pat: "Threatened by men, by society, but above all, by Lesbians."[44] Morgan was the editor of the iconic movement volume *Sisterhood Is Powerful* (1970) and had recently become a cultural feminist.[45] Elliott, for her part, was a widely beloved trans lesbian activist and folk singer, scheduled to perform on day one of WCLC.

Morgan was spoiling for a fight with pro-transfeminists from the jump, and she finally got it when she rewrote her keynote to include a long attack on Elliott, which threw the whole conference into an uproar. Most women stood by the trans woman, defending her right to participate, but one combat-trained group of lesbian separatists threatened her, at Morgan's instigation, and had to be physically restrained by other feminists. As Barbara McLean, one of the conference organizers, later noted in her "Diary of a Mad Organizer," "Beth was on the San Francisco steering committee for the conference, a part of the original group that gave birth to the idea."[46] Robin nonetheless wanted to eject her from the charmed circle of *womyn* in California—by force, if necessary. Accounts of this schismatic early-1970s moment—when Morgan's transphobia received violent support from a separatist group, the Gutter Dykes, who physically assaulted their opponents but were ultimately themselves beaten back by a surge of pro-trans solidarity—have echoed across feminist and queer studies in the past half-century.[47]

For the twenty-first-century feminist who has swallowed the narrative that transphobia was intrinsic to the women's liberation movement, reading this installment of the lesbian movement magazine is an education. Morgan's keynote is reprinted in *Lesbian Tide* in full but placed at the back in a smaller font—sandwiched between several contributions that all criticize Morgan and oppose her sabotage of the gathering. Elliott's own reflection, "On Infidels and Inquisitions," recounts, "I dreamed I was on trial before Pope Robin I. I was on trial for daring to call myself a woman and a Lesbian." But, as everyone still reeling from the events well knew, the inquisition had happened in real life, in a "Hitleresque frenzy, a purge mentality" on the podium.[48] As I recall, I first read about it in the *Trans Advocate* in 2014, thanks to the community-building archival work of Cristan Williams.[49]

In 1973, the *Diary* records the scenes to which Morgan responded as follows:

> *Friday, 9:00* Who's that on the mike!? OH GOD NO. I don't believe it! This can't be happening. This woman is insisting that Beth Elliott not be permitted to perform because Beth is a transsexual. . . . No. We do not, cannot relate to her as a man. . . . "That's bullshit! Anatomy is NOT destiny!" . . . The vote is overwhelmingly in favor of permitting Beth to perform. She begins . . . but that small but vocal anti-Beth group makes so much noise she can't be heard. I don't know when I've ever been so scared. . . . It's 3 to 1 in favor of Beth performing. . . . Beth begins to play, though I can't understand how she can even do it. She is shaking so bad.[50]

In an interview with Cristan Williams, the musicians Robin Tyler and Patty Harrison recall, "We stepped up and defended Beth. . . . Patty and I jumped on stage and we got hit, because they came onto the stage to physically beat her."[51] With tragic prescience, as the music finally begins, McLean asks herself if the transphobia that is wrecking feminism will persist: "Can it possibly be over or has it just begun?"

The next day, the organizers' stomachs are in knots. Morgan delivers a ninety-minute lecture instead of the forty-five minutes agreed upon. "Yes, we were aware of the anti-transsexual feelings within the movement," writes McLean, but as conference hosts, no one had anticipated a lynch mob: "We thought that was over a long time ago."[52] According to her own memoir, Morgan "stayed up all night" adding lots of tailored invective, such as:

> I will not call a male "she"; 32 years of suffering in this androcentric society, and of surviving, have earned me the title "woman"; one walk down the street by a male transvestite, 5 minutes of his being hassled (which he may enjoy), and then he dares, he dares to think he understands our pain? No, in our mothers' names and in our own, we must not call him sister. We know what's at work when whites wear blackface; the same thing is at work when men wear drag. . . . I charge him as an opportunist, an infiltrator, and a destroyer—with the mentality of a rapist. And you women at

this conference know who he is. Now. You can let him into your workshops—or you can deal with him.[53]

But it was Morgan who was dealt with. As one *Tide* contributor writes of Morgan, "I will not call *her* sister."[54]

The *Diary* records, "Although she lives with a man, she's trashing women who work with men. She says we should hate men. Now she's trashing Kate. Now she's trashing us over the transsexual thing. She's trashing EVERYONE. I can't believe she ever wrote anything about 'sisterhood.'" Those who invited her feel betrayed. "What have we done? An hour and a half of HATE!"[55] Remarkably, not one person in *Tide*'s May–June issue is prepared to condone Morgan's undermining of the gathering through her attempted purges of transfemmes, leftists, heterosexuals, and the Socialist Worker's Party—let alone her calls for "further polarization"[56] and "man-hating."[57]

My favorite moment occurred later on the Saturday of the conference, when the Gutter Dykes once again shoved McLean from the mic in an attempt to make 1,500 feminists again rehash the organizers' failures vis-à-vis transsexualism. "Many of the women are screaming that they don't want to hear about that any more," notes McLean. Then, out of the blue, another trans woman steps in:

> Someone is calling me. There's a blind woman who wants to come up on the stage. God, what now? I help her up. She's furious about something! I'm afraid to hear WHAT. She pounds on the podium, insists on speaking. I plead with the audience, with the Gutter Dykes. . . . Finally they let her speak. She's a TRANSSEXUAL! So emotional, trembling so bad she can hardly stand up, clutching the mike she cries out that these women are crucifying Beth and all transsexuals: "How much pain must she bear. Why do you torment her? You are more oppressive than our oppressors. . . ."[58]

"This glorious action," notes scholar Emma Heaney, "defeats the Gutter Dykes and they relinquish the microphone."[59] As Elliott testifies in the aftermath, these solidarities "kept alive my faith in womankind."[60] With regard to Morgan herself, Beth simply states, with dignity, "I personally distrust those who hate men more than they love or do anything positive for women."

But in Morgan's tirade, there's a legacy of Langham Place's refusal of the "wrong" kind of nineteenth-century feminist sister (too Scottish or Irish; too savage or wild; to emigrate with us under our banner; *not really a woman*). In her gynocentric biological determinism lurk the roots of KKK feminism, for whom "our pain" as white women "in chains" justifies infinite revenge, even via lynch mob—but only on the alien other, not the white man (certainly not against Morgan's self-described "effeminate" husband). Equally, Morgan's feminist misogyny and open contempt for "camp"[61] reveal a direct line to Wollstonecraftian femmephobia, which portrayed white women's enjoyment of dress and adornment as a kind of racial degeneration. What's more, her certainty that feminine attire, when donned from a position of choice, is the direct analog of blackface minstrelsy—a mockery of "our mothers, and *their* mothers, who had no other choice, who wore hobbling dresses and torture stiletto heels to survive, to keep jobs, or to keep husbands because they themselves could get no jobs"—echoes the pro-uniform ideology of the Blackshirt ex-suffragette policewomen, for whom wearing skirts represented an abdication of feminist power.[62]

In *Going Too Far* (1978), Morgan prefaces another reprinting of her keynote by rewriting events to paint herself as a courageous star who merely said what *everyone was thinking* about "one smug male in granny glasses and an earth-mother gown." Beth was "the only person there wearing a skirt," she spits; her "gate-crashing presence," disgracefully pandered to by Beth's fellow conference organizers, caused conference-goers to return "to their home states in disgust."[63] This insinuation—of a sly, foreign, undermining presence poisoning lesbians' community—gives breath to a fascistic femmephobia.[64] Faced with the wordless proposition that trans and cis lesbians face the same enemy and share the same struggle, Morgan refuses the contamination of "her" people, opting instead for a disavowal of common interests, even of common humanity. Elliott understood this well about Morgan: "You are treating me just like men treat women. . . . The idea that I might be the same as you threatens you, so you hold me down."[65]

But Robin Morgan was not the first feminist transmisogynist. Already in *The Female Eunuch* (1970), the macho feminist edgelord Germaine Greer had been so sure her readers shared her disgust at transfemininity that she ended her chapter on "stereotyping" by calling *all* women transsexuals, clearly intending to shock and provoke. Describing the British society lady April Ashley, who was outed as a transsexual in 1961, Greer ridiculed Ashley's artificial vagina and inability to "consummate" her marriage to the baron Rowallan.[66] "April's incompetence as a woman is what we must expect from a castrate," she wrote, "but it is not so very different after all from the impotence of feminine women." In short: "As long as the feminine stereotype remains the definition of the female sex, April Ashley *is* a woman . . . our sister and our symbol."[67] Femininity as impotence: this was supposed to be a galvanizing cry to cis women to smash the similarity—to *stop* being eunuchs, to kill the femme within.[68] "I'm sick of being a transvestite," bellowed Greer. "I refuse to be a female impersonator. I am a woman, not a castrate."[69]

Two decades later, *in The Whole Woman*, the sequel to *The Female Eunuch*, Greer repeats the idea that "as sufferers of gender role distress themselves, women must sympathize with transsexuals,"[70] even as she calls the latter "pantomime dames" and "rapists" who are attempting, just like the cross-dresser in *Psycho* (1960), an "exorcism of the mother."[71] Since 2021, Mary Harrington, for her part, has kept herself busy recycling this last bit via a series of articles such as "Trans Activism Has Mummy Issues," "The Left Has Mummy Issues," and the like.[72] Femininity = bad. The phallic cisgender maternal = good.

In both *The Whole Woman* and *The Female Eunuch*, Greer fantasizes baselessly that trans women want to kill their mothers and don't want to *be* mothers themselves, only fuckdolls. She projects suspicions she so clearly feels toward trans women onto *them*, diagnosing "hostility" (on *their* part) "toward the intact."[73] Later, Greer's writing smoothed the way for an orgy of similar pseudo-psychologizing cruelty by *Guardian* feminists such as Julie Burchill, Julie Bindel, and Suzanne Moore in the 2000s and 2010s, when the UK media pruriently platformed all these columnists, including Greer herself, as they snarled their best jokes about trans women in terms of lopped cocks, stinking post-surgical necrosis, swinging dicks, bad wigs, postmodern PhDs, bed-wetting, and suppurating holes.[74] In *A Short History of Trans Misogyny*, Jules Gill-Peterson explains that a key thing transmisogynists do to their targets involves "sexualizing their presumptive femininity as if it were an expression of male aggression."[75]

The trend peaked in 2013, the same year that Deep Green Resistance—an ecological anarcho-primitivist group in the US devoted to forest defense–style direct actions and neo-cultural feminism—imploded over the lurid and bullying transphobia of two of its founders.[76] I followed these events from within the anarchist climate justice milieu in the UK, where—together with my erstwhile writing collective, Out of the Woods—I noticed the rise of a "völkisch environmentalism," one of whose talking points was the "breaking down of everything from gender identities to national borders."[77] I now wish we had pushed harder for queer green radical feminists to think critically about the rhetorical seductions of eco-fascism. Today, both the "green nationalism"[78] that is so prevalent in Brexit Britain, and the purity impulse driving gender-critical and pornophobic lesbians to campaign to "Get the L out"[79] (of the LGBTQ+ coalition), express an eco-fascistic need for clean boundaries and unambiguous definitions.

In a historicizing discussion of "Get the L Out," the political scientist Elena Gambino has movingly shown that, contrary to common narratives about second-wave lesbian feminism, radical lesbian communities in the US frequently held themselves to sophisticated disciplines of reparation, responsibility, and accountability—for racism, for example, as well as for other interpersonal ills such as transphobia. It is a minority of feminists, then and now, who have chosen to practice something different; namely, a feminism predicated on others' exclusion from the charmed circle, be the *other* in question sex workers, indigenous queers, or trans people (if indeed the three can be distinguished in the trans-exclusionary mind). "We might name TERFish-ness a relationship of moral vulnerability," Elena writes.[80] Cis women are not only directing harms toward differently gendered feminists, but also evading accountability for these harms by refusing to acknowledge them as harms in the first place. TERFs' central claim—that they are the *real victims* of marginalization—is a classic settler-colonial gesture, wherein "victim" and "oppressor" get reversed on the basis of a definition of womanhood as unambiguous moral innocence. "Get the L Out," in this manner, seeks to withdraw to an imagined place of safety, and refuses the accountability that is and was central to queer feminism.

It is important to note that, in the 1970s, Robin Morgan's transmisogyny was not only flowing to and from the British and Australian TERF milieu of people like Greer, Beatrix Campbell (the veteran English anti-trans left feminist), and Sheila Jeffreys (the Melbourne-based English author of *Penile Imperialism* and *Gender Hurts*, whose celebration of vice-busting Victorians we discussed earlier). Crucially, Morgan was simultaneously serving as a node of transmission for another, theological strand of feminist transmisogyny headquartered in the US; namely, that of the ex–Roman Catholic professor of philosophy at Boston College, Mary Daly— and of Daly's student, Janice Raymond.

"Eunuchs Fuck Women," reads one subheading in the *off our backs* (*OOB*) interview with Daly in May 1979. *OOB* has just asked whether the cultural feminist theologian thinks "part of the problem with men is so basic that it goes back to biological-chemical differences." Daly has answered in the affirmative. "The Y chromosome is like a shrivelled X chromosome," she claims. Luckily, "mutations have a way of dying out. So maybe mutations will manage to kill themselves off eventually."[81] With all the matter-of-factness of a cult leader, Daly explains how "transsexuals" are "invading our private spaces" and "playing upon the sympathies of women" by using the "more oppressed than thou mentality." This "is not a kooky or minor phenomenon," she warns ominously. "These men [*sic*] have no penises, but their whole body, their whole mind is still a penis. Their eyes are penises, their hands are penises"—you better believe it. Despite this unusual anatomy, though, transsexuals are freakishly magnetic. "There's this seductiveness about men who appear to be feminine," Daly says. They *seem* "sensitive," but they are reincarnations of the genderbending god Dionysus, who birthed himself and lured Amazons into debauched ruin thanks to the "demonic power of Dionysian deception."[82] Trans acceptance will usher in the "Dionysian Final Solution," with battalions of "gender identity clinics" such that, for instance, "9-year-old girls who are strong will be named as deviants."[83]

"Welcome," as Robin Morgan wrote in the preface to *The Mary Daly Reader*, "to the brain orgasms of Dalyworld."[84] Daly's *Gyn/Ecology: The Meta-Ethics of Radical Feminism* (1978) takes eighteenth-century feminist misogyny and femmephobia to new extremes: feminine women, here, are lobotomized, moronic "puppets of Papa" and robotic fem-bot mutants.[85] In the book's final pages, she fantasizes a lesbian assembly, presided over by a magnificent "Chaircrone," but interrupted by "infernal infiltrators" and "demons." She calls these femmes "Obsessors," and describes their procession as carrying objects *she* deems misogynist: "tiny shoes, nylons, and spiked heels," cosmetics, jewelry, and the pill. Some are "eunuchs" and "one is carrying a placard which reads: 'I am a lesbian-feminist male-to-female transsexual. Take me in.'"[86] The "Hags begin hooting."[87] Femininity is here cleanly divorced from true, spinster-identified, hag-tastic, crone-like, amazon femaleness. Hence: "The surgeons and hormone therapists of the transsexual kingdom, in their effort to give birth, can be said to produce feminine persons. They cannot produce women."[88] But even cissexual, "self-loathing ladies titter," Daly writes. "Hags and Harpies roar." But "Fembots titter at themselves when Daddy turns the switch. They totter when he pulls the string."[89] Daly punningly riffs like this for over four hundred pages about "malfunctions (Male-Functions),"[90] gynocide, foot-binding, "mindbinding,"[91] "male sirens,"[92] and "phallo-technic society."[93]

Despite relying constantly on Webster's dictionary, Daly describes her use of language ("spinning," "whirling," and "spiraling"[94]) as itself anti-male. Reading her reminds me of Jean-Paul Sartre's observation about the anti-Semite:

> Never believe that anti-Semites are completely unaware of the absurdity of their replies. They know that their remarks are frivolous. . . . But they are amusing themselves, for it is their adversary who is obliged to use words responsibly, since he believes in words. The anti-Semites have the right to play. They even like to play with discourse for, by giving ridiculous reasons, they discredit the seriousness of their interlocutors. They delight in acting in bad faith, since they seek not to persuade by sound argument but to intimidate and disconcert.[95]

In fact, the British scholar Naomi Alizah Cohen has argued that modern antisemitism—the "socialism of fools"—and TERFism overlap in profound ways. It is no coincidence, Cohen shows, that, for National Socialists, the trans woman represented "the Jew's most abhorrent creation."[96] Nazism aligned all things Semitic with the feminine faggotry, transsexuality, and transvestism of Weimar-era Berlin's numerous "mollies" and "dolls" (lesbian masculinity and transmasculinity were actually marginal in the Nazi demonology). It was transfeminine people, specifically, whom German fascism regarded as unholy mutants formed against nature, like "Frankenstein's monster" and indeed, in this view, like Jews.

The socialism of fools and transmisogyny both turned on a construction of the natural and materially "concrete" as good, *versus* the immaterial, artificial, and abstract as bad. So, just as the Jew becomes the embodiment of capitalism's abstraction—in "left" antisemitism—"the trans woman becomes the concrete manifestation of the abstraction and denaturalization of gender."[97] Note that the virus of *artifice*—as an enemy of the people—is biologized and personified in both these forms of pseudo-materialism. Trans women and Jews alike belong to the domain of trickery, usury, dysgenics, wandering amorphousness, degeneracy, and the demonic. Aryans and cissexuals, conversely, belong to the domain of truth, earth, primal purpose, clean outlines, and palpable borders.[98] In my interpretation, Daly's "meta-ethics" are fascistic in precisely this way.

Today, Daly is a lauded figure in religious studies as well as a still-cited feminist theorist. In the twenty-first century, anthologies and retrospectives have been devoted to her thought.[99] This makes me wonder: Had the lesbian feminist Audre Lorde not publicly called out the Boston-based Jesuit college professor's racism in her "Letter to Mary Daly,"[100] who knows how much *more* influence she might have enjoyed? As it is, *Gyn/Ecology* laid the foundation for the trans-antagonistic technophobia of contemporary ecological thinkers as different as Lierre Keith and the later Silvia Federici, whose willful misreadings of Judith Butler and Donna Haraway are not substantially different from those found in the right-wing "anti-gender" mobilizations and anti-transhumanism conspiracy cults worldwide. In Silvia Federici's *Beyond the Periphery of the Skin* (2020)—in many ways a reversal of Federici's 1970s politics—trans embodiment appears as part of an aesthetically retrograde, antifeminist "craze for remakes," and represents trans people not as the historic victims and opponents of doctors, with their capitalistic agenda of social control and docility, but as enthusiastic embracers of them as "the godlike creators of our bodies."[101]

The direct inheritor of Dalyism, however, was another ex-Catholic seminarian: Daly's PhD supervisee Janice Raymond. While much ink has already been spilt on Raymond and her fountainhead text of TERFism,[102] 1979's *The Transexual Empire*, not to mention her core role in getting trans medical care excluded from American public insurance policies,[103] and her creation of a global feminist "anti-trafficking" infrastructure,[104] we cannot dispense with mentioning her here. Raymond's influence has been incalculable, not only among anti-capitalist feminists, but in mainstream liberal circles: When *Empire* came out, conspiracist and hateful as it was, it was blurbed by Daly, Morgan, and Dworkin, as well as by Morgan's friend, Gloria Steinem, who also supported the book with positive coverage in *Ms.*[105]

For Raymond, it's quite simple: "Transsexuals are *not* women. They are deviant males."[106] Beyond that, however, it all gets shambolic in an unmistakably Dalyite way. "The boundaries that have been and are used against lesbians are the boundaries of the Fathers," proposes *The Transsexual Empire*, unaccountably.[107] On the other hand, the boundaries that cis lesbians use against transsexuals are, for some reason, "genuine boundaries of self-preservation and self-centering."[108] Another hazy assertion is that, unlike the clean-cut boundary *crossings* that lesbians engage in politically, transsexuals are poststructuralist, post-Oedipal "boundary violators."[109] (Crossing lines is good, violating them is bad, got it?) If the text weren't so annihilationist, it might almost be entertaining to watch Raymond careen neurotically in and out of the foothills of a realization, similar to Greer's, that solidarity between trans and non-trans women is logical. "It could be said that *all* women who conform to [the feminine] are transsexuals, fashioned according to man's image," she writes.[110] Well, sure! But in that case, she is willing, like Daly, to say that true lesbians are purely unfeminine, and that cis feminine women are disgusting *too*—so there.

Anyway, transsexuals aren't self-created "in woman's image" in the same way that lesbians are "beginning to create ourselves in our own image." It might *seem* similar, as Raymond herself flags, but it's just not. Transsexuals are not self-made but man-made by the "medical fathers." They are "masochists," and as such have "great difficulty in believing in the validity and sanctity of their own insides."[111] Oh, right, that's another point of similarity with cis women. Curses! OK, transsexuals are strategically confusing lesbians *on purpose*. They are forcing us to define the differences between men and women, which were self-evident until *they* came along. Not today, Satan, Raymond says. We don't want to be "dragged back to answering such old questions." Some of us, as she haughtily sniffs, "have come to realize that those differences are important whether they spring from socialization or from biology."[112]

I can hardly think of a better summary of the anti-intellectualism of today's gender-critical feminists. "Until the past few years, it wasn't controversial to know or to say that there are two sexes, which are immutable," claims Nina Power, the formerly left-wing, now right-wing feminist philosopher and *Compact* editor, in her crowing provocation, "Welcome to TERF Island."[113] This is a wildly popular talking point in populist circles, but it is not true at all. It could hardly be less true. As Beans Velocci and other historians of science have patiently excavated, over the centuries, "consensus about what sex is and how to define it has been difficult to find." In itself this scientific cacophony is hardly surprising, since the natural world contains more exceptions than rules, and the tendentious motives and rationales driving inquiries into sex's true nature have been as mutually contradictory as patriarchy itself. But nor should the uncertainty trouble us since, as Velocci writes, "what sex 'really' is, if it really is anything, doesn't matter."[114] Contrary to Helen Joyce's assertion, in *Trans: Where Ideology Meets Reality*, that "sex is *why* women are oppressed,"[115] sex is not in itself the reason anything happens; rather, it is pressed into service as a concept rationalizing oppression. Defining women is not and has not, historically, been remotely necessary for feminism to proceed, and until recently, it was hardly ever feminism's game. In her magisterial hatchet job on Joyce's book (alongside Bindel's *Feminism for Women: The Real Route to Liberation* and Stock's *Material Girls: Why Reality Matters for Feminism*), the British feminist writer Grace Lavery sums it up. "Reality—the reality shared by women, actual women, in the world—really *does* matter for feminism. Metaphysical definitions of the category 'woman' really, really don't."[116]

In 2012, the world mourned the death of Adrienne Rich, a gifted lesbian poet who made the regrettable decision to help Jan Raymond as she wrote *The Transsexual Empire*. Adrienne did not originate much enemy feminism, but despite leaving the cissexist anti-porn world, she never publicly sought to repair the harm her work with Raymond did. Three days after her death, Bryn Kelly,[117] the Appalachian writer and beloved New York community activist, posted her thoughts about Rich on her Tumblr. "Lesbians in the 70s had it hard, and they still have it hard," she wrote.

> They were marginally employed then, trying to make art and change that no one understood, and that gets laughed at now. Their old cars break down all the time and there is never any money to get them fixed and they can't just bike around like they

used to. All their spaces are gone: their bookstores, their cafes, their activist centers. They do not recognize what we call feminism as anything like the feminism they know and that has meant to so much to them; and, perhaps not surprisingly, they find our theory and our praxis highly suspect. They all have breast cancer. Some of them have had it a couple times.[118]

Bryn's comradely and forgiving words remind me of the recollections of Karla Jay—one of the members of Radicalesbians, the 1970 group—about becoming close with Marsha Johnson, the decolonial gay-liberation street queen who cofounded STAR (Street Transvestite Action Revolutionaries).

"Although she knew I had mixed feelings about transvestism," writes Jay, "we became fast friends."[119] This friendship clearly speaks of Johnson's great magnanimity (which even extended, in Jay's own account, to allowing Jay to gropingly inspect her breasts!) but also attests to solidarities that formed between working-class cis and trans women who both experienced misogyny within the gay movement. Karla interviewed Marsha as a gay sister for the 1972 *Out of the Closets* anthology and recalls how she and Marsha both always volunteered to be on "clean-up" duty after gay liberation movement dances, after which they typically went out together (at 3 a.m.) to eat at an all-night diner before continuing on to various after-hours bars. Once, inside an unmarked speakeasy only Marsha knew, Karla recalls asking, "Which is the women's room?" In response, Marsha said, "Honey! Just go into whichever one smells best! That's where the good dope's gonna be."[120] Words to live by, in my opinion.

Nonetheless, it was a demoralizing and isolating experience to be a trans lesbian shortly after Adrienne Rich's death. Bryn Kelly recalls contemplating, with paranoia, her peers' apologism for Rich's still unaccounted-for episode of feminist transmisogyny. "Did she know," grieves Bryn, "did she *really* know, how damaging her collusion on this work would be to generations of low-income trans people to come? How much deep suffering and heartache it would cause? How it would bestow on us a whole new set of knives to rip each other up with?"

We may never know the answer. And as the twenty-first century descends to new depths of anti-trans horror, knowing how to draw lines that say, this feminist is our enemy, is increasingly indispensable. Yet as Bryn reminds us, "Figuring out how to live together is hard. To exist in community with people who constantly piss you off is exhausting, but ultimately: worth it." Most non-transfeminists are not enemies. In all kinds of intergenerational feminist and lesbian communities, it often happens that someone says, "Hey. Did you know you hurt me? Can we talk about that?"[121]—and is heard.

Feminism Against Cisness

The coalition emerges out of your recognition that it's
fucked up for you, in the same way that we've recognized
it's fucked up for us. I don't need your help. I just need
you to realize that this shit is killing you, too, however
much more softly, you stupid motherfucker, you know?

—FRED MOTEN, 2013[1]

What could Mary Wollstonecraft have said instead of "woman is the n—r of the world?" What *did* others at the time say, without the access she had to a publisher? I hope this book has inspired, if nothing else, a desire to find this out. An alternative history of Western feminism might be told, beginning not with *A Vindication*, but with Charles Fourier or Harriet Jacobs—and then proceeding from there through the maroon, communard, erotophilic, gender-abolitionist strands of nineteenth- and twentieth-century anti-capitalism.[2] This history would not, of course, be remotely free of schisms, missteps, contradictions, and exclusions, but it would show a liberatory rather than anti-liberatory tradition: from the milieu of Catherine Impey's *Anti-Caste* journal of the 1880s and '90s to the struggles of decolonial groups like STAR in the 1970s, from the internationalist feminism of the nineteenth-century French-Peruvian socialist Flora Tristan to the Boston-based Bread and Roses collective in the twentieth century, and from the "red love" of Bolshevik visionary Alexandra Kollontai to that of Third-Worldist family abolitionists like Pat Parker.[3] I've taken certain forms of pleasure in writing this book, but let me tell you, I can't wait to go back to reading and disagreeing with my current and future comrades instead of my enemies. Spend too long in this book's archive, and you might start thinking that most feminism was *for* cisness, which is to say, *for* an understanding of sex as imposable upon people from the outside.

Of course, enemies are sometimes family. Carol Leigh, the "Scarlot Harlot," loved feminism "like I love my mom," even as *it* mostly did not love her back.[4] Anyone familiar with Leigh's writing, or with the work of the groups she belonged to or founded—COYOTE, BAYSWAN, SWOP-USA, ACT UP—knows that she was constantly insisting that "poverty forces women into survival sex and sex for money."[5] As such, whatever Catharine MacKinnon may say, we know that Leigh invented the terms *sex work* and *pornophobia* from *within* a movement for women's liberation. Carol may, in fact, have been "sisterly" to a fault. In *Unrepentant Whore*, her memoir, Carol spends an awful lot of time almost repenting. She is generous. It is the yearning for "sisterhood" that makes her so quick, time and again, to offer to be accountable to those she may have wronged.[6] Sisterhood is what makes her entertain, so often, the idea of her faction being wrong. She regrets that her fellow "slut radicals abhor the pornophobes."[7] For her part: "I don't want to fight my sisters."

Carol sits down with a former fellow prostitute turned MacKinnonite. This friend has "been raped and arrested more times than I can fathom," and she now works "with the Vice Squad and the District Attorney, after leaving her job in the jails, where she launched the local mandatory HIV testing program for prostitutes, drawing blood from those convicted of prostitution." Carol is hurt, startled, and repelled by what her old friend is doing. Still, she forces herself to empathize: "Maybe slut-positive women *can* seem like the enemy. Maybe we *should* be treated like outcasts, excluded from the family of feminists, labeled liars."[8] Carol's so-called friend, however, does not return the favor. She looks Carol in the face and says: "Arresting prostitutes is the only way we can get services to them." In fact, "two or three days in jail is not long enough to get a woman off drugs. There must be a way to keep them in jail for longer." To top it all off, she tells Carol, "If you make it any easier for women to slip into prostitution, you'll have blood on your hands." *Blood on MY hands?* Carol thinks, biting her tongue. Nonetheless, she holds out valiantly for "a new feminist revelation, based on a union of the good girls and the sluts," a sisterhood of "my whore friends" and those currently working to jail them for their own good.

With apologies to Carol, I believe this level of optimism and kindness has been imprudent for left feminism. I agree with the anarchists Michael Richmond and Alex Charnley when they argue, in their essay "Fascism and the Women's Cause," that feminism has been one of fascism's "forms of appearance," and must, in such cases, be fought accordingly.[9] This is why I cannot rejoice when MacKinnon publishes, in 2023, "a feminist defense of transgender sex equality rights" predicated, as ever, on a version of sex that *unwomans* sex workers.[10]

In the slim, lacerating volume *Morbid Obsessions* (2022), the British fiction writer Alison Rumfitt mulls the question of points of no return, and lines of enmity that have to be drawn, painful though this is, between whorephobic feminists and feminist whores, anti-trans feminists and transfeminists. Without realizing it, she writes, gender-critical discourse shares much with trans arguments. "A lot of TERFs talk at length about not feeling like women, not feeling any sort of association with it as a category or role beyond their biology. . . . But we are past the point of ever fulfilling the dream of them realizing en masse that this is exactly what trans people often feel."[11]

In a similar vein, Rumfitt's interlocutor, the sex-worker liberationist Frankie Miren, muses that "it's hard not to be morbidly obsessed with the people who hate you, especially when they're so visible and relentless."[12] For example, how can one not fixate on the logic in play when, in 1983, the sex-worker activist Margo St. James sought to debate Kathleen Barry, the author of *Female Sexual Slavery* (1979), at one of the first ever anti-trafficking conferences? Barry refused, saying that it would be "inappropriate to discuss sexual slavery with prostitute women."[13] Presumably, the appropriate experts, and, more important, victims, are the good and normal unused women who aren't enslaved by monetized sexuality. (Barry went on to cofound the Coalition Against Trafficking in Women, which introduced the vague sense of *sexual exploitation* into UN and US policy, such that "trafficking" is now widely taken to mean all monetized sex.) Says Miren of "mega-SWERFs" (sex worker–exclusionary radical feminists) like Barry: "I've spent a lot of time wondering how you end up in that place."[14]

So have I; but as we both know, our empathy and curiosity must not stop us from mobilizing to protect ourselves and each other. Later on, *Morbid Obsessions* interviews Natalia Santana Mendes, a Brazilian *travesti* and English Collective of Prostitutes activist. Clearly, sighs Mendes, self-described neo-abolitionism is nothing but an implementation of racist police and the border regime, "making us poorer and more vulnerable to violence."[15] Sometimes, the bourgeois project that is feminist pornophobia is "radical" in flavor; at other times, neoliberal. The outcome is identical: all available evidence suggests that when pornophobes seek to intervene in the criminal legal system, the result strengthens "the institutions that perpetuate economic exploitation, colonialist notions of progress, and white supremacy."[16] Left-leaning and right-leaning feminists on the crime discussion threads of British web forums like Mumsnet are hard to distinguish. Sometimes, Miren feels, their way of pitying while jeering at the people they term "prossies" (sex workers) even merges into the language "johns" (consumers) use when they discuss sex workers with one another while "rating" them online.[17] Increasingly, the way enemy feminists talk about their feminine others gives a respectable voice to the raw (trans) misogyny their far-right Christian funders hope to disguise.[18]

Many sex workers are parents, and might wish to use forums like Mumsnet, notes Molly Smith, the author, with Juno Mac, of

Revolting Prostitutes: The Fight for Sex Workers' Rights.[19] But when they do, they are often told:

> "The less we see of prostitutes on Mumsnet the better." One user suggests: "perhaps we should form a group and chase the prossies out!" Another writes, "you whores pander to men, you undermine women, you steal our husbands, you spread disease, you are a constant threat to society and morals." One of the most shocking comments on the site, in response to a post by a sex worker, runs: "As for children being removed—so what? Why would anyone think it's a good environment for a child to be raised by someone who, according to you, chooses to allow men to fuck them for money?"[20]

The spirit of the fascist feminist Mary Richardson is clearly alive and well in Albion, but contrary to gender-critical Mumsnetters' assumptions, self-organized sex workers are *not* advocates for the sex industry, any more than cleaners are apologists for corporate sanitation giants. They simply require something all workers need as we struggle to accommodate ourselves to gender and the market *now*, while also planning a better world for the future, i.e., freedom, *in the meantime*, from stigma and police. We do not need to say that TERFs aren't feminist in order to know that they must be stripped of cultural and institutional power. In fact, the bifurcating and hierarchizing ideology of cisness, in capitalist history, has been a consistently central theme of bourgeois feminism.

In her introduction to the collection *Feminism Against Cisness*, Emma Heaney explains that feminists can very well understand—often have understood before now—sexual difference without "cisness." In other words, to say that sexual difference is material "is different than saying sexual difference is natural or eternal, far from it. It is, in fact, to say the opposite."[21] Counterintuitive as it might seem, we all already know that our sex can change; indeed, many people talk about prison, for example, as a place where men are unsexed or re-sexed, albeit this feminization is imagined as violent, imposed via rape, unchosen, and to be feared. But sex also often changes outside of prison over the course of a person's day. "A butch can experience masculinist priority amidst community in the dyke bar," offers Heaney, and that is maleness. She can then be "feminized by harassers on the subway home," and be unpleasantly reinscribed into femaleness. Within one day, a CEO can "rhetorically dominate a boardroom and be subject to brutal or subtle misogynist undermining by her husband at home."

This is because "sex" is mostly not pre-discursive. All bodies are penetrable, but sexual difference, as we all tend to think about it, is a social hierarchy based on denying this universal penetrability. Sex is on the one hand a pull of affinity—a feeling of bodily identification with people situated on one side of the binary or the other—and, on the other, it is a dehumanizing push toward classification. At the same time as we choose elements of it, sex is *subjection*, based on the idea that penetration is subordinating (paired with the ascription of penetrability to some bodies and not others). Much as we pretend that it is, sex is not, in fact, bound to specific anatomical holes. Cisness, Heaney shows, is "feminism's counterrevolution."

Sex is not cis. What Emma means by this is that the recasting of sex hierarchy as a binary biological fact always follows directly from political challenges to the sanctity of sex as an ordained social hierarchy. The eighteenth- and early nineteenth-century advocates of bourgeois women's rights, for example, biologized the genders of oriental others *because* they were trying to contain the challenge to cisness's racial order precipitated by their own political claims for emancipation. Likewise, as Heaney demonstrates in *The New Woman*, the subsequent pro-homosexual advocacy of the sexological bourgeoisie created its own *male* cisness by denigrating a deviant transfemininity as its other—a canny (and unsuccessful) attempt to escape the kind of state repression that destroyed even the upper-class Oscar Wilde. Sexual hygiene campaigns, as we've noted, concurrently sought to eliminate *hijras, amrad,* or *berdache,* while the vice police in the metropoles similarly targeted transfeminine people (*fairies* and *mollies*) for arrest. In this history, then, the transfemme is not only the "disavowed remainder of gay rights"; she is also the most viciously pursued victim of state power's project of making the modern world safe for emancipated women. "Cisness," Emma writes, "is the name for the normativity that reincorporated

gay men and feminists into the bourgeois system that their existence would otherwise threaten."[22] The phrase "feminism against
cisness" ought to be a redundancy.

My hope is that this mini-encyclopedia of Western cisfeminism
you've just read will not drive you to despair, but rather percolate in
your brain, spawning speculative fabulations of past and future feminisms against cisness and against whiteness, its twin. How might
the kinds of riotous, comradely, mutually mothering labors begun
fifty years ago by decolonial[23] revolutionary groups, like STAR in
New York, Radicalqueens in Philadelphia, and Transsexual Action
Organization in Miami, still prevail one day over their cis-imperial
counterparts? How might girlproles expropriate the adult human
female bossbabes? I try to picture what Frances Gage might have
done differently in the handling of Sojourner Truth's truth. I ask
that you envision with me the kind of counter-feminism that might
have knocked May French-Sheldon or Alice Schwarzer from their
pulpits or stopped them getting up there in the first place. Let's
discuss, next time we see each other, how anti-fascist feminists
shall crush a bishop Alma White when another white supremacist
feminist tries to claim her mantle; or how decolonial sisters can
puncture the clash-of-civilizations nonsense of Ayaan 2.0. What
kind of feminism did the "frivolous women" in the garrison town
of Grantham deserve—the sex workers, charity girls, mollies, and
mother-ers—instead of the version imposed on them by the volunteer police?[24] Likely, something like *that* is what our nativist, cissex-
ualizing present calls for. As we now know, in the 1920s and '30s,
red suffragettes took their fight right to the feminist fascism in the
Blackshirt movement. One hundred years later, we are duty-bound
to be their analogs, beating back the feminist forced-birthers, the
maternalist "parents' rights" activists, and the racist "sex-trafflick-
ing" conspiracists. We need all the help we can get.

In 2021, an art show (*Disgrace*) with the theme "feminism and the
political right" took place in London, at a small art gallery called
Arcadia Missa. The artists, Hannah Quinlan and Rosie Hastings, exhibited works depicting the antecedents of today's TERFs:

pro-empire suffragists, volunteer policewomen, and pantsuited Thatcherites.[25] Additionally, the gallery printed a trio of accompanying essays by celebrated transfeminists and critical race theorists: Lola Olufemi, Juliet Jacques, and Akanksha Mehta. Strikingly, none of the writers fawned over Hastings's and Quinlan's accomplishments or even excused the exhibition's shortcomings, a fact I find, in and of itself, pedagogical. "In the gallery," wrote Olufemi, "two white women artists put whiteness on display. They invite feedback and reflection . . . [but] they blow those fascists up so big, it's hard not to think of them as monuments."[26] Similarly, Mehta, who researches "right-wing sisterhood"[27] and directs the Centre for Feminist Research at Goldsmiths University, wrote about her skepticism:

> That sounds like a good exhibition and a worthy political project, I thought, but who is this actually for? Are we still having to tell the story of how *all* white feminism is/was a project of imperialism that not only invests itself in and emerges from racialized hierarchies and colonial violence but also, by virtue of that, only ever confines and kills the possibilities of gender justice and liberation?[28]

I appreciate why Akanksha would be frustrated. But as she knows too well, we *are* still having to tell the story. Those of us who can bear to tell it *must* tell it, again and again. This is precisely because, as Mehta continues, "it is necessary to stop exceptionalizing the right-wing and draw out the continuities and complicities of liberalism and fascism as they pertain to feminism."[29]

Mehta's essay expresses weariness at having to overcome, time and again, white shock, white innocence, and white ignorance vis-à-vis the aforementioned *continuities and complicities*. At one point, a bitter disavowal of comradeship surfaces:

> The mess we are in today didn't appear out of nowhere. Your (white) sisterhood was never ours—it was premised on our oppression and erasure. Your glorious history of "women's movements and feminist struggles" was and is an imperial history that continues to stifle and kill. The radical presents, futures, worlds, and freedoms that some of us dream of and make happen hold histories you will never be able to understand.[30]

The "never" here is too pessimistic, I hope and trust. Yet it was invaluable, to my mind, that Olufemi and Mehta criticized, so candidly, the art whose exhibition pamphlet they were published in. Not least because of their inclusion by the targets of their critique, *Disgrace* called on the non-defensive capacities of feminists who may harbor bourgeois aspirations and/or nationalist attachments, prompting us to exercise an at once self-critical and utopian imagination. The disgrace is ours, too, they imply—not only, say, Theresa May's. What, then, do we have to let go, break, lose, and grieve, before the way becomes clearer for solidarity and freedom-making?

Despite it all, feminism lives. For this reason, I will always welcome moments of tetchy decolonial pessimism over high-literary boredom. An evergreen gesture exists whereby the badness of "The Movement" in the present is decried because the critic trains her tunnel vision only on the most reactionary elements. Feminist political thought, right now, is "deeply boring" and "unthrilling," critics of this school propose.[31] Feminism today is "uninspired," "dull and unimaginative."[32] And no doubt, "pussy hats are embarrassing,"[33] just as they say—but if one looks only at the bourgeois mainstream, while simultaneously identifying with it, one will always find fodder for one's consolatory stance of underwhelmed, distanced cynicism.

Explicitly, some of the high-cultural left appraisals of contemporary feminism are "embarrassed" about a version of feminism their authors themselves espoused in their youth—a dimly remembered feminism circa 2005–15, shorn of any critique of capitalism and uncontested, apparently, by better versions of feminism. I can relate to this embarrassment, but I remember the lay of the land in adolescence very differently. Then as now, there were feminisms in the West focused on decriminalizing sex work and gestation, demanding "bread, roses, and hormones too," taking unoccupied houses, demanding gender-affirming healthcare for all, suing the police, and fighting cuts to the shelters and programs that serve fugitives from the family. I may not, admittedly, have been listening to them back then, but they were there. They were there, just as the rebellions of wayward and incarcerated girls were there in 1917—for instance in New York's Bedford women's prison—albeit unsung by most respectable suffragists of that day.

Contra the breezy dismissers, #MeToo's constituency did not only comprise professionals. As Madeline Lane-McKinley identified in 2018, there was always also a "#MeToo from below" driven by strawberry pickers, dishwashers, hospital workers, and the class action lawsuits of hotel housekeepers.[34] The class politics of whose rapes made headlines must be and were pointed out. But surely actresses, even wealthy actresses, should not work in a sector wherein rape is a tacitly acknowledged structure of labor conditions. Meanwhile, the struggle for reproductive freedom in the US has kicked into a higher gear since Roe was overturned, with organizers propagating abortifacient and contraceptive pills via underground networks and smuggling later-term abortion seekers across state lines to clinics. What is becoming clearer and clearer, too, is that this struggle for sexual and gestational autonomy cannot be separated from the struggle for gender self-determination. The paroxysm of misogyny (including feminist misogyny) attempting to stamp out transfemininity—and juvenile transmasculinity—in Britain and the US is self-evidently one of feminism's central contemporary political antagonists, and it is inextricable from the assault on the right to quit gestational labor. The mobilization against both is magnificent. In Philadelphia, where I live, a disproportionate number of trans women sprang into action when the Dobbs ruling leaked, drawing, unsurprisingly, on long years of experience creating bodily autonomy extralegally, to help strengthen repro-justice networks for and with their pregnant sisters and siblings, many of whom now reciprocate this solidarity.

From where I'm standing, the feminism I care about is in a golden age, exciting large numbers of self-described "transgender Marxists" and value-form theorists to revivify stalled debates around housework, while expanding and transforming the "social reproduction theory" popularized, by (among others) the early Silvia Federici.[35] In Rojava, the autonomous administration of north and eastern Syria, a militarily defended revolution ongoing since

2013, remains centrally motivated by feminism.[36] The gender-liberation horizon called "abolition of the family"[37] is back on the table, as is—via the Argentinian organizer Verónica Gago and other compañeras—strategic discussion of the feminist strike.[38] We are witnessing an efflorescence of conversation around "the feminist international,"[39] "feminism against work,"[40] decolonial "undercommons" feminism,[41] the relationship between marxism and intersectionality theory,[42] and "abolition feminism."[43]

When it comes to feminism, it is always easy to kill something, mock something, deflate something. Nonetheless, in print and on the streets, an extraordinary coalition is denaturalizing capitalist gender, building monstrous affinities, and seeking ways to communize care.

Acknowledgments

Since its conception in 2019, this book's gestation has been somewhat tortured, interrupted for years at a time, plagued by bad luck and logistical setbacks, waylaid by the death of its author's Mumputz, and stalled endlessly by that grieving daughter's being broke on account of being (academically speaking)—somewhat by choice—unemployed. *Enemy Feminisms* now only exists, at last, thanks to the perseverance of my agent, Ian Bonaparte, at Janklow & Nesbit, and the patience of Katy O'Donnell—and everyone working with her, notably Jameka Williams, Jim Plank, and Anne Rumberger—at Haymarket Books. I feel immense gratitude both to Ian, and to Haymarket, for taking up this project. Two writing residencies supported this project, and my heartfelt thanks go to the Vermont Studio Center, in Johnson, VT, and the Hambidge Center, in Rabun Gap, GA, for giving me space in which to read and write.

Similarly, comradely scholars at all kinds of universities and centers of learning—from Ghent, Belgium, to Gwangju, South Korea—have hooked me up with speaking gigs I've been honored to fill. The brilliant hosts of various podcasts—*The Death Panel, Ordinary Unhappiness, This Is Hell!, Politics Theory Other, Hotel Bar Sessions, The Final Straw, The Dig*, and more—have been very kind to invite me on. Also, the good people of the Brooklyn Institute for Social Research have let me teach numerous courses on enemy feminisms since 2020. Several of my BISR students have shaped my thinking on feminism more than I can say. None of this could have happened without my @reproutopia Patreon subscribers: *thank you*.

I feel substantial gratitude to Maria Murphy and Gwendolyn Beetham at the gender studies center at the University of Pennsylvania, for giving this wayward independent scholar an unpaid visiting affiliation—a library card—thereby enabling me to access the libraries I needed to write *Enemy Feminisms*. I also wish to thank a non-comprehensive list of the feminists, living and dead, who shaped this intellectual journey, whether or not they were conscious of it: Emma Heaney, M. E. O'Brien, Jules Gleeson, Nat Raha, Madeline Lane-McKinley, Lola Olufemi, Tiffany King, Katie Stone, Aren Aizura, Durba Mitra, Amy De'Ath, Kathi Weeks, Maya Gonzalez, Juliana Spahr, Kay Gabriel, Jo Isaacson, Helen Hester, Wendy Trevino, Jasbir Puar, Noah Zazanis, Pat Parker, Shulie Firestone, Andrea Long Chu, Naomi Alizah Cohen, DK Doyle-Griffiths, Linda Gordon, Melissa Gira Grant, Charlotte Shane, Jennifer Nash, Alva Gotby, Jules Gill-Peterson, Cathy Cohen, Vron Ware, Sara Farris, Gargi Bhattacharyya, Sarah Haley, Angela Davis, Liz Fekete, Kyla Schuller, Ali Phipps, Clare Midgley, Victoria Browne, Amber Hollibaugh, Françoise Vergès, Joan Nestle, Lisa Duggan, Donna Haraway, Susan Stryker.

Rich Woodall, one of my oldest friends, provided comments on several chapters. My exquisite boyfriend Thom cheerled and cooked for me. Vicky, my soulmate and nesting partner of twelve years, listened to me read aloud paragraphs as I wrote them, over and over, until she'd heard the whole damn thing. All these labors improved the manuscript considerably. That said, any errors you encounter are not these people's fault. The responsibility belongs to one particularly daft, violent, ungrateful, and intensely beloved seal-pointed foundling—Barnacle Prudence. Persons terrorized by Barnacle in the process of writing this book include (but are not limited to): Scot, Marcia, Sukaina, Kelly, Tim, Tash, Lukas, Isabel, Shuli, Maura, Michelle, Asa, Alyssa, Virgil, Bea, Artie, Ella, Will, Anemone, Kayte, Beth, Adam, Nick, Egina, Ben, Laura, Sterling, Max, Allison, Adam B, Oki, Che, Danny, Wiley, Kyle, Yianni, Abbey, Corinne, Felix, Holly, Joey, Handy, Diego, Heather, Robbie (RIP), and Voltairine. As for the many further-flung kith, those on the West Coast, upstate, in New York, Boston, Baltimore, Chicago, DC, or New Orleans, in Canada, Japan, Europe, or Palestine: you may not even know who you are, but my home, with all its feline pleasures and dangers, is yours.

Notes

Introduction: Women Are Not Horrible

1. This since-deleted tweet is quoted by Njoki Ngumi here on X (formerly known as Twitter.com), https://x.com/njokingumi/status/1094427215733891072.
2. Naomi Huffman, "Artist Jenny Holzer: 'Women Are Not Horrible,'" *Guardian*, January 4, 2023.
3. Sophie Lewis, "How British Feminism Became Anti-Trans," *New York Times*, February 7, 2019.
4. For the right-wing take on Parker's jaunt to DC, see "Terfs Take America" by "Cockburn," *Spectator*, January 31, 2019.
5. Asa Seresin, "Lesbian Fascism on TERF Island," February 11, 2021, personal website.
6. On this, see Ezra Horbury and Christine (Xine) Yao, "Empire and Eugenics: Trans Studies in the United Kingdom," *TSQ* 7(3), 2020.
7. The most popular approach to feminist history "insistently denies its relation to colonial histories and repeatedly attempts to erase its complicity with imperial ideologies from view." Tracey Boisseau, *White Queen: May French-Sheldon and the Imperial Origins of American Feminist Identity* (Indiana UP, 2004), 202.
8. Sarah Ditum (@sarahditum), "Quick question . . . who the fuck is she talking about? The Celts? Anglo-Saxons?," Twitter (now X), February 7, 2019.
9. For a good-faith engagement with Hildegard von Bingen as a feminist ancestor, refer to Huw Lemmey's psychedelic meditation, coauthored with Hildegard von Bingen herself, Alice Spawls, and Bhanu Kapil: *Unknown Language* (Ignota, 2021).
10. The existence of the French-Algerian group Les Indigènes de la République in France might have provided a clue here.
11. "Exclusive: Mermaids' research into newspaper coverage on trans issues," Mermaids UK, November 18, 2019, https://mermaidsuk.org.uk/news/exclusive-mermaids-research-into-newspaper-coverage-on-trans-issues/.
12. Some key accounts of feminisms' historic role as "handmaiden to colonialism" are: Saba Mahmood, *Politics of Piety* (Princeton UP, 2013); Nima Naghibi, *Rethinking Global Sisterhood* (Minnesota UP, 2007); Janice Boddy, *Civilizing Women* (Princeton UP, 2007); Lora Wildenthal, *German Women for Empire* (Duke UP, 2001); Antoinette Burton, *Burdens*

of History (North Carolina UP, 1994); Vron Ware, *Beyond the Pale* (Verso, 1992); Chandra Mohanty et al. (eds.), *Third World Women and the Politics of Feminism* (Indiana UP, 1991); and Anne McClintock, *Imperial Leather*, (Routledge, 1985).

13. Bonnie Burstow, *Radical Feminist Therapy* (Sage, 1992), 12.

14. Bebel attributes the apothegm to Ferdinand Kronawetter in *Der Antisemitismus* (Harvard University, 1894), 21.

15. On the Manhattan prosecutor's role in the Central Park Five case, as documented in *When They See Us* (dir. Ava Duvernay, 2019), see Zillah Eisenstein, "Watching 'When They See Us', As a White Woman," *Monthly Review Online*, June 5, 2019.

16. A sample: "White Feminism Isn't Real Feminism," *Odyssey*, August 11, 2015; "How to Tell If the Women's March Is about Real Feminism," *Vox*, January 19, 2017; "Why Commodified Feminism Isn't Real Feminism," April 3, 2018; "Extreme Feminism Is Not Real Feminism," *Florala*, October 8, 2018; "Trans-exclusionary Feminism Isn't True Feminism," *Queen's Journal*, March 6, 2020.

17. See Jessie Kindig (ed.), *The Verso Book of Feminism* (Verso, 2020).

18. Dominic Pettman, "Get Thee to a Phalanstery," *Public Domain Review*, May 1, 2019.

19. Martha Jones, "How New York's New Monument Whitewashes the Women's Rights Movement," *Washington Post*, March 22, 2019.

20. Ana Stevenson, *The Woman as Slave in Nineteenth-Century American Social Movements*, Palgrave, 2020.

21. Jessie Daniels, *Nice White Ladies*, Seal, 2021.

22. Mikki Kendall, *Hood Feminism* (Viking, 2020); Angela Y. Davis et al., *Abolition. Feminism. Now.* (Haymarket, 2023).

23. Kyla Schuller, *The Trouble with White Women: A Counterhistory of Feminism* (Bold Type, 2023); Jessie Daniels, *Nice White Ladies: The Truth about White Supremacy, Our Role in It, and How We Can Help Dismantle It* (Seal Press, 2021); Ruby Hamad, *White Tears/Brown Scars* (Catapult, 2020); Rafia Zakaria, *Against White Feminism* (W. W. Norton, 2021).

24.. Schuller, *The Trouble with White Women*, 4.

25. Melissa Phruksachart, "The Literature of White Liberalism," *Boston Review*, August 21, 2020.

26. Gloria Anzaldúa, *This Bridge We Call Home* (Routledge, 2002), 570.

27. The Chilean group LASTESIS created *Un Violador En Tu Camino*, an art protest that riffs on the Carabineros police's official slogan, "A friend in your path." See "Chile's 'A Rapist in Your Path' Chant Hits 200 Cities," *Al Jazeera*, December 20, 2019.

28. In 1970, the Black Panthers and the Young Lords seized a section of Lincoln Hospital in New York, establishing the first drug detox program at the center of the city's heroin epidemic. See M. E. O'Brien, "Junkie Communism," *Commune*, August 15, 2019.

29. In 1911, the suffragist and labor reformer Helen Todd famously demanded "bread, and roses too" for factory workers. One hundred years later, left transfeminists from Scotland to Canada modified this: "Bread, roses, and hormones, too!"

30. Feminists have long contested age segregation. See the anthology *NO! Against Adult Supremacy* (Active Distribution, 2016).

31. Victoria Law, "#FreeBlackMamas Bails Black Mothers from Jail for Mother's Day," *Waging Nonviolence*, May 11, 2019.

32. Aishah Simmons (ed.), *Love WITH Accountability*, AK, 2019.

33. Lyn Corelle and jimmy cooper intervened in a class struggle over Minneapolis's public lands, in 2021, by distributing 100 yard signs— "Make the Golf Course a Public Sex Forest!" See Lyn Corelle and jimmy cooper, *Make the Golf Course a Public Sex Forest* (Maitland Systems, 2023).

34. On feminism against whiteness: Tiffany King, *The Black Shoals* (Duke, 2019) and Oyèrónkẹ́ Oyěwùmí, *What Gender is Motherhood?* (Palgrave, 2015). On decolonial gender liberation: Lou Cornum, "Desiring the Tribe," *Pinko*, October 15, 2019; María Lugones, "Toward a Decolonial Feminism," *Hypatia* 25(4), 2010.

35. On radical reproductive freedom organizing, see Alex Barksdale, "Anarchist-Feminist Perspectives on Autonomous Reproductive and Trans Health," *Coils of the Serpent* (11), 2023.

36. See Sophie Lewis, *Abolish the Family* (Verso, 2022) and M. E. O'Brien, *Family Abolition*, (Pluto, 2023).

37. On feminism as care deprivatization: Kathi Weeks, "Abolition of the Family," *Feminist Theory*, 2021; on survival decoupled from the wage: Morgane Merteuil, "Sex Work Against Work," *Viewpoint,* October 31, 2015; on feminist decolonization: Françoise Vergès, *A Decolonial Feminism* (Pluto, 2021); on feminist decarbonization: Alyssa Battistoni, *Free Gifts* (Princeton UP, forthcoming August 2025).

38. Kay Gabriel, "Gender as Accumulation Strategy," *Invert*, 2020, and Joshua Clover and Juliana Spahr, "Gender Abolition and Ecotone War," *SAQ* 115(2), 2016.

39. Emma Heaney (ed.), *Feminism Against Cisness* (Duke UP, 2024).

40. On anti-work sex worker communism, see femi babylon and Heather Berg, "Erotic Labor within and without Work," *SAQ* 120, 2021; Heather Berg, *Porn Work* (North Carolina UP, 2021); and "Sex Workers against Work," *Other Weapons*, 2019.

41. Rasheeda Phillips, "The Future(s) Are Black Quantum Womanist," *Schlosspost*, July 2, 2018.

42. O'Brien, "Junkie Communism."

43. On Black abolition ecofeminism, see Nylah Burton, "You Can't Separate People from the Planet," *Nation*, March 4, 2022; Jennifer James, "Reproductive Justice and Abolition," *Am J Bioeth* 24(2), 2024.

44. Legacy Russell, *Glitch Feminism* (Verso, 2020); Amber Husain, "Cyborgs Without Organs," *Radical Philosophy* 209, 2020.

1. THE "ENSLAVED" ENGLISHWOMAN GOES ABROAD

1. Yoko Ono, "Woman is the N—r of the World," *Live in New York City,* [1972] 1986.
2. Aishah Shahidah Simmons, "Woman is the 'N' of the World?" *Ms.,* October 6, 2011.
3. On the reception of Maggi Hambling's "A Sculpture for Mary Wollstonecraft," including TERFs draping it in merch from the "Adult Human Female" campaign, see Eleanor Nairne, "A Naked Statue for a Feminist Hero?," *New York Times,* November 12, 2020.
4. Mary Wollstonecraft, ed. Eileen Botting, *A Vindication of the Rights of Woman* (Yale UP, 2014), 219.
5. Wollstonecraft, *A Vindication,* 60. I am indebted to Cora Kaplan's *Sea Changes* (Verso, 1986) for this analysis.
6. Susan Gubar: *"As a genre, feminist expository prose inevitably embeds itself in the misogynist tradition it seeks to address and redress."* Gubar, "Feminist Misogyny," *Feminist Studies* 20(3), 1994.
7. On the other hand, Moira Ferguson speculates that when Wollstonecraft writes that *"the bent bow recoils with violence, when the hand is suddenly relaxed that forcibly held it back,"* she *"could be hinting that women should emulate the San Domingan insurgents and fight back."* See: Ferguson, "Mary Wollstonecraft and the Problematic of Slavery," *Feminist Review* 42, 1992, 95.
8. Kaplan, *Sea Changes,* 35.
9. Gubar, "Feminist Misogyny," 1994.
10. Wollstonecraft, *A Vindication,* 151.
11. Wollstonecraft, 226.
12. Olympe de Gouges, *The Rights of Woman* (Pythia, 1989) 16.
13. Wollstonecraft, *A Vindication,* 60.
14. Wollstonecraft, 60.
15. Gubar: *"Did anyone better understand slavish passions, the overvaluation of love, fickle irrationality, weak dependency, the sense of personal irrelevance, and anxiety about personal attractiveness than Wollstonecraft herself?"* "Feminist Misogyny," 1994, 460.
16. Wollstonecraft, *A Vindication,* 32.
17. Jean Grimshaw, "Mary Wollstonecraft and the Tensions in Feminist Philosophy," *Radical Philosophy* 52, 1989, 14.
18. Wollstonecraft, *A Vindication,* 32.
19. Wollstonecraft, *A Vindication,* 79.
20. *"[I]ndirectly [women] obtain too much power, and are debased by their exertions to obtain illicit sway."* Wollstonecraft, *A Vindication,* 198.
21. Wollstonecraft, A Vindication, 198.
22. Valerie Amos and Pratibha Parmar, "Challenging Imperial Feminism," *Feminist Review* 17, 1984.

23. Carol Howard, "Wollstonecraft's Thoughts on Slavery and Corruption," *The Eighteenth Century* 45(1), 2004, 61.

24. Alexis Shotwell, "Claiming Bad Kin," *Bearing*, 3: 8–11, 2019.

25. Clare Midgley, *Feminism and Empire* (Routledge, 2007), 53.

26. Wollstonecraft, *A Vindication*, 174.

27. Angela Y. Davis, *Women, Race & Class* (Penguin, 1981), 46.

28. Barbara Taylor, "'The Men Are as Bad as Their Masters. . .'," *Feminist Studies* 5(1), 1979, 10.

29. Quoted in Kathryn Gleadle, *The Early Feminists* (Palgrave, 1995), 99.

30. Louise Newman, *White Women's Rights* (Oxford UP, 1999), 7–8.

31. Midgley, *Feminism and Empire*, 64.

32. Rafia Zakaria, *Against White Feminism* (W. W. Norton, 2021), 149.

33. Gayatri Spivak, "Can the Subaltern Speak?," in Nelson and Grossberg (eds.), *Marxism and the Interpretation of Culture* (Illinois UP, 1988).

34. Antoinette Burton, *Burdens of History* (North Carolina UP, 1994), 169.

35. William Ward, *Missionary Register*, October 1820, quoted in Midgley, *Feminism and Empire*, 75.

36. Midgley, *Feminism and Empire*, 88.

37. Still, Clare Midgley points out: "*The hegemony of this colonial discourse on sati did not go completely unchallenged by British women.*" Midgley, *Feminism and Empire*, 88.

38. Harriet Martineau, *Daily News*, June 8, 1852, quoted in Midgley, *Feminism and Empire*, 138.

39. Of the feminist figure of "Jane Bull," Burton writes: "*she was a compelling argument for political equality—one that played on British notions of fair play, liberty, and racial entitlement.*" Burton, *Burdens of History*, 46.

40. Julia Bush, "'The right sort of woman,'" *Women's History Review* 3(3), 1994.

41. Midgley, *Feminism and Empire*, 146.

42. "Stray Letters on Emigration," *The English Woman's Journal*, 1862, vol. 9, quoted in Midgley, *Feminism and Empire*, 142.

2. THE ANTI-ANTIRACIST ABOLITIONIST

1. Belle Kearney, "The South and Woman Suffrage," *Woman's Journal,* April 4, 1903, reprinted in Kraditor (ed.), *Up from the Pedestal* (Quadrangle, 1968), 265.

2. Stephanie Jones-Rogers, *They Were Her Property* (Yale UP, 2019), xvii.

3. Lillian Faderman, *Woman* (Yale, 2022), 34–5. For more on the political trajectory of the "mother of lesbian history," see my review: "A Woman is a Woman?," *The Baffler* 62, March 2022.

4. Hardenbroeck still appears in the cached version of this webpage: bossbabe.com/15-inspiring-business-women-who-shaped-the-world.

5. Jones-Rogers, *They Were Her Property*, xvii.

6. Jones-Rogers, *They Were Her Property*, 55.

7. Jones-Rogers, *They Were Her Property*, xvii.

8. On feminist marronage, see Priscilla Ferreira, "Encounters in Black Feminist Geographies That Ache and Bond," *WSQ* 49, 2021.

9. Trevor Burnarda and Deirdre Coleman, "The Savage Slave Mistress," *Atlantic Studies* 19(1), 2022.

10. *"If it takes lynching to protect women's dearest possession from drunken, ravening human beasts, then I say lynch a thousand a week."* For an attempted defense of Senator Rebecca Felton's feminism—which she advanced through her advocacy for women's suffrage, lynching, white supremacy, temperance, and agricultural and prison reform—see John Stefanek, "The Radicalism of Rebecca Felton: Reforming Southern Masculinity," MA History (unpublished), University of Montana, May 2021.

11. See, for example, Joy Ladin, "Ain't I a Woman?", TedxTalk, January 7, 2016; Pat Griffin, "'Ain't I a Woman?'" in Finn Enke (ed.), *Transfeminist Perspectives in and beyond Transgender and Gender Studies* (Temple UP, 2012).

12. Cameron Awkward-Rich, "On Trans Use of the Many Sojourner Truths," in Heaney (ed.), *Feminism Against Cisness* (Duke UP, 2024), 41.

13. Frances Gage, "Reminiscences," in *History of Woman Suffrage vol. 1* by Elizabeth Stanton, Susan B. Anthony, and Matilda Gage (eds.) (Fowler & Wells, 1881), 115–17.

14. Donna Haraway, "Ecce Homo, Ain't (Ar'n't) I a Woman, and Inappropriate/d Others," 86–100 in Butler and Joan (eds.), *Feminists Theorize the Political* (Routledge, 1992), 97.

15. Imani Perry, "Introduction," *Narrative of Sojourner Truth*, (Barnes & Noble Classics, 2005), xxxiv.

16. Haraway, "Ecce Homo," 97.

17. Haraway, "Ecce Homo," 98.

18. Nell Painter, *Sojourner Truth* (W. W. Norton, 1996).

19. *"At breakfast at the Palazzo Barbarini, Stowe told Gaskell Sojourner Truth stories in dialect. Gaskell's response was not recorded, but [William Wetmore] Story was so enchanted by Stowe's impersonation of Truth's 'ringing barytone' that he asked her repeatedly to do Truth for his friends."* Painter, *Sojourner Truth*, 154.

20. Sojourner Truth, quoted in Painter, 165.

21. Truth, 161.

22. Schuller, *The Trouble with White Women*, 250.

23. Davis, *Women, Race & Class*, 54–5.

24. Lisa Tetrault, *The Myth of Seneca Falls* (North Carolina UP, 2014), 13.

25. Lori Ginzberg, *Elizabeth Cady Stanton* (Hill & Wang, 2009).

26. Stanton, "Women of the Period," *New York World*, May 13, 1869.

27. Stanton, Anthony, and Gage (eds.), *History of Woman Suffrage, Vol. 2, 1861–1876*, (Fowler & Wells, 1881), 391.

28. Harper, quoted in Stanton et al., 391.

29. Philip Foner (ed.), *Frederick Douglass on Women's Rights* (Greenwood, 1976), 32–3.

30. Newman, *White Women's Rights*, 5.

31. Kearney, "The South and Woman Suffrage," 1903, in Kraditor, 1968, 263.

32. Carrie Catt, *Woman Suffrage by Constitutional Amendment*, (National Woman Suffrage Publishing Co., Inc., 1917), 76. In her introduction to the volume, Catt argues on eugenic grounds against enfranchising males of the lower orders while denying the vote to ruling-class ladies.

33. AP, "Suffragette's Racial Remark Haunts College," *New York Times*, May 5, 1996.

34. Newman, *White Women's Rights*, 57.

35. Kyla Schuller, *The Biopolitics of Feeling* (Duke UP, 2017), 90. On black feminist eugenics, see also Allison Berg, *Mothering the Race* (Illinois UP, 2002).

36. Ralina Joseph, *Transcending Blackness* (Duke UP, 2012); Frances Harper, "The Afro-American Mother," in National Congress of Mothers, *Work and Words of the National Congress of Mothers* (Appleton, 1897), 67–71.

37. Schuller, *Biopolitics of Feeling*, 89.

38. Schuller, *Biopolitics of Feeling*, 240n9.

39. "*If talking about racism within feminism gets in the way of feminist happiness, we need to get in the way of feminist happiness.*" In Sara Ahmed, *Living A Feminist Life* (Duke UP, 2017), 177.

3. THE CIVILIZER

1. Mary Beard (@wmarybeard), Twitter (now X), February 16, 2018, https://twitter.com/wmarybeard/status/964613592833253376. See also "Oxfam Sexual Exploitation Scandal in Haiti," *Guardian,* June 15, 2018.

2. Mrs. Sheldon quoted in *Evening Mail*, "War Babies Will Cause Revolution in Marriage Laws, Predicts Traveler," March 3, 1915. Tracey Boisseau, "'They Called Me Bebe Bwana'," *Signs* 21(1), 1995, 116.

3. *New York Times*, "What She Saw in Africa: Mrs. French-Sheldon's Lecture on her Travels, Slave Caravans, and Porters," March 22, 1892.

4. Ellen Jones, "'There Are No Black People on *Game of Thrones*,'" *Guardian*, April 6, 2019.

5. Gaby Del Valle, "How Daenerys Targaryen Became a Feminist Icon," *Vox*, April 26, 2019.

6. Elizabeth Warren, "Why the World Needs More Cersei Lannisters," *Cut*, April 21, 2019.

7. *New York Times*, "A White Lady Visits the Masai," December 11, 1892, 19. Quoted in Tracey Boisseau's Introduction in May French-Sheldon, *Sultan to Sultan* (Manchester UP, 1999), 31.

8. Fannie Williams, "A 'White Queen' at the World's Fair," *Chautauquan* 18, 1893, 342.

9. Sheldon, *Sultan to Sultan*, 96–7, quoted in Boisseau, *White Queen*, (Indiana UP, 2004), 85–6.

10. Boisseau, *White Queen*, 85-6.

11. Quoted in Newman, *White Women's Rights*, 1999, 10.

12. Newman, 106. *"Sheldon appeared as the literal embodiment of Miss Britannia."*

13. Julie Early, "Unescorted in Africa," *Journal of American Culture* 18(4), 1995, 70.

14. Boisseau, *White Queen*, 180.

15. Boisseau: *"The phrase Bebe Bwana is not found in Kiswahili and though both words individually imply a minimum of polite respect similar to the English use of Mrs. and Mr., the ungrammatical phrase carries no connotations of whiteness nor necessarily of mastery."* Boisseau, "'They Called Me Bebe Bwana,'" 121.

16. Thomas W. Knox, "A Notable Book of Travels," *Arena* 7, 1892, 109.

17. Williams, "A 'White Queen' at the World's Fair," 342.

18. Williams, 342.

19. Dea Birkett, *Spinsters Abroad*, Blackwell, 1989, 136.

20. Angela Y. Davis, "Rape, Racism, and the Capitalist Setting," *Black Scholar* 9(7), 1978.

21. Newman, *White Women's Rights*, 113.

22. Newman, *White Women's Rights*, 113.

23. Newman, *White Women's Rights,* 111.

24. Boisseau, *White Queen*, 4.

25. Boisseau, *White Queen,* 72.

26. Robert Burroughs, "The Travelling Apologist," *Studies in Travel Writing* 14: 2, 2010,139.

27. On Sheldon's amputations of armlets, see Laura Franey, *Victorian Travel Writing & Imperial Violence* (Palgrave, 2003), 141–2.

28. Julie English Early, "Unescorted in Africa," 67.

29. Edwin Arnold, "A Notable Book of Travels," *Arena*, 1892, 110.

30. Knox, "A Notable Book of Travels," 109.

31. Knox, "A Notable Book of Travels," 109.

32. Knox, "A Notable Book of Travels," 109; Clayton McMichael, "A Notable Book of Travels," *Arena*, 1892, 104.

33. Knox, "A Notable Book of Travels," 109.

34. David Swing, "A Notable Book of Travels," *Arena*, 1892, 100–101.

35. Swing, 139.

36. Swing, 202.

37. On this, refer to "The Queen, the Sheik, the Sultana, and the Female Spectator," in Boisseau, *White Queen*, 182–202.

38. Williams, "A 'White Queen' at the World's Fair," 342.

39. Georges Nzongola-Ntalaja, *The Congo from Leopold to Kabila* (Zed, 2002), 23.

40. On the 1890–1910 Congo atrocity, see Adam Hochschild, *King Leopold's Ghost* (Houghton Mifflin, 1998); and David Renton, Leo Zeilig, and David Seddon, *The Congo*, (Zed, 2013).

41. Burroughs, "The Travelling Apologist," 135.

42. Boisseau, *White Queen*, 113.

43. Rev. George Grenfell, cited in Burroughs, "The Travelling Apologist," 146.

44. Burroughs, "The Travelling Apologist,"140.

45. *New York Times*, "Defends Congo Officials: Mrs. French Sheldon Returns After 14 Months in Free State," December 18, 1904.

46. Burroughs, "The Travelling Apologist," 141.

47. Newman, *White Women's Rights*, 112.

48. On "Rhodes Must Fall," see Bhambra, Gebrial, and Nişancıoğlu (eds.), *Decolonising the University* (Pluto, 2018). On Beard, see Katie Goh, "Mary Beard and White Feminism's Crocodile Tears," *GalDem*, February 23, 2018; Ali Phipps, "White Tears, White Rage," *EJCS* 24(1), 2021; and Priya Gopal, "Response to Mary Beard," *Medium*, February 18, 2018 (tinyurl.com/priyamvadagopal).

49. On the fabrication and persistent lack of evidence of systematic rape on the part of Hamas on October 7, see Jeremy Scahill, Ryan Grim, and Daniel Boguslaw, "Between the Hammer and the Anvil," *Intercept*, February 28, 2024.

50. On Zionist feminism: Sophie Lewis, "Some of my Best Enemies are Feminists," *Salvage*, March 8, 2024.

51. Nick Pisa, "Lionesses of the Desert," *Daily Mail*, December 1, 2023; Isabel Kershner, "Israeli Women Fight on Front Line in Gaza, a First," *New York Times*, January 19, 2024.

52. *Hollywood Reporter*, "Gal Gadot Calls Out Silence Over Reports of Sexual Violence During Hamas Attack," December 3, 2023.

4. THE PROHIBITIONIST

1. Nancy Mitford, *Wigs on the Green*, Vintage, 2010 [1934], 129.

2. Josephine Butler argued that it is in relation to *work* that the class that bears the title "women" has come into being. Butler's collection of essays was titled *Woman's Work and Woman's Culture* (1869). See Grace Lavery, "Gender Criticism Versus Gender Abolition," *LA Review of Books*, July 31, 2023.

3. Judith Walkowitz, "The Politics of Prostitution," *Signs* 6(1), 1980, 123.

4. Philippa Levine, *Prostitution, Race and Politics* (Routledge, 2003).

5. Antoinette Burton, *Burdens of History*, 135.

6. Chieko Ichikawa, "Jane Eyre's Daughters," *Women's History Review* 23(2), 2014, 230.

7. Butler, LNA Annual Report, 1902, quoted in Burton, *Burdens of History*, 255.

8. It is, to put it mildly, frustrating, that people who stand merely for the legal prohibition of one industry—the sex industry—go around calling themselves "abolitionists" today. On "neo-abolition," see Elizabeth Bernstein, *Brokered Subjects* (Chicago UP, 2019); Gillian Wylie and Eilis Ward, *Feminism, Prostitution and the State* (Routledge, 2017); and Jo Doezema, *Sex Slaves and Discourse Masters*, (Zed, 2013).

9. On abolition, see Susan Buck-Morss, *Hegel, Haiti, and Universal History*, (Pittsburgh UP, 2009); Rinaldo Walcott, *On Property* (Biblioasis, 2021).

10. *"Not so much the abolition of prisons but the abolition of a society that could have prisons, that could have slavery, that could have the wage, and therefore not abolition as the elimination of anything but abolition as the founding of a new society."* Fred Moten and Stefano Harney, "The University and the Undercommons," *Social Text* 79, 22(2), 2004, 114. See also Derecka Purnell, *Becoming Abolitionists* (Astra, 2022).

11. Sophie Lewis, *Abolish the Family* (Verso, 2022); M. E. O'Brien, *Family Abolition* (Pluto, 2023).

12. Ruth Wilson Gilmore, *Change Everything* (Haymarket, 2024).

13. Butler, "A Constitution Violated" (1875), in Sharp and Jordan (eds.), *Josephine Butler and the Prostitution Campaigns*, vol. 3 (Routledge, 2002), 154.

14. James Mann, "Congressional Record—House," US 61st Congress, sess. 2, vol. XLV, January 12, 1910, 548.

15. Lorelei Lee, "Cash/Consent," *n+1* 35, fall, 2019; Lorelei Lee, "The Roots of 'Modern Day Slavery,'" *CHRLR* 52(3), 2021.

16. W. T. Stead, "The Maiden Tribute of Modern Babylon," *Pall Mall Gazette*, July 6, 1885, 3.

17. On the changes between the two acts, see Julie Laite, *Common Prostitutes and Ordinary Citizens* (Palgrave, 2012).

18. Ann McClintock, *Imperial Leather* (Routledge, 1995), 288.

19. Margaret Hunt suggests that some English purity feminists hated autonomous female sexuality no less than did their fellow White Cross pledge fanatic Anthony Baden-Powell, the ultra-misogynist Boy Scouts leader. See Hunt, "The De-Eroticization of Women's Liberation," *Feminist Review* 34(1), 1990.

20. On "organized womanhood," see Ruth Rosen, *The Lost Sisterhood* (Johns Hopkins, 1982), 51.

21. Mary Ting Yi Lui, "Saving Young Girls from Chinatown," *Journ. Hist. Sexuality* 18(3), 2009.

22. Katharine Bushnell and Elizabeth Andrews, *Heathen Slaves and Christian Rulers*, WCTU, 1907. See Kristin Kobes Du Mez, *A New Gospel for Women* (Oxford UP, 2015).

23. Walkowitz, "The Politics of Prostitution," 135.

24. DuBois and Gordon, "Seeking Ecstasy on the Battlefield," in Vance (ed.), *Pleasure and Danger* (Kegan Paul, 1984), 38–9.

25. Jessica Pliley, *Policing Sexuality* (Harvard UP, 2014), 15.

26. Victor Hugo, quoted in Butler, *Reminiscences of a Great Crusade* (H. Marshall, 1898), 36.

27. DuBois and Gordon, "Seeking Ecstasy on the Battlefield," 34.

28. *Report of the Seventh Convention of the World's Woman's Christian Temperance Union* (Tremont Temple, 1906), 40.

29. *Daily Mail*, "Israeli Morgue Worker Says Horrors Inflicted on Hamas's Victims 'Worse than the Holocaust,'" October 20, 2023.

30. Charlton Edholm, "Traffic in Girls and Work of Rescue Missions," Evangelist World's WCTU Training School, 1899, 6.

31. Elizabeth Blackwell, *Essays in Medical Sociology*, 1902, 95. Quoted in Schuller, *The Biopolitics of Feeling*, 105.

32. Jane Addams, *A New Conscience and an Ancient Evil*, Macmillan, 1912.

33. Emma Goldman, *Anarchy and the Sex Question* (ed. Shawn Wilbur), PM, 2016.

34. On QAnon sex-trafficking conspiracies, see Williamson et al., "#WayfairGate and the Growth of Sex Trafficking Panics Across Social Media," *Critical Criminology* 31, 2023.

35. Mia Bloom and Sofia Moskalenko, *Pastels and Pedophiles* (Stanford UP,2021).

36. Brian Donovan, *White Slave Crusades* (Illinois UP, 2006), 129.

37. Sanneh, "Drunk with Power," *New Yorker*, December 13, 2015.

38. Catt, WWCTU 9th Conv. 1913. Quoted in Ian Tyrrell, *Woman's World/ Woman's Empire*, 232.

39. Frances Willard, "The Race Problem," *New York Voice*, October 23, 1890.

40. Suzanne Marilley, "Frances Willard and the Feminism of Fear," *Feminist Studies* 19(1), 1993.

41. Tyrrell, *Woman's World/Woman's Empire*, 143.

42. On the basis that Willard's maternalism and public hyperfemininity was clearly, on some level, a form of "drag," some feminists—Ruth Bordin, Bonnie Dow, Tara Burton, Lillian Faderman—have tried to salvage Willard as a lesbian feminist, calling her vindication of the home "strategic."

43. Holly Fletcher, *Gender and the American Temperance Movement of the Nineteenth Century* (Routledge, 2008), 44. Tara Burton calls on us to "raise a glass"—they can't resist—"to the women whose temperance activism was, at its core, not a call for repression but rather a demand for liberation." See: Burton, "The Feminist History of Prohibition," *JSTOR Daily*, January 6, 2016.

44. Olwen Niessen, *Aristocracy, Temperance and Social Reform* (Tauris, 2007).

45. Tyrrell, *Woman's World/Woman's Empire*, 31.

46. Vron Ware, *Beyond the Pale* (Verso, 1992), 202.

47. See "Dearest Cossie" (Chapter 19), in Christopher Evans, *Do Everything*, (Oxford UP, 2022).

48. Willard, "The Race Problem," 1890.

49. Ware, *Beyond the Pale*, 209.

50. Ida B. Wells, *Southern Horrors—Lynch Law in All Its Phases*, Age, 1892, 6.
51. Willard's presidential address in Ohio, 1894, quoted in Ware, *Beyond the Pale*, 208.
52. *The Union Signal*, December 6, 1894. Quoted in: Wells, "Miss Willard's Attitude," in *The Light of Truth* (Penguin, 2014), 297.
53. Harvard historian Lisa McGirr contends that the "war on alcohol" laid the foundations of the modern prison-industrial complex, at the same time as scripting the "war on drugs" that today supplies its incarcerated population—with strong feminist participation. See: McGirr, *The War on Alcohol* (W. W. Norton, 2016).
54. Jean Turner-Zimmerman, *Chicago's Black Traffic in White Girls*, Chicago Rescue Mission, 1911; Leslie Harris, *The Rhetoric of White Slavery and the Making of National Identity* (Michigan State UP, 2023).
55. Willard, "Woman and Christianity," Annual Address, WCTU, Nov. 1890. Quoted in Newman, *White Women's Rights*, 66.
56. On Christabel's trajectory toward end-of-life evangelicalism, see Timothy Larsen, *Christabel Pankhurst* (Boydell & Brewer, 2002).
57. Tyrrell, *Woman's World/Woman's Empire*, 103.
58. Linda Gordon, *The Moral Property of Women* (Illinois UP, 2002), 73
59. Alison Phipps, *Me, Not You*, (Manchester UP, 2020), 145.
60. Emma Goldman, "The Traffic in Women," in *Anarchism & Other Essays*, 2nd ed., (Mother Earth, 1911), 200. See also Voltairine de Cleyre, *Exquisite Rebel* (eds. Presley and Sartwell), SUNY, 2005.
61. Goldman, 176.
62. Katherine Bushnell, *The Woman Condemned*, Funk & Wagnalls, 1887, 14.
63. Butler, letter to Anna Maria Priestman, 1894. Quoted in Edward Bristow, *Vice and Vigilance* (Rowman & Littlefield, 1977), 155.
64. Kathleen Barry, *The Prostitution of Sexuality* (NYU Press, 1995), 112.
65. Barry, *The Prostitution of Sexuality*, 114.
66. Sheila Jeffreys, *The Idea of Prostitution* (Spinifex, 1997), 9–10.
67. Hunt, "The De-Eroticization of Women's Liberation," 1990.
68. Blackwell, *Purchase of Women*, (John Kensil Publishing, 1887), 34.
69. For theorization of "sex workers against work," see Morgane Merteuil, "Sex Work Against Work," *Viewpoint*, October 31, 2015.
70. Sheila Jeffreys, in Rhodes and McNeill (eds.), *Women Against Violence Against Women*, (Only Women Press, 1985), 61.
71. *London Evening Dispatch*, July 15, 1895. Quoted in Tyrrell, *Woman's World/Woman's Empire*, 59.
72. On Lulu Markwell's temperance and Klan activities in Little Rock, see Ben Johnson, "The Staunchest of the Stout-Hearted Women," *Arkansas Historical Quarterly* 79(3), 2020.
73. On the cozy relationship between the WCTU and the KKK, see Carli Schiffner, "Continuing to 'Do Everything' in Oregon," PhD, History, Washington State University, 2004.
74. Tyrrell, *Woman's World/Woman's Empire*, 135.

5. THE KKK FEMINIST

1. Jessie Daniels, *Nice White Ladies*, 49. Daniels calls the "Smith & Wesson feminism my father taught me" (p. 186) a "gender-only feminism."
2. Alma White, "Woman's Chains," quoted in Susie Stanley, *Feminist Pillar of Fire* (Pilgrim, 1993), 398.
3. Alma White, *The Ku Klux Klan in Prophecy*, 1928.
4. *Woman's Chains*, "Scaling the Heights," July–August 1925, 7.
5. Sharon Otterman, "A Booming Church and Its Complicated, Ugly Past," *New York Times*, September 15, 2017.
6. *Denver Republic*, "Jumpers Jailed for Street Disturbance," February 9, 1903; *Denver Post*, "'Jumpers' Jumped and Judge Thomas Lectured," February 9, 1903. Quoted in Stanley, *Feminist Pillar of Fire*, 51.
7. "*Even detractors spoke admiringly of her business acumen.*" Stanley, *Feminist Pillar of Fire*, 78.
8. Priscilla Pope-Levison, *Building the Old Time Religion* (NYU Press, 2014), 69, 89.
9. Helen Swarth, "My Life in a Religious Commune," pamphlet (Vennard College, 1976), 42.
10. White, *The Ku Klux Klan in Prophecy*, 1928.
11. White republished these as a three-volume set as late as 1943.
12. Linda Gordon, *The Second Coming of the KKK* (Liveright, 2017), 120–2.
13. White, *Heroes of the Fiery Cross* (Good Citizen, 1928), 116–118, 144. Quoted in Gordon, *Second Coming of the KKK*, 56.
14. White, *Heroes of the Fiery Cross*, 187. Quoted in Gordon, 120.
15. White, *The Story of My Life* (Legare Street Press, 2023), quoted in Stanley, *Feminist Pillar of Fire*, 108.
16. *Searchlight*, March 24, 1923, 4.
17. Nancy MacLean, *Behind the Mask of Chivalry* (Oxford UP, 1994), 116.
18. Kathleen Blee, *Women of the Klan* (California UP, 1991), 55.
19. Blee, 180.
20. Blee, 49.
21. Blee, 49.
22. MacLean, *Behind the Mask of Chivalry*, 115.
23. Quoted in Otterman, "A Booming Church," 2017.
24. Gordon, *Second Coming of the KKK*, 122.
25. Stanley, *Feminist Pillar of Fire*, 109.
26. Lee Casey, "Bishop White of Denver—a Cromwell in Skirts," *Rocky Mountain News*, June 28, 1946, 14.
27. *Time*, "Bishop v. Drink," December 18, 1939.
28. Blee, *Women of the Klan*, 74.
29. *New York Times*, "Life of the Sect Which Intends to Reform 'The Purple Woman of Babylon,'" August 18, 1907.
30. Stanley, *Feminist Pillar of Fire*, 109.

31. MacLean, *Behind the Mask of Chivalry*, 114.
32. Blee, *Women of the Klan*, 1991: relations between the KKK and WKKK were "complicated," 61. Indiana Klanswomen's feminism advanced racial and religious hatred in "complicated, often subtle ways," 123. The Klan had "complicated views of women's proper place in society," 177.
33. F. N. Graff, "A Tribute to the Women of the Ku Klux Klan," *Dawn*, January 26, 1924, 7. Quoted in Blee, 51.
34. Elizabeth Tyler, quoted in *New York Times*, "First Lady of Ku Klux Says Women Here Flock to the Klan," September 13, 1921.
35. *New York Times*, "'First Lady of Ku Klux Says Women Here Flock to the Klan," 13 September, 1921; *Norfolk Post,* "Klan Auxiliary Planned, Kamelia For Women To Be Launched," 244(23), March 23, 1923.
36. *The Southeast Missourian*, "New Klan Will Be Formed under Simmons," June 7, 1923.
37. *New York Times*, "Join 'Invisible Empire,'" January 7, 1923.
38. Quoted in Blee, *Women of the Klan*, 2.
39. White, *Klansmen*, Zarephath, 1926, 81.
40. Seyward Darby, *Sisters in Hate* (Little, Brown and Co., 2020), 139.
41. Gordon, *Second Coming of the KKK*, 188.
42. Gordon, 117.
43. Robbie Gill, "American Women," in *KKK, Inspirational Addresses*, KKK, 1924. Quoted in Blee, 53.
44. Blee, *Women of the Klan*, 12.
45. On Gilman's feminist *maternal racial nationalism*, see Asha Nadkarni, *Eugenic Feminism* (Minnesota UP, 2014); and Louise Newman, *White Women's Rights*.
46. Charlotte Perkins Gilman, *Women and Economics* (Harper & Row, [1898] 1966), 340.
47. Blee, *Women of the Klan*, 50.
48. Blee, *Women of the Klan,* 123.
49. Gordon, *Second Coming of the KKK*, 109.
50. Nora Hickins, "'We Want No Hatchet-Wielding Amazons,'" honors thesis, University of Colorado Boulder, History, 2018.
51. White, *Ku Klux Klan in Prophecy*, 130.
52. Angela Davis, *Women, Race, & Class*, Vintage, 1983, 186.
53. Susan Brownmiller, *Against Our Will*, 2nd ed. (Ballantine, [1975] 1993), 245, 247.
54. Kristin Kandt, "In the Name of God," *AUJGSPL* (8), 2000, 784.
55. Kandt, "In the Name of God," 788.
56. Stanley, *Feminist Pillar of Fire*, 91.
57. Kandt, "In the Name of God," 792.
58. Mary Daly, *Pure Lust*, Beacon, 1983, 223.
59. Osha Davidson, "Michele Bachmann Salutes the Upside to Slavery," *Forbes*, July 8, 2011; Cathleen Falsani, "Is Michele Bachmann a Christian Feminist?", *HuffPost*, July 14, 2011.

60. See Carolina Schwarz, "Giorgia Meloni as Mother of the Nation," *taz*, January 10, 2022; Costanza Hermanin, "Women Leaders in Europe Are Always (from the) Right," *EuroNews*, January 21, 2022; Sophie Boulter, "When Fascism Is Female," *Public Seminar*, August 31, 2022; Manuela Caiani, "Giorgia Meloni and the Others," *Rival Times*, September 17, 2022.

61. Ayla Stewart, "Wife with a Purpose", blog post, 2008, quoted in Darby, *Sisters in Hate*, 133.

62. Otterman, "A Booming Church."

63. *New York Times*, "Bishop Alma White, Preacher, Author" (obituary), June 27, 1946.

64. EmPOWERed Twitter profile, @empowered2a: twitter.com/empowered_2a.

65. Margaret Kelly, "Feminism and Firearms," *Sociological Perspectives* 65(1), 2021, 79. See also Antonia Okafor Cover, @antonia_okafor, Instagram, January 3, 2023.

66. Caroline Light, "'What Real Empowerment Looks Like,'" *Signs* 46(4), 2021.

67. Claire Landsbaum, "NRA Ad Claims 'Real Women's Empowerment' Is Owning a Gun," *Cut*, July 13, 2016.

68. Caroline Light, *Stand Your Ground*, Beacon, 2017.

69. *5 Reasons Big Government is the Real War on Women*, Turning Point USA, 2016.

70. Cheryl Harris, "Whiteness as Property," *Harvard Law Review* 106(8), 1993; and Ruth Frankenberg, *White Women, Race Matters* (Minnesota UP), 1993.

71. Jessie Daniels, *White Lies* (Routledge, 1997), xii–xiii.

72. Daniels, *White Lies*, xiv.

73. Daniels, *White Lies*, xii.

74. Jessie Daniels, *Nice White Ladies*, 71.

6. THE BLACKSHIRT

1. Norah Elam (aka Norah Dacre Fox), "Fascism, Women, and Democracy," *Fascist Quarterly* 1(3), 1935.

2. Steven Brocklehurst, "The Female War Medic Who Refused to 'Go Home and Sit Still'," BBC, November 25, 2017.

3. Mary Sophia Allen, *Lady in Blue* (Stanley Paul, 1936), 24.

4. Giovanni Fasanella, *Nero di Londra* (Mauri Spagnol, 2022). See Tom Kington, "Mussolini 'Was Backed by Britain,'" *Times*, October 3, 2022.

5. On Mosley and the general strike, see Dave Renton, *Fascism, Anti-Fascism and Britain in the 1940s* (Palgrave, 2000).

6. Mosley, interrogated by the Home Office in 1940, quoted in Martin Durham, *Women and Fascism* (Routledge, 1998), 49.

7. Julie Gottlieb, *Feminine Fascism*, 2nd ed. (I.B. Tauris, 2021 [2003]), xv.

8. Gottlieb, 159.

9. Elam, "Fascism, Women, and Democracy."

10. Gottlieb, *Feminine Fascism*, 159.

11. Laura Mayhall, "Creating the 'Suffragette Spirit,'" *Women's History Review* 4(3), 1995, 319.

12. Quoted in Fern Riddell, "Sanitising the Suffragettes," *History Today* 68(2), 2018.

13. Nicoletta Gullace, *The Blood of Our Sons*, (Palgrave, 2016), 194.

14. Richard Thurlow, *Fascism in Britain*, (Tauris, 1998), 46. For more on fascism's appeal in the Depression-struck north of England, see Stuart Rawnsley, "Fascism and Fascists in Britain in the 1930s," PhD thesis, University of Bradford, 1983.

15. Arnold Leese's I.F.L. is discussed in Gottlieb, *Feminine Fascism*, 17.

16. Tammy Kovich and Butch Lee, *Antifascism Against Machismo*, (Kersplebedeb, 2023); Ewa Majewska, *Feminist Antifascism* (Verso, 2021); Mark Bray, *Antifa* (Melville, 2017).

17. Angela McPherson, "A Grandmother's Legacy," *Women's History Review* 30(4), 2021, 696. See also Susan McPherson and Angela McPherson, *Mosley's Old Suffragette*, self-published, 2011.

18. Elam, "Fascism, Women, and Democracy."

19. Elam, "Fascism, Women, and Democracy."

20. Gottlieb, *Feminine Fascism*, 165. Referring to Olive Hawks, "Youth and Womanhood Turns to Fascism," *Blackshirt* 70(24), 1934.

21. Julie Gottlieb credits this information to Jeffrey Wallder. See *Feminine Fascism*, 172.

22. On Richardson's relationship with Mussolini in 1913, see also Woonok Yeom, "Between Fascism and Feminism," in Lim and Petrone (eds.), *Gender Politics and Mass Dictatorship*, Palgrave, 2010, 111.

23. Richardson, "Statement on Forcible Feeding," *Suffragette*, February 6, 2014. Quoted in Hilda Kean, "Some Problems of Constructing and Reconstructing a Suffragette's Life," *Women's History Review* 7(4), 1998, 480.

24. See Christopher Bearman, "An Examination of Suffragette Violence," *English Historical Review* 120(486), 2005.

25. Richardson, Asa Seresin argues, presaged the feminist pornophobia of the '80s with her SWERFish instinct that some female forms must be destroyed, or hidden, to shield the dignity of other women. Seresin, "Lesbian Fascism on TERF Island," 2021.

26. Kean, "Some Problems," 1998.

27. Besides Richardson, among the many who converted from left socialism to the BUF were George Sutton, chair of North St Pancras Labour, who became Mosley's secretary, and Wilfred Risdon, an ILP organizer who became a BUF propagandist. See: Kean, "Some Problems," 484.)

28. Gottlieb, *Feminine Fascism*, 336.

29. *Fascist Week*, "Ex-Suffragette Joins the BUF: Mussolini's Predictions," 7(22), 1933.

30. Mary Richardson, *Laugh a Defiance*, (George Weidenfeld & Nicolson, 1953).

31. Richardson, November 1935, unpublished letter to trade union official, quoted in Durham, *Women and Fascism*, 46.

32. On white supremacist activist Lauren Southern's complaints about her sexist treatment by her male comrades, see Rachel Leah, "'Alt-Right' Women Are Upset That 'Alt-Right' Men Are Treating Them Terribly," *Salon*, December 4, 2017; and Lindsay Schrupp, "We Found Some Actual Feminazis—as in Feminist Nazis," *Vice*, September 22, 2015. ("The 'Stormfront Position Statement on the Treatment of the Sexes' . . . called for an end to 'women-bashing' on the site.")

33. Mrs. H. Carrington Wood, *Star*, February 1935, quoted in Durham, *Women and Fascism*, 47. Julie Gottlieb credits this information to Jeffrey Wallder. *Feminine Fascism*, 172.

34. Richardson, in *Welwyn Times*, December 1935. Quoted in Durham, *Women and Fascism*, 47.

35. Kean, "Some Problems."

36. Mrs. Wood, 1935, quoted in Durham, *Women and Fascism*, 47.

37. Robert Row, letter to Gottlieb, quoted in *Feminine Fascism*, 124.

38. Gottlieb, 133.

39. Anne Brock-Griggs, *Women & Fascism*, B.U.F., 1935. Quoted in Durham, *Women and Fascism*, 24.

40. Oswald Mosley, *The Greater Britain*, Black House, 1932, 54. The anti-fascist feminist Winifred Holtby highlighted this line in 1934 article about the BUF's appeal to women; see Paul and Alan (eds.), *Testament of a Generation*, Virago, 1985, 84. See also Martin Durham, "Gender and the British Union of Fascists," *Journal of Contemporary History* 27(3), 1992. Credit goes to Asa Seresin for noticing the echoes between TERFism and Mosley's credo.

41. Durham, *Women and Fascism*, 15.

42. Durham, 15.

43. "*BUF historiography had the greatest reverence for the Golden Age of Tudor Government and it was claimed that this had also been 'the Golden Age of women's accomplishments,*'" explains Gottlieb, quoting an article in the British Union paper *Action* (no. 151): "Women as Orators," January 14, 1939. *Feminine Fascism*, 167.

44. Martin Pugh, *Hurrah for the Blackshirts!* (Jonathan Cape, 2005), 144.

45. Pugh, 112.

46. Ginger Gibson, "Trump says immigrants are 'poisoning the blood of our country,'" NBC, 17 Dec., 2023; Andy Borowitz, "Melania Trump Seen Wearing 'I Don't Care' Jacket," *New Yorker*, 30 March, 2024.

47. Durham, *Women and Fascism*, 9. Barbara Farr also uses the phrase "fascist feminism" to describe parts of the Blackshirt movement. See: Farr, *The*

Development and Impact of Right-Wing Politics in Britain, 1903-1932, (Garland, 1987), 73.

48. Rotha Lintorn-Orman, "Women's Loyalty," *British Fascism* 4, June 1934. Quoted in Gottlieb, 21.

49. Martin Pugh, "Why Former Suffragettes Flocked to British Fascism," *Slate*, April 14, 2017.

50. Robinson and Walshe gloss Adela as "the black sheep of the Pankhurst family" in the catalog *In Her Own Words*, Peter Harrington, 2019, 56.

51. Quoted in Verna Coleman, *Adela Pankhurst* (Melbourne UP, 1992), 77.

52. Jeff Sparrow, "'Wayward Suffragette' Adela Pankhurst and Her Remarkable Australian Life," *Guardian*, December 23, 2015.

53. Mary Richardson, "My Reply to Sylvia Pankhurst," *Blackshirt* #62, June 29, 1934.

54. Gottlieb, *Feminine Fascism*, 272.

7. THE POLICEWOMAN

1. Aya Gruber, "The Troubling Alliance Between Feminism and Policing," *California Law Review* blog, September 2020.

2. Ashley Fantz and Casey Tolan, "Want to Reform the Police? Hire More Women," CNN, June 23, 2020; Cari Shane, "The U.S. Needs Sweeping Police Reform, Start by Hiring More Women," *Ms.*, August 6, 2020. See also Erin Schumaker, "'Hire More Women' Has Been Touted As a Quick Fix to Police Brutality since Rodney King," *ABC* News, August 2, 2020.

3. Leah Cowan, *Why Would Feminists Trust the Police?* (Verso, 2024), 16.

4. Listicles of feminist cop shows often include: *Veronica Mars, Stumptown, The Bridge, Agent Carter, Broadchurch, Happy Valley, Scott and Bailey, Cagney and Lacey, The People vs. OJ Simpson,* and *Unbelievable,* but the pool is enormous.

5. Bonnie McElhinny, *We All Wear the Blue* (Stanford UP, 1993), 85; Sarah Hautzinger, *Violence in the City of Women* (California UP, 2007), 224.

6. *British Journal of Nursing* 52: 1369, June 27, 1914, 569.

7. Linda Martz, "'That Splendid Body of Women,'" *Women's History Review* 29(6), 2020, 1005.

8. *BJN*, June 27, 1914, 569.

9. Nina Boyd, *From Suffragette to Fascist*, (History Press, 2013), 8.

10. See Alex Vitale, *The End of Policing* (Verso, 2021); Joe Macaré, Maya Schenwar, and Alana Yu-lan Price (eds.), *Who Do You Serve, Who Do You Protect?* (Haymarket, 2016); Kristian Williams, *Our Enemies in Blue* (AK, 2015).

11. *British Journal of Nursing* 86, January 7, 1938, 172.

12. Melissa Gira Grant, *Playing the Whore*, (Verso, 2014), 10.

13. Nina Boyle, *The Vote* 10: 314, November 29, 1915.

14. Metropolitan Women Police Association website, "History," Period Pre-1920s, metwpa.org.uk, accessed July 26, 2023.

15. Boyd, *From Suffragette to Fascist*, 2013, 146.

16. Teresa Billington-Greig, "The Truth About White Slavery," *English Review*, June 1913, 430–44.

17. *British Journal of Nursing* 81, December 1933, 349.

18. Mary Allen (ed. Julie Heynemann), *The Pioneer Policewoman* (Chatto & Windus, 1925), 25.

19. Radclyffe Hall, *The Well of Loneliness*, Anchor, [1928] 1990, 271. See Laura Doan, *Fashioning Sapphism* (Columbia UP, 2000), 76.

20. *"Female inverts have been known to wear men's uniforms and perform military service for years, and even behave as heroes."* Auguste Forel (transl. Marshall), *The Sexual Question* (Rebman, 1908).

21. Mary Allen (ed. Julie Heynemann), *Woman at the Crossroads* (Unicorn, 1934), 97.

22. Allen, 186. Raymond Douglas makes similar gestures about "unrepresentative"-ness in *Feminist Freikorps* (1999).

23. Boyd, *From Suffragette to Fascist*,189.

24. Gottlieb, *Feminine Fascism*, 154.

25. Gottlieb, 216.

26. Boyd, *From Suffragette to Fascist*, 136, 138.

27. Boyd, 181.

28. Boyd, 216.

29. Boyd, 5.

30. C. S. Lewis, *That Hideous Strength* (Bodley Head, [1945] 1965), 68–9.

31. *"She seems never to have taken her uniform off."* Joan Lock, *The British Policewoman* (R. Hale, 1979), 150.

32. Boyd: "[*Lady in Blue*] received a lengthy and effusive review in the *Policewoman's Review* (December 1936). It is unsigned, which casts suspicion on the identity of the reviewer. Could Mary herself have had a hand in its composition? The language is very much like her own." *From Suffragette to Fascist*, 166.

33. Boyd, 160.

34. Boyd, 160.

35. Naomi Jacob, *Me and the Swans* (W. Kimber, 1963), 157–8. See Doan, *Fashioning Sapphism*, 76.

36. Douglas: *"The voluntary women police movement in the post-suffrage period developed a distinctive 'authoritarian strain' of feminism."* Raymond Douglas, *Feminist Freikorps* Praeger, 1999), 3.

37. Boyd, *From Suffragette to Fascist*, 61.

38. John Carrier, "The Control of Women by Women," *Society for the Study of Labour History Bulletin* 26, 1973, 18. Quoted in Philippa Levine, "'Walking the Streets in a Way No Decent Woman Should,'" *J. Modern History* 66(1), 1994, 40.

39. Lucy Bland, "In the Name of Protection," 23–49, in Brophy and Smart (eds.), *Women-in-Law*, Routledge, [1985] 2022, 27.

40. Women's Police Service, annual report, 1917, 24. Quoted in Bland, 36–7.

41. Women's Police Service, annual report, quoted in Bland, 36–7.
42. Nina Boyle, *The Vote*, April 9, 1915. Quoted in Bland, "In the Name of Protection," 34.
43. Boyle, *The Vote*, quoted in Bland, 34.
44. Quoted in Stephanie Brown, "An 'Insult to Soldiers' Wives and Mothers,'" *J. Modern Periodical Studies* 7(1–2), 2016, 159.
45. Lock, *The British Policewoman*, 1979, 34.
46. Quoted in Bland, "In the Name of Protection," 37.
47. Allen, *Lady in Blue*, 24.
48. Allen, *The Pioneer Policewoman*, 75.
49. *Policewoman's Review* VII, June 2, 1933. Quoted in Boyd, *From Suffragette to Fascist*, 163.
50. Allen, *Lady in Blue*, 50.
51. For a full rundown of "The Home Office Inquiry," see134–70 of Allen, *The Pioneer Policewoman*.
52. Quoted in Lock, *British Policewoman,* 90.
53. Quoted in Boyd, *From Suffragette to Fascist*, 107.
54. Boyd, 107.
55. Allen, *Lady in Blue*, 148.
56. *The Woman Teacher* 17(14), 1936, 238.
57. Boyd, *From Suffragette to Fascist*, 194.
58. Quoted in Douglas, *Feminist Freikorps*, 133.
59. Allen, "Police in Germany," *Policewoman's Review* 7(2), March 1934.
60. Douglas, *Feminist Freikorps*, 124.
61. Pugh, *Hurrah for the Blackshirts!*, 297.
62. Quoted in Boyd, *From Suffragette to Fascist*, 193.
63. Boyd, 189.
64. Allen, "Women's Reserve for God, King and Country" (1933), in Boyd, 218.
65. Allen, 1940 police interrogation minutes, quoted in Boyd, 200.
66. Boyd, 7.
67. Kylie Cheung, "Kate Winslet Stopped 'Mare of Easttown' from Editing Out Her 'Bulgy' Belly," *Salon*, June 2, 2021.
68. Gigi Michie, "Kate Winslet Refuses to Hide Her Body in Mare of Easttown," *Bust*, June 3, 2021.
69. Caitlin Moran (@caitlinmoran), Twitter (now X), March 21, 2023, https://x.com/caitlinmoran/status/1638180343193784320?s=20.
70. CNN, "Former Minnesota Police Officer Kim Potter Released from Prison after Serving Time for Deadly Shooting of Daunte Wright," April 24, 2023.
71. Koshka Duff, "The Met Just Apologised After Strip-Searching Me," *Novara*, January 24, 2022.
72. Caroline Davies, "Four Met Police Officers Facing Investigation over Strip-Search," *Guardian*, June 15, 2022.

73. Leroy Logan, "We Can Stop the Police Brutality that Killed Dalian Atkinson," *Guardian*, September 29, 2022.

74. Damien Gayle, "Six Police Cleared over Death of Man Restrained in London Hospital," *Guardian*, October 6, 2017.

75. See: Aviah Day and Shanice McBean, *Abolition Revolution* (Pluto, 2022).

76. Janey Starling, "More Women in the Police Won't Reduce Police Violence," *openDemocracy*, March 28, 2023.

77. Alison Phipps, *Me, Not You* (Manchester UP, 2020), 79–80.

78. Catharine MacKinnon, "Trafficking, Prostitution, and Inequality," *HCRCLLR* 46, 2011, 306.

79. Margaret Baldwin, "Split at the Root, Prostitution and Feminist Discourses of Law Reform," *YJLF* 5, 1992, 79.

80. Anastasia Volkonsky, "Legalizing the 'Profession' Would Sanction the Abuse," *Insight on the News*, February 27, 1995, 22.

81. Carol Leigh, *Unrepentant Whore*, Last Gasp, 2004, 34.

82. Sarah Mesle, "Mare's Hair," *LA Review of Books*, 19 June, 2021.

8. THE PORNOPHOBE

1. Dorothy Allison, "The Women Who Hate Me," in Morse and Larkin (eds.), *Gay & Lesbian Poetry in Our Time*, (St. Martin's, 1988), 2.

2. Joan Nestle, "The Fem Question," in Vance (ed.), *Pleasure and Danger*, 1984, 232. On this, see Asa Seresin in our dialogue "Fascist Feminism," *TSQ* 9(3), 2022, 475.

3. Joan Nestle, *A Restricted Country*, Firebrand, 1987, 41. See also "On Rereading 'Esther's Story'" in Joan Nestle, *A Fragile Union*, Clesi, 1998.

4. Pat Califia, *Public Sex*, Cleis Pr, 2000, xiii.

5. Nestle, *A Restricted Country*, 148.

6. Alice Echols, "The Taming of the Id," in Vance (ed.), *Pleasure and Danger*, 1984, 61.

7. Amber Hollibaugh, "Desire for the Future," in Vance, 1984, 407.

8. Andrea Dworkin, "The Rape Atrocity and the Boy Next Door," in Scholder and Fateman (eds.), *Last Days at Hot Slit,* MIT, 2019, 104.

9. Dworkin, "In Memory of Nicole Brown Simpson" (1994–95), in *Last Days at Hot Slit*, 344.

10. Hollibaugh, "Desire for the Future," 409.

11. Nestle, *A Restricted Country*, 144.

12. Nestle, 150.

13. Williams, Brooke, "The Chador of Women's Liberation: Cultural Feminism and the Movement Press," *Heresies* 3(1).

14. Alice Echols, *Shaky Ground*, (Columbia UP, 2002), 7.

15. Dolores Alexander, *Chrysalis*, January 16, 1980. Quoted in: Carolyn Bronstein, *Battling Pornography, (*Cambridge UP, 2011), 220.

16. Bronstein, *Battling Pornography*, 223.

17. Bronstein, *Battling Pornography*, 224.

18. Margaret Hunt, "De-Eroticization of Women's Liberation," 45.

19. Yet dealbreakers clearly did exist. WAP's predecessor ("the Women's Anti-Defamation League," a prior attempt to set up an East Coast anti-porn scene) collapsed within months, not least because one member—Lois Gould—had argued in the *New York Times* for smut-busting partnerships with the religious right.

20. John D'Emilio, "Women Against Pornography" (1980), in *Making Trouble* (Routledge, 1992), 212.

21. Reagan invited Reisman/Bat-Ada to apply for a state grant of over $730,000. The resulting report floats pseudoscientific theories about "erototoxins" (brain-damaging chemicals caused by porn) meant to mandate a legal ban on all porn on health grounds. Reisman also endorsed anti-gay extremist Scott Lively's book *The Pink Swastika,* whose thesis is that homosexuality gave rise to Nazism.

22. Judith Bat-Ada, "'Playboy Isn't Playing,'" in Lederer (ed.), *Take Back the Night* (William Morrow, 1980), 133.

23. Dworkin, "The Root Cause," in *Our Blood* (Perigee, 1976_, 105.

24. "*In the English colonies, as I have said, every married man had one slave, his wife. As men accrued wealth, they bought more slaves. . . .*" Dworkin, "The Slavery of Women in Amerika," in *Our Blood*, 1976, 83.

25. In *Women's International Newsletter* in 1981, Leidholdt published "Where Pornography Meets Fascism," on the centrality of sadomasochism to the Nazi regime. In 1984, Sheila Jeffreys penned a similar pamphlet: "Sadomasochism: The Erotic Cult of Fascism."

26. Steinem in 1970, quoted in Lederer, 122.

27. Steinem, "Erotica and Pornography," in Lederer, 1980, 37.

28. Pamela Johnson, *On Iniquity* (Charles Scribner's Sons, 1967), 26.

29. Susan Brownmiller, "Excerpt on Pornography from *Against Our Will*," in Lederer, 1980, 33.

30. Judith Bat-Ada and Laura Lederer, "'Playboy Isn't Playing,'" in Lederer, 1980, 127.

31. Adrienne Rich, "Afterword," in Lederer, 1980, 318.

32. Judith Walkowitz is cited in *Pleasure and Danger.* Her research was readily available on the anti-porn side, should they have wanted to read it. See, for example, Judith Walkowitz, *Prostitution and Victorian Society* (Cambridge UP, 1980).

33. Or, I suppose we might say that, if the bourgeois novel is about slavery—in the sense that the novel's ascendancy is knitted together with that of the capitalist mode of production with its transatlantic colonial origins—then porn's production, too, has been inflected by slavery.

34. Jennifer Nash, *The Black Body in Ecstasy* (Duke UP, 2014), 4, 151.

35. Alice Echols, *Daring to Be Bad*, 30th ann. ed. (Minnesota UP, [1989] 2019), 137.

36. On the repro-conservative lurch among erstwhile leftists, see Barbara Ehrenreich, "Family Feud on the Left," *Nation*, March 13, 1982. See also

Sophie Lewis, "Beyond the Back-Lasch, the Beach," Patreon, March 22, 2024.

37. Sally Gearhart, "The Future—If There Is One—Is Female," in McAllister (ed.), *Reweaving the Web of Life* (New Society, 1982), 271.

38. Brownmiller, *Against Our Will*, 16.

39. Echols, *Daring to Be Bad*, 254.

40. Kathleen Barry, "'Sadomasochism,'" *Trivia*, fall 1982, 89.

41. Jane Alpert, quoted in Echols, *Daring to Be Bad*, 9.

42. "Letter from the Underground," in Jane Alpert, *Mother Right*, KNOW, 1974, 4. Emily Hobson notes this *"struck many as a betrayal of prisoners' basic humanity and led a significant number to believe she had become an informant for the federal government."* Hobson, *Lavender and Red* (California UP, 2016), 57.

43. DuBois and Gordon, "Seeking Ecstasy on the Battlefield," in Vance, 1984, 43.

44. See Carol Vance's postmortems of the ill-fated MacDworkinite collaboration with the religious right in Minneapolis and Indianapolis: "More Danger, More Pleasure," *New York Law School Review* 38(1–4), 1993; and "States of Contradiction," *Social Research* 78(3), 2011.

45. Quoted on the first page: MacKinnon, "Not A Moral Issue," *Yale Law & Policy Review* 2, 1984. 321.

46. Lisa Duggan and Nan Hunter, *Sex Wars* (Routledge, 1995), 61.

47. Robin Morgan, *The Anatomy of Freedom* (Doubleday, 1984), 109.

48. Claire Potter, "Why Can't Women Bridge the Left-Right Divide?," *Public Seminar*, May 23, 2018.

49. Califia, *Public Sex*, 123.

50. Whitney Strub, *Perversion for Profit* (Columbia UP, 2013), 265.

51. *Workers' Solidarity*, "Censor Censored—MacKinnon Law Stops Friend's Andrea Dworkin Book," #41, spring 1994.

52. MacKinnon, *Only Words* (Harvard UP, 1993), 3. Echols in 1994 called this shift from turgid academic prose to lurid "over-the-top Dworkinism" the "Dworkinization of Catharine MacKinnon." Echols, "Sex and the Single-Minded," *Village Voice*, March 1994.

53. Donna Haraway, "A Manifesto for Cyborgs," in *Simians, Cyborgs and Women* (Routledge, 1991), 158, 159.

54. Haraway, 158, 159.

55. MacKinnon, *Only Words*, 12.

56. MacKinnon, *Only Words*, 21.

57. Jennifer Nash's phrase is more tactful: *"A singular theory of representation that presumes the violence of the visual field."* Nash, 2014, 147. Susie Bright's is less so: *"MacKinnon describes the debut of the camera as if it were the creation of the H-bomb."* Bright, *Sexwise* (Cleis Press, 1995), 121.

58. Echols, "The Taming of the Id," 65.

59. Bini Adamczak and Sophie Lewis, "Six Years (and Counting) of Circlusion," *New Inquiry*, August 22, 2022.

60. Andrea Dworkin, *Ice and Fire* (Grove, 1986), 46.

61. Dworkin, *Ice and Fire*, 41, 55.

62. Dworkin, *Ice and Fire*, 48.

63. Martin Duberman, *Andrea Dworkin* (New Press, 2020), 53.

64. Dworkin, in *Letters from a War Zone* (Secker & Warburg, 1988), 35.

65. Dworkin, "Renouncing Sexual 'Equality'" (1974), in *Our Blood*, 1976, 13.

66. Dworkin, *Intercourse* (Free Press, 1987), 300.

67. Dworkin, *Intercourse*, xxxi.

68. Dworkin, "Root Cause," 1976, 102.

69. Leah Allen, "The Pleasures of Dangerous Criticism," *Signs* 42(1), 2016, 49.

70. Susie Bright, "Andrea Dworkin Has Died," *Susie Bright's Journal*, April 11, 2005.

71. Bright, *Susie Bright's Journal*, 2005.

72. Dworkin, *Woman-Hating* (Dutton, 1974), 183.

73. Dworkin, *Woman-Hating*, 185.

74. Dworkin, *Woman-Hating*, 201.

75. Dworkin, *Woman-Hating*, 188.

76. John Stoltenberg, "Andrea Dworkin Was a Trans Ally," *Boston Review*, April 8, 2020.

77. Janice Raymond, *Doublethink* (Spinifex, 2021), 46. The recantation to which Raymond refers can be seen in an interview in Cindy Jenefsky and Ann Russo, *Without Apology* (Westview, 1998), 139.

78. Janice Raymond, "Transsexualism," *Chrysalis* 3, 1977, 11–23.

79. Raymond, *Doublethink*, 47.

80. Catharine MacKinnon, "Exploring Transgender Law and Politics," *Signs* blog, May 30, 2022.

81. See Catharine MacKinnon, "Sexuality, Pornography, and Method," *Ethics* 99, 1989, 331.

82. Liberation Collective, "Lesbian BDSM, part 3," March 30, 2013. According to this collective, Califia "*is reactionary. All that [he] 'liberated' and helped mainstream in our communities is the 'lesbian' fascination for sexuality.*" Real lesbians avoid fucking.

83. MacKinnon, "OnlyFans Is Not a Safe Platform for 'Sex Work.' It's a Pimp," *New York Times*, September 6, 2021.

84. Former porn actor Cherie DeVille explains: "*Most sex workers agree 20 percent is a significant cut, but if a porn star builds their own website, purchases cloud storage for their content, and pays a credit card company to process their payments, it typically costs more than 20 percent of their income. OnlyFans provides us with a website, cloud storage, and payment processing for around the same price or* less." DeVille, "Why Does the *New York Times* Hate Porn So Much?," *Daily Beast*, September 9, 2021.

85. MacKinnon, "Trafficking, Prostitution, and Inequality," 2011. For analyses from a sex worker-liberationist perspective, see Lorelei Lee, "Bernie Sanders and My Mom and the Attack on Sex Workers,"

Establishment, April 30, 2018; and Melissa Gira Grant, "The Real Story of the Bipartisan Anti–Sex Trafficking Bill," *New Republic,* June 23, 2021.

86. Emily Witt, "After Closure of Backpage, Increasingly Vulnerable Sex Workers Demand Their Rights," *New Yorker,* June 8, 2018.

87. Dan Milmo, "MPs Urge Crackdown on Pornography to Tackle Violence against Women," *Guardian,* February 26, 2023.

88. Sophie Galer, "All Porn Is Exploitation, UK Inquiry Concludes Without Speaking to Any Sex Workers," *Vice,* March 1, 2023.

89. Quoted in Clarissa Smith and Feona Attwood, "Emotional Truths and Thrilling Slide-Shows," in Taormino et al. (eds.), *The Feminist Porn Book* (Feminist Press, 2013), 41. For more on Gail Dines, see Ana Valens, "Why Did the Boston Globe Give a Platform to a SWERF?," *Daily Dot,* September 11, 2020.

90. Some anti-porn feminist titles in English over the past twenty years: Julia Long, *Anti-Porn,* 2nd ed. (Zed, 2021); Julie Bindel, *The Pimping of Prostitution* (Palgrave, 2019); Kajsa Ekman, *Being and Being Bought,* (Spinifex, 2013); Sheila Jeffreys, *Anticlimax,* 2nd ed. (Women's Press, 2012;) Abigail Bray and Melissa Tankard-Reist, *Big Porn Inc* (Spinifex, 2011); Gail Dines, *Pornland* (Beacon, 2010); Karen Boyle, *Everyday Pornography* (Routledge, 2010); Melinda Tankard-Reist, *Getting Real* (Spinifex, 2009); Sheila Jeffreys, *The Industrial Vagina* (Routledge, 2008); Robert Jensen, *Getting Off* (South End, 2007); Pamela Paul, *Pornified* (Henry Holt, 2007).

91. Claire Potter, "Time to Re-Read Andrea Dworkin," *EuroZine,* March 8, 2022.

92. Jennifer Szalai, "A Startling and Ruthless Feminist Whose Work Is Back in the Spotlight," *New York Times,* March 12, 2019.

93. Asa Seresin, "On Heteropessimism," *New Inquiry,* October 9, 2019.

94. Sarah Fonseca, "The Yassification of Andrea Dworkin," *INTO,* June 17, 2022.

95. See Michelle Goldberg, "Not the Fun Kind of Feminist," *New York Times,* February 22, 2019.

96. Scholder and Fateman (eds.), *Last Days at Hot Slit,* 28.

97. Moira Donegan, "Sex During Wartime," *BookForum,* February/March 2019. See also "Not the Fun Kind" (moiradonegan.substack.com), referencing the kind of feminist Dworkin was not.

98. Lauren Oyler, "The Radical Style of Andrea Dworkin," *New Yorker,* March 25, 2019.

99. *My Name is Andrea* (dir. Pratibha Parmar), 90 min., 2022.

100. In Dworkin's unpublished manuscript *Ruins* (1978–83), there is a "Goodbye to All This" piece that scornfully lists the sex radicals who opposed her anti-porn cause: *"All you swastika-wielding dykettes. . ."*— quoted in Scholder and Fateman, 214.

101. Nestle, *A Restricted Country,* 122.

102. Fonseca, "The Yassification of Andrea Dworkin."

103. Nestle, *A Restricted Country*, 121.

9. THE GIRLBOSS

1. bell hooks and Kevin Powell, "Black Masculinity, Threat or Threatened," Eugene Lang College, The New School, October 7, 2015, @thenewschool, YouTube. See also bell hooks, "Moving Beyond Pain," December 6, 2021, at hooks's personal website, where she writes, *"As a grown black woman who believes in the manifesto 'Girl, get your money straight' my first response to Beyoncé's visual album,* Lemonade, *was WOW—this is the business of capitalist money making at its best."* (BellHooksBooks.com)

2. Amanda Mull, "The Girlboss Has Left the Building," *The Atlantic*, 25 June, 2020; Kate Knibbs, "Leigh Stein's Self Care and the Death of the Girlboss," *Wired*, July 1, 2020; Marie Solis, "What the fall of the 'girlboss' reveals," CNN, 2 July, 2020; Hillary Hoffower, "The fall of the girlboss is actually a good thing," Business Insider, 26 July, 2020; Anna Fielding, "Is This The End Of The Girl Boss?," *Elle*, 11 March, 2021; Samhita Mukhopadhyay, "The Demise of the Girlboss," The Cut, 31 August, 2021.

3. Roisín Lanigan, "All Hail the Girlfailure," *i-D*, February 10, 2023.

4. Alex Abad-Santos, "Gaslight, Gatekeep, Girlboss," *Vox*, June 7, 2021. The phrase satirizes Elizabeth Gilbert's 2006 memoir *Eat, Pray, Love*.

5. Eliel Safran, "10 Signs You've Girlbossed Too Close to the Sun," *Buzzsaw*, October 22, 2021.

6. "Girlboss May Be Over, But The Woman Founder Is Here To Stay," *Forbes*, 5 July, 2020.

7. On the tradwife, see my essay "Double Shift—Dialectic of the Tradwife," *Dilettante Army*, spring 2023. See also Felix del Campo, "New Culture Wars," *Critical Sociology* 49(4–5), 2023.

8. Sophia Amoruso, *#Girlboss*, Portfolio, 2014, 17.

9. Allison Elias, *The Rise of Corporate Feminism* (Columbia UP, 2022).

10. Jess Bergman, "How Bosses Ate Feminism," *New Republic*, February 20, 2023.

11. Barbara Ehrenreich, "Strategies of Corporate Women," *New Republic*, January 27, 1986.

12. Nicole Froio, "All Girlbosses Are Bastards," *Blind Field*, August 12, 2022.

13. Sophie Lewis, "How Domestic Labor Robs Women of Their Love," *Boston Review*, October 28, 2021.

14. Amoruso, *#Girlboss*, 92.

15. Amoruso, *#Girlboss* 108.

16. Amoruso, *#Girlboss* 109.

17. *"Equality does figure more centrally in Slaughter's book than it did in her 2012 article ["Why Women Still Can't Have it All"] . . . [but] market competition is central to her vision."* Catherine Rottenberg, *The Rise of Neoliberal Feminism* (Oxford UP, 2018), 157.

18. Rottenberg, *The Rise of Neoliberal Feminism* , 138.

19. Glinda Bridgforth, *Girl, Get Your Money Straight* (Broadway Books, 2000). bell hooks in 2023 says she's "a grown black woman who believes in the manifesto *Girl, Get Your Money Straight.*"

20. Steinem, quoted in bell hooks, "Dig Deep, Beyond Lean In," *Feminist Wire*, October 28, 2013.

21. hooks, "Dig Deep."

22. Sheryl Sandberg, *Lean In* (WH Allen, [2013] 2015), 8.

23. hooks and Powell, "Black Masculinity, Threat or Threatened," 2015.

24. Sophie Smith, "On bell hooks," *LRB* blog, December 17, 2021.

25. Context for hooks's landlordism is provided in *Bone Black* (1997, Women's Press): *"I inherited rental properties from my father. Although I knew that being a landlord was a position of power, it never occurred to me to refuse that power. I was not always comfortable with it, but I accepted it."*

26. *Independent*, "Ivanka Trump's book—all the most scathing reviews of *Women who Work*," May 5, 2017.

27. Michelle Goldberg, "Why Women Trash Successful Women," CNN, March 12, 2013.

28. Ali Wong, *Baby Cobra* (comedy special), Netflix, 2016.

29. Elissa Shevinsky, *Lean Out* (O/R, 2015); Dawn Foster, *Lean Out* (Repeater, 2016); Nancy Fraser, Ciniza Arruzza, and Tithi Bhattacharya, *Feminism for the 99%*, (Verso, 2019).

30. Caitlin Gibson, "The End of Leaning In," *Washington Post*, December 20, 2018; *The Atlantic*, "How Sheryl Sandberg Lost Her Feminist Street Cred," November 16, 2018.

31. NPR, "Michelle Obama's Take On 'Lean In'? 'That &#%! Doesn't Work,'" December 3, 2018.

32. *"Dear Sheryl,"* wrote Lynne Huffer, *"As a kind of feminism, your 'Lean In Circles' could be a powerful antidote [to the lack of women at your level]. Except for one problem: your happy-endings-only recipe jettisons the most important ingredient of a consciousness-raising group: the female complaint."* Huffer, "It's the Economy, Sister," *Al Jazeera*, March 18, 2013.

33. Valeriya Safronova, "Nasty Gal's Path to Bankruptcy," *New York Times*, November 11, 2016.

34. Arwa Mahdawi, "Does the Elizabeth Holmes Trial Spell the End of the #Girlboss Era?," *Guardian*, September 4, 2021.

35. Noreen Malone, "Sexual-Harassment Claims against a 'She-E.O,'" *The Cut*, March 20, 2017.

36. Lena Solow, "We're Living in the Era of the Hypocritical 'Feminist' Boss," *Vice*, April 25, 2017.

37. On Korey, see Sarah Ruiz-Grossman, "Away CEO Apologizes for Treatment of Former Staff after Damning Article," *Huffington Post*, December 6, 2019. On Gelman, see Megan Rose Dickey, "The Wing Co-Founder Admits the Co-Working Space Upheld 'the Kind of Social Inequality We Set Out to Upend,'" *TechCrunch*, October 14, 2020. On Medine Cohen, see Nikhara Johns, "Man Repeller's Leandra Medine

Cohen Steps Down Following Discrimination Allegations," *Footwear News*, June 11, 2020. On Gotch, see Khanh Tran, "Jen Gotch Resigns from Role at L.A. Brand Ban.do after Racism Accusations," *LA Times*, June 10, 2020. On Barberich, see Kerry Flynn, "Refinery29 Is Reeling from Claims of Racism and Toxic Work Culture," CNN, June 11, 2020. On Wintour, see Morwenna Ferrier, "Anna Wintour Apologises for Not Giving Space to Black People at Vogue," *Guardian*, June 10, 2020. On Emily Weiss, see Alisha Gupta, "The Sunsetting of the Girlboss Is Nearly Complete," *New York Times*, May 31, 2022.

38. Lauren Jackson, "Does Elizabeth Holmes's Gender Matter?," *New York Times*, September 17, 2021.

39. Moira Donegan, "What was the Girlboss?," *Not the Fun Kind* (Substack), August 8, 2022.

40. Carol Matlack, "In France, Kidnapping the Boss Usually Pays Off," *Bloomberg*, January 7, 2014.

41. Lily Nevo, "Girlboss Feminism Is Harmful. Mocking It May be Too," *Daily Northwestern*, May 6, 2021; Martha Gill, "'Girlboss' Used to Suggest a Kind of Role Model. How Did It Become a Sexist Putdown?," *Guardian*, August 21, 2022.

42. In Roisín Lanagan's account of anti-girlboss identification, "the girlfailure," is less overtly politicized. "*If 2022 was the year of spiritual and cultural rot, then the girlfailure was the torchbearer, a figure emerging from months spent rotting at home to give the world not 100% exactly, but at least like, 50%. On a good day.*" Lanagan, "All Hail the Girlfailure," *i-D*, 2023.

43. Froio, "All Girlbosses Are Bastards," 2022.

44. Anne-Marie Slaughter, *Unfinished Business* (Random House, 2015), 224.

45. *Globe & Mail*, "Anne-Marie Slaughter—workplaces, not women, need to change," November 27, 2015.

46. Catherine Rottenberg, "Happiness and the Liberal Imagination," *Feminist Studies* 40(1), 2014, 154.

47. Rafia Zakaria, "Same as the Old Boss," *Baffler*, June 3, 2022.

48. Sarah Arkebauer, "Female Foundering," *Baffler*, June 1, 2023.

49. Laura Beers, "Britain's New Prime Minister and the Dangers of 'Destiny's Child Feminism'," CNN, September 7, 2022. See also Rhiannon Lucy Cosslett, "Theresa May Says She's a Feminist," *Guardian*, December 13, 2016. ("*Sometimes feminism means a woman you don't agree with getting the chance to become prime minister.*")

50. Destiny's Child's version of Black girlbossism did not impress *all* neoliberal feminists. Some condemned them for baring too much skin (girls ought to listen to Ani DiFranco instead). See, for example, Andrea Steiner, "Destiny's Child: Not Ideal Feminism," *New York Times*, May 13, 2001. The contemporary neoliberal feminist establishment's effort to turn the creator of *Lemonade* (2016)—a Malcolm-X-quoting southern-gothic black trauma–exorcism—into a signifier of "feminist patriotism" is disconcerting. Yet it is perhaps also unsurprising, given Beyoncé's

performance at George W. Bush's inaugural celebration and her silence (unlike Rihanna) on abortion.

51. Elizabeth Cobbs, *Fearless Women* (Harvard UP, 2023).

52. Cobbs and Rebekah Buchanan (podcast), *"Fearless Women,"* New Books Network, March 7, 2023.

53. Noreen Malone, "Can Women Have It All? Beyoncé Says Yes," *New Republic*, January 27, 2013.

54. Cobbs and Buchanan, New Books Network.

55. Elizabeth Cobbs, *The Hello Girls* (Harvard UP, 2017).

56. David Brown, "How Women Took Over the Military-Industrial Complex," *Politico*, January 2, 2019.

57. Kevin Maurer, "She Kills People From 7,850 Miles Away," *Daily Beast*, October 18, 2015.

58. Maurer, "She Kills People from 7,850 Miles Away."

59. Panetta, quoted in Esther Wang, "Our Forever Wars Just Got More Feminist," *Jezebel*, January 2, 2019.

60. Karen Panetta, *Count Girls In*, Chicago Review Press, 2018 (blurb).

61. Rania Khalek has made variations of this pithy remark on social media, on podcasts, etc. (see @RaniaKhalek). See also: Rania Khalek, "Hillary Clinton and the Feminism of Exclusion," *FAIR*, 1 January, 2015.

62. *"As the situation in Yemen worsened, at least one firm . . . booked more than $3bn in new bomb sales. . . . American officials . . . tried three times to halt the killing by blocking arms sales to the Saudis. Their efforts were undone by the White House, largely at the urging of Raytheon."* Michael LaForgia and Walt Bogdanich, "Why Bombs Made in America Have Been Killing Civilians in Yemen," *New York Times*, May 16, 2020.

63. Rebecca Rhoads, CIO at Raytheon, controls a shell nonprofit called "Girls! Balance the Equation," working to boost females' participation in STEM sectors. Raytheon, "Girl Scouts across the Country Test Their Cyber Skills," September 26, 2019.

64. On imperial sisterhood and Edwardian girls' clubs' role in colonialism, see Julia Bush, *Edwardian Ladies and Imperial Power* (Leicester UP, 2000).

65. Eleanor Smeal, quoted in Elshtain and Tobias (eds.), *Women, Militarism, and War* (Rowman & Littlefield, 1990,) xi.

66. Catherine Powell, "How Women Could Save the World, If Only We Would Let Them," *Yale J. Law & Feminism* 28, 2017. For a debunking, see Kara Ellerby, *No Shortcut to Change* (NYU Press, 2017).

67. Jessica Contrera, "'The Kids, They Love Madeleine Albright,'" *Washington Post*, April 19, 2018.

68. Gérard Araud, quoted in Evan Osnos, "In the Land of the Possible," *New Yorker*, December 15, 2014.

69. Paola Profeta, "Pourquoi a-t-on besoin de 'Lehmann Sisters,'" *Conversation*, January 4, 2023.

70. UNWatch, "Samantha Power's Nomination Hearing: Video & Transcript," July 19, 2013.

71. Quoted in Dave Denison, "Dinner with a War Criminal," *Baffler*, June 25, 2019.

72. Richard Sisk, "Women Should Be Recognized as Natural Protectors," Military.com, March 20, 2018.

73. Sarah Lazare, "Samantha Power, Gaza, and the False Mea Culpas That Got Us Here," *Column*, December 21, 2023.

74. See, for example, "Fight of the Valkyries," *New York Times,* March 22, 2011; "Flight of the Valkyries?," *Foreign Affairs*, March 28, 2011; "Obama Pushed to War by Fight of the Valkyries," *Times*, March 27, 2011.

75. Valerie Hudson and Patricia Leidl, "No Matter Who's Elected, We Need the Hillary Doctrine," Columbia UP blog, July 15, 2015.

76. Shireen Al-Adeimi, "How Dare Samantha Power Scrub the Yemen War from Her Memoir," *In These Times*, September 18, 2019.

77. Samantha Power, "Being the Only Woman in the UN Made Me a Feminist," *Irish Times* Women's Podcast, November 13, 2017.

78. Samantha Power, *A Problem from Hell* (Basic, 2002), xxi.

79. John Hudson, "Samantha Power Confronted By Own USAID Staff for Failing to Speak Out On Gaza," *Independent*, February 1, 2024.

80. Buried on page 10 of the *NYT,* debunking its own prior exposé "Screams Without Words": Adam Rasgon and Natan Odenheimer, "Israeli Soldier's Video Undercuts Medic's Account of Sexual Assault," *New York Times*, March 25, 2024. For a far more thorough debunking of the "systematic rape by Hamas" narrative, see Jeremy Scahill, Ryan Grim, and Daniel Boguslaw on "The Story Behind the New York Times October 7 Exposé" (*The Intercept*, February 28, 2024).

81. *Newsweek*, "Madeleine Albright Saying Iraqi Kids' Deaths 'Worth It' Resurfaces," March 23, 2022.

82. Maroosha Muzaffar, "CIA mocked from all sides over new 'woke' recruitment video," *Independent*, May 4, 2021.

83. *Business Insider*, "Sheryl Sandberg Is Right—Women Are Called 'Bossy' More Than Men," April 1, 2014; Slaughter, *Unfinished Business*, 57.

84. "Humans of CIA," posted March 25, 2021, YouTube (@CentralIntelligenceAgency). (My own transcription.)

85. Janet Halley, *Split Decisions* (Princeton UP, 2006), 33.

86. Karl Marx, transl. Moore and Bibbins, *Capital, Volume I*, International, 1974, 233.

10. THE FEMONATIONALIST

1. *The Eric Andre Show*, s02, e09 (dir. Andrew Barchilon and Kitao Sakurai), aired December 5, 2013.

2. HarperCollins website for *Prey: Immigration, Islam, and the Erosion of Women's Rights* (2021).

3. Commonwealth Club, "Ayaan Hirsi Ali with Bari Weiss: Islam, Immigration, and Women's Rights," event, February 11, 2021.

4. An audio recording is stored on the Commonwealth Club website.

5. Cisca Dresselhuys, editor of the Dutch feminist magazine *Opzij*, announced in 2002 that she would not hire women who wore the hijab. Dresselhuys befriended Hirsi Ali and, according to several accounts, urged her to leave Dutch politics in favor of an international arena.

6. Sam Harris and Salman Rushdie, "A Refugee from Western Europe," *New York Times*, October 9, 2007.

7. Hirsi Ali, Axel Springer honorary prize for journalism, acceptance speech, Springer site, May 10, 2012.

8. Christopher Caldwell, "Daughter of the Enlightenment," *New York Times*, April 24, 2005.

9. Hirsi Ali, "The Last Gasp of Islamic Hate," American Enterprise Institute, September 17, 2012.

10. The interview also expounds Hirsi Ali's "clash of civilizations" feminism, according to which the Western women's movements have won the ultimate victory, whereas their equivalents in Islamic countries have won nothing: "*That is the main difference between the position of Western women and the position of Muslim women. A Western woman is not her brother's or her father's property. She's just herself.*" Deborah Solomon, "The Feminist— Questions for Ayaan Hirsi Ali," *New York Times*, May 21, 2010.

11. Rogier van Bakel, "'The Trouble is the West,'" *Reason*, October 20, 2007.

12. Elle Hunt, "Hirsi Ali Cancels Australian Tour Citing Security Concerns," *Guardian*, April 3, 2017.

13. Bill Kristol, MSNBC, "Morning Joe," 2014. Clip accessed at Media Matters.

14. Hirsi Ali, "Why Is the Southern Poverty Law Center Targeting Liberals?," *New York Times*, August 24, 2017.

15. Michael Stone, "Theo van Gogh: Free Speech Martyr," *Progressive Secular Humanist*, November 2, 2014.

16. On March 4, 2007, the *New York Times* published the entire first chapter of *Infidel*. The story begins: "As Theo cycled down the Linnaeusstraat, Muhammad Bouyeri approached. He pulled out his gun and shot Theo several times. Theo fell off his bike and lurched across the road, then collapsed. Bouyeri followed. Theo begged, 'Can't we talk about this?' but Bouyeri shot him four more times."

17. Hirsi Ali, "'South Park' and the Informal Fatwa," *Wall Street Journal*, April 27, 2010. This "desensitization" strategy has been actualized by (among others) the fascist blogger Pamela Geller with her Muhammad Art Exhibit and Contest in Garland, Texas.

18. Hirsi Ali, "Obama Should Speak Truth to Islam Because Others Can't," American Enterprise Institute, June 15, 2009.

19. Hirsi Ali, "How to Win the Clash of Civilizations," *Wall Street Journal*, August 18, 2010.

20. Laura Bush, radio address, November 17, 2001: "*The brutal oppression of women is a central goal of the terrorists. . . . Because of our recent military*

gains, in much of Afghanistan women are no longer imprisoned in their homes. They can listen to music and teach their daughters without fear. . . . The fight against terrorism is also a fight for the rights and dignity of women." See also "Cherie 'Lifts Veil' for Afghan Women," BBC, November 19, 2001.

21. Katie Herzog, "Ex-Muslim Activist Sarah Haider Says Western Liberals Are Making Things Worse," *Stranger*, June 14, 2019.

22. Hirsi Ali, "Why I Am Now a Christian," *UnHerd*, November 11, 2023. See Sarah Jones, "The Infidel Turned Christian," *Intelligencer*, November 29, 2023.

23. Braidotti described this "very intelligent, gorgeous-looking person who is fanatical about secularism" and who "fuels Islamophobia with all her might." Reading her as a prime exponent of the "Huntingtonian" clash-of-civilization narrative, Rosi noted that Ayaan "never misses a chance to ridicule the 'feminized and useless' EU and celebrate the muscular retaliatory powers of the USA." See Pascale LaFountain, "Deleuze, Feminism, and the New European Union," *TRANSIT* 4(1), November 26, 2008.

24. Hirsi Ali, "What Islamists and 'Wokeists' Have in Common," *Wall Street Journal*, September 10, 2020.

25. Hirsi Ali, "On Radical Islam, Trump Has Lost His Focus," *WSJ*, August 10, 2017.

26. Mark Perry, "Tucker Carlson on Ilhan Omar vs. Ayaan Hirsi Ali," AEI, July 11, 2019.

27. Ayaan Hirsi Ali (@Ayaan), Twitter (now X), September 27, 2018, https://x.com/ayaan/status/1045496337523822592.

28. Sara Farris, *In the Name of Women's Rights* (Duke UP, 2017), 4.

29. Paula Mulinari, "A New Service Class in the Public Sector?," *Social Inclusion* 6(4), 2018.

30. Hirsi Ali, *Nomad,* (Knopf, 2011), 243.

31. Hirsi Ali, *Infidel,* (Simon & Schuster, 2007), 295.

32. Michelle Goldberg, "The Un-Reluctant Fundamentalist," *Democracy*, Fall 2010.

33. David Cohen, "Violence Is Inherent in Islam," *London Evening Standard*, February 7, 2007. The (thwarted) "plot to murder Muslim soldiers in the British Army" to which Hirsi Ali is referring is the case of Parviz Khan, of Birmingham, who planned to kidnap and behead a Muslim soldier serving in the British Army and was sentenced to life in prison. BBC, "Soldier Kidnap Plotter Given Life," February 18, 2008.

34. Hirsi Ali, *Nomad,* 243.

35. Mehdi Hasan, "Why Islam Doesn't Need a Reformation," *Guardian*, May 17, 2015.

36. Cathy Young, "Ayaan to Liberals: Get Your Priorities Straight," *Daily Beast*, April 14, 2017.

37. Liz Fekete, "Enlightened Fundamentalism? Immigration, Feminism and the Right," IRR, 2006. "*Some feminists are being recruited to an anti-immigrant politics via aggressively promoted stereotypes of Islam.*"

38. Farris, in chapter 1 of *In the Name of Women's Rights: The Rise of Femonationalism*, details the new centrality of gender for right-wing nationalism as espoused by Rita Verdonk, Matteo Salvini, and Marine Le Pen: scrutinizing, among other things, the Lega Nord's "feminist" opposition to Turkey's entry into the EU in 2009; the PVV's ethnicization of gender emancipation policies throughout the 2000s; and the FN's contribution to feminist-backed "ban the burqa" governmental lobbies in the same period.

39. Susan Moller Okin, *Is Multiculturalism Bad for Women?* (Princeton UP, 1999), 22. In her influential monograph, Okin proposed that immigrant women living in Europe "*might be much better off if the culture into which they were born were either to become extinct (so that its members would become integrated into the less sexist surrounding culture) or, preferably, to be encouraged to alter itself so as to reinforce the equality of women at least to the degree to which this value is upheld in the majority culture.*"

40. James Angelos, "The New Europeans," *New York Times Magazine*, April 6, 2016.

41. Gudula Walterskirchen, "Bei Gewalt und Mord endet die Toleranz für religiöse Werturteile," *Die Presse*, December 1, 2019.

42. Bassam Tibi, "Junge Männer, die die Kultur der Gewalt mitbringen," *Die Welt*, May 8, 2016.

43. Bassam Tibi, "'Patriarchalische Männer sind nicht integrierbar,'" *InfoSperber*, August 29, 2016.

44. Alice Schwarzer, personal website: "The Perpetrators Were Islamists!," May 13, 2016.

45. Schwarzer, personal website: "The Consequences of False Tolerance," January 5, 2016.

46. Christiane Hoffmann and René Pfister, "A Feminist View of Cologne," *Der Spiegel*, January 21, 2016.

47. Schwarzer, personal website: "The Police Were Themselves Victims," May 13, 2016.

48. I was the translator of this book into English, which was originally entitled *Unterscheiden und Herrschen* (transcript, 2017).

49. Sabine Hark and Paula-Irene Villa, *The Future of Difference*, Verso, 2020, 3.

50. Alice Schwarzer, "Wir nehmen die Kriegserklärung an!" *Emma*, September 1, 1981.

51. Hark and Villa, *Future of Difference*, 35.

52. Hark and Villa, *Future of Difference*, 34.

53. *Guardian*, "Anti-Muslim hate groups nearly triple in US since last year, report finds," February 15, 2017.

54. Pew, "How the U.S. general public views Muslims and Islam," 26 July, Pew Research Center, 2017.

55. *Sydney Morning Herald*, "Pauline Hanson Says Islam Is a Disease Australia Needs to 'Vaccinate,'" March 24, 2017.

56. On the life of the term "rapefugees," see Monica Ibrahim, "Rapefugees Not Welcome," MSc dissertation, London School of Economics, 2017; and Ewelina Pepiak, "White Femininity and Trolling," in Polak and Trottier (eds.) *Violence and Trolling on Social Media*, Amsterdam UP, 2020.

57. Hark and Villa, *Future of Difference*, xxvi.

58. Ina Kerner, *Differenzen und Macht* (Suhrkamp, 2009), 364.

59. Shout-out to Josie Carter, my "Femonationalism" student in 2021, online at the Brooklyn Institute for Social Research.

60. *"The German feminist Alice Schwarzer . . . flew to Tehran in mid-March 1979 to support Iranian women. . . . The regime signaled its willingness to enter talks. The hastily established 'International Committee for the Protection of Women's Rights' was personally received by Khomeini and Bazargan. And yet, the 'spring of freedom' ended in March 1979. The American feminist Kate Millett was expelled from Iran; others left with the feeling that there was not much that could be done to stop the repression of women."* Frank Bösch, "Between the Shah and Khomeini," *German Yearbook of Contemp. History* 2, 2017, 154.

61. Olaf Przybilla, "Alice Schwarzer and the CDU/CSU," *Süddeutsche Zeitung Magazine*, May 17, 2010.

62. Alice Schwarzer, *Alice im Männerland* (Kiepenheuer & Witsch, 2002).

63. Alena Schröder, "Wohin die Weisheit unserer Ältesten?" *Süddeutsche Zeitung Magazine*, July 9, 2019.

64. alice-schwarzer-stiftung.de

65. en.frauenmediaturm.de/fmt

66. Christina Scharff, "Schröder versus Schwarzer?," *Feminist Media Studies*, 14: 5, 2014; see also Tristana Moore, "The Family Minister vs. the Feminist—German Women at War," *Time*, November 12, 2010.

67. Deutschlandfunk Kultur, "Überfälliger Streit der Über-Frauen," August 21, 2017.

68. Sabine Hark and Paula-Irene Villa, *Anti-Genderismus*, transcript, 2015.

69. DW News, "Alice Schwarzer confesses to Swiss tax evasion," February 2, 2014.

70. D. Stawski, "Easy Come Easy Go," *Süddeutsche Zeitung*, May 17, 2010.

71. *Der Tagesspiegel*, "Buch über Affäre von Alice Schwarzer bleibt wohl verboten," November 5, 2016.

72. Schröder, "Wohin die Weisheit unserer Ältesten?"

73. *Die Welt*, "Alice Schwarzer: 'Wer für Prostitution ist, ist auch fürs Kopftuch,'" October 12, 2020.

74. Frédéric Lemaître, "Les combats d'une féministe," *Le Monde*, November 14, 2011.

75. Alison Smale, "A Pioneering German Feminist Looks Back in Anguish," *New York Times*, March 31, 2017.

76. Hark and Villa, *Future of Difference*, 79.

77. Kerner, *Differenzen und Macht*, 362.

78. *Frankfurther Allgemeine Zeitung*, "In Cafes sitzen keine Frauen mehr," December 11, 2017. For discussion, see Charlène Calderaro, "Exploring Femonationalist Convergences," in Sifaki, Quinan, and Lončarević (eds.), *Homonationalism, Femonationalism and Ablenationalism*, Routledge, 2022.

79. Esra Erdem, "In der Falle einer Politik des Ressentiments," in Hess et al. (eds.), *No Integration? Kulturwissenschaftliche Beiträge zur Integrationsdebatte in Europa*, transcript, 2009, 187–206.

80. Die Stoerenfriedas, "Alice—Who the Fuck Is Alice," Untergrund-Blättle, January 13, 2015.

81. *"Ich dachte, nur ein Mann darf Sie nicht anfassen!"*—see *Tagesspiegel*, "Shitstorm gegen Alice Schwarzer nach Streit mit Muslima," May 9, 2019. See also Jona Zhitia, "Weißer Feminismus und Islamophobie," *Ekologiska*, September 30, 2020.

82. Lisa Nimervoll, "'schon wieder eine weiße Frau': ÖH protestiert gegen Alice Schwarzer," *Der Standard*, November 26, 2019. For further context, see Dahinden and Manser-Egli, "Gendernativism and Liberal Subjecthood," *Social Politics* 30(1), 2023.

83. Azeezah Kanji, "Ayaan Hirsi Ali, Brett Kavanaugh, and Imperial Feminism," *Al Jazeera,* October 5, 2018.

84. Adam Yaghi, "Popular Testimonial Literature by American Cultural Conservatives of Arab or Muslim Descent," *Middle East Critique* 25: 1, 2016.

85. Kiran Grewal, "Reclaiming the Voice of the Third World Woman," *Interventions* 14(4), 2012, 571.

86. Saba Mahmood, "Religion, Feminism, and Empire," in Alcoff and Caputo (eds.) *Feminism, Sexuality, and the Return of Religion* (Indiana UP, 2011), 98.

87. Mahmood, 90.

88. Lorna Finlayson, *An Introduction to Feminism* (Cambridge UP, 2016), 213.

89. *"Middle-class liberal feminism was one of the technologies of British imperial power."* Antoinette Burton, *Burdens of History*, 1994, 19.

11. THE PRO-LIFE FEMINIST

1. Daphne de Jong, "The Feminist Sell-Out," *New Zealand Listener*, January 13, 1978. Republished in Derr, MacNair, and Naranjo-Huebl (eds.), *Pro-Life Feminism*, Xlibris, 2005, 234.

2. *Huffington Post*, "'Pro-Life Feminism' is an Oxymoron," July 2, 2009; *New York Magazine*, "There's No Such Thing As a Pro-Life Feminist," November 30, 2021. See also: Joan Bray, "Pro-Life Feminism: An

Oxymoron," counter-protesting Feminists For Life, cited in *The American Feminist* 7(1), 2000, p.24.

3. Kristan Hawkins (@KristanHawkins), Twitter (now X), November 6, 2022.

4. Michael Chandler,"'Badass. Prolife. Feminist.'," *Washington Post*, January 19, 2018.

5. Emily Janakiram, "There's No Such Thing as 'Pro-Life' Feminism," *Rampant*, November 1, 2021.

6. Helen Alvaré, "Open Your Eyes, Pro-Life Feminists Are Everywhere," CNN, May 23, 2018.

7. *Feminist Buzzkills* podcast, "Progressive Anti-Abortion Uprising, aka the Fetus Thieves," June 17, 2022.

8. *Hacker News*, "Pro-life Antifa," July 19, 2022.

9. Nathan Place, "Everything We Know about Lauren Handy," *Independent*, April 6, 2022; Sofia Resnick, "Why Were There Fetuses in Her Refrigerator?," *The Cut*, May 13, 2022.

10. Katha Pollitt, "Can a Feminist Be Pro-Life?," *Nation*, March 10, 2017.

11. Rehumanize International, "Stop State-Sanctioned Violence," online store.

12. New Wave Feminists (NewWaveFeminists.com), Mission Statement. NWF describes itself as "a pro-(all) life feminist organization."

13. Feminists for Life (FeministsForLife.org), "Feminists for Life Videos"— "Revolutionize Your Campus with Resources and Support for Pregnant and Parenting Students." For more on Feminists for Life of America's college outreach program, see Laury Oaks, "What Are Pro-Life Feminists Doing on Campus?," *NWSA Journal* 21(1): 178–203, 2009.

14. Quoted in Alvaré, "Open Your Eyes, Pro-Life Feminists Are Everywhere," 2018.

15. Quoted in Ruth Graham, "'The Pro-Life Generation,'" *New York Times*, July 3, 2022.

16. Kristin Turner (@kristinnirvan), TikTok; @KristinforLife, twitter.com/kristinforlife.

17. Frederick Clarkson, "Anti-Abortion Movement Marches on After 2 Decades of Arson, Bombs and Murder," *Southern Poverty Law Center*, September 15, 1998.

18. Nina Liss-Schultz, "The Militant Wing of the Anti-Abortion Movement Is Back," *Mother Jones*, Sep./Oct., 2018.

19. Carter Sherman, "People Are Invading Abortion Clinics and 'Rescuing' Women on TikTok," *Vice*, April 26, 2023.

20. Lauren Enriquez, "How the New Feminist Resistance Leaves Out American Women," *New York Times*, February 27, 2017.

21. Lori Szala, "The Problem with Linking Abortion and Economics," *New York Times*, May 9, 2017.

22. *Jezebel*, "Why Has the *New York Times* Published 2 Op-Eds By the Same Anti-Abortion Group?," May 9, 2017; *New Republic*, "The *New York Times* Allowed an Anti-Choice Group to Write a Press Release on the Op-Ed

Page," May 9, 2017; *Slate*, "Why the *New York Times*' Post-Roe Abortion Coverage Has Felt a Little Off," August 1, 2022. See also *Mother Jones*, "The *Times*' Abortion Coverage," March 21, 2006. Here's a selection of pro-life *New York Times* opinions from the past dozen years (including only one of many by Ross Douthat): Molly Worthen, "Pro-Life, Pro-Left," September 28, 2012; Thomas Friedman, "Why I Am Pro-Life," October 27, 2012; Ross Douthat, "There is No Pro-Life Case For Planned Parenthood," August 5, 2015; Scott Arbeiter, "I'm Pro-Life, and Pro-Refugee," February 7, 2017; Charles Camosy, "You Can't Be Pro-Life and Against Immigrant Children," June 16, 2018; Charles Camosy, "I Am Pro-Life. Don't Call Me Anti-Abortion," January 9, 2019; Nicholas Kristof, "She's Evangelical, 'Pro-Life' and Voting for Biden," October 21, 2020; Trish Warren, "Why the Feminist Movement Needs Pro-Life People," November 28, 2021; Patrick Brown, "The Pro-Family Agenda Republicans Should Embrace After Roe," May 7, 2022; Matthew Walther, "Overturning Roe Will Disrupt a Lot More Than Abortion. I Can Live With That," May 10, 2022; Trish Warren, "'You Can't Protect Some Life and Not Others'," June 18, 2023; David French, "The Importance of Hope in the Pro-Life Movement," June 22, 2023. And don't even get me started on the *Atlantic*.

23. "Amicus Brief for Concerned Women of America et al.," No. 19-1392, in *Dobbs v. Jackson Women's Health*, July 28, 2021.

24. Erika Bachiochi, *The Rights of Women* (Notre Dame UP, 2021), 15.

25. Erika Bachiochi, "I Refused to Vote for Trump, but I'm Grateful for His Court Picks," *New York Times*, December 9, 2021.

26. Sophie Lewis, *Full Surrogacy Now* (Verso, 2019).

27. Reva Siegel, "The Right's Reasons," *Duke Law Journal* 57, 2008, 1688.

28. Mary Ziegler, "Women's Rights on the Right," *BJGLJ* 28, 2013, 263.

29. Lila Rose (@LilaGraceRose), April 27, 2023, quoted in Audrey Farley, "The Far Right's Dangerous Fertility Myths," *New Republic*, May 4, 2023. For Lila Rose's own manifesto for Live Action, see Lila Rose, "Battle Hymn of a Pro-Life Feminist," *Politico*, April 2, 2012.

30. Charles Svestka, @MrSVES, "The Pro Life Movement Deserves Better," YouTube, June 24, 2023.

31. Matthew Schmitz, "The Wrongs of Women," *First Things*, November 1, 2022.

32. Graham, "'Pro-Life Generation.'"

33. Madeleine McClung, "What Are Crisis Pregnancy Centers and How Are They Funded?," *Columbus Dispatch*, October 25, 2021; Karen Dewitt, "The Dark Money Behind Abortion Bans," *Ms.*, July 20, 2022.

34. "*It is in this same spirit of [Martin Luther] King [Jr.] and the original feminists [Susan B. Anthony] that young pro-life women are rising up in increasing numbers to say abortion is a radical injustice that affects us all and must end.*" Emily Buchanan, "Pro-Life and Feminism Aren't Mutually Exclusive," *Time*, January 3, 2013.

35. Ann Gordon and Patricia Holland, "The G.O.P.'s Susan B. Anthony Gender Gap," *New York Times*, February 8, 1984; Ann Gordon and Lynn Sherr, "No, Susan B. Anthony and Elizabeth Cady Stanton Were Not Antiabortionists," *Time*, November 10, 2015.

36. Buchanan, "Pro-Life and Feminism Aren't Mutually Exclusive," 2013.

37. Jane Alpert, "Mother Right: A New Feminist Theory," *off our backs* 3(9), 1973, 31.

38. Elizabeth Hedrick, "Robin Morgan, Jane Alpert, and Feminist Satire," *Tulsa Studies in Women's Literature* 33(2), 2014, 127.

39. Bachiochi, *The Rights of Women*, 1.

40. Bachiochi, *The Rights of Women*, 2.

41. Bachiochi, *The Rights of Women*, 4.

42. Bachiochi, *The Rights of Women*, 6.

43. Bachiochi, *The Rights of Women*, 15.

44. Clare Hemmings, *Why Stories Matter* (Duke UP, 2011). On "return," see 95.

45. Bachiochi, *The Rights of Women,* 111.

46. Bachiochi, 167.

47. Bachiochi, 156.

48. Ezra Klein, "Transcript: Ezra Klein Interviews Erika Bachiochi," *New York Times*, May 31, 2022.

49. Social incohesion and income inequality stem, for Bachiochi, from the widening moral gap between "the marrying rich and unmarrying poor": "*the decoupling of sex from marriage and marriage from childbearing, ushered in by the sexual revolution, unraveled a working-class culture of once-stable marital bonds.*" Bachiochi, *The Rights of Women*, 13.

50. "Ezra Klein Interviews Erika Bachiochi," 2022.

51. Scott Neuman, "Pope Calls Abortion Evidence Of 'The Throwaway Culture,'" NPR, January 13, 2014. For pro-life feminist engagements with the concept, see *Make Muse* magazine's feature "Is the Term 'Pro-Life Feminist' an Oxymoron?," February 22, 2019. For a whole pro-life book on *throwaway culture*, see Charles Camosy, *Resisting Throwaway Culture*, New City, 2019.

52. Mary Harrington, "The Three Principles of Reactionary Feminism," *Public Discourse*, April 30, 2023.

53. Victoria Browne: "*Any kind of anti-abortion argument (however complex and caveated it might be) can bolster the principles under which the mainstream anti-abortion movement claims to operate.*" Browne, "Anti-Abortion Feminism: How Is This Even a Thing?," *Radical Philosophy* #213, 2022, 40.

54. Browne in "Anti-Abortion Feminism: How Is This Even a Thing?" quoting the chief executive of Hope Clinic for Women, a "life-affirming" CPC that was targeted by "Jane's Revenge."

55. "Feminists Choosing Life of New York (FCLNY) is a state-wide human rights coalition that embraces and promotes whole life feminism and the consistent life ethic." FCLNY website (fclny.org).

56. "PAAU promotes Restorative & Transformative Justice models." (@PAAUNOW), June 16, 2023.

57. Erika Bachiochi (ed.), *The Cost of Choice* (Encounter, 2004), xv.

58. Stephanie Watson, "Abortion and Breast Cancer Risk," *HealthLine*, July 26, 2022.

59. Angela Lanfranchi, "The Abortion-Breast Cancer Link," in Bachiochi (ed.), *The Cost of Choice* (Encounter, 2004), 72.

60. Erika Bachiochi (ed.), *Women, Sex and Church* (Pauline, 2010).

61. Erika Bachiochi, "Embodied Equality," *Harvard Journal of Law & Public Policy* 34(889), 2011.

62. Erika Bachiochi, "What Makes a Fetus a Person?," *New York Times*, July 1, 2022.

63. Erika Bachiochi, "I'm a Feminist and I'm against Abortion," CNN, January 22, 2015.

64. Browne, "Anti-Abortion Feminism," 32.

65. Bachiochi, "I'm a Feminist and I'm against Abortion."

66. Bachiochi, "What Makes a Fetus a Person?"

67. Catharine MacKinnon, "The Male Ideology of Privacy," *Radical America* 17(40), 1983, 30.

68. MacKinnon, 34n23.

69. Andrea Dworkin, *Pornography* (Perigee, 1981), 96.

70. Bachiochi, "The 14th Amendment Should Protect Fetal Life," *New York Times*, July 2, 2022, A23(L).

71. Rosalind Petchesky: "Workers, Reproductive Hazards, and the Politics of Protection," *Feminist Studies* 5(2), 1979; "Reproductive Freedom,'" *Signs* 5(4), 1980; and "The Body as Property," in Ginsburg and Rapp (eds.), *Conceiving the New World Order* (California UP, 1995).

72. *NYT*, "Transcript: Ezra Klein Interviews Erika Bachiochi," 2022.

73. Laura Santhanam, "It's Time to Recognize the Damage of Childbirth, Doctors and Mothers Say," PBS, May 7, 2021.

74. World Health Organization, "Maternal Mortality," February 22, 2023.

75. Kathy Katella, "Maternal Mortality Is on the Rise: 8 Things to Know," *Yale Medicine*, May 22, 2023.

76. For more of my work on gestational labor, see any of the following: Sophie Lewis, "International Solidarity in Reproductive Justice," *Gender, Place & Culture* 25(2), 2018; "Cyborg Uterine Geography," *Dialogues in Human Geography* 8(3), 2018; "Free Anthrogenesis," *Salvage Quarterly*, June 1, 2022; "Paul Preciado's Uterine Politics," *Paragraph* 46(1), 2023.

77. Ninnia Baehr, *Abortion Without Apology* (South End, 1990), 35.

78. Katha Pollitt, *Pro* (Picador, 2014), 37.

79. Anna North, "How the abortion debate moved away from 'safe, legal, and rare,'" *Vox*, October 18, 2019.

80. Andrea Smith, "Beyond Pro-Choice Versus Pro-Life," *NWSA Journal* 17(1), 2005; Loretta Ross and Rickie Solinger, *Reproductive Justice*,

California UP, 2017; Erika Derkas et al. (eds.), *Radical Reproductive Justice*, CUNY, 2017.

81. On the history of abortion, see Kristin Luker, *Abortion and the Politics of Motherhood* (California UP, 1985); Janet Brodie, *Contraception and Abortion in 19th Century America* (Cornell UP, 1994); Londa Schiebinger, *Plants and Empire* (Harvard UP, 2007); Marie Schwartz, *Birthing a Slave* (Harvard UP, 2010); Barbara Gurr, *Reproductive Justice* (Rutgers UP, 2014); Cheree Carlson, *The Crimes of Womanhood* (Illinois UP, 2009); Heather Latimer, "Abortion Regulation as the Afterlife of Reproductive Slavery," *Feminist Studies* 49(2), 2022.

82. Nzingha H., "I'm an Abortion Doula in the Deep South, This Is What I Want You to Know," *Scalawag*, May 18, 2022.

83. *NYT*, "Transcript: Ezra Klein Interviews Erika Bachiochi."

84. On "forced life," see Eric Stanley, "Queer Remains: Insurgent Feelings and the Aesthetics of Violence," PhD dissertation (University of California, Santa Cruz, 2013).

85. Evelyn Nakano Glenn, *Forced to Care* (Harvard UP, 2010).

86. Victoria Browne, "Against Goody Two-Shoes Feminism," *Radical Philosophy* 202, 2018.

87. Crystal Raypole, "99% of Women Say They Feel Relief, Not Regret, 5 Years After Having an Abortion," *HealthLine*, January 13, 2020; Erica Millar, *Happy Abortions* (Zed, 2017).

88. Sophie Lewis, "Abortion Involves Killing," *Nation*, June 22, 2022. See also the *LRB* forum (44.14, July 21, 2022), where I argue, "*We are fighting for decriminalization, not doctors*." I also say this in "Gestational Decrim," *Salvage*, November 8, 2019.

89. Donna Haraway, *When Species Meet*, Minnesota UP, 2008, 80. See Eva Giraud, "'Beasts of Burden,'" *Culture, Theory and Critique* 54(1), 2013.

90. Erika Bachiochi, "What Makes a Fetus a Person?". Perhaps she has not experienced the moral maturity of, say: Moira Donegan, "On Zika and Abortion," *n+1*, May 4, 2016; Willie Parker, *Life's Work* (Simon & Schuster, 2017); or any of the contributors to the *LRB*'s special issue "Prejudice Rules": Edna Bonhomme, Hazel Carby, Meehan Crist, Lorna Finlayson, Erin Maglaque, Susan Pedersen, and many more.

12. THE ADULT HUMAN FEMALE

1. Janice Raymond, *The Transsexual Empire* (Teachers College, 1979), 105.

2. Mary Harrington, "The Feminist Case Against Abortion," *UnHerd*, December 23, 2021.

3. Mary Harrington, *Feminism against Progress* (Regnery, 2023), 82.

4. Harrington, *Feminism against Progress*, 214.

5. Harrington, *Feminism against Progress*, 169.

6. Harrington, *Feminism against Progress*, 133.

7. Katrina Trinko, "Mary Harrington talks transgenderism," *Daily Signal*, April 30, 2023.

8. Harrington, *Feminism against Progress*, 2023, 169.

9. Harrington, *Feminism against Progress*, 161.

10. Harrington, *Feminism against Progress*, 6.

11. Harrington, *Feminism against Progress*, 9.

12. Harrington, *Feminism against Progress*, 172.

13. Harrington, *Feminism against Progress*, 10.

14. Harrington, *Feminism against Progress*, 8.

15. Harrington, *Feminism against Progress*, 9.

16. Harrington talks about Martine Rothblatt, the Jewish trans pharma tycoon whose 2011 manifesto is called "From Transgender to Transhuman," on 139 of *Feminism Against Progress*, as well as at the *Spectator* ("The Trans War on the Body," 2021). Rothblatt is the focus of the more conspiratorial moments in the TERFism of Bilek, Stock (at *UnHerd*), Joyce, Dansky et al. Usually, Rothblatt is erroneously called a "billionaire." See Lee Leveille, "The Mechanisms of TAnon: Where it Came From," *Health Liberation Now!*, July 5, 2021.

17. Harrington, *Feminism against Progress*, 143.

18. Mary Harrington, "The Gender Resistance," *First Things*, September 14, 2021.

19. "J.K. Rowling Writes about Her Reasons for Speaking out on Sex and Gender Issues," JK Rowling (website), June 19, 2020.

20. Trudy Ring, "Yes, J.K. Rowling, the Nazis Persecuted Trans People, Burned Books," *Advocate*, March 14, 2024.

21. Louise Perry, *The Case Against the Sexual Revolution* (Polity, 2022), 22.

22. "*The word 'chivalry' is now deeply unfashionable, but it describes something of what I'm calling for.*" Perry, 96.

23. Perry, *The Case Against the Sexual Revolution*, 46.

24. Perry ,*The Case Against the Sexual Revolution*, 243.

25. Perry explains that, as a rape-crisis counselor, she used to espouse the line that rape is about power, not desire; but now, she believes the thesis—that rape is natural—argued in Palmer and Thornhill, *A Natural History of Rape* (MIT, 2000).

26. Perry blurbing Joyce: "*In the first decade of this century, it was unthinkable that a gender-critical book could even be published by a prominent publishing house, let alone become a bestseller.*" Joyce blurbing Perry: "*Brilliantly conceived and written.*" Stock blurbing Bindel: "*An impassioned manifesto.*" Bindel in the *Spectator*: "*Why liberals must stand with Kathleen Stock.*" Stock blurbing Harrington: "*One of progressive feminism's most ingenious critics.*" Harrington blurbing Stock: "*Stock writes faithfully in the tradition of the Enlightenment.*" Perry blurbing Harrington: "*Like downing a packet of Tangfastics after a lifetime of gruel.*" Bindel blurbing Perry: "*Brilliantly written, cleverly argued. . . fresh and exciting.*" And so on. See also the following reviews: Gaby Hinsliff, "Trans by Helen Joyce; Material Girls

by Kathleen Stock," *Guardian*, July 18, 2021; Rachel Cooke, "Feminism for Women by Julie Bindel," *Guardian*, August 31, 2021; Rachel Cooke, "A Potent, Plain-Speaking Womanifesto" (Perry), *Guardian*, June 6, 2022; Rachel Cooke, "Welcome to the Age of Rage" (Smith), *Guardian*, February 27, 2023.

27. Helen Lewis, "The Feminists Insisting That Women Are Built Differently," *Atlantic*, June 18, 2023.

28. Erika Bachiochi, "Sex-Realist Feminism," *First Things*, April 1, 2023.

29. For a pro-trans, still critical perspective on the Tavistock Clinic, see *Trans Safety Network*, "Questionable Expertise at Bell v Tavistock," December 20, 2020. On Shrier, see Sarah Fonseca, "The Constitutional Conflationists," *LA Review of Books*, January 17, 2021; and Jules Gill-Peterson, "Abigail Shrier Goes to Washington," *Sad Brown Girl*, March 18, 2021.

30. FiLiA, "Hannah Barnes and Time to Think," March 21, 2023; Meghan Murphy, "Abigail Shrier on Girls and the Trans Trend," *The Same Drugs* (podcast), October 20, 2020; *Feminist Current*, "Blasphemous Ideas and the Silencing of Dissent," August 30, 2020.

31. Michelle Goldberg, "What Is a Woman," *New Yorker*, July 28, 2014. See: Jos Truitt, "Why *The New Yorker*'s Radical Feminism and Transgenderism Piece Was One-Sided," *Columbia Journalism Review*, August 6, 2014. On the debunked "autogynephilia" theory, which typologizes trans women according to the presence or absence of their *autogynephilic* arousal at the thought of themselves *as women*, see: Julia Serano, "Autogynephilia" *Sociological Review* 68(4), 2020.

32. *Daily Mail*, "Megyn Kelly Posts Photo of Herself a Red MAGA-Style Hat that Reads 'Make Women Female Again,'" May 1, 2023.

33. *Pink News*, "'Gender Critical Feminist' Posie Parker Wants Men with Guns to Start Using Women's Toilets," January 30, 2021.

34. BBC, "Woman Billboard Removed after Transphobia Row," September 26, 2018.

35. Louise Perry, "Adult Human Female—Posie Parker," *Maiden Mother Matriarch* with Louise Perry, YouTube, May 1, 2023.

36. *Express*, "Sunak Insists a Woman Is an 'Adult Human Female' and 'Sex Matters' in Piers Morgan Chat," February 2, 2023; *Daily Mail*, "Rishi Sunak Says 'Biological Sex Is Fundamentally Important' Ahead of a Parliamentary Debate on Changes to Equality Law, June 9, 2023.

37. *The Guardian*, "Anti-Trans Activist Posie Parker Leaves New Zealand after Chaotic Protests," March 26, 2023.

38. For one example of TERFs disavowing Posie Parker, see the anti-trans group Woman's Place UK's statement: "Woman's Place and Kellie-Jay Keen (aka Posie Parker)," WPUK website, June 22, 2022.

39. In 2023, Keen-Minshull said on Perry's podcast, Maiden Mother Matriarch, that Nigel Farage's single issue approach was exactly what she wanted to emulate in her movement: "Why *wouldn't* we want to be him?!"

See also Mary Harrington, "What Posie Parker Learnt from Brexit," *UnHerd*, March 29, 2023. (*"When I call Posie Parker the Nigel Farage of Terfs, I mean it as a compliment."*) Sarah Franklin called this analogy in 2019. See Sarah Franklin, "Nostalgic Nationalism," *Cultural Anthropology* 34(1), 2019.

40. Meghan Murphy, "Posie Parker—Standing for Women," *Feminist Current*, January 24, 2019.

41. Monica Roberts (TransGriot), "Whyte Radfem Womyn Gone Wild," *TransGriot*, June 11, 2012. *"Are they mad because they no longer have a free ride in terms of saying whatever they want about us and thanks to the Net and the blogosphere, we trans people can push back just as fiercely?"*

42. B Camminga, "Disregard and Danger," *Sociological Review* 68(4), 2020. Camminga shows that Adichie's TERF politics have been criticized as western-centric by many African feminist writers and activists (both cis and trans), such as Panashe Chigumadzi, Shailja Patel, Ricki Kgositau, Seoketsi Mooketsi, Miss Sahhara, Thabiso Ratalane, and Sisonke Msimang. Note also: in 2013, 790 individuals and 60 organizations from 41 countries signed a "Statement of Trans-Inclusive Feminism and Womanism."

43. Beth Elliott, "Of Infidels and Inquisitions," *Lesbian Tide* 2(10–11), May–June 1973, 26.

44. Pat Buchanan, "The Living Contradiction," *Lesbian Tide* 2(10–11), May–June 1973, 6.

45. On Robin Morgan and sisterhood, see Durba Mitra, "Sisterhood is X," *SAQ* 122(3), 2023.

46. Barbara McLean, "Diary of a Mad Organizer," *Lesbian Tide* 2(10–11), May–June 1973, 36.

47. I recommend these analyses of WCLC 1973: Jules Gill-Peterson, *A Short History of Transmisogyny*, Verso, 2024, 23–5; Talia Bettcher, "A Conversation with Jeanne Córdova," *TSQ* 3(1–2), 2016; Susan Stryker, *Transgender History* (2nd ed.), Basic, 2017, 108–9; Cristan Williams, "Radical Inclusion," *TSQ* 3(1–2), 2016; Emma Heaney, "Women-Identified Women," *TSQ* 3(1–2), 2016.

48. Elliott, "Of Infidels and Inquisitions," 15.

49. Cristan Williams, "TERF Academic Rewrites History," *Trans Advocate*, February 17, 2014.

50. McLean, "Diary of a Mad Organizer," 36.

51. Cristan Williams, "That Time TERFs Beat RadFems for Protecting A Trans Woman From Their Assault," *Trans Advocate*, July 3, 2016.

52. McLean, "Diary of a Mad Organizer," 1973, 36.

53. Robin Morgan, *Going Too Far*, Vintage, 1978, 180.

54. Buchanan, "The Living Contradiction", 6. Italic mine.

55. McLean, "Diary of a Mad Organizer," 37.

56. *"My purpose in this talk here today is to call for further polarization."* Morgan, *Going Too Far*, 185.

57. *"I feel that 'man-hating' is an honorable and viable political act."* Morgan, 178.

58. McLean, "Diary of a Mad Organizer," 38.

59. Emma Heaney, *The New Woman*, Northwestern UP, 2017, 271.

60. Elliott, "Of Infidels and Inquisitions," 15. See also: *The Advocate*, "Transsexuals Hex Robin Morgan," 116, July 18, 1973, 21.

61. Morgan writes: *"The Mick Jagger/sadism fad, the popularity of transvestite entertainers, and the resurgence of 'Camp' all seem to me part of an unmistakable backlash against what feminists have been demanding."* Morgan, *Going Too Far*, 1978, 167. Morgan also claims that those who defended Elliott "as their sister" were *"into the 'brotherhood of Camp'— whatever that meant"* (p. 171).

62. Morgan, *Going Too Far*, 180.

63. Morgan, *Going Too Far*,171.

64. I discuss the femmephobia of TERFism in Sophie Lewis, "SERF 'n' TERF," *Salvage*, February 6, 2017; and "'Not a Workplace,'" Verso, May 24, 2018.

65. Elliott, "Of Infidels and Inquisitions," 26.

66. Germaine Greer, *The Female Eunuch*, MacGibbon & Kee, 1970, 62. On April Ashley, see Christopher Hutton, *The Tyranny of Ordinary Meaning* (Palgrave, 2019); and Aren Aizura, *Mobile Subjects* (Duke UP, 2018).

67. Greer, *Female Eunuch*, 1970, 63.

68. *"The characteristics that are praised and rewarded [in femininity] are those of the castrate—timidity, plumpness, languor, delicacy and preciosity."* Greer, *Female Eunuch*, 1970, 15.

69. Greer, *The Female Eunuch*, 62.

70. Germaine Greer, *The Whole Woman*, 65.

71. Greer, *The Whole Woman*, 74.

72. Mary Harrington, "Trans Activism Has Mummy Issues," *UnHerd*, September 1, 2021; "The Left Has Mummy Issues," *UnHerd*, September 1, 2022.

73. Harrington, 67.

74. Julie Bindel, "Gender Benders, Beware," *Guardian*, January 30, 2004; "Sex-Change Surgery Is the Modern Equivalent of Aversion Therapy for Homosexuals," *Guardian*, August 1, 2007; "The Great Gender-Neutral Toilet Scandal," *Guardian*, April 9, 2008; "As a Lesbian, I No Longer Want to Be Lumped in with a List of Folk Defined by 'Odd' Sexual Practices," *Guardian*, November 7, 2008; Suzanne Moore, "Why Does Nobody Want to Feel Like a Natural Woman Any More?," *Guardian*, February 19, 2011; Julie Burchill, "Hey Trans People, Cut It Out: Where Do Dicks in Terrible Wigs Get Off Lecturing Us Natural-Born Women?," *Spiked*, January 15, 2013 [previously at *The Observer*]; "The Observer Withdraws Julie Burchill Column As Editor Publishes Apology," *Observer*, January 14, 2013; "Two Top Female Writers, an Insult about Brazilian Transsexuals and a Firestorm on Twitter," *Daily Mail*, January 13, 2013;

"*Guardian* Writer Julie Burchill Defends Suzanne Moore Saying She Was 'MMonstered' by 'Chicks with Dicks' on Twitter," *PinkNews*, January 13, 2013; "Germaine Greer Says Her Views on Transgender People Are 'Opinion, Not Prohibition,'" *Guardian*, October 24, 2015; Ugla Jónsdóttir, "Trans People Are Exhausted of Debating Facts with People Like Germaine Greer on *Genderquake*," *Guardian*, May 9, 2018; Julie Burchill, "I Knew I Was Right," *Spectator*, April 19, 2018; Suzanne Moore, "Women Must Have the Right to Organise: We Will Not Be Silenced," *Guardian*, March 2, 2020; "Why I Had to Leave the *Guardian*," *UnHerd*, November 25, 2020.

75. Jules Gill-Peterson, *A Short History of Trans Misogyny* (Verso, 2024), vii.
76. Lierre Keith and Derrick Jensen, "The Emperor's New Penis," *CounterPunch*, June 21, 2013.
77. Out of the Woods Collective, "Lies of the Land," in *Hope Against Hope* (Common Notions, 2017), 97. Quoting Paul Kingsnorth, "The Lie of the Land," *Guardian*, March 18, 2017.
78. James Trafford, "Against Green Nationalism," *OpenDemocracy*, March 29, 2019.
79. The organization "Get the L Out UK" argues on its website that "the only way to end anti-lesbianism is to get the L out of the 'GBT community.'" For analysis, see Jules Gleeson, "Lesbians Going Their Own Way?," *New Socialist*, July 19, 2018.
80. Elena Gambino, "Politics as 'Sinister Wisdom,'" *Contemporary Political Theory* 20(3), 2021, 542–3.
81. Mary Daly, interviewed by Carol Anne Douglas, *off our backs* 9: 5, May 1979, 23.
82. Mary Daly, *Gyn/Ecology* (Beacon, 1978), 67.
83. Daly, interviewed by Douglas, 1979, 23.
84. Robin Morgan, "Preface," in Rycenga and Barufaldi (eds.), *The Mary Daly Reader*, NYU Press, 2017, xiii.
85. Daly, *Gyn/Ecology*, 1978, 13.
86. Daly, *Gyn/Ecology*, 420.
87. Daly, *Gyn/Ecology*, 419.
88. Daly, *Gyn/Ecology*, 68.
89. Daly, *Gyn/Ecology*, 17.
90. Daly, *Gyn/Ecology*, 30.
91. Daly, *Gyn/Ecology*, 8.
92. Daly, *Gyn/Ecology*, 408.
93. Daly, *Gyn/Ecology*, 9.
94. Daly, *Gyn/Ecology*, 3.
95. Jean-Paul Sartre, *Anti-Semite and Jew* (Schocken, [1946] 1995), 20.
96. Sartre, *Anti-Semite and Jew*, 20.
97. Naomi Joni Alizah Cohen, "'The Eradication of 'Talmudic Abstractions,'" *Invert* 1, 2018.

98. The American anti-porn ecofeminist Jennifer Bilek is a case in point. At her website, where she purports to expose the Jewish billionaires funding global transgenderism, Bilek contrives to frame anti-trans agitation as a pro-female *decolonial* crusade and biophilic moral duty that goes hand in hand with the environmentalist Extinction Rebellion movement, in the tradition of her own original movement, the anticivilization ("anti-civ") network Deep Green Resistance. "Women have become occupied territory," she writes, taking eco-primitivist anti-industrial eschatology squarely into the realm of ecofascism: "Like the Americas in the 1500s. Women are fighting to hold on to their sex-segregated spaces, just as the indigenous sought to hold on to their land, many of them not even realizing that destroying sex-segregated spaces is not the colonizers' ultimate objective." (The "ultimate objective" of the colonizing "genderists" is nothing less than the destruction of humanity, or so Bilek gleefully reveals.) "Womanhood is Occupied Territory," *The 11th Hour* blog, November 27, 2021. Notwithstanding her outlandish conspiracism, Bilek's voice permeates mainstream gender-critical feminism. Dozens of well-established gender-critical feminist and "LGB" charities and personalities have promoted Bilek's antisemitic theories about the "biophobic" "genderist" plots of trans Jewish moguls Martine Rothblatt and Jennifer Pritzker. One researcher at the University of California, Christa Peterson, has tirelessly evidenced this mainstream uptake of Bilek, and in 2021 her list included Helen Joyce, LGB Alliance Canada, Object UK, Keep Prisons Single-Sex, Transgender Trend, ReSisters UK, Trans Widows' Voices, Sheila Jeffreys, Mary Harrington, Heather Brunskell-Evans, Save Women's Sports, Jean Hatchet, Kara Dansky, Julian Vigo, Jane Clare Jones, and Women's Human Rights Campaign. In May 2023, a comprehensively detailed report by the antifascist watchdog Health Liberation Now! (HLN) demonstrated that Bilek's boosters in the anti-trans groups Women's Liberation Front (WoLF) and Women's Declaration International (WDI) have the ear of none other than Reem Alsalem, the UN Special Rapporteur on Violence Against Women and Girls. See: Lee Leveille, "Rights For Me, Not For Thee," *All Or None—A Call for Global Solidarity with Trans and Gender-Diverse People*, Health Liberation Now!, May 26, 2023; and Christa Peterson, "The XX Factor," ep. 4, "The Transhumanists' Immortality Projects?!" with Katy Montgomerie, February 27, 2021.

99. Rycenga and Barufaldi (eds.), *The Mary Daly Reader* (NYU Press, 2017); Mary Hunt, "Celebrating and Cerebrating Mary Daly (1928–2010)," *Journal of Feminist Studies in Religion* 28(2), 2012.

100. Audre Lorde, "An Open Letter to Mary Daly" [1979], in *Sister Outsider*, (Penguin, 2020), 54–9.

101. Silvia Federici, *Beyond the Periphery of the Skin*, PM, 2020, 55, 59. For two critical perspectives on the anti-trans argument of this collection, see Cory

Knudson, "Beyond the Periphery of the Skin," *Full Stop*, May 28, 2020; and Hannah Boast, "The Doctor's Knife," *Radical Philosophy* 210, 2021.

102. Responses include: Jules Gill-Peterson, "Toward a Historiography of the Lesbian Transsexual," *Journal of Lesbian Studies* 26(2), 2022; Cristan Williams, "The Ontological Woman," *Sociological Review* 68(4), 2020; Cameron Awkward-Rich, "Trans, Feminism," *Signs* 42(4), 2017; and of course Sandy Stone, "The Empire Strikes Back," *Camera Obscura* 10(2), 1992.

103. Cristan Williams, "Fact Checking Janice Raymond," *Trans Advocate*, January 9, 2016. Williams debunks Raymond's claim that her two reports for the National Center for Health Care Technology and the Office of Health Technology Assessment, commissioned in 1980, made only a small contribution to the government's decision to exclude trans medical care from public insurance policies. *"It was Raymond's NCHCT report that allowed the OHTA report to assert that trans medical care was ethically controversial. . . . We can safely conclude that the policies Raymond helped create contributed to the death and suffering of trans people."*

104. On Jan Raymond's Coalition Against Trafficking in Women, see: C. Libby, "Sympathy, Fear, Hate," *TSQ* 9(3), 2022; Kamala Kempadoo, "The Modern-Day White (Wo)Man's Burden," *Journal of Human Trafficking* 1, 2015; Aziza Ahmed and Meena Seshu, "'We Have the Right Not to Be "Rescued. . .",'" *Anti-Trafficking Review* 1, 2012; Laura Agustín, "Migrants in the Mistress's House," *Social Politics* 12(1), 2005; and Julia Davison, "'Sleeping with the Enemy'?," *Social Policy and Society* 2(1), 2003.

105. Steinem's blurb: *"As a scholar, Janice Raymond explains the 'how' and 'where' of transsexualism. As a compassionate critic and feminist, she also analyses the 'why': the false and cruel sex roles, so restricting of full humanity, that some individuals choose to surgically mutilate their bodies in order to escape."* See also Gloria Steinem, "If the Shoe Doesn't Fit, Change the Foot," *Ms.*, February 1977.

106. Janice Raymond, *The Transsexual Empire* (Teachers College, 1979), 183.

107. Raymond, *The Transsexual Empire,* 109.

108. Raymond, *The Transsexual Empire*, 110.

109. Raymond, *The Transsexual Empire*, 108.

110. Raymond, *The Transsexual Empire*, 106.

111. Raymond, *The Transsexual Empire*, 144.

112. Raymond, *The Transsexual Empire*, 114.

113. Nina Power, "Welcome to TERF Island," *Compact*, March 22, 2023. In Power's book, *What do Men Want?,* Penguin, 2022, she trots out the old canard that trans ways of being reflect a desire to entrench, instead of "get beyond," gender roles (p. 33). Power has since been outed as a fascist in a UK court.

114. Beans Velocci, "The Battle over Trans Rights Is about Power, Not Science," *Washington Post*, October 29, 2019.

115. Helen Joyce, *Trans* (Oneworld, 2021), 2.

116. Grace Lavery, "Gender Criticism versus Gender Abolition," *LA Review of Books*, July 31, 2023.

117. Rest in power, Bryn Kelly. See: *GO* Staff, "Remembering Bryn Kelly," *GO*, April 8, 2016.

118. Bryn Kelly, "Diving into the Wreck," re-printed in Gabriel and Abi-Karam (eds.), *We Want It All* (Nightboat, 2020).

119. Karla Jay, *Tales of the Lavender Menace* (Basic, 1999), 93.

120. Karla Jay, interview by Gwen Shockey, Addresses Project, March 8, 2018.

121. Bryn Kelly, "Diving into the Wreck," 2020.

CONCLUSION: FEMINISM AGAINST CISNESS

1. Fred Moten and Stefano Harney, *The Undercommons*, minor compositions, 2013, 140–1. See also Stephen Dillon, "'I Must Become a Menace to My Enemies,'" *GLQ* 28(2), 2022.

2. In *Abolish the Family* (2022), I attempt one such counter-narration in my "potted history."

3. On the "kinky science fiction writer" Charles Fourier, see M. E. O'Brien, "Communizing Care," *Pinko*, October 15, 2019; on Flora Tristan, see Kevin Duong, "Flora Tristan," *Age of Revolutions*, June 17, 2019; on Bread and Roses, see Meredith Tax, "A Parable of Women's Liberation," *Against the Current* 134, 2008; on *Anti-Caste*, see Caroline Bressey, "Victorian 'Antiracism' and Feminism in Britain," *Women* 21(3), 2010; on STAR, see Nat Raha, "Necessary Labour," *Transfeminisms,* Goldsmiths, February 11, 2015; on Kollontai, see Liza Featherstone, "A New Generation of Radicals Is Rediscovering Alexandra Kollontai," *Jacobin*, March 31, 2022; on Pat Parker, see Rae Alexandra, "The Oakland Poet Who Brought Lesbian Feminism to the Fore," *KQED*, April 30, 2018.

4. Carol Leigh, *Unrepentant Whore* (Last Gasp, 2004), 29.

5. Margo St. James founded COYOTE (a backronym which stands for Call Off Your Old Tired Ethics) in San Francisco in 1973: *"A loose union of women—both prostitutes and feminists—to fight for legal change."* Carol Leigh cofounded BAYSWAN (Bay Area Sex Worker Advocacy Network) in 1996.

6. On the internationalist yearning for sisterhood—and its imperialist obstructors—see Durba Mitra's powerful essay on Robin Morgan's three *Sisterhood* anthologies, "Sisterhood is X," *SAQ* 122(3), 2023.

7. Leigh, *Unrepentant Whore*, 30.

8. Leigh, *Unrepentant Whore*, 29.

9. Michael Richmond and Alex Charnley, "Fascism and the Women's Cause," *LibCom*, July 10, 2023.

10. Catharine MacKinnon, "A Feminist Defense of Transgender Sex Equality Rights," *Yale J. Law and Feminism* 34(2), 2023. As Emma Heaney argues in both the *New Woman* and *Feminism Against Cisness,*

the exceptionalization of this form of work sets the forms of social life it produces apart from the category of cis womanhood.

11. Alison Rumfitt, in Frankie Miren and Alison Rumfitt, *Morbid Obsessions* (Cipher Press, 2022), 43–4.

12. Frankie Miren, in *Morbid Obsessions*, 37.

13. Melissa Gira Grant, *Playing the Whore* (Verso, 2014), 40.

14. Miren, in Miren and Rumfitt, *Morbid Obsessions*, 37.

15. Natalia Santana Mendes, interview, in *Morbid Obsessions*, 84.

16. Elizabeth Whalley and Colleen Hackett, "Carceral Feminisms," *Contemp. Justice Review* 20(4), 2017.

17. Miren, in *Morbid Obsessions*, 45–6.

18. On this, see Joanna Wuest, "Social Conservatives and Radical Feminists Allied Against Trans Personhood," in *Feminism Against Cisness* (Duke UP, 2024) edited by Emma Heaney. Wuest examines new developments in the coalition between TERFs, Christian legal organizations, conservative nonprofits, and Trump administration officials: specifially, a mobilization of feminist, antiracist, and even intersectional arguments against the very notion of trans experience and identity. Groups like The Family Policy Alliance and the Alliance Defending Freedom are using #MeToo-style rhetoric while funding TERF groups like the Women's Liberation Front and leveraging intersectional antiracist ideas against the expansion or erosion of sex and gender.

19. Molly Smith and Juno Mac, *Revolting Prostitutes* (Verso, 2019).

20. Pastachips, "If You Think Punter Forums Are Grim You Should See How This Parenting Website Talks about Sex Workers," *Medium*, November 29, 2021.

21. Emma Heaney, "Sexual Difference Without Cisness," in *Feminism Against Cisness*, 11.

22. Heaney, *Feminism Against Cisness*, 11.

23. Heaney and Margaux Kristjansson, "1970s Trans Feminism as Decolonial Praxis," in *Feminism Against Cisness*, 56–79.

24. I propose the formulation "mother-er" to reflect the anti-essentialist sense in which mothering labors—with their collective potential for revolutionary generativity—are tied neither to the patriarchal institution of motherhood nor to the biology of gestational parentality. Sophie Lewis, "Mothering against Motherhood," *Feminist Theory* 24(1), 2023.

25. In the twelve etchings—plus film, fresco and pencil drawings—that comprise *Disgrace*, "*posh women are depicted cavorting at a garden party, baking cakes to support the empire, breeding perfect privileged children and mobilising in fascist black shirts. . . pinch-faced puritans and scantily clad liberals battle over the morality of sex work and pornography, and a decade later when a woman in a power suit is shown clambering over bodies to cannonball a social housing block.*" Elizabeth Fullerton, "'There's a Lefty, Rose-Tinted Glaze around Feminism,'" *Guardian*, October 11, 2021.

26. Lola Olufemi, "Notes on Dirt and Disgrace," in Hannah Quinlan and Rosie Hastings, *Disgrace—Feminism and the Political Right* (Arcadia Missa, 2021), 52.

27. Akanksha Mehta, "Right-Wing Sisterhood," doctoral thesis, SOAS, University of London, 2017.

28. Akanksha Mehta, "Pre-Existing Conditions—Feminisms, Empire, Futures," in Quinlan and Hastings, *Disgrace*, 2021, 28.

29. Mehta, 37.

30. Mehta, 38.

31. Caitlín Doherty, "A Feminist Style," SideCar, *New Left Review*, July 7, 2023.

32. Becca Rothfeld, "An Activist Practice," SideCar, *New Left Review*, July 27, 2023.

33. Becca Rothfeld, "Feminism and Kitsch," *The Drift*, January 31, 2022.

34. Madeline Lane-McKinley, "#MeToo From Below," *Commune*, October 13, 2018.

35. Silvia Federici and Marina Sitrin, "Social Reproduction," *ROAR* 2, June 25, 2016; Tithi Battacharya (ed.), *Social Reproduction Theory*, Pluto, 2017; Nat Raha, "Transfeminine Brokenness, Radical Transfeminism," *SAQ* 116(3), 2017; Emma Heaney, "Materialist Trans Feminism against Queer Theory," in Emma Heaney, *The New Woman*, Northwestern UP, 2017; Vek Lewis and Dan Irving, "Strange Alchemies," *TSQ* 4(1), 2017; DK Doyle-Griffiths, "Labor Valorization and Social Reproduction," *CLC* 22(2), 2020; Kay Gabriel, "Gender as Accumulation Strategy," *Invert* 1: 21–35, 2020; Beverley Best, "Wages for Housework Redux," *Theory & Event* 24(4), 2021; Jules Gleeson and Elle O'Rourke (eds.), *Transgender Marxism*, Pluto, 2021; Mikey Elster, "Insidious Concern," *TSQ* 9(3), 2022; M. E. O'Brien, Nat Raha, Xin Liu, and Grietje Baars, "Transversing Sexualities and Critiques of Capital," *Women, Gender and Research* 1, 2022; Christopher Nealon and Colleen Lye (eds.), *After Marx*, Cambridge UP, 2022; Marianna Fernandes et al., "Social Reproduction, Women's Labour and Systems of Life," *Dialogues in Human Geography*, 2023; Jo Giardini, "Trans Life and the Critique of Political Economy," *TSQ* 10(1), 2023; *The Trans Marxist Issue* (*TSQ* 11:2, eds. Ira Terán and Emrys Travis), 2024.

36. On Jineolojî, see Rahila Gupta, "The Kurdish Feminist Revolution," *New Internationalist,* February 23, 2023; Nadje Al-Ali and Isabel Käser, "Beyond Feminism?," *Politics & Gender* 18(1), 2022; Gönül Kaya, "Why Jineolojî?," *Internationalist Commune*, November 22, 2017.

37. Erin Maglaque, "Red Love, for All," *New Statesman,* September 23, 2022; Lily Sánchez, "Why We Should Abolish the Family," *Current Affairs*, September 5, 2022; Jordy Rosenberg, Eman Abdelhadi, and M. E. O'Brien, "The Horizon of Human Emancipation," *BOMB*, August 4, 2022; Sophie Lewis, "Of Innocence and Experience," *Tank* 94, March 2, 2023; Katie Gibson, "Bringing Abolition Home," *Blind Field*, June 6, 2023.

38. Madeline Lane-McKinley, "9 Notes on "Gender Strike," *Blind Field*, April 28, 2017; Marina Montanelli and Michael Hardt, "The Unforeseen Subject of the Feminist Strike," *SAQ* 117(3), 2018; Luci Cavallero and Verónica Gago, "The Political Invention of the Feminist Strike," *Viewpoint*, March 23, 2021; Aaron Jaffe, "From Social Reproduction Theory to Social Reproduction Strikes," *Socialism & Democracy*, 2023.

39. Maylei Blackwell, Laura Briggs, and Mignonette Chiu, "Transnational Feminisms Roundtable," *Frontiers* 36(3), 2015; Verónica Gago et al., "The Earth Trembles," *Critical Times* 1(1), 2018; Verónica Gago, *Feminist International* (Verso, 2020); Jo Littler and Verónica Gago, "We Want Ourselves Alive and Debt Free!," *Soundings* 80(13), 2022.

40. Heather Berg, "'Today Solidarity Means, Fight Back,'" *Essays in Philosophy* 24(1–2), 2023; Madeline Lane-McKinley, *Comedy Against Work* (Common Notions, 2022); Kate Willett, "Slacker Uprising," *Broken Pencil*, August 3, 2022; Marian Jones and Robin D. G. Kelley, "Sabotage, Slowdowns, and Theft," *Lux* 4, April 2022; Wilson Sherwin, "'Nothing but Joy," *Souls* 22(2–4), 2020.

41. Pilar Villanueva, "Why Decolonial Feminism," *Toward Freedom*, February 4, 2019; Bárbara Martínez-Cairo and Emanuela Buscemi, "Latin American Decolonial Feminisms," *Les Cahiers ALHIM* 42, 2021; Laís Rodrigues, "Decolonial Feminism," *Estudos Feministas* 30(1), 2022; Yuderkys Miñoso and Ruth Pión, "Decolonial Feminism in Latin America," *Hypatia* 37, 2022; Kimberly Romano, "La Lucha y La Memoria," *NACLA*, April 21, 2023.

42. Jennifer Nash, *Black Feminism Reimagined* (Duke UP, 2018); Lise Vogel, "Beyond Intersectionality," *Science & Society* 82(2), 2018; Holly Lewis, *The Politics of Everybody* (Zed, 2022); Ashley Bohrer, "Toward a Decolonial Feminist Anticapitalism," *Hypatia* 35(3), 2023.

43. TruthOut, "Angela Y. Davis, Gina Dent, Erica Meiners and Beth Richie Talk Abolition Feminism," *TruthOut*, February 7, 2022; Brittany Battle, "'Everything I Believe In Is Rooted in Love,'" *QC* 11(3), 2022; Amna Akbar, "Long and Variegated Struggles," *LA Review of Books*, June 28, 2022; Rachel Kushner, "Is Prison Necessary?," *New York Times Magazine*, April 17, 2019; Angela Y. Davis, "Women's March Speech," *Guardian*, January 22, 2017.

Index

About the Author

Sophie Lewis is a writer, utopian, feminist and freelance independent scholar living in Philadelphia. Her first two books, both published by Verso Books, were *Full Surrogacy Now: Feminism Against Family* (2019) and *Abolish the Family: A Manifesto for Care and Liberation* (2022). Sophie's essays and articles routinely appear in academic journals like *Feminist Theory* as well as literary ones like *n+1*, *Harper's*, and the *London Review of Books*.

Sophie has a PhD in Geography from Manchester University, as well as an MA in Politics from the New School, and a BA in English literature from Oxford University, which was followed by an MSc in Environmental Policy (also at Oxford). Dr. Lewis teaches short courses on feminist theory at the Brooklyn Institute for Social Research, open to all and online. She also has a visiting affiliation with the Center for Research on Feminist, Queer and Transgender Studies at the University of Pennsylvania.

As a member of the Out of the Woods ecological writing collective, she contributed to the collection *Hope Against Hope* (Common Notions, 2019). Her writings have been widely translated and anthologized. You can find all her lectures and articles at lasophielle.org, and become a subscriber at patreon.com/reproutopia.

About Haymarket Books

Haymarket Books is a radical, independent, nonprofit book publisher based in Chicago. Our mission is to publish books that contribute to struggles for social and economic justice. We strive to make our books a vibrant and organic part of social movements and the education and development of a critical, engaged, and internationalist Left.

We take inspiration and courage from our namesakes, the Haymarket Martyrs, who gave their lives fighting for a better world. Their 1886 struggle for the eight-hour day—which gave us May Day, the international workers' holiday—reminds workers around the world that ordinary people can organize and struggle for their own liberation. These struggles—against oppression, exploitation, environmental devastation, and war—continue today across the globe.

Since our founding in 2001, Haymarket has published more than nine hundred titles. Radically independent, we seek to drive a wedge into the risk-averse world of corporate book publishing. Our authors include Angela Y. Davis, Arundhati Roy, Keeanga-Yamahtta Taylor, Eve L. Ewing, Aja Monet, Mariame Kaba, Naomi Klein, Rebecca Solnit, Olúfẹ́mi O. Táíwò, Mohammed El-Kurd, José Olivarez, Noam Chomsky, Winona LaDuke, Robyn Maynard, Leanne Betasamosake Simpson, Howard Zinn, Mike Davis, Marc Lamont Hill, Dave Zirin, Astra Taylor, and Amy Goodman, among many other leading writers of our time. We are also the trade publishers of the acclaimed Historical Materialism Book Series.

Haymarket also manages a vibrant community organizing and event space in Chicago, Haymarket House, the popular Haymarket Books Live event series and podcast, and the annual Socialism Conference.

www.ingramcontent.com/pod-product-compliance
Ingram Content Group UK Ltd.
Pitfield, Milton Keynes, MK11 3LW, UK
UKHW041849230425
457795UK00006B/13